The Curriculum and the Child

In the **World Library of Educationalists**, international experts themselves compile career-long collections of what they judge to be their finest pieces – extracts from books, key articles, salient research findings, major theoretical and practical contributions – so the world can read them in a single manageable volume. Readers will be able to follow themes and strands of the topic and see how their work contributes to the development of the field.

John White has spent the last 35 years researching, teaching, thinking and writing about some of the key and enduring issues in Philosophy of Education. He has contributed over 30 books and 143 articles to the field.

In *The Curriculum and the Child*, John White brings together 16 of his key writings in one place. Starting with a specially written Introduction, which gives an overview of John's career and contextualises his selection within the development of the field, the chapters cover:

- mind
- state and curriculum
- well-being
- politics
- curriculum subjects.

This book not only shows how John's thinking developed during his long and distinguished career; it also gives an insight into the development of the fields to which he contributed.

John White is Emeritus Professor of Philosophy of Education at the Institute of Education, University of London.

Contributors to the series include: Richard Aldrich, Stephen J. Ball, John Elliott, Elliot W. Eisner, Howard Gardner, John K. Gilbert, Ivor F. Goodson, David Labaree, John White, E. C. Wragg.

World Library of Educationalists series

The Curriculum and the Child

The selected works of John White

John White

 Routledge
Taylor & Francis Group

LONDON AND NEW YORK

First published 2005
by Routledge
2 Park Square, Milton Park, Abingdon, Oxon OX14 4RN

Simultaneously published in the USA and Canada
by Routledge
270 Madison Ave, New York, NY 10016

Routledge is an imprint of the Taylor & Francis Group

© 2005 John White

Typeset in Sabon by
Newgen Imaging Systems (P) Ltd, Chennai, India
Printed and bound in Great Britain by
MPG Books Ltd, Bodmin

British Library Cataloguing in Publication Data
A catalogue record for this book is available
from the British Library

Library of Congress Cataloging in Publication Data
A catalog record for this book has been requested

ISBN 0–415–35663–6 (hbk)
ISBN 0–415–35664–4 (pbk)

CONTENTS

ACKNOWLEDGEMENTS

The following articles have been reproduced with the kind permission of the respective journals

'Education and nationality' (1996), *Journal of Philosophy of Education*, 30(3): 327–43.

'Education, the market and the nature of personal well-being' (2002), *British Journal of Educational Studies*, 50(4): 442–56.

'Education, work and well-being' (1997), *Journal of Philosophy of Education*, 31(2): 233–47.

'Intelligence and the logic of the nature–nurture issue' (1974), *Proceedings of the Philosophy of Education Society of Great Britain*, VIII(1): 30–51.

'Puritan intelligence' (2005), *Oxford Review of Education*, 31(3).

'The education of the emotions' (1984), *Journal of Philosophy of Education*, 18(2): 233–44.

'The problem of self-interest: the educator's perspective' (1986), *Journal of Philosophy of Education*, 20(2): 163–75.

The following chapters have been reproduced with the kind permission of the respective publishers

'Education and personal well-being in a secular universe' (1995), *Inaugural Lecture* published under this name by Institute of Education, University of London.

'Motivating children' (2002), *The Child's Mind*. London: RoutledgeFalmer.

'Rethinking the school curriculum' (2003), *Rethinking the School Curriculum*. London: RoutledgeFalmer.

'Should mathematics be compulsory for all until the age of 16?' (2000), in S. Bramall and J. White (eds), *Why Learn Maths?* London: Institute of Education, University of London.

'Should schools determine their own curricula?' (1976), originally in *Proceedings of Philosophy of Education Society of Great Britain*, Vol. X. This version is from a reprint of this in H. Sockett (ed.), *Accountability in the English Educational System* (1980). London: Hodder.

'The aims of education in the liberal democratic state' (1990), *Education and the Good Life*. London: Kogan Page.

'The arts, well-being and education' (1992), in P. H. Hirst and P. A. White (eds), *Beyond Liberal Education*. London: Routledge.

'The end of the compulsory curriculum' (1975), *The Curriculum: the Doris Lee Lectures*. London: Institute of Education, University of London.

'The roots of philosophy' (1992), in A. P. Griffiths (ed.), *The Impulse to Philosophise*. Cambridge: Cambridge University Press.

INTRODUCTION

It must have been the lack of coherence in my own schooling that first prompted me to think about the aims of education. What were all those bits and pieces of learning supposed to be about? Those four languages and their grammars. The courting habits of the earthworm. The Second Crusade. Attempting and failing to jump over the buck. That sixth form essay for the headmaster on 'Eating Onions' (his choice of title) . . . .

I now understand the earthworm. Since the more familiar rabbit was not in our syllabus, we were expected to extrapolate what was sexually in store for us from the shenanigans of an even lowlier species. Such minor illuminations aside, I have no idea what my school thought it was doing or how it saw its bits and pieces fitting together. It probably didn't care if they did fit or didn't fit – as long as it pushed enough of us through to decent universities.

This is where my interest in educational aims must have begun. It has already lasted more than four decades. This is partly because the question goes so deep; and partly it is because the educational world always has to be urged not to ignore it. School tests, public examinations and league tables preoccupy governments and schools today as much as Oxbridge entrance papers absorbed the attention of B..... School in the middle of the last century.

Aims cannot be sidelined. Schools and governments have to know where they are going before working out how best to get there. So, where do they turn? There are always plenty of aims-pontificators ready to help. Some go for learning for its own sake, others for the child's happiness, vocational preparation, or democratic citizenship. Some want to reserve 'real' education for the few intellectually capable of it. Others begin from grand psychological theorisings about the multiple abilities children have wired into their brains and so on.

What an education system needs is a way of filtering such recommendations so that only worthwhile ones are left. But who will be the filterers? And how can one prevent them from contaminating the process with their own idiosyncrasies? How can one find people sufficiently dispassionate to do the job?

This is where my own profession comes in. Philosophers of education have a role in helping the filtering process. This is not easy. It is tempting to let one's own pet views warp one's thinking – in which case one risks joining the aims-gurus. In the end, this may be inevitable. But philosophy of education is committed to the thought that it can do better, that some measure of objectivity is possible in this tricky area and its own discipline is well placed to provide it.

It has at least two reasons for thinking this. One is that a large part of the job of any philosopher is to sift through others' arguments, checking whether their conclusions follow from their premises, being attentive to obscurities, locating and questioning assumptions.

Philosophers are as well placed to do this with arguments about school aims as with claims in epistemology or the philosophy of language. The second point is that the question of what should be the aims of education is an ethical question and a key branch of philosophy is ethics. This discipline can help us to find our way around the values underpinning educational aims and conflicting points of view about them.

None of this equips philosophers of education to make definitive pronouncements on what the aims should be. Some of them *have* done this. In his *Republic*, Plato lays it down with great confidence that the education of the ruler has to proceed towards acquiring ever more indubitable and abstract kinds of knowledge, since Plato believes this will infallibly equip him to govern well. These days, philosophers of education are – or at least should be – more modest. They accept that any conclusions they come up with about aims are themselves up for grabs and need to be subjected to stringent critique.

Can we take it as baseline that what children learn at school should at least *do them some good*? Most people would find this uncontroversial enough, including those – virtually everyone – who think schooling should also be for the benefit of other people than the pupil. This leads immediately into philosophical depths. What counts as 'benefit' here? Whether we have in mind the child or other people, we are talking about their well-being. What *is* well-being?

I have been preoccupied with this last question since my first ventures into philosophy of education. Several factors triggered it. One was my own experience of schooling, as a pupil myself and as a young teacher. I have already said something about the former. How helpful to me were the bits and pieces I picked up at B..... School in living a fulfilling life? Were the French lessons I taught the boys of Beal Grammar Technical School in Ilford in the early 1960s conducive to a full and vibrant existence for them? Even if they had been taught by Mr Jones, the head of languages – with twenty years more experience in the classroom behind him than my six months – was the French they were compelled to study justifiable in terms of their own good? Perhaps it was. The problem was that I had no way of knowing.

The second trigger was more sociological. In those years, when comprehensive schools were rare as yet, secondary schooling was divided between the selective or grammar school sector in which I mainly studied and worked – and the secondary modern system, which catered for 80 per cent and more of the population. Secondary moderns had a less academic curriculum, with much more space for practical, that is manual, activities. Was the schooling that their pupils received good for them? Or was it – as I was inclined to believe – designed to hold them back, to gentle them towards the manual jobs that the economy needed?

I had already begun teaching philosophy of education before the third factor came into play. At that time, the late 1960s, the theory of the school curriculum most favoured in my field was that it should be based on various forms of understanding, including mathematics, history, literature, the physical sciences and other areas, all to be pursued for their own sake. The justification given by Richard Peters and Paul Hirst for this prescription, which rested on a Kantian claim that it must be true if some form of self-contradiction was to be avoided, failed to satisfy me. Their curriculum proposal smacked of paternalism. It seemed to advocate foisting a particular version of human fulfilment – the scholar's ideal – on the pupil population as a whole. Were there not, after all, other ways of leading a flourishing life? Perhaps a more defensible suggestion was that one purpose of schooling is to open students' eyes to a number of different life-ideals rather than imprison them in one of them.

For various reasons, therefore, I found myself drawn towards thinking about personal well-being and its place among the aims of education. I was hampered for many years by the lack of literature in general philosophy on this concept. Until the 1980s philosophical ethics was virtually synonymous with moral philosophy. Questions about our moral obligations, rival ways of justifying them, their objectivity or subjectivity, dominated the field. Relatively few philosophers wrote about what was often called 'prudence' as contrasted with 'morality', that is, about what counts as a good life for ourselves as distinct from issues about our duties to other people. In the last two decades discussions about the nature of human fulfilment have become much more prominent in general philosophy. Their influence is evident in several essays in this book.

I still believe, as I did forty years ago, that the concept of personal well-being is pivotal to sound thinking about education – at every level, from the classroom to national policy-making and beyond. It obviously comes into the picture if a child's education aims at helping him or her to lead a fulfilling life. But it also features insofar as it is about preparation for work or citizenship, for both of these are about benefiting other people.

British culture, like other cultures, is confused about what it is to lead a flourishing life. In our case, this is partly because we are only recently emerging from a Christian world-view. This has held out a vision of personal fulfilment in another life, while emphasising the fulfilment of our moral duties in this one. This outlook is now much on the wane. For most of us, well-being is of this world and of this world alone. It is something to be achieved in the very short time that we each have. But what is it? Is it happiness, contentment? Is it something at which we should consciously aim? Should we live in accordance with some kind of long-term plan? What part in well-being should wealth, or high culture, being with friends, hard work, seeing the world, good food, social recognition, body image or other factors play? How much of my life should I devote to my own good, how much to that of others'?

The education service is in a fix. It needs some kind of settled conception of personal well-being to make sense of what schooling should be about; but in the culture there is massive uncertainty. Little wonder that the system judges its progress by what can be easily measured; and the aims that it does have are grand mission statements that have little bearing in practice.

If policy-makers think about philosophy of education at all, they probably see it, too, as disconnected from the 'real world' of schooling. Yet this fails to recognise its vital role. Confusion about how best to live is not endemic: philosophy has ways of bringing some order to the area.

One example is the relationship between one's own well-being and that of others. Does the work of schools fall into two parts, one that helps the pupil to flourish and the other to do with developing moral sensibilities? This seems to mean that the two areas are separable. But are they? Can you lead a flourishing life if you do not care a button for other people?

For most of us, a large part of what makes life personally fulfilling is engaging in social activities that also benefit other people, sometimes mainly the participants themselves – as in friendship, and sometimes, in addition, mainly other people – as in certain kinds of work. But is this intertwining essential? Could not one in principle live successfully for Number One and not bother about others – perhaps even using people, against their own interests, as means of making one's own life fuller? If we ask these questions *in the context of children's education* – rather than more generally – does this alter what we might say? I discuss these matters in Chapter 9.

I mentioned earlier the decline of our Christian heritage and the emergence of secular conceptions of well-being. This was the springboard for my inaugural lecture in 1994 as Professor of Philosophy of Education at the Institute of Education. This now appears as Chapter 10. I was struck by the thought that in past centuries our picture of how to live well has been set within a cosmic framework, without which it made no sense. In a more secular society, how far does a different understanding of well-being still need some such background, even if a personal deity may be lacking in it? If it does, what consequences might this have for school education? In particular, what contribution might aesthetic education make?

Another Christian legacy to contemporary British – and not only to British – culture is the notion of work originally linked with Puritanism, which had become so influential in middle-class thinking by the nineteenth century. For many dissenters a life of unremitting labour – outside the home for men, within the home for women – was associated with the desire for, and perhaps expectation of, personal salvation. It was a manifestation – perhaps the chief manifestation – of one's duty to care for others, to bring about social improvement. The notion that life revolves around work is still strong in Britain today, a country with longer working hours than those of many others. It still deeply affects the culture of the school, both in its compulsory industriousness and in its orientation towards examination – and thereafter career – success. Chapter 11 explores the place of work in our concept of well-being. Is it a vital constituent, or could we in theory flourish without it? Does it make a difference whether the work is autonomous or not? What picture of work and its place in human life should schools be transmitting?

With educational aims in mind, several chapters in the book, including those just mentioned, investigate possible ingredients in personal well-being – altruism, work, a cosmic framework. How far are these things in principle dispensable elements in the concept? If they are, should educators encourage pupils to think of them as optional, or is this leaving things too open? A formally similar preoccupation drives Chapter 15. A remarkable feature of our age is that huge numbers of people engage in the visual arts, literature and especially music, either as consumers or as producers. Some say this is because art is filling a spiritual vacuum left by a declining influence of religion. Whether or not this is true, some kind of artistic activity is widely seen as part of one's personal fulfilment. Is it *necessarily* part of it? If so, children should be brought up to see a life without art as unimaginable. If not, should educators limit themselves to opening children's eyes to artistic activity as *one kind of option among many*, to be jettisoned if they so choose?

These arguments about possible ingredients in well-being require a fuller exploration of the concept in general. This is provided in Chapter 12. It contrasts two radically different theories about what it is to flourish, after basic needs for things like food, clean air, shelter, health, a minimum income, perhaps liberty are met. One theory goes for an objective list of ingredients which, perhaps in different combinations and with different weightings, contribute to any individual's fulfilment. We have already encountered some possible candidates: aesthetic activity, work, altruistic concern, close personal relationships. Other frequently favoured items are the pursuit of knowledge, self-understanding, physical activities and bodily pleasures. The second theory is less restrictive. It holds that no external list of goods can trump the individual's subjective perspective. How far a person leads a flourishing life depends on how far he or she succeeds in satisfying informed desires of most personal importance, whatever these may be – wearing designer clothes for an evening out then throwing them away, buying the latest album because it is the latest, collecting thimbles and so on. The subjective view is at the root of those justifications of the market economy which stress the market's contribution to human well-being. Which of the two views – the objective or the subjective – informs the aims of schooling is of great consequence. People in education often see their endeavours as at odds with, and challenged by, those of the market: But if the subjective view is followed, schools, markets and advertising agencies could well be in the same business, each of them making it easier for people to make informed choices about, and possess, the kinds of goods they most prefer. Which account of well-being, if either, is the more defensible?

Although I have spent most time on aims to do with the well-being of the learner, there are, of course, other goals of equal, or some would say greater, significance – for instance, equipping pupils to help *other people* to flourish (insofar as this is separable – see above). Patriotism is an aim with both pupil-directed and other-directed aspects. It is defended in Chapter 13. The excesses of twentieth-century chauvinism have made many on the liberal left antipathetic towards patriotism – as at odds with liberal virtues of personal autonomy and equal respect. But can it not be detached from chauvinism? Can it become a defensible school aim? If so, how might this work out in the British context? To which country, for instance, should those English children who choose to do so feel attached – the UK, Britain or England? This chapter was written before Scottish and Welsh devolution, but the issues it raises are perhaps even more relevant now.

* * *

Who should decide what the aims of schooling should be? When I first began teaching philosophy of education in the late 1960s, all maintained schools were free – at least in theory – to decide their own curricula. In an article in *New Society* (White, 1969) I wondered whether this was defensible. Might not some children – I was thinking mainly of those in secondary modern schools – be sold short? Should there not be some kind of public guarantee that all of them have access to what I called 'the forms of experience which constitute the higher culture – the arts, mathematics, the human and physical sciences, philosophy....'? I elaborated this description of a state-controlled curriculum at book length in *Towards a Compulsory Curriculum* (White, 1973). It was there that aims to do with the pupil's well-being first became salient in my thinking.

About that time it struck me that I had no idea for how long, historically, schools had been free to determine their own curricula. The received wisdom was that this autonomy was an entrenched part of our liberal English tradition – and a contrast to the detailed state control that one found in France and other countries. But was the conventional view correct? I thought I knew that in the late nineteenth century the government imposed standards in the 3 Rs on its new elementary schools. But I could find nothing in any history of education about when any shift of control to the schools may have taken place. Making use of a history degree that I never imagined I would need once I had discovered philosophy, I decided to try to unearth the facts myself. The results are found in Chapter 5.

Up to this point, the mid-1970s, I had not spelt out in detail the case for state control, which by then seemed to me stronger than ever. I did so in what is now Chapter 6. I still stand by its central arguments. It is interesting to review these from a 2005 perspective, 16 years after the introduction of the National Curriculum, as they still have lessons for us. First, at what level should any state control be imposed? There is every reason why teachers should be left free to determine detailed matters of syllabuses and pedagogy: they are in the best position to do this and professionally equipped to do so. But they lack expertise when it comes to the broad framework of the curriculum. This is because such macro-decisions are enmeshed with beliefs about the kind of society that it is hoped the curriculum will help to bring about. 'Decisions about curriculum frameworks are inescapably connected with *political* views about the nature of the Good Society.' There is no reason why teachers should be privileged over postmen or doctors when it comes to making politically sensitive choices: in a democracy, every citizen, and not just a section of the citizenry, has an equal right to share in these.

Among possible objections to political rather than professional control, I noted in this same chapter the danger that 'any state control could only reflect the subjective preferences of those who drew it up'. Although I suggested that this is not necessarily the case, what happened *in fact* in 1988 was not far from this. The Secretary of State for Education Kenneth Baker, in opposition to Mrs Thatcher, who favoured only English, mathematics and science, successfully pressed for a broader National Curriculum of ten traditional school subjects. He gave no rationale for this. Apart from a few empty words, the new curriculum was aimless. It was also remarkably similar to the school curriculum that Stalin imposed on the Soviet Union, as Chapter 7 points out. As with the latter, it gave government wide powers to lay down the details of curricular programmes. In terms of the distinction made in

Chapter 6, the Baker solution took powers from teachers which were rightly in their purview, while failing to spell out any overall aims, necessary as these are to the 'broad framework' area which is the state's only legitimate province.

The 1988 settlement was far from the kind of national structure I had advocated for two decades. It made me realise that the argument for state control I had worked out hitherto was incomplete. The comparison with Stalin's curriculum was enlightening. A defensible national curriculum, I came more clearly to see, has to be in line with democratic values. The main argument on which I had relied since the 1970s, was that no sectional element could validly decide on educational aims: these were the province of the citizenry as a whole. This presupposes a democratic state. The 'Good Society' of the future, which a public curriculum should help to shape, must be, if the argument is to work at all, a democratic society. This means that civic aims appropriate to a democracy – including aims discussed above concerning the well-being of the learner – must be at the heart of the curriculum. It also means that any subsidiary part of a 'broad framework', to do with prescribed components of the curriculum, must be justifiable in terms of overall aims related to democracy.

In the late 1990s, under pressure from teachers who wanted a better idea of what the National Curriculum was for, the new Labour government equipped the latter with an extensive list of aims. These came into force in 2000. As Chapter 8 explains, although they have their limitations they make a fair fist of encapsulating democratic values. But Baker's ten subjects, plus one or two others, still provide the curriculum content. How well do they, including their detailed programmes and targets, match the overall aims now grafted on to them? Not well at all, to judge from a close study of the documentation. The new aims have given us a yardstick by which to assess the adequacy of the school curriculum. If the government is serious about them, it should reform the content of the curriculum so as to bring it into line with them. After four years, it has done nothing yet, but continued pressure may force its hand or that of its successor.

The mismatch between overall aims and curriculum specifics has underlined for me the inappropriateness of much of the traditional subject-based curriculum foisted on the nation in 1988, being an almost perfect replica of the scheme introduced in 1904 for the new state secondary school. Many people, not only in England, but across the world, take it as read that schools should be teaching mother tongue, mathematics, science, technology, history, geography, a modern language, art, music, physical education and perhaps religious education. We have come to think in terms of block entities like these – and for the most part accept that they should each be taught for most of the pupil's school career, or, in the case of indispensable items like mother tongue and mathematics, for the whole of it. But why? Is there a good reason for this, or do we just freewheel lazily across the decades unwilling to consider any alternative?

Take mathematics. In England this is now compulsory for children aged 5–16 years and there is talk of the government extending it to 18 for those still at school. But how justified is this stance? The official case for the subject's importance falls apart, as Chapter 16 shows. Beyond primary stage, where basic arithmetic is obviously appropriate, it becomes increasingly difficult to justify it as a compulsory subject. This latter idea, which originated within philosophy of education against a wider background of reflection about the aims of education, is now being defended by leading figures in the world of mathematics education.

When I first argued for a compulsory curriculum in 1969, mathematics was prominent in my wish list, as an earlier quotation demonstrates. I was too ready in those days to favour the highly intellectual, often abstraction-favouring, approach to the curriculum which has been so influential in British culture, and whose latest manifestation is the 1988 scheme. I am not implying at all that this traditional view is wholly misguided, only that its credentials need to be put to the test. At point after point, as with mathematics, the standard curriculum has become a totem, a taken-for-granted feature of the educational landscape.

When justifications fail, turn to explanations. This is why philosophy of education and history of education fit so well together. Just as my failure to find solid reasons for schools' curricular autonomy led me in Chapter 5 to explore how this autonomy came about, as a future project I would like to burrow further into how the traditional curriculum originated and developed, and why it has become so powerful, especially over the last century. In the British context, the role of the dissenting communities in England and the Presbyterians in Scotland from the seventeenth century onwards comes into the story. It has to do with the importance radical protestants attached to a detailed knowledge of the world of God's creation for its own sake as a condition of personal salvation, and their consequent replacement, in their grammar schools and academies, of a classics-based curriculum with one based on science, mathematics, English, history, geography, religion, logic and other subjects. (The arts were a later addition – as one might expect, given the origins of this curriculum in puritan thinking.) The line of thinking here is embryonic; and I realise the influence of Dissent is only one element in the story. In a different context, I say more about puritanism when I come to Chapter 4 below.

Another compulsory subject I favoured in 1969 was philosophy. As with mathematics, the very abstraction of the subject seemed important to me then. I argued that it was subjects like these, which are unintelligible without participation unlike, say woodwork, or drawing whose nature can be grasped to some extent from the outside, should be mandatory. They enlarge the options available to people as possible ingredients in their plan of life – and if pupils do not participate in them, they will necessarily not be able to appreciate them as possible options (White, 1973). I now see all sorts of problems with this argument. In 2004, I would support on quite other grounds some philosophical thinking in the curriculum – not necessarily as a separate subject. The clientèle I have in mind for it embraces older secondary students, perhaps not all of them. Philosophy can help to give them a mental map, an overall conceptual framework in which they can make better sense of what they are and how they can live well, as both individuals and citizens. In Chapter 14 I challenge, by contrast, the fashionable interest in philosophy for much younger children, sometimes as young as five.

* * *

The book is about the child as well as about the curriculum. Its first four chapters are about psychological matters. While the rest of the book draws mainly on one or another branch of value philosophy – aesthetics, political philosophy, and especially ethics – this section consists, with one exception, of applied philosophy of mind.

I first became interested in the topic of intelligence because of its role in selecting children for élite schooling, especially via the English 'eleven plus' exam, still very much in operation when I entered the teaching profession. The theory behind this derived from Cyril Burt and originally from Francis Galton. Burt held that intelligence is 'innate, general, cognitive ability' which sets individually differing limits on what one can intellectually achieve. If he is right, there is no point in giving many children an intellectually rigorous secondary education, since this is above their mental ceiling. Burt's theory had been widely criticized on empirical grounds, but the objections I make in the second half of Chapter 1 are conceptual. The main argument is that his claim that we all have our own ceiling of ability is both unverifiable and unfalsifiable. It is not a scientific claim but a metaphysical one, on a par, perhaps, with a statement like 'God exists'. In this chapter I also agree with my co-symposiast, Gilbert Ryle, in rejecting the construal of intelligence as *general* ability, concerned especially with abstract thinking. Prowess in philosophy and in mathematics, for instance (see Chapters 14, 16), does not necessarily show more intelligence than practical achievements in gardening, fitting bathrooms, or planning holidays.

Thirty years later, I returned to the Galton–Burt conception from a different perspective. I was intrigued why a notion so lacking in justification had been so influential – and has continued to be so to some extent despite allegations in the 1970s that Burt had falsified his data. Once again, a failed justification turned me in the direction of historical explanation. How did the early pioneers of intelligence and intelligence testing come to have their ideas? A thought buzzing about my mind from time to time since the late 1960s has been that there are certain parallels between these ideas about intelligence and ideas from the puritan tradition. Notions of predestination, for instance, and of an 'elect' on the road to personal salvation had echoes in modern ideas of innate limits to intelligence and of an élite of bright youngsters *en route* to success in life. Chapter 4 takes up this hunch and explores possible parallels in greater detail. It spells out the surprising finding that virtually all the intelligence pioneers in the Galtonian tradition, in both the UK and the US, came from puritan family backgrounds. What weight should be given this, however, is more obscure.

The two chapters of this book not yet considered are in very different styles, directed to very different readerships. They illustrate something of the range of work we cover in philosophy of education – a gamut running from theoretical discussions which try to break new philosophical ground and which are presented in academic journals for colleagues' critical assessment, through to writings for teachers and policy-makers in more popular books and press articles. Part of my subject's fascination, which has kept me in its thrall to it over the last 40 years, has been the opportunities it has given of moving up and down this gamut – now responding to conceptual and logical flaws in a new policy initiative, now laying siege once again to some intractable concept of pivotal importance for education, like human well-being.

Richard Peters ran the degree course in philosophy and psychology for which I studied in the evenings at Birkbeck College, University of London in the early 1960s. In 1965, he became my colleague when I began teaching under him at the Institute of Education. I am indebted to him in so many ways, not least for the enduring interest I have always had in the educational applications of the two branches of philosophy that engaged himself, ethics and philosophy of mind. In my early years I struggled to define a position of my own on central issues in our field, independent of Peters' framework. I have already mentioned my rejection of his Kantian argument for the pursuit of truth for its own sake as central to the curriculum. In Chapter 2, on a related matter, I distance myself from his wariness about the place of the emotions in education, giving them a far more positive motivational role. Motivation is also the topic of Chapter 3. Here, I move some way along the gamut described above, towards trying to make some impact on the educational world. The chapter is from a recent book intended for teachers and parents on various aspects of the child's mind.

References

White, J. (1969) 'The curriculum mongers: education in reverse', *New Society*, March 6.
White, J. (1973) *Towards a Compulsory Curriculum*, London: Routledge and Kegan Paul.

PART 1

THE CHILD'S MIND

CHAPTER 1

INTELLIGENCE AND THE LOGIC OF THE NATURE–NURTURE ISSUE

Proceedings of the Philosophy of Education Society of Great Britain (1974), VIII(1): 30–51

I suppose the first step in discussing the logic of the nature–nurture issue is to define what the issue is; and this is not a simple task. And perhaps, we shouldn't take it as read from the beginning that there is *one* thing at issue here. Perhaps there are several issues. Or perhaps there are none. On the side of 'nature' it does indeed seem that there are at least *two* different claims, not necessarily incompatible: (i) that intelligence is innate ability (Burt's view), (ii) that individual differences in intelligence are largely determined by genetic factors: the 'mainstream' view, held by, for example, Jensen, Eysenck, Butcher and Burt (again). What is at issue, then? Is it whether intelligence is, or is not, innate ability? Or whether innate determinants of individual differences in intelligence out-weigh environmental ones? Would someone arguing for 'nurture' be claiming that these differences are largely environmentally produced? Or would he object to this whole attempt at quantification?

I

All this is very unclear. To help sort things out, let me begin with a necessarily brief, but I hope not too dogmatic, account of the concept of intelligence. One popular view, deriving from Ryle's *Concept of Mind*, is that 'intelligence' is a 'disposition-word' and that statements containing disposition-words are analysable into hypothetical statements about behaviour. Thus T. R. Miles writes, ' "X is intelligent" can be taken as equivalent to "If X is placed in particular circumstances he produces responses of a particular kind" e.g., if he is present at a group discussion he makes appropriate remarks, if presented with a difficult crossword puzzle he can usually solve it, and so on'.[1] A feature of Miles' 'if-then' analysis of intelligence, which distinguishes it from those of Mark Fisher and of Ryle himself, is his apparent commitment to the *general* nature of intelligence.[2] Where Ryle talks of the intelligence of the sharpshooter and Fisher that of the golfer, Miles' intelligent man must display his intelligence in widely different activities. Before taking up this issue of whether intelligence is general or specific, let me mention an important problem for Miles' and for all 'if-then' analyses of the concept. This is: how are we to understand the 'and so on' at the end of Miles' statement? No doubt a long list of further examples could be given. But it would be necessarily incomplete. It seems that what must hold this list together is that all its items are applications of the general formula 'if he were in circumstances Y, he would act *intelligently*'. The circularity is manifest. It is clear that the concept of an intelligent person must be understood in terms of the concept of an intelligent act. This conclusion also raises problems for the notion of 'general' intelligence. If one can act intelligently in any particular situation, for example, in playing chess, then one does not have to bring in any reference to a *number* of types of situations – group discussions, solving crosswords etc. – into one's account of an intelligent act. One might, always, of course, decide to write all-round ability into one's concept of the 'intelligent' man; but this would be to introduce a *different* concept.

I mentioned above that the 'and so on' constitutes a problem not only for Miles' but also for all 'if-then' analyses. It does so, for instance, for Ryle's analysis, if indeed it is of an 'if-then' sort. For Ryle being intelligent is activity-specific. Let us examine, for instance, Ryle's example of the soldier exercising his intelligence in scoring a bull's eye: 'Was it luck or was it skill? If he has the skill, then he can get on or near the bull's eye again, even if the wind strengthens, the range alters and the target moves.'[3] In terms of the 'if-then' scheme, 'X is shooting intelligently' is equivalent to 'If the wind strengthens, then X tends to do A if the range alters, X tends to do B if the target moves, and so on'. The 'and so on' is still troublesome, as it was with Miles, but Ryle's account contains a further difficulty. For the above equivalence could be satisfied by a person who had been taught a variety of routines, to be applied in different situations in a quite mechanical way, one situation triggering off one response, another another. He could, moreover, learn response A to an increase in wind-strength in such a way that he never considered it as connected with response B to an alteration in range, and so on. Each item of routine behaviour could exist in isolation from the others.

Such a man would not be an intelligent marksman, but a person who had simply learned a number of routines. If he were acting intelligently, what he did in one situation would have to be *connected* with what he did in another. What is lacking in Ryle is a principle of unity, something to hold together the different bits of behaviour manifested in different situations. (In many ways his theory of intelligence is not unlike Hume's theory of the self.) The man who argues intelligently is not *merely* 'ready to recast his expression of obscurely put points, on guard against ambiguities..., taking care not to rely on easily refutable inferences, alert in meeting objections' etc.[4] Again, he could do these things in isolation; in arguing intelligently each of these forms of behaviour must be related to a common endeavour – to the pursuit of truth, for instance. And one cannot give any account of this relation without talking about how the agent *understands* what he is doing, about how he sees the different situations he is in and his responses to them. What connects the different moves which Ryle's intelligent arguer makes is that he *sees* them all as related to his central concern. We may redescribe them as follows: he must *see* his obscurely expressed points *as* obscurely expressed (and so hindering the pursuit of truth); *see* ambiguities (which also hinder this); *see* easily refutable inferences *as* easily refutable (and so not advancing the pursuit of truth) etc. Briefly, he has to see various things as falling or not falling in the class of things promoting the pursuit of truth. Not only this: the things which he sees as belonging to this class must in fact belong to it. It would not be a mark of intelligence, for instance, to see a *clearly* expressed point as obscurely expressed.

By analysing intelligence in terms of tendencies to behave in certain ways, Ryle omits the very feature in virtue of which we call such behaviour 'intelligent': the agent's 'inner' view of what he is doing. Putting together now the two difficulties in the 'if-then' analysis which we have singled out, we see that (i) the concept of an intelligent person is to be understood in terms of the concept of an intelligent act, and (ii) the concept of an intelligent act is to be understood in terms of the concept of seeing one thing as connected with another. This conclusion implies that a behaviouristic account of intelligence must fail: reference must be made to the awareness implicit in this seeing-as.

Now there are problems in ascribing the view I have been attaching to Ryle. Although he seeks to analyse intelligence in terms of overt behaviour rather than private phenomena, it is not clear which kinds of private phenomena he has in mind. Does he mean *any* private phenomena? If so, this would appear to include the form of awareness just mentioned. Or does he mean only 'intellectual' phenomena, that is, acts of theorising or deliberation? It is evident that he means *at least* these; and to this extent his objections to the 'official doctrine' of intelligence are well made: intelligence is not analysable in terms of deliberation. But this does not imply that it is not analysable in terms of other private phenomena, for example, seeing connexions. It is not clear how far Ryle would allow the latter claim. He says of his intelligent arguer that 'underlying all the other features of (his) operations there is the cardinal feature that he reasons logically, that is, that he avoids fallacies and produces valid proofs and inferences, pertinent to the case he is making' (p. 48). He goes on, 'What is true of arguing intelligently is, with appropriate modifications, true of other intelligent operations. The boxer, the surgeon, the poet and the salesman apply their special criteria in the performance of their special tasks, for they are trying to get things right' (p. 48). Both these passages seem to imply that an intelligent operation is one where the agent has a certain end in view and follows certain rules conducive to that end. Whatever he does, then, he must *see* as conducive to this.

I will leave the difficulties of interpreting Ryle's theory at this point. But the remarks just made about intelligent operations raise another problem. How far are intelligent operations goal-directed? Peters claims a necessary connexion between 'intelligence' and 'goal-directedness' on the grounds that the 'adaptiveness or relevant variation (of goal-directed movements) in relation to change (perceived changes in the goal and in conditions that lead to it) is part of what we mean by "intelligence" '.[5] But I am not at all sure that intelligent operations necessarily involve either goal-directedness or variations in behaviour. One may find these in *some* cases, in those of intelligent squash-playing or intelligent generalship, for instance. But they are either or both absent in other cases. Pavlov's dog, on one interpretation of what was happening to him, may be said to have exhibited intelligence in hearing a bell as a sign of food; but he did not vary his behaviour in relation to a goal because he did not engage in any behaviour at all.[6] Neither therefore, is there any question of means-end behaviour. Though the sound of the bell was certainly *connected* with the dog's end of satisfying his hunger, it was in no way a means of achieving this end.

A second counter example: a man who has recently made an amateur film about Edward Jenner, the discoverer of vaccination, is reading the nursery rhyme 'Where are you going to, my pretty maid?' to his little granddaughter, and comes across the line, ' "My face is my fortune, Sir," she said'. He connects this with the fact that in the old days milkmaids were known to be immune to smallpox. This is an intelligent thing to do; but once again, although the connexion he makes is itself no doubt connected with his interests, his intelligent act has nothing to do with adapting means to ends. Both examples, in fact, show that the route to understanding the nature of intelligence does not lie through the notion of means-end behaviour. Judgements, whether perceptual, as in the first case, or non-perceptual, as in the second, can equally be described as intelligent. What picks these and all other phenomena out as intelligent is that they all involve some kind of seeing of connexions, that is, application of concepts. Not *merely* this, to be sure; in seeing connexions which do not exist and in applying concepts incorrectly, one is not performing intelligently. Intelligence is *correct* concept-application.

I have just equated concept-application with the seeing of connexions; and I must now say something to elucidate and justify this equation. One might be tempted to say, 'I can see that in *some* cases seeing connexions can be redescribed as applying concepts. The intelligent arguer, for instance, sees the exposure of an ambiguity as connected with the promotion of truth. Alternatively one may say that he sees this as falling under the concept of a means to this end. If I say, for instance, 'What dreadful weather!' I use the words 'dreadful weather' to connect an instance of poor weather with other instances of the same thing. Similar connecting is involved in all use of concepts. But not all seeing connexions is redescribable as concept-application. Pavlov's dog may have connected the sound of a bell with food, but, bring language-less, he had no 'concepts to apply'. In reply to this point, I should make it clear that as I am using 'concept' I am not restricting concept-possession to language-users. Insofar as animals can be said to perceive something as something (e.g. the sound of a bell as a sign of food), they can be said to perceive different particulars as members of a class (e.g. different particular sounds as all signs of food). I am using 'concept-possession' to include such primitive classificatory abilities. Pavlov's dog shows his intelligence in applying the concept 'sign of food' to the sound of the bell. A caveat is needed here. The dog has not 'applied' a concept in any active sense of the term. That is, he has not *used* a concept in the way in which I have just now used the concept of a caveat. The dog's conceptual abilities are, in Price's words, 'tied', not 'autonomous'. They are activated by the presence of instances: lacking a language, the dog cannot use concepts in the absence of their instances.

A further objection is likely to be made at this point. Seeing connexions may involve concept-application and vice versa. It may be true that to act intelligently one must correctly see connexions (or apply concepts). But surely this is at most a *necessary* condition of intelligence. A person who uses a public telephone for the first time may well see a connexion between the operations he performs and his end of communicating with someone. But it is hardly something of which one would ever say, 'How intelligent of him'. This is because we usually only call behaviour 'intelligent' if it in some way transcends normal expectations, for example, if a person applies his understanding in judgements which are abnormally quick or abnormally sophisticated. This objection has focussed on the kinds of occasions when we use the word 'intelligent'. But it is not clear how much light observations of this sort throw on the *meaning of* a concept. To take another example, we talk about people's *motives* when there is, or may be, something untoward about what they are doing: we ask for the motives of a criminal, but not of a man going into a restaurant. But the fact that we would never *talk* about people's motives for the quite ordinary and readily intelligible things they do does not imply that they do not *have* motives for these things. The man's motive in going into the restaurant is his desire to satisfy his hunger. The very obviousness of the motive explains why we have no need to mention it. We must beware of the same fallacy (which Searle calls 'the assertion fallacy')[7] in analysing the meaning of 'intelligence' in terms of 'transcending normal expectations'. Putting a coin in a slot in a call-box never is *called* 'intelligent', but this does not imply that it is not intelligent. Once again, it is the very *obviousness* of its being an intelligent thing to do which makes it not worth saying that it is. Intelligent performances, like actions from motives, are such omnipresent features of our lives that it is scarcely surprising that we do not often trouble to call them what they are.

This last point also helps to resolve another difficulty. For Ryle, routine or 'single-track' behaviour, like ordering arms, posting a letter or opening a door with a key is not the kind of thing that can be done intelligently. For MacIntyre in *one* sense of the word 'intelligent' action is the successful carrying out of routines. (He also identifies two further senses: the details do not concern us here.)[8] On this I would agree with MacIntyre that routine behaviour can be intelligent, but disagree that there is any other sense of 'intelligent' used here than that applicable to the intelligent arguer, for instance. In both 'single-track' and 'multi-track' cases, the agent's behaviour is concept-guided; in both, he sees some connexion between what he is doing and certain ends. There are, after all, intelligent and unintelligent ways of putting a key in a lock; one has for instance, to hold the key horizontally and the right way up and not try to jam the rounded end into the hole. The intelligent way involves seeing the connexion between the position of the key and the successful completion of the task.

This brings me back to an earlier issue. Many writers have argued that written into the concept of intelligence is the concept of flexibility (or variability, adaptability). More specifically, they have argued for a conceptual connexion between intelligence and flexible *behaviour*. I do not accept the more specific claim, for reasons already mentioned. But the more general claim is acceptable enough. This is, again, because of the connexion between intelligence and concept-possession. To possess a concept is, among other things, to be able to see its different instances as instances of the same thing. Flexibility is a feature of concept-possession to the extent that the conceptualiser is prepared to apply his concept not rigidly, just to one particular object, for example, but to object after object of the same type. Now the *disparateness* of the instances falling under a concept can vary from concept to concept. Some concepts have very disparate instances (e.g. game, table, blue); others have very similar, or even identical ones (e.g. ultramarine). None, however, is less of a concept for lacking disparateness; its possession still brings with it the flexibility mentioned above. The application of these points to the discussion of intelligence and routine behaviour should be clear. In putting a key in a lock one has to see the key's being in a certain position as conducive to one's end. Understanding this rule enables one to apply it again and again, whenever one puts a key in a lock, even though the situations to which one applies it are virtually identical. In intelligent arguing, however, there are many different *kinds* of things, as we have seen, which can be seen as conducive or not conducive to one's ends. The latter concept is in this case more disparate. Both kinds of behaviour may be intelligent, since both contain the flexibility of the kind described. To insist that disparateness as well as flexibility be written into the concept is to conflate a particular *kind* of intelligent performance with intelligent performance in general – a conflation often due to committing the 'assertion fallacy' mentioned above.

One might object here that I have overlooked an important reason why some would wish to challenge the intelligence of routine actions. It is not primarily their 'single-tracked' nature which is relevant, but the fact that because they are single-tracked, they can be performed automatically, as a matter of habit. Accepting the account of intelligence given so far, one might admit that the *first* time one puts a key in a lock one may be doing this intelligently, in that one makes a judgement that its being in a certain position is connected with one's goal. But the more the action becomes habitual, the less it can be described as intelligent, since one comes to perform it without making such judgements. The expression 'seeing connexions', in other words, must be interpreted in an occurrent sense: to act intelligently it is not enough to see (i.e. understand) connexions; one must be *aware* of the connexions, here and now.

I would agree that we must interpret 'see' in an occurrent sense if we are talking about intelligent performances. But I am not convinced that successful behaviour of an 'automatic' sort ever excludes seeing connexions in this sense. *Some* connexions can get taken for granted. The key-turner, for instance, does not constantly keep on seeing the connexion between the key's position and successful turning. But he must at least constantly keep on perceiving the key, each time he uses it, as being (now) in the right position for insertion in the lock. 'Automatic' activity is never automatic in the sense that it is performed without any such present awareness.

The great diversity of definitions of 'intelligence', among both psychologists and philosophers, is well known, or, as some would say, notorious. To many it seems as if there are as many definitions as there are writers on the subject – that the concept is hopelessly confused and intractable. But the account given above may show that the position is not so desperate. It is true that some would and others would not ascribe intelligence to animals, to routine behaviour, to behaviour that does not transcend normal expectations. Some would define it in terms of dispositions to behave, others in terms of seeing connexions. Some would confine it to means-end behaviour; others would extend it to cover acts of judgement unrelated to occurrent ends. To some extent the differences of opinion so far stem from different mistaken presuppositions about the nature of meaning, for example, (i) the apparent conflation of an analysis of the *sense* of 'intelligent' with a discussion of the *criteria* for its applicability, found in accounts by Ryle and those influenced by him, and (ii) the conflation of meaning and use (usage) found in the view which stresses the transcendence of normal expectations. Apart from this, there is a common thread running through all these very different accounts, a thread which also runs through several *further* accounts of intelligence which will be discussed later in this paper, when I look at some of the psychological work in this field. The common thread is successful concept-application or the seeing of connexions. Some accounts concentrate on the seeing of certain *kinds* of connexions (e.g. between means and ends); others concentrate on certain aspects of the use of concepts (e.g. flexibility, or the speed with which connexions are made); some disputes turn on different notions of what it is to have a concept (e.g. disputes over animal intelligence). All these last points are illustrated in several further differences of opinion. Some see intelligence as very much an intellectual matter: one finds this in Plato, in the Cartesian tradition which Ryle attacks, and in many of the tests constructed by intelligence testers. Opponents stress the non-intellectual intelligence shown in the performance of physical skills, like playing tennis, for instance. This disagreement may well turn on differences of view about the nature of concepts and their possession. Following the very broad account of concept-possession I outlined earlier, where this is not necessarily connected with the use of language, the tennis player may be said to be applying concepts in the various kinds of sign-cognition which play so large a part in his game. (As Price points out, sign-cognition is not something confined to animal behaviour, but plays an important part in some of the most sophisticated of human activities.)[9] On this view, to have concepts it is enough to be able to see *x* as *f*, for example, to see the peculiar flight of a tennis-ball as a sign that it will bounce in such and such a way. If, however, one insists that such a recognitional ability is not sufficient for concept-possession, but that one must also understand the connexions between concepts, then one may be inclined to restrict the application of 'intelligence' to more intellectual matters, to the solution of the kind of mathematical and logical problems one finds in intelligence tests, for instance. A still further restriction results from the Platonic insistence that the kind of 'understanding of conceptual connexions' required for concept possession transcends that of the problem-solver and must be that of the *philosopher*: here nothing short of a 'higher-order' awareness of conceptual relationships will do.

I have said nothing so far about the contrast made between intelligence and stupidity. A stupid action is one where the agent fails in some way to apply relevant concepts. But stupidity is not the only contrast. When we say (rightly or wrongly) that dogs and monkeys are intelligent animals but ants and amoebae are not, we are surely not saying that ants and amoebae are *stupid creatures*. To say the latter would imply that they possess concepts but fail to apply them. But ants, like rocks, are not intelligent in the more basic sense that they are not the kinds of entities who can possess concepts in the first place. Their 'behaviour' is explicable not in terms of concept-possession, but in terms of mechanical processes.

It is clear, then, that we have here two different, though related, concepts of intelligence. (1) An intelligent creature is one who lacks the capacity to form concepts. (2) An intelligent act is one where the agent applies concepts successfully. Indeed, a *third* distinction suggests itself. For between (1) and (2) lies concept-possession. A person (or animal) may acquire certain concepts; and whether he goes on to apply them successfully or unsuccessfully is a further question. He may possess chess-playing concepts, regardless of whether he plays chess on any particular occasion. Concept-possession as a third sense is perhaps close to Ryle's identification of 'being intelligent with 'knowing how to do something'. It is also the sense on which educators and psychologists rely when talking of children 'acquiring intelligence' or of the 'growth (development) of intelligence' in the child. When, too, one is urged to 'use one's intelligence' it is one's conceptual equipment that is meant by the term.

We have, then, *three* concepts of intelligence, a distinction we owe originally, and in a somewhat different form to Aristotle.[10] Beginning with the clearly biological one, we have (i) intelligence as the capacity to *form* concepts (this is innate in some animals but not in others) and (ii) intelligence as the capacity to operate with concepts. This is (as a matter of fact) an *acquired* capacity. And since different activities – like playing chess or fishing or studying philosophy – bring their own conceptual equipment with them, intelligence must be specified according to the activity: one can acquire intelligence in sharpshooting, but lack it in trigonometry (perhaps because one has never learnt this). Finally there is (iii) intelligence as the actualisation, that is, the correct application, of conceptual capacities mentioned under (ii).

II

How far do these distinctions help us in sorting out the 'nature–nurture' problem? It looks as if there may be a pretty simple solution to it. Is intelligence an innate capacity? Well, doesn't it depend on which concept one takes? Intelligence as the capacity to form concepts – the first sense – is clearly innate; intelligence in the other two senses is acquired. I am doubtful how far Hebb, in his well-known distinction between 'Intelligence A' and 'Intelligence B', is right in making the former innate by definition.[11] I see no reason in principle why a substance could not be injected into ants, say, to give them the power to form concepts. They would then have this capacity, but not innately. But *as a matter of fact*, if not of logic, intelligence in one sense is innate and in another sense acquired.

It would be gratifying to think one could solve the 'nature–nurture' issue as quickly as this. But it would be odd if one could. For it would be surprising in the extreme if this long-standing controversy which has generated so much heat and so many millions of learned words, turned on no more than a simple ambiguity in the word 'intelligence'.

The controversy, in fact, goes deeper than this. To see this, let us look more closely at the first of the two claims I mentioned at the beginning of this paper in support of 'nature' rather than 'nurture'. The second of these claims – that innate determinants of IQ differences outweigh environmental ones – I shall come to later. It was in fact put forward at a later date than the first claim, deriving originally from Francis Galton and found notably in Cyril Burt's writings, that is, that intelligence is an innate capacity of some sort – in Burt's formulation, that it is 'innate, general, cognitive ability'. Now, despite appearances, it is clear, I think, that intelligence as so defined is *not* intelligence in the first of the three Aristotelian senses, that is, is *not* intelligence as the (innate) capacity to form concepts. For intrinsic to the Galtonian concept of intelligence is that individuals may differ in this intelligence: one person may be more intelligent than another. The notion of possible degrees of intelligence is not written into the concept of intelligence as the (innate) capacity to form concepts. Animals, including men, either have this capacity or they do not. Human beings (in almost all cases) have it.

There is an important linguistic point to make here, so as to avoid a possible confusion. I am claiming, against Galton or Burt, that it does not make sense to say that human beings (all those, i.e., who are able to form concepts) differ in innate capacity as I have defined 'capacity' so far. But 'capacity' is an ambiguous word. In one sense, it simply means 'power': men are born with the power of forming concepts, a power not found in plants and rocks. But in another sense, it means more than this. In saying, for instance, that a milk bottle has a 'capacity' of one pint, I am implying not merely that it has the power of holding one pint, but also, more importantly, that it *lacks the power to hold more than this*. There are upper limits, if you like, on the amount it can hold.

The Galtonian concept of intelligence sees it as an innate capacity in the latter of these two senses. We are born not simply with conceptual powers, but with individually varying upper limits beyond which we cannot develop. We can each hold only just so much intellectual substance; some of us may be quart size, as it was, others pint size, others quarter-pint size. A recent example of such a conception of intelligence is found in a paper of Cyril Burt's, written in 1955 and reprinted in Wiseman's *Intelligence and Ability*. Having defined intelligence as 'an innate, general, cognitive factor', Burt goes on to add: 'The degree of intelligence with which any particular child is endowed is one of the most important factors determining his general efficiency all throughout life. In particular it sets an upper limit to what he can successfully perform, especially in the educational, vocational and intellectual fields'[12] (pp. 280–1).

I cannot stress too strongly the difference between this Galtonian concept of intelligence and the first of my 'Aristotelian' senses. To say, in the Aristotelian way, that we have an innate capacity to form concepts (or to see connexions) does not imply that there is any upper limit, peculiar to the individual, on what concepts we may form or on what connexions we might see. It does not imply an innate capacity in the milk-bottle sense of 'capacity'. It may be true that in *one* sense any concept-using creature must be limited in what he can achieve. If one agrees with Kant's thesis in his *Critique of Pure Reason*, we must all be limited, as far as our theoretical knowledge goes, to what falls within the bounds of our possible experience. If so, being an intelligent creature, that is, having the innate capacity to form concepts, *does* imply upper limits of a sort. This is a conceptual truth, establishable *a priori*. But the Kantian claim is different from the Galtonian one, in that there is no mention in Kant of the possibility of *individual differences* in one's upper limits. The limits are the same for all concept-using creatures, simply in virtue of their being concept-using creatures. In the Galtonian conception, however, we each have our own, individually distinctive, innately produced ceiling of potential.

Having separated out the Galtonian conception from others with which it is too easily confused, we may proceed to examine it more closely. This, as we shall see, will take us into the heart of the 'nature–nurture' issue. Intelligence, on this view, is innate cognitive capacity in the 'milk-bottle' sense.

The crucial problem now is: does intelligence in this Galtonian sense exist? Clearly we cannot take it that it does without evidence. What kind of evidence would be necessary to confirm or refute this claim? At this point we need to break down the claim into two component parts: (i) that for each of us there are upper limits of intellectual development (which may differ from individual to individual) and (ii) that these upper limits are fixed by an *innate* capacity (called 'intelligence'). Both of these sub-claims require evidential support.

Let me concentrate on the first of these. What criteria would have to be satisfied to show that a person has an upper limit in this sense (regardless, for the moment, of how this limit is produced)? Poor achievement on its own would clearly not be a criterion. If a child fails to understand a certain theorem in geometry – Pythagoras' perhaps – we cannot assume such understanding to be forever beyond him. He may well come to grasp it tomorrow perhaps because his teacher has tried to explain it to him in a different way, or for some other reason. But suppose all sorts of teaching methods were tried and none of them worked. Would *this* be sufficient to show that he had reached a ceiling? Is there not still always the possibility that some method may work of which we are not now aware? I suppose there always is. But it seems to me that, beyond a certain point (and I am not clear where that point is) doubts like this may become otiose. Some extreme mental defectives *do* seem to have intellectual ceilings, in that they are unable to develop from the level of sign-cognition very far, if at all, towards the use of symbols. Here the evidence is the failure of all sorts of different methods of helping them over this hurdle. Perhaps this evidence is insufficient. If so, one might conclude that the claim that at least some people have upper intellectual limits is *unverifiable*. I do not think I want to say this. But the Galtonian claim is in any case stronger than this: not that some, but that *all* of us are so limited. Is *this* a verifiable proposition? One difficulty is that this now applies to normal individuals as well as mental defectives: and with normals it is so much more difficult to tell when the criterion I have been urging has been satisfied because, unlike mental defectives, normals possess a conceptual equipment which teachers can make use of in trying to devise different methods of getting them over intellectual hurdles. It is not clear to me just when, if at all, one would be justified in concluding that a normal individual had reached his ceiling and that no further teaching efforts would be of any use.

A second difficulty over the verifiability of the claim that *all* have ceilings is that it seems that there must be at least one person whose ceilings cannot be shown (always assuming that ceilings in general can be determined). For to establish that X has a ceiling one must have failed in attempts to get him beyond this ceiling – which implies that one can oneself operate conceptually beyond this point. So there must always be at least one person of whom it cannot be shown that he has a ceiling. For if there were no such person, then who could have shown that the man or men with the highest ceiling had such a ceiling?

It looks, therefore, as if the claim we are examining is in principle unverifiable. But neither does it seem to be in principle *falsifiable*. For what could possibly falsify the proposition that we all have intellectual ceilings? Nothing, as far as I can see. If one took the most brilliant man in the world, whose grasp of new ideas seemed boundless, even this would not be enough to falsify it. Even he, clearly, might have his *Pons Asinorum* somewhere, even though no one could ever know what it was.

If this argument is correct, the proposition that we all have our own upper limits of ability is both unverifiable and unfalsifiable in principle. So, too, therefore, is the proposition that we all have innately determined upper limits, that is, that there is such a thing as Galtonian intelligence. So too, indeed, is the more specific claim that we all have upper limits which vary along a normal curve. To say that these propositions are unverifiable and unfalsifiable in principle is to underline that they cannot be *empirical* hypotheses. They are, rather, metaphysical speculations in the Kantian sense that they transcend the bounds of any possible experience. Positivists might claim that they are meaningless utterances. Not holding a verifiability theory of meaning, I would not want to go as far as this. But in their unverifiability and unfalsifiability, they are similar to the claim that there is always some unconscious motive for what we do, a hypothesis which some Freudians might hold. Or to the claim that every historical event has been preordained by God, or is the product of economic forces. Or to the claim that Jesus Christ was the Son of God. All of these claims, as far as I can see, *might be* true. But no possible evidence could prove them right or prove them wrong.

Propositions of this kind are often found at the centre of ideological systems of belief, for example, Marxism, Christianity, psychoanalytic theory. This is not surprising. To say that a proposition like 'God exists' cannot be falsified is to say that no one can produce any good reason for claiming that it is not true, or if you like, it is to say that its truth cannot rationally be denied. But if its truth cannot rationally be denied, its truth is surely undeniable. In which case one might be inclined to conclude it surely must be true.

This line of thought may help to explain why adherents of different ideological systems often cling so tenaciously to their beliefs, even where these depend on unverifiable propositions like the one mentioned. But it is, of course, fallacious. What is undeniable in the sense that it cannot be falsified is not necessarily undeniable in the sense that it *must be true*.

Like the religious and political propositions I have mentioned, the proposition that we all have innately determined upper intellectual limits has become the hub of a new ideological system. Around it, too, have accreted all kinds of other propositions, both descriptive, for instance about the constancy of IQ, normal distributions and so on and prescriptive, for example, about the different kinds of educational provision which ought to be made for children of different 'innate capacities'. As such a system grows in complexity and the more its supporters occupy themselves with discussions about details, about the more peripheral parts of the system, the greater the likelihood that the basic beliefs, presupposed to these peripheral ones, get taken for granted and so made all the harder to question or relinquish. If two people, for instance, are arguing whether God is one person or three, they are each committed to the belief that God exists. If two others are arguing whether one's IQ is a valid indication of one's intellectual ceiling, they are each committed to the belief that we have such ceilings.

I now want to link all this up with a discussion of the second claim made on the side of 'nature', mentioned earlier – the claim that individual differences in intelligence are determined largely by genetic factors. 'At last!', some may be thinking: 'this is surely what the "nature–nurture" issue is all about. Whether we have or haven't intellectual ceilings is neither here nor there. What is, is *how far* individual differences in intelligence (as measured by IQ) are attributable to innate or environmental factors'.

But *is* this the 'nature–nurture' issue? Suppose one enters the lists. A dominant school of thought today claims that genetic factors outweigh environmental ones, by about three to one. Suppose one challenges this emphasis on the genetic, arguing that environmental factors are more influential. What, if anything, is one committing oneself to in joining the debate?

To see this, we will have to look more closely at what it *means* to say that individual differences in intelligence are determined largely by genetic factors. First of all, 'intelligence' here stands for 'measured intelligence': a person of high (or low) 'intelligence' is, on this definition, simply a person of high (or low) IQ. There is an important question as to how far a test of 'intelligence' in this technical sense is a test of it in any ordinary language sense. It seems to me that it tests, at most, only restricted areas in which intelligence can be displayed, for instance the area of formal logical relations. It does not test one's intelligence, say, as a boxer or as a tennis player. In addition, a low score on a test fails to discriminate between intelligence in the second and third of my Aristotelian senses. That is, it is not evident simply from a subject's answers whether he scored badly because he *lacked the conceptual equipment* to do tests of this sort or he *possessed the equipment but failed*, on this occasion, to apply it.

But leaving these doubts on one side it is still not at all clear what it means to say that individual differences in IQ are largely determined by genetic factors. This is especially so, where this is taken to mean that over 50 per cent of the variation is determined by the genes and 50 per cent by the environment. (A commonly found ratio in the literature is $75:25$ in favour of 'nature'.) Can causal factors be quantified? Suppose we are asking what caused a fire in a warehouse. Does it make sense to say that it was due, say, 50 per cent to the lighted cigarette end, 30 per cent to the presence of inflammable material, and so on? It does not make much sense to me, either in this case or in the intelligence case.

But if we leave out precise proportions, we can at least attach *some* sense to the claim in question. It certainly makes sense to say that variations in the height of individual adults are largely determined by genetic factors, more by these than by environmental ones. It is a move towards unintelligibility to then ask: but what is the precise proportion? For to say in this case that genetic factors are more influential than environmental ones is not to say that they account for more than 50 per cent of the sum-total of causal factors, but that they fix the upper limit of physical growth for each individual, while environmental factors, like diet, can only operate below that limit, to bring people up to it, or leave them stunted.

The application of this to intelligence should be clear. The claim that individual differences in IQ are largely determined by innate factors only makes sense, I believe, if it means that innate factors fix the upper limits of one's intellectual development while environmental factors operate only within this innately determined framework. But this presupposes the existence of intelligence in the Galtonian sense, that there are individually differing upper intellectual limits. Whoever enters the lists over whether innate or environmental factors are more influential is equally committed to a belief in this. In joining issue at all one cedes victory to the nativists, since one admits the truth of the untestable belief which is the bedrock of their position. It is more rational, perhaps, not to begin to take sides. Or, at least, not to attack the nativistic position by coming down in favour of 'environment' (what would it mean, after all, to say that environmental factors counted for, say, 60 per cent?) but, rather, by drawing attention to the untestable assumption on which the whole nativistic position rests. The claim that 75 per cent of the variation between individuals in IQ is genetically determined is based on studies of identical twins to a large extent. In case it should seem that I am ignoring direct reference to these studies, let me spend a minute or two looking at this evidence. The nub of the argument is that there is a high correlation (0.75) between the IQs of monozygotic twins reared apart. Since, it is held, their environments are very different, the factor explaining this similarity in IQ is the factor they have in common, that is, their genetic endowment.

As far as I can see, this argument rests on an unjustified assumption. Suppose one does indeed find a correlation of 0.75 between IQs of identical twins. Or suppose, to make the issue more clear-cut, there is even a correlation of 1.0: each twin has exactly the same IQ as his co-twin. This in itself would not support the genetic case. For suppose one twin from each pair were given intensive coaching in answering intelligence tests and as a result, when both these twins and their co-twins were retested, the coached twins scored on average 20 IQ points above their co-twins. This would, of course, significantly reduce the correlation between IQs. So the assumption lying behind *actual* twin research is that none of the twins' IQs could alter sufficiently to change the 0.75 correlation. But, as far as I know, this assumption is quite without foundation. No varied attempts have been made, and have failed, to change the twins' IQs by coaching. Far from this twin research being able to *show* us that people have their own intellectual limits, it is clear, I think, that this assumption is built into the research itself.

In searching for what is at issue in the 'nature–nurture' controversy, I have tried to show that the fundamental issue is whether or not we all have our own upper limits and that this is undecidable. I have tried to rebut the suggestion that the issue is whether genetic factors out-weigh environmental ones, since to make *this* the issue is to presuppose this assumption. But the 'nature–nurture' controversy has also often been presented as revolving round a different issue; the issue of whether or not one's IQ is 'fixed', that is, represents the upper limits of one's possible development. If the IQ can be improved, this is thought to be a point in favour of 'nurture' rather than 'nature'. Hunt identifies the issue in this way in his *Intelligence and Experience*. He discusses the arguments for and against what he calls the 'belief in fixed intelligence'. His 'evidence dissonant with fixed intelligence', includes evidence against the constancy of the IQ and evidence on the improvements in IQ due to schooling. For Hunt the 'nature–nurture' issue is one which can be settled by empirical research. But this, I think, is to misconstrue the nature of the controversy. The recent resurgence of nativistic literature, by Jensen and others, shows how little evidence like Hunt's against a fixed IQ has damaged the nativistic position. If one claims, as recent writers do, that *most* of the variation in individual IQs is genetically determined, this is not to deny that environmental influences have *some* effect; so any improvement in individual IQs can easily be accommodated in the theory.

The 'nature–nurture' issue cannot be settled by empirical research. There is indeed a danger that immersion in research may strengthen the hand of the Galtonians, by drawing attention away from the irrefutability of their doctrine. Hunt himself provides an interesting example of this. He rejects the belief that the IQ indicates one's upper mental limits. But he could still quite consistently hold that there *are* such upper limits, and there is in fact some evidence in his book that he does believe in the existence of Galtonian intelligence. He writes, 'The genes set limits on the individual's potential for intellectual development, but they do not guarantee that this potential will be achieved and they do not, therefore, fix the level of intelligence as it is commonly measured.'[13] Paradoxically, therefore, Hunt is still on the nativistic side of the fence.

It is misguided, therefore, to locate the 'nature–nurture' issue in disputes either over the relative weight of genetic and environmental factors on IQ differences, or over the fixedness of the IQ. The real issue is whether we all have our own upper limit. But to call this an 'issue' is itself, perhaps misguided. Since it cannot be falsified, no one can seriously take issue with it. The most one can do is to indicate just this. Some self-styled 'environmentalists' seek to rebut the Galtonian doctrine by claiming that there are no upper limits of ability. But this, it seems to me, goes too far, for this claim is just as unverifiable and as unfalsifiable as the claim that such limits exist: atheism on this issue is no more rational than theism. There is, perhaps, after all, no 'nature–nurture' issue, since there is no scope, at this level, for rational disagreement. Those who accept the Galtonian claim as true have forsaken rationality for the domain of faith. There is no reasoning with them.

Notes and references

1 Miles, T. R., 'On defining intelligence', in Wiseman, S., *Intelligence and Ability*, p. 163 (Harmondsworth, Penguin Books, 1967).
2 Fisher, M., 'Intelligence', *Proceedings of Philosophy of Education Society*, Vol. I, 1966.
3 Ryle, G., *The Concept of Mind*, p. 45 (London, Hutchinson, 1949).
4 Ryle, G., op. cit., p. 47.
5 Peters, R. S., *The Concept of Motivation*, p. 112 (London, Routledge, 1958).
6 I am assuming that the dog's salivation would not count as 'behaviour'. On this, see Hamlyn, D. W., 'Behaviour', *Philosophy*, 1953.
7 Searle, J. R., *Speech Acts*, pp. 141 ff. (Cambridge, Cambridge University Press, 1970).
8 MacIntyre, A. C., 'Purpose and intelligent action', *Proceedings of the Aristotelian Society*, Supplement Vol., 1960.
9 Price, H. H., *Thinking and Experience*, pp. 101 ff. (London, Hutchinson, 1953).
10 Aristotle, *de Anima*, II. 5., 417a 21.
11 Hebb, D. O., *The Organisation of Behaviour*, pp. 294 ff. (New York, Science Editions, 1961).
12 Wiseman, S., op. cit. As well as Burt's article (pp. 260–81), see also the extracts from Gallon's *Hereditary Genius*, ch. 3 (pp. 21–32).
13 Hunt, J. M., *Intelligence and Experience*, p. 7 (New York, Ronald Press, 1961).

CHAPTER 2

THE EDUCATION OF THE EMOTIONS

Journal of Philosophy of Education (1984), 18(2): 233–44

Richard Peters' claim in his essay on 'The education of the emotions' (Peters, 1972) that there is a twofold task involved in the education of the emotions – the development of appropriate appraisals, and the control and canalisation of passivity – is a consequence of the way he thinks of both emotions and education. I shall argue that this double conceptual constraint leads him into an altogether too narrow an account of how the emotions can be educated. This critique will lead us both into a richer, alternative account of the topic and also into a more extensive investigation of Peters' philosophy of mind.

The concept of emotion falls, Peters claims, under the category of passivity. We talk, for instance, of the emotion of fear. We also talk of fear as a motive, as when someone runs away from a barking dog. What differentiates fear as an emotion from fear as a motive? For Peters the difference is in terms of passivity and activity. When we talk of fear as an emotion we refer to cases where people are overcome by fear, reduced by it to teeth-chattering or blanching inactivity; where it is a motive, it is, as in the example given above, a motive for *action*. The same mental state is present whether we have to do with fear as an emotion or fear as a motive. Whether rooted to the spot by the sight of the snarling dog or taking to one's heels, in each case one sees the animal as a threat to one's well-being. Peters follows most other philosophical writers on emotion in holding that emotions have, or at least typically have, a 'cognitive core'. To feel an emotion is at least to see the object of one's emotion in a certain light; and each emotion incorporates its own distinctive kind of appraisal, fear bringing with it the thought that something is a threat to one, anger the thought that something has frustrated one, and so on.

Peters' account of education in the article is familiar: ' "education" suggests the initiation of people into what is worthwhile in a way which involves some depth and breadth of understanding and knowledge' (p. 474). Together, his concept of emotion and his concept of education narrowly circumscribe what the education of the emotions can consist in. Since emotions and motives belong on different sides of the passivity/activity fence, it can have nothing to do (with one exception, which I shall discuss later) with the development of motivation: it must be restricted to operations on passive states of mind. What kind of operations? Since education basically involves developing knowledge and understanding, educating the emotions must consist in bringing these passive states of mind under the sway of truth and reason.

This can be achieved in two ways. First, by the development of appropriate appraisals. Since the judgments or appraisals which we saw above to constitute the 'cognitive core' of emotions may be false or unfounded, education in this sphere consists in bringing pupils to replace their false and irrational thoughts by true and well-grounded ones. In recognising and reacting to emotions in themselves and in others pupils must also be brought to perceive emotions which *actually exist*, not seeing jealousy in a person, for instance, when he or she is not jealous at all. Their love of truth, finally, will lead them to be sincere in the revelation of their own emotions to others.

The second, closely related, way of educating the emotions is the control and canalisation of passivity. The development of appropriate appraisals 'is made doubly difficult because of the countervailing influence of more primitive, wild types of appraisal that warp and cloud perception and judgment and aid and abet self-deception and insincerity' (p. 479). Presumably the thought here is that some appraisals are so 'primitive' as to be beyond the reach of reason. A child may be able to be talked out of her ill-founded fear of frogs, but more deep-seated fears are often intractable. Such emotional states get in the way of the pursuit of truth essential to education. One can try to control them, Peters suggests, in several ways. In this context we can leave on one side non-educational techniques like conditioning. Educational techniques include developing the kind of self-understanding advocated by Freud and developing other, 'self-transcending', emotions which can loosen the hold on us of the more primitive ones. Since the same state can be a motive as well as an emotion, one can also try to control emotions by developing appropriate action patterns: rather than 'writhing with sympathy' or 'fuming with moral indignation', one can become motivated by sympathy or moral indignation to act in certain ways, thus preventing oneself from being dominated by passivity. Finally, one can learn to canalise such expressions of emotion into speech and symbolic gesture, including forms of art. Rather than fuming, for instance, one can express one's moral indignation in a piece of satire.

It is essential to Peters' argument about control and canalisation that certain emotions and certain motives are taken to be of more educational value than others. Not just *any* emotion can be employed by the educator to control the more primitive ones, but only 'self-transcending' emotions, 'notably love, respect, the sense of justice and concern for truth' (p. 480). Not just *any* motives should be encouraged in the quest to control passivity, only 'positive sentiments such as respect, benevolence and the sense of justice' (p. 481).

Why are these particular emotions and motives thought to be of educational value? Peters does not spell this out, but it seems clear from his other writings that it must be to do with the conceptual connexion he makes between education and the development of reason. Justice, benevolence, respect for persons and truth-telling all appear in Peters' ethical theory as the names of ultimate principles which can be shown by use of transcendental arguments to be presupposed to any rational morality.

What *aims* lie behind the educating of the emotions as Peters sees it? The various ways of developing appropriate appraisals all lead pupils out of error and towards a concern for truth. Why is *this* important? There could, in principle, be two sorts of reason: pursuing or possessing truth could be valuable in its own right, or it could be valuable as means to, or part of, something larger. When a child comes to see that her fear of frogs is irrational since frogs are not dangerous, is this insight intrinsically valuable, or is it important to her in the wider management of her life? Many, including myself, would wish to say the latter. But it would be difficult for Peters to take this line, at least within the confines of his own theory of the emotions, since relating someone's fears to the management of their life entails understanding fear *as a motive*. In this way of looking at the matter, one tries to remove the child's fear of frogs because one does not want her to grow up needlessly timid, to shy away from frogs when she sees them in a friend's garden, etc. It is her forms of *activity*, her behavioural dispositions – timidity and confidence, for example – which we as educators are trying to shape. But the shaping of activity and the motives which underlie it is, as I have repeatedly stressed, outside Peters' remit.

We are left with the alternative that for Peters the establishment of true rather than false judgements, not only about the objects of the pupil's emotions, but also about emotions perceived in others, is valuable for its own sake. Certainly nothing in his discussion of these topics points to any other justification. Elsewhere in his writings the central aim of education appears to be the pursuit of truth not for instrumental reasons but for its own sake. It would be reasonable to see this more general theory as having application in this specific area of the education of the emotions: the pursuit of truth for its own sake is Peters' hallmark of education, whether the pupil is engaged on science or history or is concerned with his own and others' emotions and their objects.

When he turns to the control and canalisation of passivity, Peters does emphasise the importance of building up patterns of action based on appropriate motives. Here, he appears to come close to those, mentioned above, who see the education of the emotions as shaping dispositions, traits of character. But the appearance is deceptive. We are dealing with two radically different and historically deeply rooted conceptions of education. On the one side we have education as the formation of character, on the other education as an initiation into the pursuit of knowledge for its own sake. If Peters emphasises motives and dispositions in the present section, it is only as a means – one means among several – of preventing the pupil from being overwhelmed by passivity. Why is it undesirable to be so overwhelmed? It is because, as we have seen, this tends to 'warp and cloud' perception and judgment. We come back to the overriding importance of being free from false beliefs, to all appearances as an end in itself.

An alternative to Peters' theory has begun to emerge. It is based on different premises, both about the nature of emotions and about the nature of education. On the latter, its concept is broader than Peters'. Education is upbringing in general, not the more specific enterprise, such as is found in universities and in many schools, of engaging pupils in the pursuit of truth for its own sake. It is concerned with the all-round formation of the person, with 'the whole man'. It seeks to shape the pupil's central dispositions and interests, to lay down and lock together the girders of character.

Its conception of the emotions is different, too. Emotions and motives do not fall under two mutually exclusive categories – passivity and activity – so that emotions cannot be motives and vice-versa. On the alternative account we are considering, emotions can be and often are motives. We see a snarling dog and are afraid. We may be so afraid that we are rooted to the spot. Here the emotion – fear – which we are experiencing indeed leaves us passive, unable to act. But the same emotion in a less intense form may urge us to run away. Here our emotion is our motive.

Some of the leading features of the alternative account are already emerging. Education as upbringing has to do with the formation of character. In this view parents and teachers bring up young children to be people of a certain sort. In two main ways. They want them to possess certain virtues, to be courageous and confident rather than cowardly and timid, to be resolute, temperate, just, wise, kind, compassionate and so on. And they also want them to grow up to have attachments, commitments to particular objects, whether these be careers, sports, intellectual and artistic activities; friends, lovers, their own children, or indeed themselves; neighbourhood- and work-communities; their town, country, international organisations. (The specific virtues and attachments listed are meant only as examples, not as prescriptions.) Of course they want them, too, to possess all sorts of skills and all sorts of factual knowledge. On the account of education, I am sketching these will come on the back of the virtues and the attachments: just as one cannot be courageous unless one knows what to do in different frightening situations, so one cannot be a committed basketball player without having acquired the game's particular skills.

The emotions are intimately connected with this conception of education as fostering virtues and attachments. Many virtues are formed by the shaping of particular emotions. Courage, for instance, has to do with how one learns to manage one's fears. There is nothing mechanical about this. Courageous people are not those who always stand their ground and never run away. They learn to adjust their reactions and behaviour to the different kinds of fearful situations which they face. They are not afraid of things of which there is clearly no reason to be afraid, like ghosts or rabbits; they learn to withstand the fear they feel of other things where it is appropriate to do so, sometimes by drawing on stronger motives (e.g. a front line soldier guided by thoughts of honour) and sometimes by taking care not to reveal to others the fear that they feel (e.g. a mother with young children in a forest in a thunderstorm). And when they are faced with something as dangerous as an escaped wild tiger, they do what is appropriate to that situation – and take to their heels. Courageous people can thus be *motivated* by fear on occasions: it is not the case that courage has always to do with the control of an emotion which simply affects one, in a passive way.

Some emotions are related to virtues much more often as motives than courage is. Sympathy, for instance. In shaping this as an ingredient of such virtues as thoughtfulness, friendliness or cooperativeness, educators have good reason to encourage pupils to act out of sympathy on many occasions. But here, too, acquiring these virtues requires the same kind of *judgment* that we saw in the case of courage. Sometimes one's sympathy, like one's fear, has to be kept in check, or regulated appropriately: people in positions of power like judges, politicians or civil servants must be careful to maintain their impartiality when tempted unduly to favour individuals or groups of individuals towards which they feel a particular sympathy.

Emotions enter into virtues, therefore, sometimes passively and sometimes as motives. There are no tidy boundaries here, there being variations in the proportion both between emotions and within particular emotions, depending on what is appropriate to different situations. This notion of appropriateness to a situation is central here. It comes from Aristotle's remark in the *Nicomachean Ethics* (Book 2, ch. 6) that 'to feel emotions at the right times, with reference to the right objects, towards the right people, with the right motive, and in the right way, is what is both intermediate and best, and this is characteristic of virtue'. Judgement is of the first importance. This is not to say, of course, that in every fearful situation, say, the courageous person works out *de novo* what to do: he or she has built up dispositions of different kinds to cope with different types of situation. But he or she cannot react purely automatically, but has to keep an intelligent eye open to know which dispositions to draw on and what subtle changes in the situation call for equally finely discriminated responses. Like Peters' theory, this alternative sees the education of the emotions as bringing them under the sway of reason. But it does so in a different way: we are not talking now about the intrinsic pursuit of truth, but about that practical wisdom which learns to manage, control and direct the emotions in an intelligent way as part of the larger project of promoting one's own and others' well-being.

So far in this alternative account I have spoken only of the connexion between emotions and virtues. I have said nothing yet about attachments. But before we leave the virtues, I should stress that not all virtues are as directly tied to particular emotions as courage is to fear, thoughtfulness to sympathy, or temperance to the desires for food, drink or sex. Being reliable, honest, truthful, just are different. These are 'artificial' rather than 'natural' virtues, in that' possessing them is to be disposed to follow the interpersonal rules necessary to sustain a community, like promise-keeping, telling the truth, or impartiality in the distribution of goods. But even though not directly tied to particular emotions, these artificial virtues may still have *some* connexion with them. In bringing up children to be honest, reliable and fair, we may well want them – it would indeed be odd if we did not – to *want* to be those things, and want to be them not in the grim, emotionally neutral way that a Puritan may want to do his duty, but seeing their being honest etc. with some prospect *of pleasure* in their being so (see Gosling, 1969, chs 6, 11). If, then, we want our pupils to be pleased when they come up to the mark in these ways, ashamed or guilty when they fail to do so, we are building on such emotions as these in inculcating into them the artificial virtues.

Hardie (1980) points out in his *Aristotle's Ethical Theory* that by the 'character' of a person we should understand primarily a 'system of sentiments' and interests, not a collection of virtues and vices (p. 121). We do not know much about Hitler, for example, if we know only that he was courageous and abstemious: to understand the moving forces in his character we have to know about the ends to which he was committed, about his *attachments* in the term which I used previously. At the same time it would be wrong to draw too clear-cut a distinction between virtues and attachments. For attachments bring virtues with them. In loving my country, I display courage in defending it; just as my devotion to science goes along, for instance, with intellectual honesty and fairness in my treatment of other researchers in my field (MacIntyre, 1981, ch. 14).

If education is to embrace the formation of attachments, it should be obvious that here, too, it must set about shaping the pupil's emotions and associated behaviour. This is partly because, as we have seen, attachments are sustained by virtues and virtues are founded on emotions, and partly because, as Hardie, following psychologists of sentiment like Shand, McDougall and Sprott, points out, a "sentiment" [or 'attachment' as I have been using the term] is an "organised concentration of interest" round one object. It involves not a uniform range of emotions, as does an Aristotelian virtue, but an interconnected variety of emotions appropriate to a variety of relationships. Thus anyone who has a sentiment of attachment to a society, such as a college, will be pleased by its successes, saddened by its failures, and gratified by the misfortunes of its rivals' (op. cit.: 121–2).

Education in attachments pivots around the emotion, or emotions, of love. Pupils come to love objects of different sorts. Sexual love will draw them towards other people. Love in the sense of cherishing will attract them not only to other individuals but also to social objects like schools or nations as well as to intellectual disciplines (Elliott, 1974), natural scenery, types of sport, and so on. If love is central, it brings with it the whole complex of emotions, peculiar to each object of attachment, to which Hardie refers. It is because I love the philosophy of education that I am pleased when it prospers, depressed and anxious when its future seems uncertain, indignant when its critics unjustly malign it.

This and similar examples show, incidentally, that it is misleading to claim, as Peters is sometimes inclined to do, that the education of the emotions should seek to foster only 'positive' emotions like compassion, love of truth or respect. Indignation and anxiety are also sometimes appropriate and need to be encouraged. Negative emotions are a necessary element in the formation of attachments: love is inextricable from anxious concern. As we saw earlier, too, developing the virtues may bring with it the encouragement of negative emotions on occasion: the courageous person may well be right to feel afraid from time to time.

Which theory, Peters' or its alternative, is to be preferred? This depends largely on which has the more acceptable account both of the nature of education and of the nature of emotion. What education is taken to be partly involves value-judgements about ends. These stand in need of justification. Why the central aim of education should be taken to be the pursuit of truth has been much discussed in recent philosophy of education: it is clear that there are manifold difficulties facing this claim (White, 1982, ch. 2). Education as upbringing, that is, character-formation, is far less contentious. There will be all kinds of disagreements about the *kinds of* virtues and attachments to be fostered, but I know of no one who would deny that children need to develop *some* virtues and *some* attachments. And this is all that the alternative position requires.

On the nature of emotion the latter is also more acceptable. For Peters, fear (e.g.) as an emotion cannot be fear as a motive, since emotions fall under the category of passivity and motives, under that of activity. His claim is counterintuitive: in ordinary speech we make no such distinction. It seems to make entirely good sense to say that emotions can be motives, that, for instance, the anger which afflicted me is the reason why I hit *him*. What grounds, then, does Peters have for apparently saying the opposite?

His argument, like the one just given, rests on considerations drawn from ordinary language; but in a different way. The nub of Peters' position is that when we use the word 'emotion' we do so to pick out our passivity (Peters, 1972: 469), whereas we use 'motive' only when an explanation for an action is at issue (ibid.). These are empirical claims and as far as that about the word 'emotion' is concerned I remain sceptical. Certainly there is no awkwardness or linguistic infelicity in talking of different 'passions' leading us to do this or that – given that is that we are looking at literary or philosophical writings of the eighteenth or nineteenth centuries, since the term 'passion' is now in little use in this sense. Neither is there any problem about talk of 'feelings' motivating us as well as overcoming or over-whelming us. ('I felt so ashamed, I just had to confess there and then.') Can we similarly find plausible examples of the use of 'emotion' in the context of motivation? What about 'I have never been much affected by the more altruistic emotions: if I had, I would have led a worthier life?' The example is contrived; but it is enough to suggest that the term 'emotion' like its synonyms 'passion' and 'feeling', can connote activity as well as passivity. One difficulty is that 'emotion', unlike 'feeling', is something of a technical term devised by philosophers and psychologists, so has less secure a place than, say, 'feeling' in ordinary language. But even if we conceded to Peters that the word 'emotion' was used to connote passivity, this would merely be a point about word-usage. It would not support the more substantive claim that *emotions themselves* – the fear or joy or contempt that one feels – are purely passive phenomena. It is quite consistent to claim that such emotions have an active as well as a passive side to them *and* that, for whatever reason in the history of linguistic usage, the term 'emotion' (but not 'fear' or 'joy') is used only when referring to passivity.

That the *concept* of emotion connotes activity as well as passivity even though the use of the *word* 'emotion' (perhaps?) lacks such an association should by now, I think, be abundantly clear. If this is so, Peters' account of the education of the emotions falls behind its competitor not only on the nature of education but also on the nature of emotion.

To understand more fully why Peters' account of the education of the emotions is so very different from the alternative account, we have to see rather more of his underlying theory of human nature.

On the alternative account the emotions, brought increasingly under rational control in the way indicated, are the building blocks of character. Peters relegates them to a far more peripheral part of our nature. What for him is central?

Putting together pieces of the jigsaw found in his various writings, the picture looks like this. Human nature has a passive side and an active side. Emotions are passive. Some mental states – fear, anger, love, etc. – which are labelled 'emotions' if passive, can also be called 'motives' if they provide an explanation of actions. But not all explanations of actions are motives. Motives are a special class of reasons for actions. We do not ask for people's motives in playing chess or in giving Christmas presents to their friends. This is because they are doing the done thing: their behaviour does not call for justification. It is only where there is something untoward about an action that we ask for a motive. The term 'is used in contexts where conduct is being assessed and not simply explained, where there is a breakdown in conventional expectations' (Peters, 1958: 35).

There are problems parallel to those arising with emotions over Peters' analysis of motivation. He directs his attention to the conditions under which we use the *word* 'motive', rather than more directly with the implications of the concept of a motive. Whereas it may be true that we only ask for a 'motive' when we feel there is something unobvious or untowards which needs to be explained, it is quite consistent with this, and surely true, that people *have* motives for quite conventional actions even if, naturally enough, there is no point in asking for them. (A person's motive may be that she *wants* to do the done thing.)

Leaving the adequacy of Peters' analysis on one side, however, the interesting point for us is that motives, like emotions, cannot be at the core of his theory of human nature, but must be more peripheral. Motives have to do with a 'breakdown in conventional expectations'. It is then *acting conventionally* that is at the centre of things.

'Man is a rule-following animal' states Peters (op. cit.: 5) 'His actions are not simply directed towards ends; they also conform to social standards and conventions.' Not only that; but these standards and conventions 'enter into and often define the end' (ibid.) as in the case of passing an examination or getting married.

Conventional, rule-following behaviour provides the foundation, the bed-rock of Peters' theory of human nature. Upon that foundation is erected the superstructure of rationality. Not all rules and conventions are rationally justifiable. The path one ought to follow in life – not least in educating the young – is to sift away those rules which cannot be rationally grounded and live by those which are. Peters' ethical theory is mainly taken up with identifying and justifying the criteria, in the shape of higher-order moral principles, which enable us to sift lower-level rules in this way.

Closely connected with the concepts of rules and rule-following in Peters' scheme is the concept of habit. In his discussion of the two forms of life in 'Reason and habit: the paradox of moral education' one finds the same fundamental contrast between the sphere of the merely conventional and the sphere of rationality: 'on the one hand there is an emphasis on habit, tradition and being properly brought up; on the other hand there is an emphasis on intellectual training, and on the development of critical thought and choice' (Peters, 1981: 45). Moral education is described as a process whereby children 'must enter the palace of Reason through the courtyard of Habit and Tradition' (op. cit.: 52).

Peters' fundamental conception of human nature, therefore, is of a two-tier structure with the habitual following of conventional rules at the bottom and the rational life at the top. In passing from one to the other, one does not *abandon* habits and conventions. One's day-to-day life is, indeed, woven around them – rational ones to be sure. 'The art of living consists, to a large extent, in reducing most things that have to be done to habit; for then the mind is set free to pay attention to things that are interesting, novel and worthwhile' (op. cit.: 56). To be thus liberated is to lead the life of reason. This has a procedural aspect as we saw just now – one lives by rationally defensible moral principles like benevolence, justice and telling the truth; and it also defines the ends it is most worthwhile to seek – Peters' 'worthwhile activities', those which any rational person must follow, all to do with the pursuit of truth for its own sake.

Schematically we can present the elements of Peters' theory of human nature as shown in Table 2.1.

It is clear from this that while habit and convention provide the basis from which education as the development of rationality must proceed, Peters sees little or no positive role for the emotions in education, whether we are using 'emotion' in this sense or in the more usual sense whereby emotions can be motives. Emotions as forms of passivity can, as we know, 'warp and cloud perception and judgment' and need therefore to be controlled and canalised; in this, as in the correction of the false appraisals they sometimes involve, reason can get to work in one form or another (see Table 2.1) so as to prevent emotions from interfering with rational development.

In one way, despite what has just been said, emotions may have a central place in Peters' conception of education, if only as the source from which all learning proceeds. Whether he *does* want to claim this is not too clear, but we do know, at least, that

(a) wishing is to be distinguished from wanting in that the former falls under the concept of passivity and the latter under that of activity (Peters, 1972: 472–3);
(b) emotion implies wishing, but not wanting (ibid.);
(c) in the course of a child's upbringing wants emerge from wishes (ibid.: 149).

Table 2.1

		Tier 2	Rational activity
Same mental state (e.g. fear, can be passive or active)			
Emotions	Motivated actions	Tier1	Conventional actions, habits
	Deviations from Normality		Normality
Passivity		Activity	

This does not clinch the case for emotions as the basis of everything else, since we are not told whether there could be wishes unconnected with emotion. But it at least leaves it possible, perhaps even likely, that Peters sees emotions as such a source.

But there is something odd about claim (c), that wants 'emerge from' wishes. Since activity and passivity in Peters are categorically distinct, what sense can be made of a transition from one to the other? This mystery apart, Peters' account would seem to make human nature at its most basic level something wholly passive. This flies in the face of empirical evidence that human beings, like other animals, show active tendencies – in food-seeking, for instance – even at birth. One difficulty here has to do with the concept of wanting which Peters employs. This, like many of his psychological concepts, diverges from the more familiar concept on which other philosophers as well as common sense, rely.

For Peters, wanting *x*, unlike wishing for *x*, implies grasping that *means y* can be taken to bring about *x* (Peters, 1972: 149). It also brings with it the concept of *reasons*, since one now understands bringing about *x* as a reason for doing *y*. Wanting, finally, involves *standards*: 'the ends wished for come to be conceived in more determinate ways and according to standards definitive of reality thinking' (Peters, 1973: 88); 'wishes become wants when social standards defining ends and efficient and socially appropriate ways of attaining them become imposed on this autistic amalgam' (Peters, 1981: 32–3).

But this provides too rich a concept of wanting. Not all wants imply understanding means-end connexions, grasping reasons, conforming to rules. Hungry new-born fledglings want food, yet none of these implications hold of them. Wanting, or desiring, is a primitive concept. The conceptual links which Peters makes in fact go the other way: none of the three things he picks out is possible without wanting something. Peters' concept of wanting is close to but not, I think, identical with the ordinary concept of intending, where intending to do *y* normally involves wanting *x* and believing that *y* is a means to *x* (McGinn, 1982: 94–5).

It makes sense to claim that wants in Peters' sense 'emerge from' something conceptually simpler; but what they emerge from is wants in the more ordinary sense, together with belief about what will satisfy them. They do not, at all events, emerge from wishes. Peters states that wishing, unlike wanting (in his sense), does not involve the thought of taking means to ends. Is this true? A hungry man in a desert may wish for food. What does this imply? Two things, I think: (a) that he wants food and (b) that he believes that he can't get food. Other examples support a similar analysis: the child who wishes she could be playing in the park wants to do so, but knows (and therefore believes) that her mother will not let her; someone wishing he hadn't done something wants the past to be different but knows this is impossible. Wishing therefore presupposes wanting, and in addition a belief about the impossibility (physical, legal, conceptual etc.) of achieving what one wants. If this is right, then Peters' claim that wishing does not involve the thought of taking means to ends must be wrong: it involves it well enough, and in addition the thought that in this case taking means to the end is ruled out. Wishing is thus a more complex concept than Peters allows: it is not a passivity-concept rather than an activity-concept, since it involves activity-concepts like wanting and taking a means to an end.

How does all this leave the putative connexion between emotion and wishing? *Neither* concept, pace Peters, involves passivity rather than activity. Both concepts include both wants and beliefs. The beliefs necessary to wishing are more sophisticated than those necessary to emotion: a cat or dog can in some embryonic sense see something as *threatening*, and thus be capable of fear; but only a more advanced concept-user, perhaps only a language-user, could see something as *impossible*. While wishing cannot be the bedrock of all human learning, the desires and beliefs found in the more basic of our emotions may well be.

Peters' attitude towards the emotions is irresistibly reminiscent of Kant. He shares the views that human beings ought to realise their rational natures and that they are often impeded in this task by non-rational influences, their passions and inclinations. Kant's rationale for his view depends on his 'two-world' view of man as consisting of a noumenal self and a phenomenal self. Peters does not use this distinction, but for him there is still something of a bifurcation in our nature: on the one hand the area of convention and reason, and on the other that of emotions and motives. Generally speaking, as with Kant, he holds that it is the job of the first part of our nature to keep the second part from sullying it or diverting it from its proper tasks. As with Kant, certain of our emotions – Kant's 'reverence for the law', Peters' 'rational passions' involved in the pursuit of truth, like a love of clarity or a hatred of irrelevance (Peters, 1973: 74ff.) – accompany rather than hinder the life of reason, but strictly speaking, on his theory of the emotions, they can have no more active, that is, motivating role.

I say 'strictly speaking' here, because in some of his later writings, Peters seems to allow a more positive role for emotions and motives in education than in his first investigations of these concepts (Peters, 1958, 1961). In the article on the 'Education of the emotions' (Peters, 1972) we already see one divergence. I mentioned above his view that the wilder appraisals found in some emotions can be canalised and controlled by developing associated motives: it is better, he says, to act out of sympathy than merely writhe with sympathy. Here sympathy, along with respect, benevolence and a sense of justice all count as motives. Peters only once refers to such things as these as 'motives'. Otherwise he calls them 'positive sentiments'. This is an indication, perhaps, of uneasiness about a possible inconsistency here. If motives, as portrayed in Peters (1958), are reasons for actions 'where there is a breakdown in conventional expectations', there is surely some strain in describing sympathy, respect and benevolence as 'motives'. In later writings, this early analysis of 'motive' appears to have been left even further behind. In 'Moral development: a plea for pluralism', we read, for instance, of virtues, such as compassion, which are also motives for action (Peters, 1981: 94).

Some emotions, too, come to have a more positive role in education, with the old hard- and fast-line between emotions and motives now softening. I have in mind the 'rational passions' mentioned above. The love of order, concern about getting things right and hatred of confusion that accompany the pursuit of truth are not just passive byproducts of the activity: they urge the inquirer onwards, are motives or reasons for what he does. It is significant, perhaps, that Peters does not write of the 'rational emotions', preferring to rely on a more old-fashioned term which, as he implies (Peters, 1973: 80) bridges the gap between passivity and activity.

In his employment of a bridging term like 'passion' and in his use of 'motive' in a less restricted way, Peters has come in his later writings away from his original conceptual scheme for describing human nature to something nearer that embodied in the alternative theory. Even here, the only emotions and motives that are explicitly derestricted are those attendant on the life of reason, the rational passions on the one hand and motives like benevolence and a sense of justice, which are enshrined in following the supreme principles of a rational morality. We are still some way from the alternative, Aristotelian, picture of the shaping of one's whole repertoire of emotions to form the virtues and attachments which make up one's character.

These latter three concepts – of virtues, attachments and of character – so central to the alternative account of the education of the emotions, cannot be constructed out of the conceptual equipment of Peters' original account. The Aristotelian concept of the virtues depends on a concept of emotion which embraces both passivity and activity: Peters' insistence on using only concepts which fall neatly on one side or other of this line makes the employment of virtue concepts impossible: it is not surprising, therefore, in his ethical theory that he favours a morality of rules and principles rather than one based on the virtues (Wamock, 1971, chs 5, 6).

A similar argument could be mounted to show that the concept of an attachment or sentiment, at least in the sense found in the alternative account, is also unemployable. Peters does, it is true, use the term 'sentiment' (cf. Peters, 1972: 480), but only in the different sense of 'a settled disposition to make appraisals of a certain sort' (in other words as referring to a continuant emotion rather than an occurrent one).

The concept of character is especially interesting in this connexion. Unlike the concept of a virtue, it is one to which Peters has devoted a lot of attention in different writings. In his essay on 'Moral education and the psychology of character', for example, he says of the terms 'character' and 'character-trait' that their significance is primarily adverbial. They usually indicate a *manner or style* of behaving without any definite implication of directedness or aversion – unlike the terms 'motive', 'attitude' and 'sentiment' (Peters, 1981: 25). When we talk about a person's 'character' we talk about things like his honesty, punctuality, considerateness, meanness (see also Peters, 1958: 5), not about his greed or sexual desire which are to do with the *goals* he tends to pursue, not his manner of pursuing them. A person's inclinations and desires, Peters tells us, belong to his 'nature', not his 'character' (Peters, 1981: 25–6).

In Peters' bifurcation of human nature, 'character' plainly belongs not with emotions and motives, but with conventions, rules and habits. It is thus a very different concept of character from that which embraces virtues and attachments and in which people's *ends* figure as well as the dispositions on which they rely to attain them. This is not at all a merely linguistic point, that Peters is using the word 'character' in one way and the alternative account in another. The underlying issue is, I think, ethical. What is of central importance in human life? In all his writings Peters lays weight on the *procedures* we follow in doing what we do, on following rules rather than not following rules and then on following rules rationally rather than blindly. Repeatedly, as again with Kant, ideological considerations are played down. We are enjoined, for instance, not to seek *the aims* of education, but to reflect, rather, on the principles of procedure involved in educating (Peters, 1959). This Kantian outlook also colours Peters' philosophical psychology, shifting all his central concepts – emotion and motive, wanting and wishing, character – away from their usual connotations to ones more in line with his ethical beliefs.

As with Kant, problems arise over the most central concept of Peters' philosophical psychology and ethics, the concept of rationality. Acting rationally is not to be understood in terms of satisfying one's wants: Peters' rich concept of wanting, as we have seen, incorporates within it the idea of having reasons for acting. Detached from desire, the concept of reason in both Kant and Peters becomes obscure, the transcendental arguments *of Ethics and Education* leaving the reader as unenlightened as Kant's delineation of the noumenal self in the *Critique of Practical Reason* and the *Groundwork*.

Only a brief sketch has been provided so far of the alternative account of the education of the emotions. The topic is vast and it would be impossible to do it justice in what remains of this essay. The place of virtues and sentiments in a wider theory of educational aims would have to be explored. There could be more detailed investigations of the shaping of particular emotions, aesthetic emotions or self-esteem, for example. Sociological work on the types of emotions most commonly found in contemporary society – the sorts of fears people tend to have, the things which horrify them or for which they feel contempt etc. – would enable us to see in what ways conventional patterns will have to shift so as to fit a rational set of educational aims. The role of particular disciplines, not least literature and drama, in emotional education is another underdeveloped area (but see Hepburn, 1972).

Many other growth points will occur to one. Rather than saying any more about these, I will finish by making two connected and more general points:

(1) In criticising the central place which Peters gives to rules and conventions, I do not wish to imply that the education of the emotions should have nothing to do with these. If we revert to our earlier example of how pupils' fears and fear-reactions are shaped as they acquire courage, we can see several places at which standards come in. Emotional learning is patently heavily dependent on one's linguistic abilities: knowing what frogs are, for instance, helps one to see they are not to be feared. Linguistic rules apart, we are guided by conventions within the culture or cultures to which we belong to produce this or that response in different affective situations. A 'stiff-upper-lip' schooling might teach us to try not to reveal our grief over the death of a loved one; brought up in Thailand, we would be encouraged to share it with the rest of the community. A soldier is trained to withstand frightening situations in which, for others, flight would be the expected response. Our emotional dispositions are patterned by conventions. But to say with Peters that we enter the palace of Reason through the courtyard of Habit may be misleading here. We do not learn to follow what conventions are expected *and then* learn to apply reason. Acquiring courage, as we said earlier, involves judgment. Conventions take us only part of the way: we have to acquire the difficult art of knowing what to do when; and this, as we have seen, means applying our powers of practical reasoning to do what we consider best in situations not fully covered by social rules. Reason guides us, therefore, into Habit's courtyard. Assuming, that is, that by 'habit' one is talking of what Ryle would call the 'multi-track' dispositions involved in acquiring one of the virtues, rather than something more mechanical like scratching one's nose or lighting one's pipe. (Peters' use of 'habit' seems to cover both.)

None of this implies that reason has no other role in the education of the emotions. The pupil can also come to reflect on the acceptability, according to one criterion or another, of the dispositions he or she acquires or the conventions which regulated them. Someone brought up, for instance, in the status-oriented ethos of our society may realise that his feelings of self-esteem depend in large part on his seeing others as beneath him in the social hierarchy and resolve to reject this attitude as unworthy.

(2) A major problem in educating the emotions in a society like ours is that conventions about how to react or what to do in different affective situations are often either uncertain or no longer in existence. In a more traditional society, like Thailand, as I began to imply above, there are still complex rituals which people whose close relatives have died must follow, all intended to enable them to

cope with their grief. In Britain, as many have pointed out (e.g. Scruton, 1980), owing to the erosion of traditional patterns and to what is now in some quarters almost a taboo on talk about death, those in grief are often at a loss to know what to do. Where conventions have not eroded, they often lack the stability of less anomic societies, owing to moral disagreement about them within the community. Self-esteem based on contempt for inferiors is a case in point. Another concerns anger and its control. The way one reacts to others' interrupting one, may often depend on the weight one attaches to one's own good as compared to theirs: different ideologies at work within society – liberal individualism, Christianity in its different forms, communitarianism and so on – point in different directions. Since few of us live within the framework of a single ideology but have been influenced by many, it is scarcely surprising that we often do not know how to respond.

As writers as politically far apart as Roger Scruton and Alasdair MacIntyre have pointed out, we need to establish new forms of conventional expectations to enable the education of the emotions, and with it, in MacIntyre's case, the life of the virtues, to flourish (MacIntyre, 1981, chs 14, 15). How we do this, if at all possible, is obviously an enormous practical problem which takes us far beyond the concerns of this essay. Not just *any* conventions will do, of course. In some areas new conventions *are* growing up to fill the vacuum. While tabloid papers seek to regiment our fears, our hopes, our sense of envy and of horror along always predictable paths, in money matters, prudence and thrift have often given way, especially through media pressure, to the passion to consume and possess: what for the Greeks was the vice of *pleonexia* is no longer seen by us as unworthy (MacIntyre, 1981: 171). But it is precisely these questions – of which existing conventions are worthy or unworthy, and of how to build up new ones on sound ethical foundations, with which the education of the emotions must in future get to grips.

References

Aristotle *Nicomachean Ethics*.
Elliott, R. K. (1974) 'Education, love of one's subject and the love of truth', in *Proceedings of the Philosophy of Education Society*, Vol. 8, No. 1.
Gosling, J. C. B. (1969) *Pleasure and Desire* (Oxford, Clarendon Press).
Hardie, W. F. R. (1980) *Aristotle's Ethical Theory* (2nd edition) (Oxford, Clarendon Press).
Hepburn, R. W. (1972) 'The arts and the education of feeling and emotion', in Dearden, R. F., Hirst, P. H. and Peters, R. S. (eds) *Education and the Development of Reason* (London, Routledge).
McGinn, C. (1982) *The Character of Mind* (Oxford, Oxford University Press).
MacIntyre, A. C. (1981) *After Virtue* (London, Duckworth).
Peters, R. S. (1958) *The Concept of Motivation* (London, Routledge).
Peters, R. S. (1959) 'Must the educator have an aim?', in his *Authority Responsibility and Education* (London, Allen and Unwin).
Peters, R. S. (1961) 'Emotions and the category of passivity', *Proceedings of the Aristotelian Society*, Vol. LXII.
Peters, R. S. (1972) 'The education of the emotions', in Dearden, R. F., Hirst, P. H. and Peters, R. S. (eds), *Education and the Development of Reason* (London, Routledge).
Peters, R. S. (1973) *Reason and Compassion* (London, Routledge).
Peters, R. S. (1981) *Moral Education and Moral Development* (London, Allen and Unwin).
Scruton, R. (1980) 'Emotion: practical knowledge and common culture', in Rorty, A. K. (ed.), *Explaining Emotions* (Berkeley, CA, University of California Press).
Warnock, G. (1971) *The Object of Morality* (London, Methuen).
White, J. (1982) *The Aims a/Education Restated* (London, Routledge).

CHAPTER 3

MOTIVATING CHILDREN

The Child's Mind (2002). London: RoutledgeFalmer

What is motivation?

Children are active creatures, often surprisingly so. Tobias Lindseth Melsbu, for instance. In August 2001, when he was aged three, he was reported to have driven the family minibus back home after nursery school. Tobias, from Ramsund, a Norwegian town, 125 miles north of the Arctic Circle, took the keys, turned on the ignition and cruised home. He took in a slope, two 90-degree turns, a creek and a sharp swing into the family driveway. He crashed into the garage door but was unhurt. He had developed his driving skills while sitting on his mother's lap as she drove.

Tobias, I guess you could say, was highly motivated to drive the minibus. He also steers us neatly into an area of mental life which covers action, activity, desire, motivation. So much of the work parents and teachers do with children revolves around activities they engage in – not often bus driving, it is true, but things like dressing, eating, playing games, drawing, and thinking about problems in science.

In very early childhood parents have to help children to understand the notion of agency itself – not in any philosophical sense, but as built into the correct use of words such as 'dressing', 'drawing', 'lifting', 'being cruel'. Children have to learn to use such words about both their own behaviour and that of others'.

They also need to know how actions are to be explained. 'Why did Daddy laugh like that?', asks the five-year-old; 'Why did Hitler invade Poland?', asks the sixteen-year-old history student. On occasion parents and teachers, too, need to find out why children act as they do. 'Why does Hannah keep disappearing off upstairs?' 'Why is Neil so aggressive today?'

One context, then, in which educators must deal with motivation is thinking about what makes children behave as they do. Another is encouraging or getting them to do something – sometimes when they do not want to. These two things – explaining children's actions, and motivating them – are closely connected. Grasping the factors involved in why children act as they do gives you a lever that you can use in urging them to do what you would like them to do.

It is tempting to think of this lever in the causal terms we are used to in the physical world. If you know why someone's headache was cured – through aspirin – you can use this knowledge if someone else gets a headache in the future. Some discussions of motivation in educational psychology see it after a causal pattern like this. Whether this makes good sense we shall have to see.

Before looking at motivation, something more basic. This is the notion of human agency itself. Children have to grasp this concept in their early years. What is it they come to understand about it?

Human agency

Suppose a young child – say between two and three – sees her mother writing a letter. How does she understand what is going on? We adults would say, as I have just said, 'She is writing a letter'. We know what writing is and what letters are. The little girl does not yet have this understanding, or only the, first beginnings of it. She sees her mother doing something – making marks on paper – but cannot bring to this the understanding we have as adults. Perhaps she sees her as drawing little shapes. Or perhaps her mother has told her she is 'writing a letter' or 'inviting Laura to your party' and the child makes what sense she can of what she is told.

Is there one correct answer to the question 'What is the mother doing?' – in the way that there is one correct answer, in primary school arithmetic, to 'What is 7 + 8?' Is the correct answer 'writing a letter'? This might seem the most natural way to answer, but it is also true that she is making marks on paper and that she is inviting someone to a party.

Human actions are capable of many true descriptions. This is also true of other things. What I see when I look out into the garden is 'a tree', 'an apple tree', 'a mature specimen', 'a dark shape'. The peculiar feature of human actions is that the descriptions have to be in terms of what the agent *has in mind* in doing what she is doing. People can make marks on paper for all sorts of reasons. In the present case, the mother is making them with the intention of communicating with someone, more specifically with the intention of inviting someone to a party.

Inducting children into what agency is involves bringing them – gradually – to understand people's intentions in acting as they do. Human actions typically have a structure. They do not exist as isolated events, but are undertaken for *reasons*. Reasons are not isolated phenomena either. They are connected with a host of other aspects of the agent's life.

The mother is writing a letter. Why? She wants to invite a child to a birthday party. The reason is not self-standing. Behind it are her unspelt-out reasons for wanting a party and for wanting this particular child to come to it. All this takes us into a web of further considerations – her caring attitudes towards her own child, the place of children's birthday parties in the culture, her child's relationship with the other child.

So far the focus has been on the mother's wants or desires. But these do not give a full account other reasons for writing the letter. They do not explain why she chose *this* way of trying to get the child to come to the party. She could have gone round to her house, telephoned or e-mailed her mother, put a notice in the local paper. What were her reasons for writing a letter? She believed it is the proper thing to do on such occasions. There is also her belief, almost too obvious to spell out, that sending a letter is an effective means of letting someone know something. She also has further background beliefs – that the postal service is generally reliable, for instance.

Her beliefs as well as her wants enter into her reasons for action. Together they form a structure. In this case, she understands what she is doing (writing the letter) as a means to an end (inviting the child). Behind this goal lie further things that she wants – to please her child, to do what is expected of her in the community. She wants the end and believes that writing the letter is an effective and appropriate means. There are also background beliefs she has about both the means and the end. She believes that Britain has a postal service; that people in her community expect her to organise a party.

This everyday example helps in seeing what goes into the notion of human agency. Some of its features, as we shall see, are not found across the board, but the involvement of our beliefs and desires in what we are doing is of central importance.

This last point shows that human agency, like most other mental phenomena, brings with it intentional objects. Beliefs are always beliefs *that* something is the case. Desires are also desires *that*, even though language sometimes hides this, as in English. The mother who wants to write a letter desires that she write one. As with all intentional objects, this state of affairs need not exist. She may want to write it, but is then prevented.

There is more to human action than believing and wanting. I may want an ice cream and believe I can get one by going out to the man in the ice-cream van. But I may not actually go out because I also want to do something else for which I have a stronger preference – lie in bed, finish watching a TV programme. Action also requires something else. I must also at least *intend* to buy the ice cream. Not merely that, for intentions too can come to grief.

In uncovering the mother's web of beliefs and desires I am not implying she has any of this consciously before her mind when doing what she does. Some of these things – wanting the child to come to the party – may be more present to her than others, like believing that Britain has a postal service. But quite possibly, she has none of them directly in mind. The invitation may be the fourteenth she has written that morning.

Even wholly habitual actions like tying your shoelaces still bring with them beliefs and desires. The shoelace-tier wants to be properly dressed and believes that tying his laces is a part of this. Although he is not conscious of these things at the time, at least he must know them. If asked why he is tying the laces, these are the kinds of thing he mentions. The mother similarly knows her reasons for writing the letter and can articulate them if required. Human agency depends on the possession of language.

All this, once we begin to think about it, is very familiar. But very young children are still largely outside these thought-structures. They have to be inducted into the whole business of tying laces and writing letters, so as to understand the reasons people have in general for doing these things and what intentions particular individuals have in doing them. They need to get inside the structures of desires and beliefs that make such actions intelligible.

The examples given so far have been of intentional actions – things that people have intended to bring about (even though they may not have formulated such intentions to themselves). I said earlier that human actions typically have a certain structure. We have now seen how this is built around reasons, and how beliefs and desires enter into these. But there are exceptions.

If a child *unintentionally* knocks over a bottle of sauce, he has no reason for doing this. Hence he has no wants that may be satisfied by doing so or beliefs about this being a means to a desired end. In cottoning on to the notion of human agency, the young child has to learn the difference between intentional and unintentional behaviour – and with it differences in blame and responsibility which each of these brings with it.

I have talked about the young learner coming to understand *human* agency. Non-human animals are agents, too. As with human beings, we can make a broad distinction in their case between the things they do and the things that simply happen to them. If a dog gets kicked, feels toothache, finds himself wedged in a hole, he is not an agent – unlike when he bounds across a field, eats his food, chases an intruder. How, if at all, is non-human agency different from human?

There is a traditional answer that has come down to us from Descartes. Animals are mindless machines. A dog's running after someone is to be understood as a chain of causal connexions at the physical level. Human beings, on the other hand, are capable of action brought under the control of reason. What happens when someone runs for a bus is this. As soon as he rationally decides to do this, an act of willing in his mind operates on the brain in such a way as to cause muscle movements to his legs.

This will not do. It is just not true that some kind of mental act – deciding or willing – always initiates our rational actions. We often do things out of habit – change gear while driving, spread butter on our bread – where we are not on each occasion *making decisions* to do these things, let alone willing that they come about.

To come back to the difference between human and non-human agency. If we are willing to ascribe to non-human animals something of a mental life – to talk of dogs and cats feeling pain, seeing, hearing and smelling things, being afraid of things – then there should be no problem about seeing their active states – their running, digging for bones, coming up to be stroked – as also manifestations of their mentality. Non-human animals – some of them, at least – have wants. Hungry cats want to eat, sleepy dogs to sleep. We explain animals' behaviour by their wants. Why is my cat standing by the back door? Because he wants to be let out into the garden. Why is he rubbing against my leg? Because he wants to be fed. *So far*, the pattern of explanation is similar to explanations in human cases: we explain why agents do the things they do in terms of their desires.

But only so far. Lacking language, animals cannot *express their reasons* for doing what they do – if indeed they can be said to have reasons. My cat wants to go out into the garden. Perhaps in some embryonic sense he believes that standing by the door is an effective means of getting me to open it for him. Do his desire plus his belief add up to his having a reason for action? Or can we not speak this way of cats or dogs because they are not language-using creatures? Must having a reason require being able to express that reason?

Whatever the answer, at least we know that *human beings* can normally give a linguistic account of the reasons they have for acting as they do. If asked why she was writing a letter the mother can reply that she wants to invite a child to a party. She is able to formulate her wants (and, if need be, her relevant beliefs) in language and thus explain her behaviour.

Not, of course, that human beings always *do* express what they have in mind. For the most part we do not. The crucial point is that we *can* do so. If asked, we can give an account of why we are doing what we are doing. A man puts ground coffee into the filter on the coffee machine. He does this every morning, never thinks about it. But if someone – from another culture, perhaps – were to ask him why he is going through this operation, he would have no difficulty in answering 'Because I want a cup of coffee' or in spelling out his belief that the operation was part of a process whereby coffee could be made.

Motives as explanations

I have looked, very briefly, at what human actions are. Now I shall move on to how we explain them.

Although these may look like two separate topics, they are inseparable. To show this, I go back to the point that the same action can be described in many ways:

 (i) She is making marks on paper.
 (ii) She is writing a letter.
(iii) She is inviting someone to a party.

If we want to explain (ii) we can invoke (iii). This gives the reason why she is writing the letter. Here the explanation of the action is another description of it. It is not always like this. Another explanation of why she is writing the letter is that she wants her child to be happy. This is *not* another description of what she is doing. The important fact remains, however, that explanations *are* often redescriptions. ('Why is he drinking that coffee? He is slaking his thirst.')

In this respect, explaining human actions is *quite unlike* explaining events in the physical world. When asked why gases expand when heated, our answer cannot be a further description of the event. It has to go beyond this, into underlying laws of nature.

Asking why a child acted in such and such a way is normally to ask for her *motive*. Her motive is her reason for acting as she does. Sometimes the motive may take the form of a redescription. ('Why is he writing in that book? He is doing his GCSE coursework.') At other times it may go beyond this. ('Why has she put her hand up? Because she wants to attract the teacher's attention.')

We have already seen how beliefs and desires enter into people's motives. Motives can be of different sorts, and the way beliefs and desires occur in them differ accordingly.

Very often the explanation of a child's behaviour will be in terms of some future end to which he sees his action as a means. 'Why is Steve showing off? Because he wants to impress the girls.' His desire to impress and his belief that making funny remarks is a good way of impressing both come into the explanation – as well as further beliefs and desires that may be in the background.

Why did Tobias Lindseth Melsbu drive the minibus home? Perhaps because he wanted to get there quickly, or to impress his mother. Again, his beliefs also come into the frame: that he knows how to steer, that Mummy will be pleased with him.

But not all motives are instrumental. No doubt Tobias's were not wholly so by any means. Driving the minibus would also be good fun. 'Why is Julia singing at the top of her voice? No reason, she's just enjoying herself, that's all.' Although we say 'no reason', we really mean 'no further reason'. She *has* a reason, all right, for such lusty singing, but the reason is intrinsic: she just wants to do it for its own sake. In this case, there are no additional reasons to do with beliefs about appropriate means to ends.

All this is beginning to unravel some of the complexities of the concept of motivation. More will become evident as we go on. A distinction just made was between instrumental and intrinsic motivation. Are these two categories together exhaustive? Could there be non-intrinsic motives which are not instrumental? As I shall try to show later, this is a key question for teachers and parents.

The folk-psychology of motivation

Before coming to this, a warning against too reductive an account of motivation. Some philosophers have suggested that explanations of human actions are resolvable into combinations of desires and beliefs, full stop. Why do people act as they do? Because they want Y, believe that X is a means to Y, and so do X. We have already seen that this account falls down when applied to intrinsic motivation. More generally, it fails to do justice to the complexities of the situations that people often find themselves in when they do things. All sorts of factors come into the motivational story.

A teenager goes berserk in a classroom, lashing out at everyone, throwing chairs around, shouting abuse. Why did he do this? We find out that a fellow student had just touched him on a raw spot. He was feeling low in any case, partly because of domestic circumstances, partly because he never gets on well in this particular class. There is much more to the story than that – more, indeed, that we would need to refer to in giving a comprehensive explanation. These things would all come into his reason for acting *as* he did. It is because motives are many-faceted and complex rather than able to be regimented into a few basic components that novelists often cast more light on them than philosophers or psychologists of reductionist inclination.

Classroom teachers are as well placed as parents to see the force of these remarks. In non-routine cases such as the one described, only someone like themselves, *au fait* with the whole situation in which the out-of-the-way behaviour occurs, is able to provide anything like a full explanation of it.

If any of them think there are people better placed than themselves – academic psychologists? – they should have more confidence in their own powers. Understanding motivation is not a recondite matter, the province of behavioural science or some other specialism. It has to do with sensitively applying everyday psychological concepts – beliefs, wants, perceptions, emotional responses, means-to-ends, doing something for its own sake – to capture all the complexities.

Although we only use the word 'motive' in English when asking for people's reasons in cases that are untoward in some way ('What was his motive for killing his wife?'), it still remains true that other, quite ordinary, actions can have motives – even though we do not refer to them as such. Although we would normally never *ask about* a child's motive in switching on a light, that does not mean that she does not *have* a motive. Perhaps it is so banal that it is taken for granted: she wants to do something in the room and it is too dark. Motives have to do with reasons for action. Her reasons involve her desires – to look for the cordless phone, go to bed, feed the gerbil – as well as her belief that switching on the light will enable her to see such objects; and perhaps other considerations, too.

In everyday cases like these, teachers and parents do not need experts in motivation to help them make sense of children's behaviour. Their own immersion in a culture where moving a piece of plastic on a wall provides illumination means that they can take the child's reasons for doing this as read.

This is not at all to say that experts have nothing to offer. Teachers have, for instance, found work on children's self-perception helpful – studies suggesting that pupils' low opinion of their own intelligence, or their low self-esteem in general, lie behind their poor performance in the classroom. Whether this psychological research has told them something they found brand-new is a further question. The chances are that they know a good deal about these things from their own experience. What psychology can do is to take them beyond this experience and show them that their own beliefs or half-beliefs are confirmed in other settings where there are greater controls on idiosyncratic perceptions. A large part of psychological work of this sort has to do with reinforcing and clarifying ideas that educators have already. It is partly in the business of confidence-building and self-understanding.

In this respect it has much in common with a book like this one. Both take it for granted that practitioners already have the psychological equipment they need in order to carry out their work. This is drawn from the psychological concepts we use in everyday language, from immersion in their culture, from reading fiction, and from their day-to-day transactions with children, partners, friends and colleagues. Philosophers help them to become more explicitly aware of their conceptual apparatus. Psychologists focus on specific kinds of belief or attitude (children's beliefs about their own inadequacy, for instance). Neither discipline uncovers facts previously wholly unknown to the reader – as a chemist does or a historian. Both help to make the implicit more explicit, the confused less tangled.

Other psychologists of motivation move in more scientific realms. A motto for parents or teachers turning to psychology texts for guidance on motivation could be 'beware of chapter headings'. Some textbooks fill most of their chapter on the topic with physiological data on hunger, thirst, sex and aggression. These desires, shared at their root with some non-human animals, do indeed generate reasons for action. How far teachers and parents need to go into their biology or physiology is another question. Most human motives, including those by which children are guided, go far beyond these biological drives. The reasons why we all do what we do are often highly complex and reflect values and beliefs acquired from many sources, not least the culture in which we live.

Sometimes, admittedly, children's behaviour can only be explained by factors requiring scientific investigation. It might be caused by epilepsy or other physical diseases. In these cases we are beyond the realm of motives, for children do not have reasons for going into fits. This is not to say there are not reasons why they have them. But here reasons are simply causes – in the same sense that there is a reason why water turns into ice at a certain temperature. Even though there *is* a reason for this, the water does not *have* a reason.

It is also true that, where children do indeed have motives, these may be too complex for educators relying only on their own psychological resources. In some cases of sexual abuse, for instance, they need expert psychological help to sort out the twisted array of factors in their students' background. Specialists also come in where motives proper have to be separated from physiological or other causes where these are closely intertwined – as where a child's behaviour can be partly, but not wholly, attributed to taking drugs.

The only other point to make about the psychology of motivation is to issue a safety warning, if such is needed, about textbooks that obscure far more than they illuminate. No names, no packdrill. But if readers should find themselves getting horribly lost among lists of 'internal processes' such as instincts, hierarchies of needs drives and cognitive dissonance, or among diagrams with arrows of causation leading from 'need reduction' to 'drive' to 'activity' to 'satisfaction' and back to 'drive', they can be reassured that the problem does not lie with them.

Types of motivation: intrinsic and extrinsic

There are many ways of classifying motives. I mentioned – above the division between biological and non-biological ones. Here, with education in mind, I want to focus on another kind of classification, expanding on what I was saying earlier about instrumental motives and intrinsic ones. I asked whether these two categories exhausted the field or whether there could be extrinsic reasons that are not instrumental.

I think there can be. An extrinsic reason is one that is not intrinsic – where intrinsic motives have to do with what is done for its own sake, not for the sake of something else. A child may play the piano simply out of enjoyment and not because he is preparing for a music lesson or for a concert performance. Enjoying playing the piano is here an end in itself. Extrinsic reasons are reasons which refer to ends outside the activity itself.

There are three importantly different types of extrinsic reason. The first is involved where the action or activity undertaken is a *replaceable* means to an end. A teacher is planning a group trip to the Science Museum. How will he go?

By train and tube or by minibus? He thinks it through and chooses the train. If asked 'Why are you catching this train?', his answer is that he wants to get to London. This is an example of a straightforward means-end reason where the means selected is replaceable by another. But not all extrinsic reasons are of this sort. Sometimes the means is irreplaceable. Someone is filling in the answer to a crossword clue. Why? Because she wants to complete the crossword. Here the means – answering clue number 7 across – is an integral *part* of the end – answering all the clues. Nothing can substitute for it.

The distinction between these first two types of extrinsic reasons is between those which are (purely) *instrumental*, that is, where one means can take the place of another, and those referring to *wholes* of which the action or activity is an integral part. This is of great importance educationally, as will become clear.

The role of whole-part reasons in our lives goes way beyond crossword puzzles. Suppose the answer to the question 'Why did that woman kiss her daughter as she left for school?' is that she was expressing her affection for her. This is a reason for her kissing, but what kind of a reason is it? 'Expressing affection' does not refer to a goal to attain to which kissing is one particular means, replaceable by other ways of showing affection such as hugging or gentle words. It is a reason that serves to locate the kissing as part of a larger picture, to do with a certain kind of relationship.

Whole-part reasons are found, unsurprisingly enough, where there are whole-part features in our lives. Two examples of wholes have been given: doing crossword puzzles and being in a loving relationship. Other examples would be: creating, performing or attending to a work of art; belonging to a nourishing enterprise or social group – a school or firm, for instance, or a football club or a nation; playing a game of chess or snooker.

We come to the third kind of extrinsic reason. This one is wholly or chiefly orientated to *the past*. A teacher intervenes in a physical attack of one pupil on another. 'Why did you lash out at him?' 'I was in a blinding rage: he was reading my private diary.' Here the lashing out is an immediate response to a perceived hurt. It is not undertaken primarily with a view to bringing about some future end, as would be, for instance, a calculated design to teach someone a lesson so that he would think twice before doing the same thing again.

Among the emotions, some are future-orientated, like fear or hope, others look to the past, like anger, grief, remorse or shame, while yet others dwell in the present, like joy, or straddle past, present and future like certain kinds of love. Insofar as emotions motivate people to do things – as distinct from affecting them more passively – they fit into the categorisation of motives given so far. They provide us with intrinsic reasons (like joy) and among extrinsic reasons instrumental ones (like fear), whole-part ones (like love of one's family or country), and backward-looking ones (like shame or anger).

I have mentioned so far a number of different kinds of motive: intrinsic reasons and three types of extrinsic, that is, instrumental, whole-part, and past-orientated. Will this categorisation do? Is there not a sense in which all our motives come down to whole-part reasons? Consider playing the piano for its own sake. Is 'for enjoyment' the last reason that can be given in a chain of reasons? After all, playing the piano for enjoyment is not wholly detached from other areas of life. It has its part in a wider canvas filled with other intrinsic as well as extrinsic goals. Similarly with travelling by train to get to London. There are larger considerations behind this ultimately connected in some way with the whole of a person's life.

It is tempting but mistaken to take this as showing all motivation to be part-whole. Some people may treat their lives like works of art, of which they are the (self-)creators. Just as in a painting or poem, so in the unfolding story of their life the parts have to be crafted together to make a harmonious whole. For them piano playing for enjoyment is not, or not only, an end in itself, but has its place in a greater totality. Usually, though, people are not self-creators in this way. The things they enjoy for their own sake are parts of their lives, certainly, but they do not see in them a contribution to a totality. For most of us, 'Because it is enjoyable' is a reason which stands in no need of further reasons behind it.

One last remark. Although I have analytically separated various types of intrinsic and extrinsic motive, these do not usually occur separately from each other. A child may be playing the piano *partly* for enjoyment and *partly* because she is practising for a music exam. We often have mixed motives for what we do.

Motivation in education

Understanding motives

The intrinsic and extrinsic reasons that pupils and teachers have for acting as they do are often immediately intelligible from the context. We know why children collect trays and cutlery in the canteen, why Jonathan asked those silly questions in class, why the head of history sits in that chair in the staff room. Strangers to the school or strangers to British or modern Western culture might find some of these things puzzling and would need to ferret out the agents' relevant desires and beliefs.

Sometimes we participants are also puzzled. We do not know why that child is behaving out of character, or suspect that the reason she gives us may not be her real reason. We, too, may need to find out about her beliefs and/or desires. Why did Ellie surreptitiously eat those grapes in class? If we discover that she has just come to believe that eating fruit every hour throughout the day is a good recipe for slimming, we have a possible belief-desire pair to help explain her odd behaviour. There may be more severe cases of unintelligibility where the school needs professional psychological help. Yet even here the pattern of attempted explanation is the same – penetrating the bizarre belief – system of a schizophrenic person's mind, trying to find out what he really wants.

There are also ethical issues falling under this section about when it is right to try to find out what pupils' or colleagues' motives are and when doing so would invade their privacy. I will leave these on one side.

Motivating children

More problematic for many teachers is how to motivate their pupils to engage in learning activities. Some of their problems are more intractable than others. Every teacher has to find some way of involving children in schoolwork and good lesson planning provides part of the answer. But how can they cope with students who are apathetic, or just do not want to know, or find anything to do with school a turn-off?

These are all practical matters and practitioners are the ones who can give most help. But philosophical considerations may be useful in establishing a conceptual framework for these more specific suggestions. I have four of them in mind.

Preliminaries

Motivating pupils is getting them to engage in activities by furnishing them with reasons for doing so that are meaningful to them. I phrase this with deliberate care.

If you want a child to work at algebraic equations, it is not helpful to tell him he will need to understand algebra in order to become a maths teacher, true though this might well be, if he has no desire to become one. The reasons you give must be such as to make him want to do the algebra: they must be meaningful to him in this sense.

Motivating pupils is not always or only a matter of linking the activity to some desire, intrinsic or extrinsic, to which it was not linked before: it sometimes involves working on their beliefs. A girl at secondary school would like a well-paid job and sees doing well at science as a route to one; but she has given up on science because she thinks of it as a boys' subject. Challenging this last belief may be all that is necessary for her to be able to throw herself into it.

Being motivated has to do with having reasons for some action or activity. Strictly, you cannot motivate children to *learn* something, because learning is not an activity but an *achievement* – usually, coming to know something one did not know before. Teachers want pupils to learn, say, German word order and they do this by setting them various tasks. Children have to be motivated to engage in *these tasks*.

A point about goals. During the liquidation of the kulaks Soviet children were incited to denounce their parents. One of them, Pavlik Morozov, became hero-worshipped for doing so. Being able to motivate pupils may or may not be a good thing. It depends on the desirability of what is learnt. This is a point where the philosophical psychology of education abuts onto the philosophy of educational aims.

How to motivate

Motivating pupils is getting them to engage in activities by furnishing them with reasons for doing so that are meaningful to them. These reasons are largely compounds of desires and beliefs. All this implies an active stance on the part of the teacher or parent, who has to hook up an activity with desires and beliefs that children have already, or change these desires or beliefs where appropriate. It also implies some understanding of the desires and beliefs that weigh with particular learners, rather than operating in some more global way which ignores individual differences.

This way of looking at motivation – as an active and nuanced intervention into particular pupils' mental structures – is poles apart from theories that leave more to nature and less to culture. It may suit some child-centred thinkers to believe that children will become interested in deepening their understanding or their aesthetic experience all in good time, once their needs for love or self-esteem are adequately met. Or that you cannot expect young children to be other than egoistic in their outlook because they are not yet at a stage of development where altruism becomes possible. But education is not a standing-back and letting benign nature take its course. It is necessarily a shaping, an intervention, an initiation into cultural practices.

Pupils can be motivated via attention to their beliefs; or by attention to their desires.

What children think

Normally, when people engage in activity *A* to fulfil a desire *B* – mowing the lawn, for instance, to keep the garden tidy – certain beliefs on their part are taken for granted. They must think that *A* is a way of bringing about *B*, that they have the ability to do *A* (they have the strength to cut the grass, they know how to operate the mower), that they can muster the effort required to do *A* (they are not too tired), that *A* is an appropriate activity for them to engage in (it is their own lawn they are cutting, not their neighbour's), that there are no insuperable external impediments (the lawn is not waterlogged).

Beliefs like these are so obvious that they hardly seem worth mentioning. This is why talk of motives often bypasses agents' beliefs in favour of their desires.

Where one or other of these commonplace beliefs is missing, however, motivation may fail. However strong the agent's desire to do *A* (in order to bring about *B*, or whatever), if he thinks that doing *A* is not in within his power, that *A* is unachievable by anyone, or that it is wrong to do *A*, he will not have a sufficient reason for doing *A* and may end up not doing it. If he is to come to do it, his beliefs must alter appropriately.

This is true, not least, of learning tasks. Perhaps a pupil would really like to learn to swim – so that he could go off with his friends to the outdoor pool and bathe in the sea in the summer. Suitable desires are in place, but he shies away from swimming lessons because he thinks he is hopeless at anything physical, and in addition he will sink and possibly drown once he gets out of his depth. Motivating a pupil like this is a matter first of understanding the beliefs that impede him and then of encouraging him to see they are baseless.

What children want

Pupils also need appropriate desires. We can now apply our earlier, desire-based, typology of motives to issues of motivating pupils. We discussed extrinsic and intrinsic motives. Among extrinsic motives we distinguished purely instrumental from part-whole and from backward-looking motives. Backward-looking motives are unlikely to be used to motivate students. I cannot imagine a teacher trying to get a pupil to do a piece of work out of revenge, anger or grief. But all the other types of motive are of great importance in education.

PURELY INSTRUMENTAL MOTIVES

Not long ago, Latin was a requirement for admission to certain British universities. What motivated many young people to study it was their desire to get into Oxford or Cambridge. If Sanskrit had been prescribed in Latin's place, they would have probably buckled down to this instead. Doing Latin was a replaceable activity.

These days Latin is less in evidence, but some students at school or university choose subjects because they think they are most likely to lead to a well-paid job. They are not interested in accountancy courses in themselves but grind through them for the sake of the rewards. If doing sociology or media studies were guaranteed to net them a huge income in their first year and accountancy graduates were two a penny, their choices would be quite different.

Purely instrumental motives are also used to motivate much younger pupils. A primary child works hard at spelling because her teacher is keen on this and praises children for good work. If the teacher had thought correct spelling a bourgeois fetish and gave recognition for creative writing, she would have thrown herself into this.

If expectations of reward or punishment are used as motivators, those who use them should realise that, as far as the learner is concerned, the learning activity is replaceable by any other that is more likely to produce the reward or prevent the punishment.

One thing at issue here is the commitment the learner has towards the learning activity. Some of the things pupils learn are intended as permanent and irreplaceable pieces of mental equipment on which they will draw throughout their lives. Being able to read, write and count are obvious examples. So, too, you might argue, would be treating others with respect, having an understanding of how your society works, being responsive to aesthetic qualities in art or nature. (I am moving into controversial territory, to do with the philosophy of educational aims. But the examples are less important than the general point that much educational learning is meant to be permanent and irreplaceable.)

The point I am driving at is this. If we want pupils to come to have a proper attitude to these permanent and irreplaceable kinds of learning (whatever they are), that is, to *come to see them as permanent and irreplaceable*, it seems a bad bet to rely on motivation that treats them as replaceable. If other forms of motivation were available it would seem more sensible to resort to those.

But sometimes this objection is overridable. Very young children love doing what brings parents' and, later, teachers' approval. There is no harm in capitalising on this motivation – quite the contrary – provided (i) that the activity in question has to do with permanent and irreplaceable equipment, and (ii) that as soon as possible the child is encouraged to engage it for other than instrumental reasons. For example, children can begin to decipher letters and words because they get good parental feedback and then come to enjoy doing this for its own sake or because they begin to see the whole business of reading as part of what it is to become like other people.

A danger in relying on purely instrumental motivation in young children is that it encourages authoritarian behaviour in them. The reason why they are doing what they are doing is that someone wants them to do this – and if this person wanted them to do something else, they would do that instead. This, too, points towards replacing instrumental by other forms of motivation.

INTRINSIC MOTIVES

Pupils can also be brought to engage in an activity because they find it interesting or enjoyable for its own sake. Young children like listening to stories, drawing, playing games. Some older students throw themselves into mathematics or history because they find these things fascinating in themselves.

Intrinsic motivation is understandably what many teachers value. It is worth cultivating for more than one reason. Most obviously, it helps to generate committed absorption in the learning activity. Children learning to write can get great pleasure from copying the shapes of letters if they are in the hands of a teacher who associates them with pigs' tails, step ladders and other objects. Yet forming letters is not something in which the teacher wants them to develop an intrinsic interest throughout their lives. From the child's point of view the activity may be delightful in itself, but from the teacher's its value is as a skill to be harnessed to other ends. At some point the children's interest must shift in this direction.

A second reason for encouraging intrinsic motivation has to do with the aims of education in a liberal society. These are many-sided, of course. Among them is the aim of introducing pupils to a range of intrinsically interesting activities from among which to choose those they wish to follow as major concerns in their lives. These could include all sorts of things, from playing or following sport to craft activities to studying history to gardening or the arts. An important component in a nourishing life is the whole-heartedness of a person's engagement in activities of major importance to them. Acquiring such a sense of total absorption in one or more activities as a child can, with luck, give that child the taste for it in other areas. Education has much to do with the proliferation of enthusiasms.

Some people leave school with little in the way of any. To prevent this, a first task of school education is to ensure that the delights of intrinsically motivated activity are experienced throughout a person's school career – not allowed to grow thin as the child becomes an adolescent. A second task is to extend experience of intrinsic motivation across a widening range of activities from which the self-directed adults whom the pupils will become can choose their preferences.

Whether all the staples of the secondary curriculum are best suited to promote these aims is another question. Some are all but irrelevant. There is, it is true, an intrinsic aspect to learning to speak or read a foreign language, but this is of small account as compared to its practical uses. Mathematics is pleasurable in itself for some people, adults included, but they tend to be few. Given this limited appeal, there is no good reason I can see why we should expect every student to get intrinsic buzzes from it. This is not to say that teachers should not aim at such a reaction, only that if they do not succeed with many pupils they should not lose sleep over it. As long as every pupil is equipped with experience or understanding of a *broad range of* intrinsically interesting activities, the liberal aim I mentioned is met. This is compatible with some possibilities, such as mathematical pleasures, remaining outside their ken. Artistic activities are different in that virtually everybody – again, I am thinking mainly of adults – finds some intrinsic interest in something in this broad field. I am assuming here we are not making too tight a ring round 'artistic activities' and restricting these to the more arcane reaches of serious art: there is no sharp borderline between the latter and entertainment art.

Would it be enough for teachers to rely on intrinsic motivation? I do not think so. Suppose a secondary school student came to love not only mathematics for its own sake, but also history, literature, music and science. She might keep all these activities in discrete compartments, turning with delight from one to another. This could be a good outcome as far as it went, but would it be good enough?

What it leaves out is the element of evaluation, of learning to weigh the relative importance to oneself of this project or that. Evaluation is a condition of becoming a relatively integrated person rather than a being whose life fractures into a collection of unconnected enterprises. It is not enough to immerse yourself in many things for their own sake: at some point, your reasons for being involved must also include some reference to the part that the activity plays in your psychic constitution as a whole. (This need not go so far as seeing your life on the model of a work of art.) This leads us to another kind of motive.

LEGO TRUCKS AND ANIMAL FRIEZES: PART-WHOLE MOTIVES

In his fine essay on 'The fragmentation of value', Thomas Nagel writes:

> If you have set out to climb Everest, or translate Aristotle's *Metaphysics*, or master the *Well-Tempered Clavier*, or synthesise an amino acid, then the further pursuit of that project, once begun, acquires remarkable importance. It is partly a matter of justifying earlier investment of time and energy, and not allowing it to have been in vain. It is partly a desire to be the sort of person who finishes what he begins. But whatever the reason, our projects make autonomous claims on us, once undertaken, which they need not have made in advance.
>
> (1979: 130)

Nagel's examples are all of part-whole motivation. The process of climbing Everest is no doubt rewarding in itself, but this is not the only, and certainly not the main, reason that a climber will give for doing what she is doing. She has in mind the final achievement, reaching the summit. What she is doing now is a part of that whole enterprise.

Nagel's examples are also all rather grand and out of the ordinary. But parents and teachers know the force of what he is saying from more mundane situations. Wanting to finish a Lego truck, reading a novel, a history project, a piece of writing, an experiment in science – all these things can be powerful motives for children.

They are perhaps at their most powerful when the wholes in question are most archetypically wholes. Created objects, including aesthetic objects, best fit this bill. A Lego truck is complete in itself and so is *Animal Farm*. A history project is also a bounded entity, but there is always a certain arbitrariness about its borders, the product of practical requirements. In this it is like a set of problems given out for maths homework. Completing the latter, too, can be a motivator, but there need be no intrinsic unity about the set.

If pupils are motivated in this part-whole way, the assumption is that they have started on the activity in the first place. What has motivated them to do this? Perhaps a reason drawn from one of our first two categories: (i) purely instrumental and (ii) intrinsic. A teacher may persuade a reluctant child to read the first few pages of a story by relying on desire for praise or recognition, knowing that, once hooked, the child will need no further prompting to finish the whole thing. Or a learner may simply be fascinated by the subject matter in general – science, music, or whatever – and *that* is why she has embarked on the particular project.

But sometimes this third category (iii) of part-whole motives can also spark off an activity in the first place. Building the Lego truck could be part of a larger enterprise of making a toy village. What makes some children want to learn to read may be some inchoate sense that doing so – and they may only have the dimmest of apprehensions of what it is all about – will make them more like all those people around them for whom it is obviously important to be able to do whatever it is they are doing with these strange shapes. They want to read so as to become – as we might put it – part of this community of initiates.

Social part-whole motives, of which this is an example, are of especial interest to educators. So many curriculum activities can be approached from this direction. A primary class is busy painting animals to go in a frieze around the classroom. The children are not only enjoying creating their bears and zebras for its own sake: they are doing this, too, as part of a communal enterprise.

Communities or groups can differ in size. Secondary school children can be encouraged to see their history lessons – indeed their science or mathematics lessons – as equipping them as citizens of Britain or Portugal. There are also communities centred on different kinds of social practice. Young footballers can see themselves as belonging to Spurs or Newcastle United or a wider confraternity of enthusiasts. Young poetry lovers can grow into an awareness of an unseen community of creators and responders, spread out across centuries and continents. They can read their Keats or their Yeats not only for intrinsic enjoyment but also as proto-members of this group.

These social motives cannot get off the ground unless the students *care* about belonging to these collectives or communities. Again, we come back to underlying aims of education. There is a strong case, which must be argued elsewhere, for children being brought up concerned for the well-being of others whose communal life they share, whether at the level of family, friends, local community, national community, humanity as a whole.

Parents and teachers who think this way will wish to develop the attitudes, emotions and beliefs that enhance this altruistic concern – for instance sympathy, love, loyalty, trust, a belief in the equal intrinsic importance of every person. It is these that provide the fundamental motivation at issue. The more it is in place, the greater the motivational scope open to the educator when it comes to particular activities. He or she is not driven back, as is the parent or teacher of more individualistic temper, more narrowly attentive to the worldly success, happiness or well-being of the child, towards the purely instrumental or the intrinsic. Here, perhaps, is part of the explanation of the sheer enthusiasm for learning so noticeable in a country like Taiwan, with its strong communal traditions.

Like earlier categories discussed, social part-whole motives can be put to bad as well as good uses. Red Nose Day is one thing; the Red Guards were another. Pavlik Morozov, mentioned above, was motivated to shop his own parents by his vision of himself as part of the Communist cause. In present-day Britain, motivation can arise from the demands of your gang or from the expectations of public opinion as worked on by the mass media. It should be a part of every student-teacher's training to reflect on when social motivation is desirable and when it goes too far.

In this section I have looked at part-whole motives and their place in education. Although I have concentrated on social motives, I also noted the motivation that comes from wanting to finish an uncompleted task. This leads me to another type of part-whole motivation.

Self-creation is an uncompleted task, not least for young adolescents only recently embarked on it. As pointed out earlier, being moved for wholly intrinsic reasons to engage in a range of activities, from athletics, say, to rock music and science, is not enough. Persons are not compartmentalisable. If students themselves are not self-motivated to relate their discrete commitments to a more global picture of what they might become, their mentors have some responsibility to help them to do so. This again takes the argument back to the aims of education. For students to be able to respond to such promptings, they have to have some care for themselves as whole persons in the first place.

As always, reliance on this type of motivation can go too far. Human lives do not share all the features of works of art, even though they share some. Someone's love of scuba-diving has a high value in itself for the diver: its significance does not lie chiefly in the part it plays in his overall structure of desires. In this way it is unlike a patch of colour in the corner of a painting.

Here, as elsewhere, teachers and other guides of young people need delicacy of judgement in the motivational appeals they make. They should be wary of imprisoning their charges in compartmentalised activities, but cautious, too, about encouraging a Hamlet-like over-reflectiveness about the unity of their selves.

ONE DAY YOU'LL SEE WHY

Before leaving this section, a word about a way of motivating that is ancient history among schoolteachers but which does not fit neatly under any of the other headings.

Teachers trying to put over some recondite material in mathematics, say, or science sometimes say 'You may not understand at the moment why you have to learn this, but one day you'll see why and be glad of it'. If a child is swayed by some such appeal, how does this happen?

Belief is central here. She believes 'teacher knows best'. But desire must come into the story, too. What does she believe teacher knows best *about*? Well, she may not be very clear about this, but it must have something to do with what will be good for her or right for her to do. The child wants what is good for her in the future and believes that her teacher knows what this is. Being only ten or twelve years old she has only the dimmest of pictures of what her future well-being might consist in. It is understandable that she falls in with what an apparent authority on this urges her to do.

The basic issue here is whether the teacher *does* know what is best for her. There are not, so far as I know, experts on the good life. In *some* contexts, true, teachers may well be on fairly firm ground in making this sort of motivational appeal. If it is a question of literacy, for instance, or of everyday arithmetic, it is a fair bet that the child will be glad he or she has learnt these things.

But schools and teachers have sometimes trodden more uncertain territory: in the past, Latin and Greek or the rote-learning of Bible passages; in the present, parts of the secondary curriculum. Not by any means that pupils' trust in their teachers' wisdom always depends on things these teachers say explicitly. Sometimes the very ethos of the school reinforces it. I remember in my own case how it seemed to be taken as read at the age of twelve that I would do best to drop science for ever; and later – on entry to the sixth form – that two years of medieval history were the ideal prospect for me. How wrong the school was on both counts!

Developing children's reasons for action

Motivation also belongs to educational content in its own right. Parents and teachers have a responsibility to induct children into an understanding of what count as good reasons for action.

At first the very youngest children operate much in the way that animals do. They have certain (innate) wants and act in accordance with these. Gradually, as they develop the necessary language and conceptual ability, they come to act for reasons. They can tell you why they are looking in the cupboard, thereby revealing their implicit grasp of the desire- and belief-structures we rely on in explaining human behaviour (they are looking in the cupboard for biscuits; and they believe that this is where the biscuits are kept).

As they grow older, their upbringers can help them to expand these structures into more complex and sometimes more appropriate forms. Existing desires become more determinate: enjoying physical exercise becomes specified into playing volley-ball or rollerblading; while brand-new desires – to play a musical instrument, to construct mathematical proofs, to flirt – become grafted onto old. Undesirable desires get sifted out. Acceptable ones get chained together in complicated, hierarchical structures of means-end and part-whole relationships.

Beliefs undergo similar transformations. Children acquire more and more information in different domains, much of which can be incorporated into reasons for action. False or unfounded beliefs are winnowed away. (Older children may smoke so as to gain the approval of their peer group. Is the belief correct? If smoking is a means of gaining approval, is it on balance a good means? Why is it important to gain the approval of the group?) Those beliefs that pass muster are bound by logical links within increasingly sophisticated thought-structures. Or such, at least, is the ideal, however much some children fall short of this in practice.

More than just this work on expanding desire- and belief-structures is required. Pupils have to learn to choose between desires when they conflict, make one rather than another the motivating desire from which they will act. They want to smoke and they want to be healthy. They need to acquire *second-order* desires of desiring their health-desire to trump the smoking-desire. As they grow older and their desires multiply, they are likely to face more, and more intractable, conflicts between them. In their earlier years, their parents and teachers were on hand to help them resolve them. Now, gradually, they will take over this office themselves and make their own autonomous judgements as to what to do.

Developing children's understanding of their own and others' actions

There is an asymmetry between our understanding of our own motives and our understanding of others'. By and large our own motives are open to us. We know why we are writing this letter to the tax office or buying a bus ticket to Wood Green. If we saw a stranger doing these things, we would not immediately know why. We would have to have recourse to evidence, in the shape of what he or she said their reasons were, for instance.

This claim needs to be qualified in two ways. We do not always know our own motives. A man may tell himself he is interested in a woman only because of her intellect, wanting for whatever reason to repress his awareness of being sexually attracted to her. Also, others' motives are by no means always as opaque as in the examples given. If I see my neighbour watering her garden during dry weather, I need no detective work to tell me she wants her plants not to suffer.

These remarks open up new directions for motivational education. The watering example reminds us of the significance of cultural background. We all know – at least in broad terms – what people have in mind when they spray water from a can, or when they tap numbers into a mobile phone, or pull a trolley out from a rack in the supermarket. There is a taken-for-granted background here that we all share, but which for a tribesperson from a totally different culture would be unintelligible.

Very young children are something like the tribesperson. I heard a little girl in an art gallery recently asking of a Degas nude why they put up rude pictures like this. As I walked past, her mother was carefully explaining about the patches of light on the skin. She was initiating her daughter into what will become for her a taken-as-read horizon shared with all lovers of Western art.

Children need to be inducted into their own culture's motivational structures. They will soon become second nature to them. But their education needs more than this. There are at least three kinds of opacities which they will require extra guidance to dispel. The first has to do with their own unconscious motives. I am not thinking of the deeply embedded forms of repression associated with psycho-pathology, but of more commonplace examples of self-deception that affect us all. In pupils' own interests they should be made aware that they may have motives which they are reluctant to admit to themselves. Literature is one resource for this.

Second, a shrinking and increasingly multicultural world brings with it greater demands on being able to interpret the behaviour of people from other cultures. This is a matter partly of learning about other taken-for-granted backgrounds, partly of avoiding stereotypes or refusing to step outside your own cultural horizons so as to make the exotic more familiar.

Third, the motives of those who share your own cultural horizons are not always as patent as those of the gardener or the mobile-phone user. Sometimes they may *seem* patent, as in the case of a bogus police officer I recently encountered as a member of a jury, who called at a flat claiming to be investigating robberies in the area while his accomplice was busy stealing an engagement ring from another room. Pupils need to be intellectually equipped against the con artist, the deceptively friendly salesman or advertiser.

At other times motives are from the outset more indiscernible. We just cannot understand why a friend should be so uncharacteristically blunt with us, or why the Prime Minister should timetable the prorogation of Parliament as he did. Here, too, pupils need to acquire appropriate intellectual resources – a general, nuanced understanding of human nature in the first case, insight into British party politics in the second.

All these points indicate the sophistication which pupils need to attain in their understanding of their own and others' motives. Modern society contains plenty of institutions ready, each for its own reasons, to present a simplified, stereotyped picture of the motivational scene. Soap operas, tabloid newspapers, advertisements show people dominated by – usually short-term – desires for money, sex, power, recognition, comfort, security. Political movements can pin crude low motives on undesirable groups, as the Nazis did on the Jews or Stalin on his political enemies. Pupils need to be armoured against such reductionisms through initiation into the subtleties and complexities of the world of motives.

I have argued for this initiation on the grounds of the extrinsic benefits it produces for our own well-being or in our role as citizens. But there is an intrinsic aspect as well. For most of us, other people's motives are objects of fascination in their own right. Gossip trades on this. So do history books, plays, novels, films, detective stories. Parents and teachers should, and do, see to it that children are equipped to enjoy all these delights.

Summary and key points

Philosophical perspectives on motivating children are best approached via the more general notion of human agency. Inducting children into what agency is involves bringing them – gradually – to understand people's reasons for acting as they do. These reasons include both beliefs and desires. Reasons for action are not always consciously before the agent's mind. Non-human animals are agents, too, although whether they can be said to have reasons for their behaviour is unclear. Motives as reasons for action can be either intrinsic or extrinsic. Extrinsic motives can be either purely instrumental, or part-whole, or past-orientated.

Motivating children to learn is a practical task on which philosophy can give no specific advice. It can, however, provide a helpful framework. Attention can be paid both to children's beliefs and to their desires. The chapter discusses the advantages and drawbacks of relying on purely instrumental, intrinsic and part-whole motivation. Education is also partly a matter of expanding children's reasons for action in desirable directions. Teachers and parents also have the task of helping children to understand motives in other people and in themselves.

Further reading

There are several good philosophical accounts of human agency, motives and related concepts. Brief discussions are in McGinn, C. (1982) *The Character of Mind*, Oxford: Oxford University Press, ch. 5; Searle, J. (1984) *Minds, Brains and Science*, London: British Broadcasting Corporation, ch. 4; Kenny, A. (1989) *The Metaphysics of Mind*, Oxford: Oxford University Press, ch. 3; Hamlyn, D. W., 'Motivation', in Cooper, D. E. (ed.)

(1986) *Education, Values and Mind: Essays for R. S. Peters*, London: Routledge and Kegan Paul.

Strangely, as far as I know, the general topic of motivation has not previously been discussed at any length in the philosophy of education literature. The essay by Hamlyn, just referred to, is basically in general philosophy. But see MacIntyre, A. (1999) *Dependent Rational Animals*, London: Duckworth, chs 8, 9 on how young children learn to become independent practical reasoners. Chapter 6 of the same book argues against Kenny (op. cit.) that non-human animals *can* have reasons for action.

CHAPTER 4

PURITAN INTELLIGENCE

Oxford Review of Education (2005), 31(3)

Francis Galton believed that there are individual differences in general intellectual ability which, like differences in height, have innately determined upper limits. His successors on both sides of the Atlantic, beginning with Pearson and Burt in Britain, and Goddard and Terman in the USA, held the same belief.

As a philosopher, I have long had problems with its justifiability. If we leave aside its divergence from our ordinary notion of intelligence, which is neither general nor always intellectual, there are intractable epistemological difficulties with the claim about upper limits, as this is neither universally verifiable nor falsifiable (White, 1974, 2002, ch. 5).

When justification for a claim appears inadequate, it is often appropriate to look for an explanation of how the claim came about. At this point philosophy passes the baton to history.

I

Galton first published his idea about individual differences in ability in a magazine article in 1865 (Galton, 1865). He spent the rest of his life seeking evidence for it, beginning with his *Hereditary Genius* of 1869 and its surveys of family-related eminent achievements. The idea was the cornerstone of something much grander. Galton had read his cousin Charles Darwin's *The Origin of Species* (1859) and wished to apply Darwin's ideas to the evolution of human beings. While the evolution of our own species would take place anyway, Galton believed that we could help the process by deliberate intervention. We could – and not only could, but should – encourage our finest intellectual stock to breed and discourage our meanest from doing so. The idea with which we began – that there are innate, and limiting, differences in intellectual ability – is a basic assumption in this proposal.

Galton later came to call his scheme 'eugenics'. He devoted his later years to the eugenics movement, of which Pearson, Burt, Goddard and Terman became enthusiastic adherents. Terman's approach is typical for this group:

> all the available facts that science has to offer support the Galtonian theory that mental abilities are chiefly a matter of original endowment...It is to the highest 25 percent of our population, and more especially to the top 5 percent, that we must look for the production of leaders who will advance science, art, government, education, and social welfare generally...The least intelligent

15 or 20 percent of our population...are democracy's ballast, not always useless but always a potential liability.

(Terman, 1922, paper quoted in Minton, 1988: 99)

While Burt's work on intelligence testing helped to place children, especially the brightest, in the correct educational stratum for their abilities, Goddard's career embraced testing immigrants to the USA on Ellis Island in 1913 to exclude those of poor intellectual stock.

Locating views about intelligence and the IQ in the wider story about the eugenics movement satisfies to some extent the demand for explanation. But only to some extent. We still need an explanation of eugenics itself. Why did Galton's application of Darwin take the form it did?

II

In an article for the *Times Educational Supplement* in 1969 I wrote

The proposition that all men have genetically determined intelligence is not unlike the Calvinist belief that for all of us our future state is predestined by God. In both, one finds the notion of a mysterious something, either 'out there' or 'in the genes', which sets limits to what men will do.

The official doctrine of intelligence is a modern re-edition of an older Puritanism. Nature has replaced God; an élite, the elect; Mensa the community of the saved; and intelligence testers, the Puritan high priests. It is time we shook such primitive notions out of our minds.

(White, 1969: 4)

I found out recently that the comparison I made with predestination had – famously – been made in 1922–3 by Walter Lippman, the American columnist. He wrote

most of the prominent testers claim not only that they are really measuring intelligence, but that intelligence is innate, hereditary, and predetermined. They believe that they are measuring the capacity of a human being for all time and that this capacity is fatally fixed by the child's heredity. Intelligence testing in the hands of men who hold this dogma could not but lead to an intellectual caste system in which the task of education had given way to the doctrine of predestination and infant damnation.

(*The New Republic*, 15.11.22)

III

Are comments about predestination, the elect, and damnation anything more than journalistic flourishes? Perhaps not. There are certainly *parallels* between the Galtonian doctrine of intelligence and the thought-world of the Puritans.

The predestinarian doctrine was prominent in English and, later, American Protestantism from the late sixteenth century, especially in its more radically Calvinist circles. It has a double aspect: some are predestined to salvation, the others to damnation. There is no middle ground. The saved, moreover, are few in number and the many are damned. The saved are the 'elect', those whom God has selected for eternal life. The damned are those of whom the Protestant came to say, with formerly with more literalness than most of those using the phrase today, 'There but for the grace of God go I' (George and George, 1961: 55). Cyril Burt wrote

> The degree of intelligence with which any particular child is endowed is one of the most important factors determining his general efficiency all throughout life. In particular it sets an upper limit to what he can perform, especially in the educational, vocational and intellectual fields.
>
> (Burt, 1959: 281)

There is certainly a *negative* predestination here – by our heredity rather than by God. For all of us, there are limits which we cannot transcend, which will affect our performance in life.

What of salvation and damnation? Although the intelligence testers believed in a continuous gamut of ability from high to low, most of them were especially interested in the *extreme ends* of this range – in Galton's phrase 'the extreme classes, the best and the worst'. Galton wrote in 1890

> Greater interest is attached to individuals who occupy positions towards either end of a marshalled series than to those who stand about its middle. An average man is morally and intellectually an uninteresting being...is of no direct help to evolution, which appears to our dim vision to be the goal of all living existence.
>
> (Pearson, 1914–30, Vol. II: 384–5)

On the one hand there were the 'gifted', 'the eminent', 'those who have honourably succeeded in life', 'presumably...the most valuable portion of our human stock'. On the other, the 'feeble-minded', the 'cretins', the 'refuse', those seeking to avoid 'the monotony of daily labour', 'democracy's ballast'. On the eugenic programme, the former were to grow and flourish, the latter encouraged to wither. A famous example of this dualism is found in Goddard's study of the so-called 'Kallikak' family, members of one branch of which, over several generations, were mentally defective or ne'er-do-wells, while members of the other were virtuous and upright (Goddard, 1912).

The eugenicists devoted most of their attention to the highly able as the vanguard of human evolution. They saw them as a group, a class. This coincided to a large extent with the class of more affluent, educated families – the belief is especially strong among the English eugenicists – although one function of intelligence testing was to identify gifted members of the lower classes so that they could receive a 'selective' or 'élite' education through 'the salvation of scholarships'.

Puritan salvation was of the individual soul, but its collective nature was also emphasised. Parents wished their children and their grandchildren to be among the saved. Whole religious communities, especially among Congregationalists and Quakers, believed their future, if they lived well, to be among the elect. I bypass the agonisings so many Puritans had over whether, if predestined creatures, they could do anything at all – whether by moral living, faith, or industriousness – to promote their chances of election, agonisings that led Quakers, Methodists and others to jettison predestination.

By the eighteenth century the industriousness and business ability of many of the English Puritans – now called 'dissenters' after their exclusion from public life after the Test Acts of 1662 – made many of them rich, not least, again, among the Quakers (Vann and Eversley, 1992: 9, 111–14), and by the nineteenth century, though less markedly, the Congregationalists. As hoped-for members of God's elect, dissenters increasingly cut themselves off, both theologically and socially, from the poorer classes below them. The same process of exclusiveness was at work in the same period in Puritan New England in the same period. 'Poverty is a great affliction, and Sin the cause of it' (quoted in Miller, 1953: 396). Although the lower classes were in general harshly treated, pains were taken to support the 'deserving poor', that is, those most likely to be among the saved. Is there a parallel here with 'the salvation of scholarships'?

This brings us back to education. Seeing the many forms in which human intelligence is manifested, not least in the practical affairs of everyday living and working, it is striking that the eugenicists set such store by *intellectual* ability, especially of a more abstract sort. One can see this from the content of intelligence tests, with their predilection for logical, linguistic and mathematical problems. The eugenicists had a conception of intelligence close to the traditional preoccupations of schools and educators. They also held that the intellectual élite needed an appropriate education, for instance in the selective secondary schools set up in England after 1904. None of them held that high innate ability is enough on its own, agreeing with Galton in his emphasis on 'capacity for hard labour' (Galton, 1978: 38).

In writing about the Puritan family in seventeenth-century New England, Morgan wrote

> For a people who believed in predestination and the absolute sovereignty of God the Puritans ascribed an extraordinary power to education.
>
> (Morgan, 1944: 51)

As Protestants, they believed that their children had to be able to read the Bible themselves (pp. 45–6). Lack of knowledge was seen as man's chief enemy – again a reaction to the perceived intention of the old Roman Catholic regime to keep people ignorant. For the Puritan the acquisition of knowledge, especially of the scriptures, was a necessary route to salvation (p. 46). They thought it should begin early and intensively. Their sons also had to discover their own particular God-given talents and gifts so as to identify the specific vocation for which He had chosen them. (For girls it was taken as read that their calling were to be a housewives.) Some boys, who were intelligent enough and whose parents were rich enough, might put off the choice of a calling until later by going to Harvard College. 'Anyone with a "liberal" education would adopt a "liberal" calling, that is, a calling which required no manual labor and no long period of apprenticeship' (op. cit.: 30). In eighteenth-century Britain the equivalents of Harvard and its successor were some of the Dissenting Academies, set up after the exclusion of the Puritans from Oxford and Cambridge in 1662, and the four Scottish universities. All these institutions provided a broad general education for dissenting families in which the most abstract studies were prominent. (On this, see also Section V later.)

A final parallel concerns vocation. The intelligence pioneers all had a great interest in vocational matters. Galton's *Hereditary Genius* is structured around eminent individuals in a range of top-flight professions. Like most of his followers, Galton did not believe that specialised talents were inherited. He held that people wrongly think that 'because a man is devoted to some particular pursuit, he could not possibly have succeeded in anything else' (Galton, 1978: 24). What is inherited is general ability. This fits one for a range of possible occupations, not for a specific vocation.

The same idea is found in Terman (1919: 17–18), who thought the time close when intelligence tests would be used for determining vocational fitness. He did not believe this could be done in any fine-tuned way, such that tests could say 'unerringly exactly what one of a thousand or more occupations a given individual is best fitted to pursue'. But he did hold that further researches will ultimately determine the minimum IQ needed for success in each main occupation. 'All classes of intellects, the weakest as well as the strongest, will profit by the application of their talents to tasks which are consonant with their ability' (p. 21). Burt, too, had an abiding interest in vocational selection. In 1919, he was appointed the first head of the vocational section of the new National Institute of Industrial Psychology (Burt, 1952: 67).

The idea that vocations should be roughly related to one's talents or gifts is a *leitmotif* of the intelligence testers. The three terms just used, 'vocation', 'talent' and 'gift' are all of religious origin. The idea just mentioned has a close parallel in a key puritan belief.

A vocation is a 'calling' from God. It is a central concept in Calvinist thought, marking the revolution which this way of thinking made in overturning Roman Catholic asceticism (George and George, 1961: 126–43). It takes two forms, the 'general' calling and the 'particular' calling. The former applies only to the elect: God has called them to keep faith with the gospel. The latter applies to everyone, saved and unsaved. Its chief form consists in an occupation – for example, husbandman, merchant, physician and carpenter. A calling in this sense has two important features. It must be useful to society; and it must correspond to the individual's 'gifts' – the talents which he or she has been given by God. A calling is not simply a kind of job, as we would understand this today. What is important is how one sees the job. Performing it is a central religious duty. It is in this that the revolution from Roman Catholicism consists. Whereas for the later middle ages the highest form of Christian life was the contemplative activity of the monk in withdrawal from the everyday life of work and family, the Puritan celebrated the latter in all its ordinariness as the chief site of religious duty.

This section has explored various parallels between ideas associated with Galtonian intelligence and intelligence testing on the one hand, and with Puritan thinking on the other. There are similarities between the Calvinist notion of predestination and the idea that one's degree of innate intelligence may rule out for one the possibility of a professional career and with it a certain standard of living. There are similarities between the puritan obsession with salvation on the one hand and the intelligence theorists' preoccupation with 'eminence', 'reputation', 'giftedness', 'rescuing' bright working class youngsters through IQ tests and the scholarship system. Both groups were attached to the virtues of the work ethic and had no time for the idleness and moral looseness associated with the reprobate in the one case and those of low IQ in the other. Both saw the conjugal family as an important institution for the transmission of desirable features across generations: in the religious case, a presumption of salvation, and in the psychological, a presumption of high intelligence. Both favoured an intellectually demanding education for its favoured group; and both saw it as equipping its recipients for a worthwhile vocation.

All these are at most parallels, echoes across the centuries which may, or may not, be coincidental. Is more than coincidence at work?

IV

All the early psychologists of intelligence had puritan family roots. I begin with the British.

Francis Galton (1822–1911)

Until he read *The Origin of Species* in 1859 or later, Galton was a believing Anglican, who had married into an eminent Anglican family (Fancher, 2001: 4). His father had also been an Anglican, having originated as a Quaker. Beyond that point, Galton's Quaker roots stretch back in impressive lineage to the early days of the movement in the mid-seventeenth century. Of his sixteen great-great-great grandparents on the paternal side, at least eleven and possibly thirteen were early members of the Society of Friends (Pearson, 1914–30, Vol. I: 27). They include the influential seventeenth-century Scottish Quaker Robert Barclay, for whom salvation was dependent on obedience to the inner light in passive waiting on God (Watts, 1978: 461). Other Barclays on that side of the family set up and developed Barclays Bank. By the eighteenth century the Galtons had interests in the manufacture of guns and in the slave trade. In 1795 Galton's grandfather, Samuel Galton F.R.S., was disowned by the Quakers for his gunmaking activities, although he went on attending meetings until his death in 1832. He and his wife, Lucy Barclay, 'lived and died as Quakers' (Pearson, 1914–30, Vol. I: 45). After his disowning he went into banking, as did Galton's father, Samuel Tertius Galton. The elder Samuel was a member of the celebrated Lunar Society of Birmingham, which devoted itself to scientific and technological advance. Here he was a colleague of Erasmus Darwin F.R.S., grandfather to Charles Darwin and also to Francis Galton, since the latter's father had married Erasmus Darwin's daughter.

To what extent did Galton's Quaker background help to shape his thinking? His Quaker biographer, Karl Pearson, sometimes mentions its effect on his character, as in his reference to Galton's 'Quaker stubbornness' (Pearson, 1914–30, Vol. I: 57). More generally, the standpoint from which both the 1865 article and *Hereditary Genius* are written is that of a comfortably-off author who sees himself as belonging to a small, highly educated élite and who draws a sharp distinction between that élite and the shapeless, potentially dangerous mass below. He is someone who has a lot of time for achievement – especially intellectual achievement – of a high order, for 'reputation'. As he writes in *Hereditary Genius* (p. 6), 'I look upon social and professional life as a continuous examination. All are candidates for the good opinions of others, and for success in their several professions.' These are qualities found in the high-class Quaker society from which he sprang. In a critique of his own community in 1859 John Rowntree

> revealed that what underpinned the Society of Friends was the assumption that the Quaker way of life was a route to [material] success. It comprised in effect an élite of preselected personal and social qualities which, while replenishing itself from generation to generation, had proved itself incapable of maintaining popular support. A wide base to the Society would have undermined that success.
>
> (Walvin, 1997: 132)

Although Galton gave up his Christian beliefs after reading Darwin, he remained religious for the rest of his life. The ending of *Hereditary Genius* is sympathetic to the view that

> the constitution of the living Universe is a pure theism, and...its form of activity is what may be described as cooperative...all life is single in its essence, but various, ever varying, and interactive in its manifestations, and...men and all other living animals are active workers and sharers in a vastly more extended system of cosmic action than any of ourselves, much less of them, can possibly comprehend...they may contribute, more or less unconsciously, to the manifestation of a far higher life than our own, somewhat as – I do not propose to push the metaphor too far – the individual cells of one of the more complex animals contribute to the manifestation of its higher order of personality.
>
> (Galton, 1978: 376)

Again,

> Man has already furthered evolution very considerably, half unconsciously, and for his own personal advantages, but he has not yet risen to the conviction that it is his religious duty to do so deliberately and systematically.
>
> (Galton, 1907: 198)

Pearson confirms this:

> It was a great revolution in thought that Galton was proposing and probably few grasped its extent in 1883. He had in mind a new religion, a religion which should not depend on revelation....Man was to study the purpose of the universe in its past evolution, and by working to the same end, he was to make its progress less slow and less painful in the future.... If the purpose of the Deity be manifested in the development of the universe, then the aim of man should be, with such limited powers as he may at present possess, to facilitate the divine purpose.
>
> (Pearson, 1914–30, Vol. II: 261)

Galton's new religion shared with that of his dissenting ancestors the notion that it is one's religious duty to be socially useful and thereby to promote God's purposes.

Cyril Burt (1883–1971)

Cyril Burt was also of Puritan stock, as with Galton on his father's side. He tells us in his autobiographical sketch (Burt, 1952: 55) that his mother was an Anglican and that his father, along with most of his, Cyril's, other male relatives, was a Congregationalist.

His childhood passed more directly under the influence of Congregationalism than Galton's did under that of Quakerism. His father was in the medical profession. 'In his eyes', Burt tells us (Burt, 1952: 55), 'I was, like my sister, unquestionably destined from birth to follow him as a doctor.' The father was a keen classical scholar, who taught Burt 'the Latin declensions morning by morning while still in my cot, with stories from Livy or Nepos as a reward'. His grandfather on his father's side was also a Congregationalist. He was as keen on early learning as his son, since a few years later than the cot experience, 'my grandfather, who was a great admirer of German science and philosophy, made me learn the German declensions and recite the song from *Wilhelm Tell*' (p. 55). Of all the Puritan groups, the Congregationalists had been traditionally been the most committed to learning and teaching – across a broad range, not only in theology. This seems clearly reflected in Burt's own family. His early education reminds one of the Congregationalist belief in seventeenth-century New England, that 'Satan never hesitated to begin his assaults upon children in their infancy, "and therefore if you would prevent him, do not you delay, but be dropping in instruction as they are able, and as soon as they are able to understand any thing"' (Morgan, 1944: 53). 'Children were taught as fast as they could learn' (ibid.).

Burt tells us that 'the last six generations have included six surgeons or physicians, three ministers of the church on the male side' (p. 54). Connexions between science and religion thus go deep into his family past. In the dissenting tradition, the two were closely linked, since science, it was held, revealed the structure of God's created world. This is especially true of the Congregationalists, who were the leading organisers of Dissenting Academies from the seventeenth through to the nineteenth century. Science gained more and more prominence in their curricula as the eighteenth century progressed.

How far was Burt himself interested in religion as well as science? In his long retirement from 1950 until 1971, theology became one of his three major non-professional interests, along with astronomy and music. He described himself as Christian, as regards denomination 'Liberal Anglican', and as regards theology, Unitarian (Hearnshaw, 1979: 207). He became quite proficient in Hebrew, read widely in theology and sketched out a book to be called 'The Pros and Cons of a Religious Metaphysic' (p. 208). He also published several essays on psychical research, which by his last decade had become 'an integral part of his metaphysical system' (p. 224). He was a Cartesian dualist, holding that there are two types of consciousness, a passive form dependent on brain processes, and an active form – which he called 'psychon' – 'with a possibly infinite life-time'.

> Not only might the psychic fields of different individuals overlap, thus accounting for telepathic experiences, but there might well be a sort of 'over-soul' – 'a kind of group mind formed by the subconscious telepathic interaction of the minds of certain persons now living together perhaps with the psychic reservoir out of which the minds of individuals, now deceased, were formed, and into which they were re-absorbed on the death of their bodies'. This active 'psychon' was something that acted according to its own laws. Psychology was, therefore, a science in its own right, and not dependent on material data.
>
> (pp. 224–5)

Based on his view that 'psychon' could direct bodily action since voluntary choice could causally bring about changes in the brain, Burt believed, in his own words,

> in the supreme importance of consciousness in deciding the direction and furthering the progress of animal evolution.
>
> (quoted in op. cit.: 225)

We have met the idea of the identity of individual consciousness with something supra-individual in Galton. He, too, thought that evolution was consciously directed, not accidental. It looks as if Burt took over from his mentor not only the conception of intelligence as innate, general intellectual ability, but also something of the wider metaphysical scheme into which that conception fitted and which supplied it with a rationale.

If this is right, then ultimately, for Burt, psychology and theology are mutually inextricable. Hearnshaw tells us that he believed psychology was 'a science in its own right, and not dependent on material data'. What Burt appears to mean this is that the study of the human mind can give us glimpses of that trans-individual consciousness that governs the universe.

Burt's élitist social and political attitudes are consonant with his Congregationalist background. The Congregationalists were the direct descendants of the predestinarian Calvinists of the first Elizabeth's reign. Like the Quakers, they believed they belonged to the elect – dubbed by Chesterton 'the awful aristocracy of the elect' (Routley, 1961: 63). They restricted membership of their church accordingly (Watts, 1978: 169, 291); and like the Quakers, they traditionally tried to keep marriage within their faith (pp. 329–30). They also tended, again like the Quakers, to look after their own poor (p. 337) while being indifferent to poverty in general, seeing it as part of the Providential plan (Jones, 1962: 192). Socially, from the seventeenth century 'Congregationalism was very much the religion of the economically independent' (op. cit.: 126), including merchants and tradesmen. Like the Quakers, they made up for their exclusion from much of public life by 'a fervent devotion to business' (p. 127). By the nineteenth century they 'found themselves joining in the general adulation of worldly success' (p. 288). It was the Congregationalists who became particularly associated with the defence of the 'Victorian virtues' of hard work, thrift, teetotalism, sabbatarianism, respect towards the family and suspicion of the theatre (pp. 290–4). An observer in 1902 wrote that their denomination was 'more than any other the Church of the middle classes' (quoted in Bebbington, 1989: 110). By contrast, the Baptists 'had a more proletarian profile' (Briggs, 1994: 265–6; see also 268–78).

We have already seen how the exclusionist attitudes of the Quakers – their inclination to see themselves as a religiously privileged group, sure of their own salvation – appear to be reflected in Galton's preoccupation with evolutionarily privileged people. It would not be surprising, if so, if Galton's eugenic vision also appealed to Congregationalists, with their own adulation of success and similar sense of innately given specialness.

William McDougall (1871–1938) and Karl Pearson (1857–1936)

In his autobiographical sketch Burt mentions William McDougall and Karl Pearson as significant figures in his early training as a psychologist of the Galtonian school (Burt, 1952: 60–2). It was through meeting McDougall at Oxford that Burt decided to take Psychology with him as a special subject for his final examination. While at Oxford McDougall himself worked among other things on devising 'a series of mental tests that should be, as far as possible, independent of language and learning, and universally applicable' (McDougall, 1930: 210). But his main work in psychology, as it developed through his career, was on the purposiveness embedded in innately given instincts. He was a eugenicist who, after emigrating to the USA at the beginning of the 1920s, wrote a book on national eugenics called *Is America Safe for Democracy?* which evoked hostility for its racist views (p. 213). Like Burt, he was interested in psychical research, and although agnostic in religious matters, became increasingly inclined to believe in the reality of telepathy (p. 220).

McDougall, like Burt, came from dissenting stock. His father, who ran a profitable chemical business, 'was successively a member of most of the leading Christian sects' (p. 191). He shared the views of other northern manufacturers, who were 'class-conscious, conscious of power and of their peculiar interests', and attached to the Liberal party. McDougall remembered his paternal grandfather, who had founded the chemical business, as 'a stern and very pious old gentleman whose hobby was the writing of articles to show that the Bible miracles were compatible with the teachings of science' (p. 191). He had been a pupil of John Dalton, the chemist and author of the atomic theory. Dalton was a Quaker, who had lectured in mathematics and science at the Manchester Academy from 1793 to 1800 (McLachlan, 1931: 258) and was active at another dissenting academy in Blackburn in 1819 (ibid.: 272).

Karl Pearson was Galton's biographer and, like Burt, a disciple. He was a professor at University College London from 1884 until 1933, at first in Applied Mathematics and Mechanics and then, from 1911 until 1933, as the first Galton Professor of Eugenics, a chair endowed by Galton. In 1901 he joined Galton and a colleague from UCL in founding the journal *Biometrika*. He was 'an active social-ist...But he was more a socialist in the abstract and, as an intellectual snob, believed that social progress would inevitably favour those who worked mainly with their brains rather than their hands' (Gillham, 2001: 273).

Pearson was a main influence on Burt's early work on statistical aspects of mental testing (Burt, 1952: 61, 62); and it was he who, along with Galton and others, drew up a scheme, finally accepted by the London County Council, for adding an educational psychologist to the inspectorate, the post which Burt was the first to occupy (p. 63).

Karl Pearson, like Galton, was of Quaker stock on his father's side. His son and biographer mentions his many visits to the Yorkshire Dales, where 'he loved to mix more serious work at statistics with walks along the tracks and bridle-paths between the dale-side farms where his Quaker ancestors had lived and died' (Pearson, 1938: 2).

I turn now to the pioneers of intelligence testing in the USA.

Henry Herbert Goddard (1866–1957)

H. H. Goddard was America's first intelligence tester, a eugenicist and author of *The Kallikak Family* (Goddard, 1912).

He was born in New England, of Quaker parents who could both trace their families back to English roots in the seventeenth century (Zenderland, 1998: 16). His father had been a farmer but was reduced to being a day labourer. He died when Herbert was nine and 'were it not' he wrote, 'for the Society of Friends (Quakers) it would probably have gone hard with us...The Friends always take care of their poor' (p. 17). His mother was a committed Quaker; and her commitment grew during Herbert's childhood in the wake of nation-wide Quaker revivalism in the 1870s which deeply affected their Maine community. The 'great change' which had been wrought in her caused the local Friends to recognise her 'gift in the ministry' (she preached in the local Congregational Church among other places).

Goddard was educated by the Quakers at Oak Grove Seminary, the Friends School in Providence and later at Haverford College. He resented the latter's reputation as, in his own words, 'a convenient way to keep sons of rich Philadelphia

Quakers out of mischief' (p. 20), and disliked its narrow, 'guarded', education. Despite this, he graduated from Haverford with a BA, followed by an MA in mathematics, and got married, his wife soon coming to share his Quaker faith (p. 25). Goddard became principal of a Quaker school in Ohio and two years later principal of his old school, Oak Grove Seminary.

It was while at Oak Grove that Goddard heard an address to local teachers given by G. Stanley Hall, one of the first American psychologists and at that time president of Clark University (p. 28). Goddard was inspired, as were many others, by Clark's child-centred, science-based approach to education and in 1896 went to Clark University to study with him, gaining a doctorate within three years. In an ethos of free enquiry, Hall inducted Goddard into scientific thinking, especially in evolutionary psychology.

> Despite the stark differences distinguishing Quaker from Clark pedagogy, Goddard's education in science remained surprisingly consistent. Like other Protestants, Goddard's Quaker teachers had taught a version of natural theology, in which the order found in the physical world illuminated God's orderly mind. Science, Goddard learned, meant discovering the laws of nature.
>
> (p. 30)

Goddard's Quaker schooling in Providence had included classes in geology based on evolutionary ideas deriving from Darwin. This prepared him well for his later studies, 'for he evidently perceived no open warfare between his Christian heritage and his new career as a scientist studying evolutionary theory' (p. 31).

The intellectual autonomy of Hall's regime did nothing to shake Goddard's faith, given that Hall himself, brought up on strict Congregationalist lines as a child (Ross, 1972, ch. 1), had recently returned to Christianity and now saw himself as providing a psychological reinterpretation of Christian ideals, supplying, as he put it, 'modern methods of studying the soul' (ibid.). The same application of a new science to old subject-matter appears in the topic which Goddard chose for his doctoral dissertation: 'The Effects of Mind on Body as Evidenced in Faith Cures' (p. 33).

Goddard maintained close ties to the Quakers in the following years (p. 39). His biographer writes that

> he never fully abandoned the modes of thinking acquired in his childhood. In his later years, both his negative and his positive responses to his early Quaker experiences would be evident in his actions. For the rest of his life, this scientist would always despise rigid pedagogy and strict theological dogma. In a deeper sense, however, his religious background would become intertwined with his very understanding of what a psychologist was.
>
> (p. 42)

She suggests that

> By the time he graduated, Goddard had found his vocation. He left Clark in 1899 a disciple less of the church's version of the Gospels than of G. Stanley Hall's. Moreover, Goddard embraced his new psychological calling with an evangelical zeal which matched his mother's. He now believed in an evolutionary version of the faith of his fathers.
>
> (p. 43)

Zenderland's biography shows abundant evidence of the further intertwining of Goddard's commitment to both science and religion in his early work as an educator, especially in his work in the Child Study movement (pp. 46–9). What is more pertinent to the present investigation is the tenacity of his belief in the eugenic significance of individual differences in intelligence and the zeal with which he developed and promoted intelligence testing. We may note his belief in these tests as a way of identifying the 'feeble-minded', not least among immigrants arriving in America; his polarisation of the highly able virtuous and the moronic vicious in the Kallikak book; and his vision of a society in which everyone pursues his vocation at his own mental level.

Like Burt and Galton, Goddard came from a branch of Puritanism that took for granted its members' election. The social philosophy of all these men was premised on the nurturing of a small group of gifted individuals, the constraining of the least intelligent, and the stratification of callings according to mental ability. Each found his calling in science; each threw himself with a lifetime's passion into the eugenic mission.

Lewis Terman (1877–1956)

Lewis Terman was also a pupil of G. Stanley Hall at Clark University and a Galtonian. He developed and publicised the Stanford-Binet test, applied it to tracking systems in school, and worked for many years on the intellectually gifted. He, too, was a eugenicist with a polarised interest in producing leaders at one end of the ability spectrum and curtailing feeble-mindedness at the other.

Like the other psychologists who shared his social outlook, Terman came from protestant stock. He was born and brought up on a farm in Indiana. His father enjoyed reading the Bible although seldom attended church (Seacoe, 1975: 2). Each side of his family could trace its roots in America to around 1700. The fact that his paternal grandfather John H. Tarman, of Scotch–Irish descent, had changed his name to John Bunyan Terman (Minton, 1988: 3) indicates a Puritan connexion. Terman's mother was of protestant ancestry on both sides of her family – German (Pennsylvanian 'Dutch') and French Huguenot. Along with her husband she was firm on protestant family virtues like order and discipline and hard work (Seacoe, 1975: 3). In his late teens, as a young teacher, Lewis Terman lost all interest in organised religion and became increasingly agnostic (p. 6).

Other American psychologists

G. Stanley Hall (1844–1924) was, as we have seen, the teacher of both Goddard and Terman at Clark University. His Congregational background has been already mentioned. He was a pioneer of American scientific psychology, having launched the first psychological laboratory in the USA, its first journal of psychology, and the American Psychological Association (Schultz and Schultz, 2000: 201). His particular interest was in evolutionary theory especially as applied to child psychology. His most influential work is *Adolescence* (1904). This includes his famous 'recapitulation theory', that children's development repeats the life history of the human race, from near-savagery to civilisation.

James McKeen Cattell (1860–1944) was also a pupil of G. S. Hall and an early devotee of mental tests following his meeting with Galton, who inspired him to investigate individual differences. Cattell's father was a Presbyterian minister and President of Lafayette College, an institution with Presbyterian connexions where

Cattell himself studied. Of other famous American psychologists associated with intelligence studies, *R. S. Woodworth*'s father was a Congregational minister (Woodworth, 1932: 359), *Thorndike's* a Methodist minister (Jonçich, 1968, ch. 1) and *Thurstone's* a Lutheran minister in Sweden (Thurstone, 1952: 295). *Yerkes* was greatly influenced by his mother. She 'wished me to enter the church. Almost certainly she would have become a foreign missionary had she been free to choose a career' (Yerkes, 1932: 385).

Conclusion

Goddard apart, there is no *conclusive* evidence for any of these men of the influence of puritan beliefs on their psychological and educational work. But the fact, coupled with their own social attitudes, already outlined, that *all* of their families shared a similar thought-world – mainly in the more exclusivist forms of puritan-inspired belief – may point in that direction.

V

A wider investigation of this topic would need fully to explore the religious background of other intelligence pioneers in the same tradition. This is a task beyond this paper. But a few indications may be helpful.

Charles Spearman (1863–1945) is the most famous of the British pioneers as yet unmentioned. The originator of factor analysis and the concept of general intelligence (g), he held chairs in psychology and philosophy of mind at University College, London, from 1907 until 1931. The religious background of his family is uncertain. I have seen no evidence of nonconformity. Given his connexions with the army (he was a professional soldier before he became a psychologist), as well as the fact that his father, the Right Honourable Sir A. Y. Spearman, was a senior civil servant in the Treasury in the 1830s, his establishment background suggests Anglicanism, but I have no firmer evidence of this.

More recent British psychologists in the same tradition, and also fellow-eugenicists – include *Godfrey Thomson* (1881–1955) and *R. B. Cattell* (1905–1998). Again, I have found no clear evidence of family religion, although the industrialist background in each case may point to nonconformity. Thomson's grandfather had helped to set up a chemical works with his cousin in Tyneside (Thomson, 1969: 1–2); while Cattell's father and grandfather were both 'engineer designers running their own business in the English Midlands' and also liberal in politics (Cattell, 1974: 61). In the case of *P. E. Vernon* (1905–1987), there is clear evidence of puritan links:

> My grandfather was a Baptist minister in London, whose three eldest children all became medically qualified, including my father...He was a puritanical, authoritarian figure, who seldom had any time for his children, and of whom I was thoroughly frightened; though I realise now that I resemble him in many ways and have been much influenced by him.
>
> (Vernon, 1978: 303)

A word, finally, on *Jean Piaget* (1896–1980). Although he is not in the Galtonian tradition, he is a psychologist of intelligence who began work in intelligence testing at the Simon-Binet laboratory in Paris, using tests devised by Cyril Burt. His writings have several features in common with work of the Galtonians: an element of predestinarianism in his biological notion of stages of mental development which cannot be attained until previous stages have been completed; and an interest in general, abstract-logical aspects of mental life. Piaget's mother, Rebecca, née Jackson, was of English origin. One of her ancestors, James Jackson (1772–1829), was a Quaker (Jackson, 1893: 152), who ran a steel-works in Birmingham. He was invited by the French Government in 1814 to move to France and bring his industrial expertise with him. He set up a family steel-making business in Saint-Etienne (Barrelet and Perret-Clermont, 1996: 42). Belonging to an upper middle-class protestant family, Rebecca herself was very devout (Piaget, 1952: 239). She became a member of the free evangelical church of Neuchâtel (Barrelet and Perret-Clermont, 1996: 23). She passed on her Christian Socialist ideas and activist orientation to her son. Jean Piaget was brought up in a rigorous Protestant faith (p. 112), which generated his earliest book *La mission de l'idée* in 1915 (pp. 112–13).

VI

Godfrey Thomson (1947: 17) wrote that 'although intelligence expresses itself in different forms, in its highest aspects it is always concerned with abstractions and concepts and relationships'. The content of intelligence tests, with their prominent logical, linguistic and mathematical items, mirrors this widely held definition. Why is it that Galtonian intelligence has come to have this feature – despite the patent truth that intelligent behaviour can take countless forms, few of which require the ability to handle abstractions?

The fact that so many of the intelligence pioneers, from Galton onwards, were themselves trained in abstract thinking, especially in mathematics, may well be relevant. A deeper and more general point is that abstract thinking was especially prized within the Puritan communities. Look at Perry Miller's account of social arrangements in seventeenth-century New England:

> Whether arguing from right reason or from the law of Scripture, Puritan leaders came to the same conclusion, to an authoritarian state, a society of distinct classes, ruled by a few basic laws administered by the wise and learned of the upper class through their mastery of logic, their deductions from the basic laws being as valid as the laws themselves, and resistance to their conclusions being the most exorbitant sin of which the lower classes were capable.
>
> (Miller, 1939: 429)

What stands out here is the reference to 'a mastery of logic'. To modern readers, at least to those not caught up in Galtonian eugenics, this looks odd in the extreme. Why should logic, that most abstract of intellectual fields, be so socially important?

To understand this, we have to grasp the crucial importance of logic in the Puritan world view. The origins of this are in the sixteenth century, but 'the reign of logic...continued unbroken' until the nineteenth (Miller, 1939: 115). Harriet Beecher Stowe, writing in 1869 about an older generation of New Englanders, says

> If there is a golden calf worshipped in our sanctified New England, its name is Logic; and my good friend the parson burns incense before it with a most sacred innocence of intention. He believes that sinners can be converted by logic, and that, if he could once get me into one of these neat little traps aforesaid, the salvation of my soul would be assured. He has caught numbers of the shrewdest infidel foxes among the farmers around, and I must say that there is no trap for the Yankee like the logic trap.
>
> (Stowe, 1869: 224, quoted in Miller, 1939: 115)

A key figure in the story is the sixteenth-century French logician Ramus (Pierre de la Ramée). He believed that one could map out the nature of God's world, beginning with the most abstract categories and then, by a repeated process of dichotomisation, arriving at more and more determinate classes and finally at concrete entities themselves. His theory is massively problematic. Why should one think the classification of phenomena should proceed by *dichotomies*? Yet it was hugely influential in Puritan thinking on both sides of the Atlantic. An early Ramist, Alexander Richardson, used the term '*intelligentia*' to label the capability behind Ramus's first act of the mind, to 'see the simples in things', that is to see how specific phenomena are to be grasped in terms of the increasingly more general categories under which they fit. More generally, having faith depended, for the Protestant, on the individual's unmediated understanding of his or her relationship to God and place in the divine scheme. Ramist logic was the key to this understanding. It showed how individual items of knowledge about the world could be plotted on an all-encompassing map. Puritans took it for granted that anything that anything they observed or discovered in the world could be fitted into such a scheme.

With the progress of the scientific revolution, the Puritans gradually abandoned Ramism as a key to understanding the universe. In the eighteenth century the Puritans' educational establishments, not least the English Dissenting Academies and the Scottish universities, began to teach science proper as the way of revealing God's creation. Yet the attachment to logic – no longer Ramus's as in the earlier Academies – continued, as an inspection of the curricula of these institutions well into the nineteenth century will show. Attachment to abstract thinking had become a central feature of the thought world of Dissent.

Ramist logic, it was held, not only revealed the features of the outer, perceptible world, it was also the key to understanding the inner world of the mind. As Miller puts it,

> Ramus taught that logic is the formalized or regularized version of the natural intelligence. Dialectic is employed instinctively by all men, though as it is refined in the textbooks it can be employed only by the learned.
>
> (Miller, 1939: 144)

In other words, human beings naturally think in a Ramist-like way. Their minds are attuned by God to be revelatory instruments, able to lead their possessors, through reason, to an understanding of God and of God's world. The logic systematises this common ability, producing a higher-order, theoretical manifestation of what operates at an instinctive level.

The Janus-nature of Puritan logic, looking one way outwards to the observable world, the other inwards to the mind, helps to explain the later dissenters' fascination with science on the one hand and with what was called in their colleges 'pneumatology' – the science of spirits – on the other. This was a hybrid subject, one part of it concerned with 'the Powers and Faculties of the Human Mind, and the Instinct of Brutes'; and the other with 'the Being of God, and his natural Perfections' (Doddridge, 1763).

Understanding the essence of the human soul to reside in that power of abstraction which distinguishes men from beasts helps one to fathom the nature of the divine mind.

There is no direct evidence that I know that pneumatology – the well – attested precursor of scientific psychology – influenced Galton's conception of the mind. All that is clear is that his notion of inherited mental abilities could not well have derived from the prevailing associationist psychology of his time, with its rejection of innate factors. How far was Galton influenced by the psychology of his ancestral culture – the pneumatology that his grandfather Samuel Galton no doubt studied at his dissenting academy in Warrington?

Whatever we might say about Galton – and for that matter, Pearson and Burt, there is firmer evidence of a direct link between Puritan psychology (and logic) and the first scientific psychologists in America. The traditional Puritan preoccupation with the soul or mind was carried through into the Mental and Moral Philosophy curriculum, which had become a compulsory course in American universities and colleges in the early nineteenth century. 'The reason for this was that these institutions (invariably having denominational affiliations, most frequently Presbyterian) felt it necessary to counter the materialist and atheist arguments of many leading European thinkers by demonstrating the consistency of Christianity with philosophy and logic' (Richards, 2002: 53).

It was the responsibility of the college president to deliver the Mental and Moral Philosophy course to senior students.

> Preconceived theological views and evangelistic purposes combined to deprive the course of anything resembling earnest philosophical investigation. One student described the course as embracing 'man in his unity, and God in his sovereignty', and he was not exaggerating.
>
> (Rudolph, 1962: 141)

Mark Hopkins, president of Williams College, described his course to a gathering of alumni as beginning with the physical man and leading, in Rudolph's words (ibid.), 'through the byways of mental faculties, grounds of belief, logic, and emotion, to the ultimate destination, the moral government of God'.

The pioneers of the scientifically orientated 'new psychology' in America after 1880 have been cast as 'breaking the stranglehold of this sterile force' (Richards, 2002: 53), but it seems from recent research that the continuities are as important as the divergences:

> My own view is that, while Psychology established itself as a replacement for Mental and Moral Philosophy ..., there were some important respects in which it continued to play a similar 'moral education' role. Furthermore, many textbooks published as 'Psychology' between 1880 and 1900 closely resemble their predecessors in agenda and structure, even if they are more secular in approach and more 'scientific' in tone. In other words, there were fairly high levels of continuity between old and new, and the New Psychology's revolutionary rhetoric was frequently more an expression of aspiration than achievement.
>
> (op. cit.: 54)

One of the most celebrated college presidents of the late nineteenth century was G. Stanley Hall of Clark University. As a charismatic teacher indebted to his puritan heritage and eager to found a new scientific psychology, he bridged the old world and the new.

VII

How far has the argument proved that the psychology of intelligence had roots in Puritanism? At the very least, I would suggest, it has shown it to be a plausible hypothesis, stronger in some cases – perhaps in Goddard's – than in others. I am aware that the – to me – surprising discovery that virtually all the major players in the story had Puritan connexions may prove, after all, to be no more than coincidence. Meanwhile, the hypothesis looks worthy of further pursuit.

Acknowledgements

I am most grateful to Norman Franke for genealogical evidence on Burt's family; to Henry Minton and Dr Lewis Terman for help on Terman's background; to Jane Green for raising the question whether, given the nature of his work, Piaget may have had puritan connexions; and to M. Thierry Veyron of the Bibliotheque Municipale de St Etienne, France, for information about Piaget's Quaker connexions.

Bibliography

Barrelet, J.-M. and Perret-Clermont, A.-N. (1996) *Jean Piaget et Neuchâtel*, Lausanne: Payot.

Bebbington, D. W. (1989) *Evangelicalism in Modern Britain: A History From the 1730s to the 1980s*, London: Unwin Hyman.

Briggs, J. H. Y. (1994) *The English Baptists of the Nineteenth Century*, Didcot: The Baptist Historical Society.

Burt, C. L. (1952) 'Cyril Burt' in Boring, E. G. *et al.* (eds) *History of Psychology in Autobiography*, Vol. IV, Worcester, MA: Clark University.

Burt, C. L. (1959) 'The Evidence for the Concept of Intelligence' in Wiseman, S. (ed.) *Intelligence and Ability*, Harmondsworth: Penguin.

Cattell, R. B. (1974) 'Raymond B. Cattell' in Lindzey, G. (ed.) *History of Psychology in Autobiography*, Vol. VI, Englewood Clliffs, NJ: Prentice Hall.

Doddridge, P. (1763) *Lectures on Pneumatology, Ethics and Theology* included in Doddridge, P. (1803) *Works*: Vol. IV published in Leeds.

Fancher, R. E. (2001) 'Eugenics and other Victorian "Secular Religions"' in Green, C. D., Shore, M. and Theo, T. (eds) *The Transformation of Psychology*, Washington, DC: American Psychological Association.

Galton, F. (1865) 'Hereditary Talent and character', *Macmillan's Magazine*, Vol. 12.

Galton, F. (1907) *Inquiries into Human Faculty and its Development*, London: Dent (first published 1883).

Galton, F. (1978) *Hereditary Genius*, reprint of 1892 edition, first published 1869, London: Friedmann.

George, G. H. and George, K. (1961) *The Protestant Mind of the English Reformation*, Princeton, NJ: Princeton University Press.

Gillham, N. W. (2001) *A Life of Sir Francis Galton*, Oxford: Oxford University Press.

Goddard, H. H. (1912) *The Kallikak Family: A Study in the Heredity of Feeble-mindedness*, New York: Macmillan.

Hearnshaw, L. S. (1979) *Cyril Burt: Psychologist*, London: Hodder and Stoughton.

Jackson, William Fritz (1893) *James Jackson et ses Fils: notice sur leur vie. et sur les établissements qu'ils ont fondés ou dirigés en France*, Paris: Chamerot et Renouard.

Jonçich, G. M. (1968) *The Sane Positivist: A Biography of Edward L., Thorndike*, Middletown, OH: Wesleyan University Press.

Jones, R. T. (1962) *Congregationalism in England 1662–1962*, London: Independent Press.

Lippman, W. (1922) 'The Abuse of the Tests', *The New Republic*, 15 November.

McDougall, W. (1930) 'William McDougall' in Murchison, C. (ed.) *History of Psychology in Autobiography*, Vol. I, Worcester, MA: Clark University.

McLachlan, H. (1931) *English Education under the Test Acts: Being the History of Nonconformist Academies 1660–1820*, Manchester, NH: Manchester University Press.

Miller, P. (1939) *The New England Mind: The Seventeenth Century*, New York: Macmillan.

Miller, P. (1953) *The New England Mind: From Colony to Province*, Cambridge, MA: Harvard University Press.

Minton, H. L. (1988) *Lewis M Terman*, New York: New York University Press.

Morgan, E. S. (1944) *The Puritan Family*, Boston: Trustees of the Public Library.

Pearson, E. S. (1938) *Karl Pearson: An Appreciation of Some Aspects of his Life and Work*, Cambridge: Cambridge University Press.

Pearson, K. (1914–30) *Life, Letters and Labours of Francis Galton* (3 Vols), Cambridge: Cambridge University Press.

Piaget, J. (1952) 'Jean Piaget' Burt' in Boring, E. G. *et al.* (eds) *History of Psychology in Autobiography*, Vol. IV, Worcester, MA: Clark University.

Richards, G. (2002) *Putting Psychology in its Place*, New York: Routledge.

Ross, D. (1972) *G. Stanley Hall: The Psychologist as Prophet*, Chicago, IL: University of Chicago Press.

Routley, E. R. (1961) *The Story of Congregationalism*, London: Independent Press.

Rudolph, F. (1962) *The American College and University: A History* (1990 edition), Athens, Georgia: University of Georgia Press.

Schultz, D. P. and Schultz, S. E. (2000) *A History of Modern Psychology* (7th edn), Fort Worth, TX: Harcourt College Publishers.

Seacoe, M. (1975) *Terman and the Gifted*, Los Altos: William Kaufman.

Stowe, H. B. (1869) *Oldtown Folks*, Republished New Brunswick: Rutgers University Press 1987.

Terman, L. M. (1919) *The Measurement of Intelligence*, London: Harrap.

Thomson, G. H. (1947) *The Trend of National Intelligence*, London: The Eugenics Society.

Thomson, G. H. (1969) *The Education of an Englishman*, Edinburgh: Moray House.

Thurstone, L. L. (1952) 'L.L. Thurstone' in Boring, E. G. *et al.* (eds) *History of Psychology in Autobiography*, Vol. IV, Worcester, MA: Clark University.

Vann, R. T. and Eversley, D. (1992) *Friends in Life and Death: The British and Irish Quakers in the Demographic Transition, 1650–1900*, Cambridge: Cambridge University Press.

Vernon, P. E. (1978) 'The Making of an Applied Psychologist' in Krawiec T. S. (ed.) *The Psychologists*, Vol. 3, Brandon, Vermont: Clinical Psychology Publishing Company.

Walvin, J. (1997) *The Quakers*, London: John Murray.

Watts, M. R. (1978) *The Dissenters: Vol. I: From the Reformation to the French Revolution*, Oxford: Clarendon Press.

White, J. (1969) 'Intelligence – the New Puritanism' *Times Educational Supplement*, 24 October.

White, J. (1974) 'Intelligence and the Logic of the Nature–Nurture Issue' *Proceedings of the Philosophy of Education Society of Great Britain*, Vol. 8, No. 1.

White, J. (2002) *The Child's Mind*, London: RoutledgeFalmer.

Woodworth, R. S. (1932) 'R. S. Woodworth' in Murchison, C. (ed.) *History of Psychology in Autobiography*, Vol. II, Worcester, MA: Clark University.

Yerkes, R. M. (1932) 'R. M. Yerkes' in Murchison, C. (ed) *History of Psychology in Autobiography*, Vol. II, Worcester, MA: Clark University.

Zenderland, L. (1998) *Measuring Minds: Henry Herbert Goddard and the Origins of American Intelligence Testing*, Cambridge: Cambridge University Press.

PART 2

THE STATE-CONTROLLED
CURRICULUM

CHAPTER 5

THE END OF THE COMPULSORY CURRICULUM

The Curriculum: the Doris Lee Lectures (1975). London: Institute of Education, University of London

1

The *Morning Post* of 22 May 1926, stated in a leading article, 'A very remarkable omission occurs in the new code just issued by the Board of Education. It is the omission of curricula. The Board is wisely leaving the framing of the course of instruction in the elementary schools to the Local Authorities and to the teachers.' This 'remarkable omission' seems to have been noticed only by this paper. The *Schoolmaster*, it is true, did reprint the *Morning Post's* comment in its issue of 28 May, thanking its writer for his 'outspoken common sense'. The week before, however, in its first reactions to the new code, the *Schoolmaster* did not find the omission of curricula worthy of comment; but for the *Morning Post, it* might have ignored it completely. Apart from this, the omission was not picked up either in *The Times* or the *Daily Telegraph* or, more surprisingly, in *The Times Educational Supplement*; neither was it taken up in any parliamentary debate of that time.

This near-universal silence is surprising if one considers the importance of the change that the new code had introduced. Although it was true, as the *Schoolmaster* stated, that 'for some years the policy of the Board of Education has been to relax the hide-bound regulations which characterized the early Codes', the crucial point was the one which it went on to make: 'but now, for the first time, the whole curriculum is left to the discretion of the school authorities for determination'.[1] Since before the 1870 Education Act, the State in the shape of the Board of Education had laid down the broad framework of what the elementary schools were expected and were permitted to teach. The Code of 1922, in force until 1926, had reiterated what had been official policy since Morant's curriculum changes in 1904, that elementary schools should normally teach English language, Handwriting, Arithmetic, Drawing, Practical Instruction in Handicraft, Gardening, Domestic and other subjects, observation lessons and Nature Study, Geography, History, Singing, Hygiene and P.T. and Moral Instruction. A certain flexibility was allowed in the statement that 'it is not necessary that all the subjects be taught in every school or class',[2] but this apart, the normal requirements were clear enough. In the 1926 Code, however, all mention of subjects was eliminated, with the exception of Practical Instruction. It stated simply that 'the secular instruction in a School or Centre must be in accordance with a suitable curriculum and syllabus framed with due regard to the organization and circumstances of the School or Schools concerned'.[3]

This change of principle in 1926 affected not only the elementary schools but also the teacher training colleges. Here we find a similar pattern. The 1922

Regulations, in force until 1926, laid down detailed requirements about courses. In the 1926 *Regulations*, we merely find that 'courses of education and training must be in accordance with a suitable curriculum'.[4]

But not every part of the maintained system was given curricular autonomy in 1926. The third main element, the secondary schools, was bound by a prescribed curriculum until 1945. This was virtually unchanged during the period 1904–45. Except with previous permission of the Board, each secondary school was to teach 'English language and literature, at least one language other than English, geography, history, mathematics, science, drawing, singing, manual instruction (boys), domestic subjects (girls), physical exercise and organised games.'

The principle of the school's autonomy to decide its own curriculum is one which goes almost unquestioned in England today. It is often held to be a 'traditional' feature of the English educational system, differentiating it from most continental systems, where the curriculum is laid down by the State. But the 'tradition' only goes back, for the elementary school, until 1926; for the secondary schools, it is a bare thirty years old.

This is not to say that before 1926 English elementary schools were subject to the lesson-by-lesson control of the French and other systems. They were not. Not only were teachers allowed to handle the listed subjects as they best saw fit; in addition, not every subject on the list had to be taught in every school or class. But despite this autonomy, the State still controlled the broad framework. It was able to impose on the elementary schools a total curriculum radically different from the secondary curriculum, one more concerned, in Eaglesham's words, with 'education for followership' than 'education for leadership'.[5] The architect of all this was Robert Morant, in his curriculum reorganization of 1903–5. His central objective was to prevent elementary schools from developing in a secondary direction, as many had been doing before 1900.[6] *His* version of a state-controlled elementary curriculum was one which deliberately omitted subjects of a secondary type. The most notable example was science. Between 1890 and 1900 the amount of science teaching in elementary schools increased dramatically.[7] After 1904 Morant made it impossible, simply by not including science in the list of elementary subjects.[8] He used the state's powers to regulate the curriculum so as to keep the lid on the intellectual pretensions of the elementary system. Since he had the power where it mattered – that is, over the general framework – he was less concerned about what went on *within* this framework. And if some schools dropped one or two of the listed subjects, this was no threat at all to the general policy. The important thing to ensure was that the schools did not teach subjects *outside* the list prescribed.

By 1926, Morant's system had been in operation for over twenty years. In May of that year, it was jettisoned overnight. Afterwards, the State could no longer keep the lid on elementary education by telling schools what they should teach – or not teach. The only exception was Practical Instruction, which had been made a statutory requirement in all schools by the 1918 Act.

We might suppose that such a fundamental change of policy was preceded by a protracted public debate, in Parliament and in the press, on the pros and cons of state-controlled curricula: here, perhaps, we should find its explanation. But there was no such debate. The change was sudden and unexpected. In particular, the new regulations were published before Parliament knew what they contained.[9] We must look for an explanation elsewhere.

An obvious place to start looking is the Board's circular accompanying the new elementary *Code* in April 1926.[10] Not only *were curriculum* regulations omitted in this Code: many of the regulations on other topics were omitted too. The circular explained all these omissions by stating that henceforth only those regulations which were *mandatory* on local authorities as a condition of parliamentary grant would be included. On the curriculum in particular it stated that the list of subjects 'derives its authority from general agreement rather than from any exercise of the Board's statutory powers'.[11]

This, then, is the official reason for the change: the list of subjects had no statutory authority and so could not be insisted on as a condition of grant. The circular pointed out the powers that Local Education Authorities (LEAs) already had to vary the curriculum and concluded, therefore, that any uniformity was the product of a 'general consensus' rather than the will of Parliament.

What are we to make of this argument? What *does* seem clear, from the Board's records in the P.R.O., is the discovery – if it was a discovery – that the list lacked statutory authority, was not made before the summer of 1925. This must be so, because the 1922 *Code* had been revised in draft by May 1925 and at that point *included* the familiar list.[12] By July 1925 it had been decided to rearrange the Code so as to separate the 'mandatory' from other regulations. (Subsequently all non-mandatory regulations were dropped altogether.) By November, the criterion of distinction was determined to be the use of the word 'must'. If a regulation then in force stated that something 'must' be done, it was said to be mandatory. If 'should', or 'should as a rule' was used, it was merely 'hortatory', not 'mandatory'.[13] As it happened, the 1922 *Code* stated that the elementary subjects (except Practical Instruction) 'should', rather than 'must', be taught.

All this gives us some of the background to the 1926 change of curriculum policy, but it still does not answer the vital question why the change occurred. What caused the Board to change its mind between May and July 1925? Did it *discover* previously unknown facts about its legal powers? Or did it invent, or at least sharpen, certain distinctions to bulwark a policy change which had been decided on for other reasons?

The evidence points to invention. If the Board had wished it, without any transgression of statutory power, the Code of 1926 could have been merely a reissue of its predecessor. On the curriculum, for example, it is true that no subject (except for Practical Instruction) had been laid down by statute: But what *had* been laid down by statute at least since 1870 was that the regulations of the Board were to contain the conditions under which grant was payable.[14] So the list of subjects in the pre-1926 Codes *did* derive its authority from the Board's statutory powers, despite the counterclaim in the Circular. It is true that there was flexibility: not every subject had to be taught in every school or class. But to state, as the Circular did, that the list derived its authority from general consensus, was completely to ignore the statutory backing for compliance with regulations. The fact that the Code said that subjects 'should' rather than 'must' be taught, does nothing to remove their statutory authority.

Further evidence that the legalistic distinctions subserved an independent policy change comes from the parliamentary reaction of C. P. Trevelyan, the ex-President of the Board in the 1924 Labour administration, to the publication of the 1926 *Code* and other Regulations.[15] He objected strongly to the sweeping away of standards that this entailed. He did not refer specifically to the omission of subjects: where he did go into details was on the omission of building and staffing standards. The motive which he claimed lay behind the changes was a *financial* one. Up till then, he pointed out, the standards (of all kinds) laid down in the regulations were under *parliamentary* control. Henceforth, they would be at the discretion of the Board and the local authorities. Parliament could no longer insist on minimum standards being met: if a local authority wished, for instance, to save money by building sub-standard schools, there was no longer any parliamentary check on its being able to do so.

This, then, is another and very different possible explanation of the 1926 simplification of regulations. Perhaps financial motives, not constitutional ones, were dominant. How much there is to be said for this motive as far as the *curriculum* regulations go we shall examine in a moment.

2

A question not so far raised is: who was responsible for the change in curriculum policy in 1926? Was it the civil servants at the Board? Or was it the politicians? There is evidence to support the latter claim. In May 1925, soon after the first draft of the new elementary Code was ready – the draft that kept close to the 1922 version – we read in the Board's papers that 'the President is holding up the draft'.[16] In January 1926, a memorandum from a senior official, Sir Edmund Phipps, states: 'We propose to deal with all the Content of the Curriculum by means of a reference to the "Suggestions for Teachers." It is the President's idea to keep "subjects" out of the Code.'[17] Unfortunately Phipps does not go on to say, if he ever knew, what the President's reasons were for so specific a recommendation. The President of the Board of Education at that time was Lord Eustace Percy, who held the office throughout Baldwin's administration of 1924–9. This evidence that Percy took a personal hand in removing curriculum subjects from the regulations is supported by the contents of a document he drafted for discussion at the Board in July 1925. It was called 'Heads of Policy' in regard to the training of teachers.[18] Its first paragraph stated that 'The Board will not itself take any part in prescribing the courses of study or training or the nature of the examinations or other tests by which the qualifications (of elementary teachers) are determined...'

Until this time it had been taken for granted that the Board would control training college curricula. A Departmental Committee on the Training of Teachers had recently reported that the Board's *examining* function should pass to Joint Boards, including university representatives;[19] but there was never any suggestion that the Board should relinquish its power to decide the over-all shape of training college curricula. Percy's initiative and originality in this matter seem evident. The plan to free both elementary schools and training colleges from a prescribed curriculum seems to have been his. The dates of the relevant documents suggest that he made up his mind to do so in the summer of 1925.

3

Why did he do so? Unfortunately he has not, as far as I know, left any record which specifically answers this question. But he does say something more generally about his educational policies in his 1958 autobiography, *Some Memories*.[20] Here Percy minimizes the significance of what he did. He describes his policy changes as 'adding a few finishing touches' to a process of emancipation from central control which was already going on.[21] But the change in curriculum policy can scarcely be described as a 'finishing touch'. To drop state prescription of elementary and training college curricula was not to tinker about with a detail. It was to remodel the educational system on an entirely new foundation.

If through modesty or forgetfulness Percy is misleading in 1958 about his achievements in 1926, we are still left with our outstanding question about his motive. It is pretty clear at least that it had nothing to do with so-called 'progressive' educational ideas. Not only did he specifically attack them in his auto-biography[22]: contemporary evidence also shows that Percy had very traditional views on the content of curricula. Although he gave the schools and training colleges autonomy, he favoured, apparently paradoxically, very much the same mixture as before. But more of this later.

We must come back at this point to Trevelyan's allegation that the simplifica-tion of regulations in 1926 was undertaken for *financial* reasons. Was *this* Percy's motive? Did he change the control of all sorts of matters so that Parliament could no longer insist that certain standards were observed, so that education would be run on the cheap?

There is probably a good deal of truth in this suggestion as far as the general simplification is concerned. But while financial reasons sound plausible enough to explain the relaxation of, say, building or staffing standards, it is not so easy to see how the omission of subjects could help to save money. Unless it is made clearer just how it *was* financially advantageous to remove subjects, this hypothesis must rest unsupported although it is still a possibility. A slightly different hypothesis might be that Percy decided on the over-all changes for financial reasons and discovered that for reasons of consistency curriculum subjects had to be omitted. This hypothesis, too, is a possibility. Its weakness is that it ignores the two pieces of evidence which show that Percy specifically wanted to keep subjects out of the regulations: the decision was not *forced* on him; it was made on his own initiative.

4

We have so far failed to discover any obvious reason why Percy decided to drop lists of subjects from the regulations. And it is hard to see what motive he could have had. The Conservatives had long been concerned to keep the lid on elemen-tary education. State, that is parliamentary, control was a useful way of doing this: as I stated above, for over twenty years before 1926, it was used to *exclude* certain content. By making schools autonomous, Percy seemed to be flying in the face of this policy. Elementary schools could now in principle teach what they liked – even the science or the foreign languages found in the secondary curriculum, or even, say, economics, or political studies. Wasn't all this to take the lid off, rather than keep it on? And if so, what on earth was Percy up to?

Now it was true that after the changes the Board still had the right of approving school curricula, so it could still try to keep the lid on. But with so many schools to vet, it would still seem to have been harder to do so than under the old system. If the Conservatives' policy was still to contain elementary education, how was it at all to their advantage to free curricula?

There is one way in which it might have been. The political situation in 1925 was very different from what it had been twenty years earlier. Socialism was now a powerful political force, both in the world as a whole, with the Russian Revolution of 1917, and in Britain in particular with a Labour government already in office for a brief period in 1924. True, this was only a minority government; but given the growing popularity of the Labour Party, a majority Labour government in the near future was very much on the cards.[23] If Parliament still controlled the content of education, the socialists could change the regulations so as to remove the barri-ers between the elementary and secondary curricula. They would be able to intro-duce curricula more in line with socialist ideas. To forestall this, it was no longer in the interests of anti-socialists, including Conservatives, to keep curriculum policy in the hands of the State. The Morant system of a state-controlled division between curricula could only work as long as anti-socialists held political power. Once the socialists came to power, it might well be better, from the Tories' point of view, if curriculum control was taken out of Parliament's hands. There would be danger here, of course. The lid could not be kept on in the same way, that is by statutory control. But, even so, there might be other ways. If they could devise a workable system of non-statutory controls, the Conservatives had everything to gain and nothing to lose from taking curricula out of the politicians' hands.

This is, of course, only a hypothesis. With hindsight, we can see that it might well have been a rational move, if he had thought of it, for Percy to free curricula for this reason. The big question is: *did* he think of it?

There is evidence not only of Percy's anti-socialism, but also of his fear that curricula might become infected with socialist ideas. His autobiography shows us how seriously, in the 1925–6 General Strike period, he took the rise of extreme left militancy and, in particular, the threat of extreme left domination of curricula: he mentions the successful resolution at the 1926 Labour Conference, calling for an investigation into 'how far, under a workers' administration...a proletarian attitude and outlook on life might be cultivated' in the schools.[24] In his contemporary speeches and writings he follows the same line, attacking the left-wing Teachers' Labour League in its demand that imperialist teaching be abolished, and inveighing against the theoretical treatment of economics and citizenship.[25] In this latter area, he argues that teachers should be given maximum freedom: once governments begin to make prescriptions, 'we run the risk of all those evils that we have seen in the Prussia of the past and in the Russia of today'.[26]

Now it might be hypothesized that Percy freed curricula not as a party political manoeuvre, but for an altogether nobler motive, to prevent schools from becoming vehicles of state-controlled political indoctrination – of whatever kind. But it is hard to see Percy as the champion of the intellectual autonomy of the masses. His objection to courses in economics, citizenship, social and economic history was not merely to *slanted* courses: he did not think that these subjects were appropriate *at all*.[27] It is quite possible that what really worried him was not political indoctrination but political enlightenment.

Perhaps one should not assume that this distinction, between indoctrination and enlightenment, was itself very clear to Percy. Perhaps his reaction to the left-wing threat sprang from a confused set of motives. Perhaps, too, Percy was troubled not only by the threat from the extreme left but by the threat of *any* Labour government. For there was enough reason even in Labour's official educational policy, which was far from militant, to justify the curriculum changes. Labour's policy in 1925 was based on its 1922 policy statement, *Secondary Education for All*.[28] This argued that the existing dualism between elementary and secondary education should cease and that the education system should be remodelled, so as to include a secondary stage for all children after 11.

This meant that after 11 children would no longer be 'marking time' but would be given a 'proper secondary curriculum'. This was not to be a *common* curriculum for all children. There would be a certain amount of diversity between schools, which were to have 'biases' in different directions.[29] But the diversity did not extend as far as letting the schools teach what they liked. Although the document does not go into detail, it is clear that it would not have tolerated the continuance of the old elementary curricula under a new name. It is essential to remember that in advocating 'secondary education' for all, the Labour Party was pressing for education of a certain *type*, more liberal, more intellectually demanding than elementary: the phrase did not have only its later, thinner meaning of 'education beyond II'.[30] It is also essential to note that the Labour Party's intended way of realizing its policy was by an extension, that is, a less rigid and academic version, of the existing Secondary Regulations.[31] It would, therefore, have been a perfectly rational policy on the Conservatives' part to begin to free curricula from parliamentary control, since doing so would make the Labour programme unworkable. There is more than enough evidence in other areas to show that one of the main objectives of Conservative education policy at that time was to prevent the coming of secondary education for all.[32] One might even go so far as to claim that it would have been odd if the Conservatives had *not* seen the political significance of freeing curricula, since no more effective spanner could have been thrown in Labour's works.

Was it a spanner, though, since Labour could, in principle, have reintroduced state control once returned to power? This is true enough, but since it was known that the teachers and the teachers' unions had long pressed for more and more freedom from Whitehall's constraints, it would have become increasingly hard for Labour to do so without coming to seem an enemy of the profession.[33] So emancipating school curricula, if the Conservatives *did* undertake it for the reason I hypothesized, was by no means such an ineffectual weapon as it might seem.

I can imagine another objection to this whole line of thought. It seems to imply that Labour had pretty determinate ideas about what secondary curricula should be like, and that these ideas posed a threat to their opponents. But, as we know, by 1926 Labour was at one with the Conservatives in praising the curricular recommendations of the Hadow Report.[34] Was Labour's policy really such a threat, after all? And if it wasn't, how plausible is it to see the 1926 emancipation of curricula as a response to this policy?

I shall have more to say, later on, about Labour's policy. But what I want to stress now is that whether Labour's policy *actually was* a threat is not to the point. What is, is whether Percy in 1925, *perceived* it as a threat. It may be that, as things turned out, the Labour policy was easier to undermine than anyone could rationally have expected at that time.[35] The crucial question is whether Percy saw Labour's declared policy of bringing all children under revised Secondary Regulations as *likely* to involve the imposition of unwelcome curriculum requirements. This, surely, seems very far from implausible – especially if we take into account Percy's avowed alarm at the leftward move of the Labour Party at that time: this might result not only in an extension of the Secondary Regulations, but in their radicalization.

5

But to say that it was *rational* for the Conservatives to free curricula so as to make secondary education for all unrealizable is not to say that they *did* do it for that reason. We are still left with a hypothesis only, a hypothesis for which I have as yet produced no conclusive evidence. Not that I am going to produce anything *conclusive* in the rest of this lecture: I may as well admit that right now. But there are further considerations, both for and against the hypothesis, which may help you in its assessment.

First, if the hypothesis is correct, as I hinted above, one would expect the Conservatives to turn to *other* methods of keeping the lid on elementary curricula than state, that is parliamentary, control. An obvious instrument here would be the Board of Education, its area of discretion now widened since the abolition of parliamentary-controlled curriculum regulations in 1926. Despite the school's new freedom, the Board's *Handbook of Suggestions*, which contained detailed suggestions on the elementary curriculum, maintained the old anti-intellectual tradition until after the Second World War.[36] The priority of manual over intellectual skills is reflected in the number of pages which the 1937 *Handbook* devotes to the different subjects. Gardening, for instance, has 30 pages, practical arts and crafts 61, physics 3/4 of a page. All practical, that is manual, activities together have 130 pages, all science together, 3 pages.

The Board also helped to keep training college curricula on traditional lines despite their emancipation in 1926. In 1928, a departmental committee reported that although the detailed provisions formerly in the Regulations about curriculum subjects had disappeared, 'we understand that the Board will be disposed still to regard them as a normal standard by which to judge whether a curriculum is suitable...'.[37]

In both elementary schooling and in teacher training, therefore, the Board was able to preserve something like the old curricula even in the absence of state control. Its power was in one way *strengthened*, not weakened, by the emancipation. For the emancipation was essentially from *parliamentary* control. As a Labour Party advisory committee rightly predicted, in May 1926, of the simplification of the Code regulations in general, their net effect would be to allow the Board to control what happened on the periphery without being accountable to Parliament.[38]

There were other ways, too, in which the Board could control curricula. Although it no longer prescribed subjects after 1926, new regulations still reserved to it the right to *approve* curricula. It also still controlled the HMIs. A further source of influence lay in its official reports, circulars, pamphlets and other official publications. The Hadow Report of 1926, for instance, injected all kinds of recommendations about content into the elementary system, recommendations whose effect, as many have pointed out, was to shore up the old dualism.[39]

Not only the Board in general, but Percy himself in particular, sought to influence the shape of school curricula in the new era of autonomy. Percy's public speeches soon after the 1926 changes show a preoccupation with the content of education. I have already mentioned his attack on the theoretical treatment of economic and political questions in elementary schools. This was at the North of England Education Conference in January 1927. It was another example of how official influence could be exerted on the shape of the curriculum even when it was decontrolled. A few months later, in a speech at Olympia, we find Percy urging businessmen to put pressure on schools to teach curricula relevant to commercial and industrial needs. The Board, he said, was currently working out standards for the new forms of post-primary education, but 'our success...must depend...upon the advice and assistance...from organized Commerce and Industry and upon the standards which organized Commerce and Industry can set for these schools'.[40]

On the one hand, therefore, we find Percy removing elementary curricula from parliamentary control; on the other we find him encouraging new forms of influence both within the Board and outside it How far was this shift from statutory to non-statutory forms of control a *deliberate* move on Percy's part? There is a certain amount of positive evidence in his autobiography, although the relevant section is about his policy in general, not about the curriculum in particular. In this book Percy describes the part he played in emancipating local authorities from central control. He compares this change in policy with Lugard's introduction of 'indirect rule' in the administration of Nigeria. He also points out a new danger that 'indirect rule' might bring, 'that educational policy might in practice be worked out by negotiations with a national Association of Educational

Committees ...' which he implies, might become a political force in its own right and 'shut out Whitehall from real tactical control'. He found, however, that the situation was not as dangerous as it might have been, since most of the directors of education with whom he had to deal avoided 'the temptation to play at caucus politics'.[41]

The phrase about 'shutting out Whitehall from real tactical control' is instructive since it implies that the Board is still to rule, even though the rule is to be indirect. Always fond of equestrian images, Percy once described his new policy to Churchill, then the Chancellor, as letting the horse go on a lighter rein.[42] The horseman, note, is still to be in command: it only *seems to* the horse that it is freer than before. Equally, it might have seemed to the Nigerian people in Lugard's time that giving powers to their chieftains made them more autonomous; but in doing so, Lugard did not weaken, but actually strengthened, his over-all command of affairs. (A partial parallel can be seen today in the South African policy towards the Bantu chiefs.)

The passage also indicates that Percy was aware of the *risk* in 'indirect rule', the risk that, after all, forces on the periphery would realize the scope they had for independent action and might thus threaten the power of the centre. (Perhaps there is a contemporary parallel here in the growth of concerted policies in the South African Bantustans.)

6

This concludes the evidence supporting the claim that the Conservatives *did* try to ensure that the lid was kept on elementary schools' aspirations after 1926. I must stress again that this is still very far from verifying the larger hypothesis, that they freed curricula so as to make secondary education for all unworkable. I have, moreover, not yet mentioned what is perhaps the most important consideration *against* accepting this hypothesis. It is this. If Percy's target *was* Labour's policy of secondary education for all, why was there no adverse Labour reaction to this particular move? Since there was none, have I not vastly exaggerated its importance?

A full examination of Labour's educational policy would need another lecture. I shall limit myself to three points. I shall not stress, incidentally, the defence that the 1926 elementary Code was published in the same month as the General Strike, true though this is. No doubt the Labour Party was preoccupied at this time with bigger things than a new elementary Code. But, even so, if my main hypothesis is right, one would expect some reaction from Labour, if only a delayed one. So, to return to my three points.

First, it is not quite true that there was no Labour opposition. I have already mentioned Trevelyan's very hostile speech about the excision of regulations from the Code, indicating that parliamentary authority would be thereby diminished.[43] The Labour Party Advisory Committee was more specific about the *curriculum* regulations, objecting to the disappearance from the Code of any reference to the general principles and objectives of education.[44] This said, however, I cannot deny that if the main hypothesis is right, it seems odd that Labour did not make much more of a fuss about the change.

On the other hand – and this is my second point – there is evidence in recently discovered facts about the origins of the Hadow Report, that the Labour Party, and perhaps especially Trevelyan and Tawney, could have been less than alert in identifying really momentous threats to the policy of secondary education for all. This evidence shows that the generally held view that the Hadow inquiry originated with Trevelyan as the Labour President of the Board in early 1924 is false.[45] It originated in the last few weeks of the outgoing Conservative administration in late 1923.[46] Its terms of reference were such as to *contradict* the policy of secondary education for all. They were to consider 'the organization, objectives and courses of study for children up to fifteen years of age in *other* than secondary schools...'.[47] In separating secondary schools from non-secondary schools in respect of curricula and objectives, this directive clearly contradicted the Labour policy and, if implemented, would make that policy harder to achieve. There is, moreover, evidence that it was *intended to* have this effect. One of those who helped to draft the reference, Percy Jackson, Chairman of the West Riding Educational Committee, said at the time that an inquiry of this kind would be 'useful in dispelling the socialist and Labour war-cry of "Secondary Education for All", and it was important to dispel that notion, if possible, before the Labour Party came into power'.[48]

Despite the terms of reference, one of Trevelyan's first acts as President was to give the Hadow inquiry his formal approval, even though it totally undermined his party's policy. A similar negligence must also be ascribed to Tawney. It is one of the as yet unsolved mysteries of recent educational history why the main architect of *Secondary Education for All*, who was also a member of the Hadow Committee, apparently failed to see this glaring contradiction. Even by 1926, when the published Report proved to live up to all the expectations which Percy Jackson and other Conservatives had about it, the Labour Party failed to smell a rat. Tawney was a signatory to it; Trevelyan welcomed it.

Neither Trevelyan, nor Tawney, it seems clear, were perceptive enough *to* see what their Conservative opponents saw with utter clarity: that the key to the success or failure of secondary education for all was the control of curriculum policy: if a dualistic curriculum pattern could be retained, secondary education for all was a dead duck. If Labour leaders were so unperceptive over Hadow, it is not really so surprising that they did not see the way in which the elimination of subjects from the 1926 Code was an equally severe obstacle to their policy.

Thirdly, we should remember that *secondary* curricula were still controlled by Parliament after 1926. Since Labour's policy was to bring all children under a more flexible form of the existing Secondary Regulations, Labour planners, even assuming they paid much attention to the omission of subjects in 1926, may reasonably have concluded that there was no threat to their policy. If there was no place for the elementary system in their plans, then why bother if its curriculum was decontrolled? As long as Parliament still maintained the power to determine the content of *secondary* education, that was all that was needed.

I will have to leave it to you at this point to make up your own minds about the viability of the main hypothesis. As I have tried to stress, there is no conclusive evidence in its favour. I should not wish you to leave here *believing* that Percy's motive was to dish the Labour Party. I would hope, at most, that you think that it is an unproven hypothesis seriously worth considering.

Whatever the *motives* behind the 1926 omission of subjects, the long-term *effects* have been to impede the realization of secondary education for all. If the Conservatives did not liberate curricula with this intention, at least the change has enabled them to keep secondary education for all at bay for half a century, a feat which would have been quite impossible under state control. For if the curricula of elementary, later secondary modern, schools, had been kept within bounds by clear-cut regulations, it surely would not have taken their Labour opponents so long to see the importance of insisting on a common secondary school. As it was, a quarter of a century passed before they did so. Meanwhile, the freeing of elementary curricula in 1926, together with the Hadow Report of that year, created a new optimism on large parts of the left that the elementary schools could gradually evolve towards secondary status – an optimism which in many quarters was not extinguished, but even rekindled, by the coming of the secondary modern school and the ideology of 'equal, though separate'. Even today, in a system moving towards universal comprehensivization, curricular dualism can still persist in the shape of selection by curriculum rather than selection by schools. The continued existence of curricular autonomy still allows dualist policies to continue.

Except for these comments about the *effects* of the 1926 change, I have concentrated throughout on its possible *motives*. A further question arises about the motives behind the later renunciation of state control over *secondary* curricula. As I said, these were freed in 1945 when the Secondary Regulations disappeared. Why were they freed? This is a big question and I only have two brief points to make about it. First, they did not *have to* be freed. There was no *necessity* about the disappearance of the Secondary Regulations. The Spens Report of 1938, for instance, had argued not that they be abolished, but that they be reconstructed.[49] Second, there is some evidence that it was Butler's idea to decontrol secondary curricula. A comment he made on an office draft of the 1943 White Paper underlines *his* awareness of the importance of a curriculum policy and the solution which he favoured.[50] He wanted it to be made clear that in four areas in particular reform was to depend to a very large extent on 'administration' rather than legislation. Curriculum content was one of these, alongside teacher training, the universities and the public schools. It was to be one of these four virtually autonomous areas. Butler specifically mentioned on the draft the responsibility of the Norwood Committee for educational content. Brian Simon has recently described the unmistakably shady way in which its Report was adopted as official policy in 1943.[51] It is well known that the Norwood Report in its distinction between the curricular needs of psychologically different types of children over 11 provided an ideological framework for the post-war tripartite system. One plausible interpretation of these facts is that Butler's curriculum policy, as shown in his decontrol of secondary curricula and his support for Norwood, was intended to prevent socialists from ending the old dualism between *élite* and non-*élite* by parliamentary regulation, while preserving the dualism by a continuation of 'indirect rule'.[52]

But perhaps you feel you have had too much of my first 'conspiratorial' hypothesis about Percy to be able to take a second, about Butler. Whatever you feel, I would not like you to write off all that I have said as merely 'conspiracy theory'. A conspiracy theory, properly so-called, holds that *all* major historical events come about through deliberate, behind-the-scenes long-term machinations, by the 'capitalists', for instance, or International Jewry.[53] Now I certainly would not be a conspiracy theorist by this definition. I am not interested in such global claims about historical causation in general, but only in the causes of one particular event. To be a conspiracy theorist in the global sense is surely irrational. But is it any less irrational to hold that no historical events are the product of long-term hidden strategies?

Acknowledgements

I am grateful to Professor Brian Simon of Leicester University and to Bill Bailey of Garnett College for their extremely helpful comments on an earlier draft of this paper.

Notes and references

1 *The Schoolmaster*, 28 May 1926, p. 848.
2 Board of Education, *Code of Regulations for Public Elementary Schools*, 1922, art. 2.
3 *Code*, 1926, art. 10.
4 Board of Education, *Regulations for the Training of Teachers*, 1926, art. 2.
5 Eaglesham, E. J. R. (1967) *The Foundations of Twentieth-Century Education in England*. (Routledge) chs 4, 5.
6 See, Eaglesham, E. J. R., op. cit.; pp. 40, 51.
7 Between 1890 and 1900, the number of pupils under the London School Board taking elementary science as a 'class' subject, that is, one which schools could offer if they wanted to as an addition to the basic curriculum, increased from 2,224 to 173,462. *Final Report of the School Board for London*. 1904, p. 127.
8 See Elementary *Code*, 1904, art. 1. Contrast with the 1903 *Code*, art. 15(b), by which various branches of science could be included in the curricula of elementary schools.
9 From 1870 to 1918 draft codes of regulations had been laid on the table of the Commons for a month before coming into force, so as to allow opportunity for amendment. In 1922 and later, this procedure was replaced by the rule that regulations be published forty days before coming into force. From Simon B., *The Politics of Educational Reform, 1920–1940* (Lawrence and Wishart, 1974), p. 57.
10 *Circular 1375*, 29 April 1926.
11 Op. cit., para. 5(a).
12 P.R.O. Ed. 11/101.
13 P.R.O. op. cit., Report of Regulations Committee, 4 November 1925.
14 Education Act, 1870, art. 97. Education Act, 1918, art. 44.
15 Parliamentary Debates. House of Commons, vol. 198, 22 July 1926, cols 1457–60.
16 P.R.O. Ed. 11/101. Memo of 19 May 1925.
17 P.R.O. op. cit. Memo. of 26 January 1926. Phipps to Watkins. For more public evidence of Percy's objection to a 'standardized curriculum', at least for older children, see his Commons speech of 23 July 1925. Parliamentary Debates. House of Commons, vol. 186, col. 2455.
18 P.R.O. Ed. 24/1814. July 1925. See also Commons speech cited in note 17, col. 2458, where Percy says that variety may be important in teacher training colleges as well as in schools.
19 Board of Education, *Report of the Departmental Committee on the training of Teachers*, May 1925.
20 Percy, Lord E., *Some Memories* (Eyre and Spottiswoode, 1–958).
21 Percy, op. cit., pp. 120–1.
22 Percy, op. cit., pp. 105–6.
23 In 1923 Sidney Webb solemnly told the Labour annual conference that 'from the rising curve of Labour votes it might be computed that the party would obtain a clear majority...somewhere about 1926'. Hence Labour had only to wait, and the revolution would come of itself, such again, according to Webb, was the 'inevitability of gradualness'. Taylor, A. J. P., *English History, 1914–1945* (Oxford University Press, 1965), pp. 200–1.
24 Percy, op. cit., p. 103.
25 See his speech at North of England Educational Conference, Liverpool, 6 January 1927. 'Do we wish', he asked, 'to teach the child, even if we could, to reason theoretically about the production of goods and the performance of services by other people, or do we not rather wish to teach him first, in practice and in the concrete, to produce goods and perform services himself?' (pp. 5–6).
26 See note 25, op. cit., p. 7.
27 See note 25.
28 Tawney, R. H. (ed.) *Secondary Education for All* (Allen and Unwin, 1922).
29 Op. cit., p. 30.
30 Op. cit., pp. 28–9.
31 Op. cit., p. 30. See also *From Nursery School to University: a Labour Policy* (1926), p. 24.
32 See Simon, B., op. cit., chs 1, 2.
33 See *The Schoolmaster*, 28 May 1926, p. 848.

34 Parliamentary Debates, House of Commons. Vol. 202, 16 February 1927 cols 1026–8. See also Simon, B., op. cit., p. 135.

35 It is instructive to compare Labour thinking up to 1922 with its thinking in and after 1926. Here are some examples

In 1917, the party conference resolved that there should be (1) free, compulsory, universal secondary education, and (2) no specialization until the last year of the secondary school course, when a bias could be given in a direction technical, professional or commercial, as part of a general education (Labour Party Advisory Committee on Education, Memorandum 1). In 1922, Barbara Drake's Fabian Pamphlet, *Some Problems of Education*, strongly criticized the London Education Committee's proposal to specialize further in practical work in the upper standards of its elementary schools, pointing out that 'thousands of children will be given a mainly practical diet, whose intellectual capacities demand stronger meat' (Pamphlet 198, pp. 11–12).

Contrast these statements with the following. In 1926, the Labour Advisory Committee published a report on *The Education of Children over 11*, which stated: 'A definite change begins at about 11 as between boys and girls and then a more varied curriculum is necessary than in the first four standards of the elementary school. A relatively clear differentiation takes place between the practical and academic type of mind, and this should also necessitate a wide choice of curriculum.'

In 1931, the pamphlet, *The Labour Government and Education: Two Years Progress*, stated: Hitherto there has been undue concentration of attention upon academic ability and insufficient recognition of the importance of creative ability.

> ...Under the new organization the boys and girls whose interests and abilities lie mainly in doing things and making things with their hands have as much consideration and scope as those to whom academic work makes a stronger appeal.
>
> Practical work – for example, woodwork, metalwork, gardening, cookery, laundrywork, housecraft – is for all pupils an important part of the course in the new Post Primary schools; and for the benefit of the more practically minded boys and girls there will be increasing opportunities of specialization in one or more practical subjects.
>
> (p. 8)

36 The *Handbook* was last published in 1944, being clearly intended for use in the period of reorganisation after the 1944 Education Act.

37 P.R.O. Ed. 24/1818. Report of the Committee on Universities and Training Colleges, April 1928, para. 23.

38 'The general effect will be to transfer authority for educational policies from Parliament to the President of the Board, and instructions to local education committees now laid before Parliament in the form of draft regulations, may, in future, be conveyed by the President in letters marked "private and confidential" or through other channels equally inaccessible to public opinion', *Labour Party Advisory Committee on Education*. Memorandum 146, May 1926. (Drafted by Barbara Drake.)

39 See Banks, O., *Parity and Prestige in English Education* (Routledge, 1955), Simon, B., op. cit., in n. 9., Selleck, R. J. W. 'The Hadow Report, a study in ambiguity' in *Melbourne Studies in Education* (ed. Selleck), 1972.

40 P.R.O. Ed. 24/1274. Percy's speech at Advertising Convention at Olympia, 20 July 1927, esp. p. 8.

41 Percy, Lord E., *Some Memories* (Eyre and Spottiswoode, 1958), pp. 121–3.

42 Ed. 24/1389.

43 See note 15.

44 Memorandum 146A.

45 Studies incorporating the new evidence include Simon, B., op. cit., p. 74ff. and Selleck, R. J. W., op. cit. See also Barker, R., *Education and Politics, 1900–1951: a study of the Labour Party* (Oxford University Press, 1972).

46 For the original material on the origins of 'Hadow', see P.R.O. Ed. 24/1226.

47 Hadow Report on *The Education of the Adolescent*, 1926, p. iv.

48 P.R.O. Ed. 24/1226. Minute of deputation of Consultative Committee to Selby–Bigge, 23 November 1923.

49   Spens Report on *Secondary Education*, 1938, pp. 311–15, 377.
50   P.R.O. Ed. 136/400. Butler's comments on draft of the White Paper, p. 2.
51   Simon, B., op. cit., p. 328.
52   One impressive example of the way in which 'indirect' control over curricula could be used to hamstring the progress of secondary education for all was the publication of the pamphlet *The Nation's Schools* by the new Ministry of Education in May 1945. This enjoined LEAs to organize secondary education on tripartite lines and, coming as it did just before the election of the new Labour Government, committed the latter to the Norwood solution for several years.
53   Popper, K., *The Open Society and its Enemies* (Routledge, 1945), Vol. 2, pp. 94–5.

CHAPTER 6

SHOULD SCHOOLS DETERMINE THEIR OWN CURRICULA?

Proceedings of Philosophy of Education Society of Great Britain (1976), Vol. X.
This version is from a reprint of this in H. Sockett (ed.), *Accountability in the English Educational System* (1980). London: Hodder

The object of this chapter will be to examine the credentials of the familiar claim that the content of education should be a matter for the professional, that is to say, for the teacher. This is a universal belief not only in the teachers' organizations (explaining teacher dominance in the Schools Council) but also among politicians. It is a belief which stands in need of justification, for although it is usually taken for granted, its truth is not self-evident.

Section I: teacher autonomy

Who should decide what the overall shape of a school's curriculum should be? Should it be the headmaster alone? Or the staff as a whole? Or parents? Or pupils? The Schools Council? A Teacher's General Council? The Department of Education and Science (DES)? Parliament? – Or who?

What, first, is the system in this country? In practice, except for the statutory inclusion of religious education (RE), schools decide their own curricula. Theoretically, powers are vested in Local Education Authorities (LEAs) via governors and managers; but in fact it is the schools which decide. Here there is a gamut of cases, between the headmaster acting autocratically and a more democratic system in which all the staff participate.

Many would argue that schools are not in fact as autonomous as they seem. Secondary school curricula, in particular, are dominated by the requirements of external examination, especially from the third or fourth year onwards.

At this point, we must highlight a crucial distinction, already referred to in passing, between (a) the control of syllabus details and (b) the control of the general framework of the curriculum. It is true that as regards (a) many schools *are* constrained by pressures from external examinations. But schools are still largely autonomous as regards (b) they can decide, for instance, whether to have a common core curriculum, how long it should last, and what its content should consist of. As we all know, there are great variations between schools on these points.

How a school decides to organize this general framework can determine whether it keeps control in its own hands or whether it lets it pass elsewhere. The more a school approaches a 'cafetaria' curriculum system, the more the power to decide what the whole curriculum shall be for any individual pupil passes to that pupil and/or his parents. The more emphasis, conversely, there is on a common curriculum, the more this power is retained by the staff of the school.

So much for the factual background. Let us turn back to prescriptive questions about who should determine curriculum content. Let us in particular concentrate on the question whether *teachers* (including head-teachers) ought to do this.

One familiar view here is that teachers have no right to impose any content on their pupils (either in sense (a) or sense (b)), since any such imposition would be an interference with a pupil's right to develop in his own way. This is an extreme libertarian position which underlies a number of contemporary points of view, from biologically based growth theorists to deschoolers, sociologists of knowledge and the ideologues of Penguin Education.

Now I don't want to enter into a full-scale critique of this position, especially since a main difficulty in it is well known: it rests on the implausible assumption that the pupil is always in a position to know what kind of content is most suitable for him. What is interesting about the position for present purposes is that it challenges the principle of teacher autonomy in matter of content. If teachers are free to organize curricula as they wish, what guarantee is there that they are not swayed in their decisions by preconceptions arising from their social origins, for instance, or from professional traditions, which are at odds with what is good for their pupils? Why, after all, should *teachers* be in any privileged position over content? And if there is no satisfactory answer to this question, then why should not the pupils themselves or the pupils' parents decide content, since it is, after all, the pupils who are most directly affected by whatever decisions are made?

Can this challenge to teacher autonomy be countered? To some extent it can. If it is asked why *teachers* rather than, say, postmen or doctors should make curriculum decisions, the answer may seem pretty obvious: postmen and doctors are not professionally equipped to make these decisions, but teachers are. This seems to me a cogent answer if we are concerned with (a) above, control of syllabus details. Classroom teachers have to marry educational content to the cognitive structures which their pupils already possess. There are all sorts of individual and group differences between pupils in the same age group in, for instance, what they already know and in what kinds of things will motivate them to learn. Syllabuses have, therefore, to be tailored to meet these differences. On this topic, it is true, teachers *are* professionally equipped to make decisions, whereas postmen and doctors are not. But it does not follow from this that they are any better professionally equipped than other people when it comes to (b), deciding the general framework of the curriculum.

There is one good reason for this. This is that decisions of this sort, when taken together, help to shape the character of society as a whole. Suppose, to take extremes, all teachers agreed to a dualist curriculum framework, whereby, as in Plato or in prewar England, the few get an intellectually oriented curriculum and the many get the opposite. Society would then be likely to consist of a knowledgeable élite and relatively ignorant masses. Or suppose all agreed to put every child through a common curriculum until sixteen; the character of society would be very different. Again, contrast a situation where a 'cafetaria' curriculum was the general rule with one where a Herbartian system was the accepted thing, that is, one where morality was the end of education, promoted through a common general education in different forms of knowledge and sympathy. Whereas a 'cafetaria' system might help to create a society of self-centred individuals, each intent on doing what he most wanted to do, the Herbartian system might tend to quite the opposite effect. Each of these frameworks is linked to a different conception of a good society. What emerges from this is that teachers cannot make responsible decisions about total curriculum frameworks without considering what kind of society they think is desirable. Granted, not all teachers would ever in fact be in such unanimity as these four extreme examples presuppose. But this does not affect the main point. If a school decides on a certain framework, knowing that other schools are likely to make quite other decisions, in line with quite other conceptions of a good society, then the school is either glad that other schools are making other decisions or it would prefer all other schools to make the same decision as itself. Each of these attitudes embodies a conception of a good society. Even if a school claimed that the content of education was not connected with any such conception, being wholly concerned, say, with the pursuit of theoretical and aesthetic activities for intrinsic reasons, even this policy would have social consequences of which the school should be aware. For one thing, decisions would have to be made about whether this content was for all or only for a few; for another, a society of individuals who held that theoretical and aesthetic pursuits were all important might well be, like the Castalians in Hesse (1970), less morally and politically concerned than one in which the education had been of another sort. That the first sort of society is more desirable than the second is itself a value judgment about a good society.

In short, therefore, decisions about curriculum frameworks are inescapably connected with *political* views about the nature of the Good Society. If this is so, then teachers have no professional expertise which justifies leaving these decisions in their hands. If there could be moral experts, then as long as we ensured that there were a sufficient number of these to make curriculum decisions in schools, I might be less alarmed than I am about teacher autonomy in this regard. But I do not believe in the existence of moral experts. Teachers, it seems to me, are not *qua* teachers in any better position than anyone else, postmen and doctors or whoever, to make decisions directly affecting the shape and character of our society.

It is understandable that as this truth, that teachers have no special right to decide curricula, seeps further into the consciousness of those of us professionally or otherwise concerned with education, objections to teacher control of the curriculum should become more and more vocal. This is what I believe has been happening recently. To date the attacks have come largely from extreme libertarian, or anarchist, wing, proclaiming that power should pass from the tyrant-pedagogues to the people, that is to say to pupils and their parents. Teachers themselves are often the first to respond to such an appeal. Why, after all, should they cling to powers they cannot in all conscience justify? Hence, perhaps, a partial explanation of the widespread preference for 'cafetaria' curricula. But this is a shortsighted and at bottom irresponsible solution to a problem of conscience. If teachers are in no privileged position to decide whole curricula for any individual, then neither, for the same reasons, are pupils or their parents. Neither, incidentally, are school counsellors, who often find themselves having to help pupils pick their way through the menu of 'cafetaria' curricula, since neither pupils nor their parents can make the decisions required (so far no one else has been dreamed up to whom the counsellors can pass the buck).

Attacks on teacher autonomy come not only from the libertarian wing. Teachers' power over curricula need not only pass downwards, to pupils and parents. It could also pass upwards, to public bodies to which the schools were subordinate.

Section 2: initial objections to state control

Elsewhere in Europe it is generally the *State* which lays down the general framework of school curricula. Are there any reasons why it should not do so in Britain as well?

Some might appeal to differing national traditions. But this will not do. Apart from the difficulties of naturalism in arguments from tradition, the claim that Britain has a longstanding tradition of school autonomy simply is not true. Until 1926, the State in the shape of the Board of Education, laid down curricular frameworks for both elementary schools and teacher-training colleges. It continued to do so for secondary schools until 1945; and in further education it still keeps its old powers.

Others might say that state control of curricula would be 'totalitarian'. Fred Jarvis of the NUT, for instance, apparently holds this view. But is there any substance in it? It is true that state control *could* lead to totalitarianism in the sense that all pupils could be indoctrinated in a particular form of state worship, whether Hitlerite or Stalinist. But it *need* not. One of the educational objectives publicly laid down could be to promote a critical appreciation of the principles of democratic government. This would be a far cry from 1984. In addition, state-controlled curricula exist in many countries which are scarcely models of totalitarianism, like Sweden, for example. As I said, such curricula have also existed and still do exist to some extent, in Britain.

A third objection might be that there is bound to be disagreement about what the content and objectives of the curriculum should be, so any state control could only reflect the subjective preferences of those who drew it up. This is an argument which needs to be taken very seriously. But it is hardly an argument supporting school autonomy, because if it is true, then any curriculum which a school has autonomously devised will necessarily merely reflect the subjective preferences of the headmaster or staff. In any case, is it true that there is bound to be disagreement? There may be disagreement about some things but not about others. There is not likely, for instance, to be any disagreement about the inclusion of the three Rs. If the argument breaks down here, it may break down elsewhere; the extent of universal agreement may be greater than critics seem to expect. Lastly, the argument assumes that a prescription could only avoid the taint of subjectivity if there were no disagreement with it. But why so? Not everyone would agree that the earth is round, but that does not mean that there is nothing to choose between this proposition and a flat earth theory on the grounds that both are inescapably subjective.

A fourth objection might be that state control would diminish the quality of teaching; it would tend to become dead and inert, and opportunities for experimentation would decline. Continental experience of state-controlled curricula bears this out. This is why one finds so many European teachers admiring the autonomy their counterparts have in Britain. In assessing this argument it is important to bear in mind the distinction, made earlier, between control sense (a) and control sense (b). The argument is at its strongest when concerned with sense (a). If the State controls syllabus details (as it often does on the continent) teachers will indeed lose their freedom – which I argued above was essential – to devise means of marrying content to individual minds. Experimentation will be impossible and teaching will doubtless suffer. But since the issue under discussion is state control only over *general* curricular frameworks, the argument is irrelevant. There would still be plenty of scope for initiative and experiment. Indeed, since teachers would be working within a clear framework of objectives, it could even be that the quality of teaching, far from declining, actually improved. Teachers, under a state-run system, might have a much better idea of what they were supposed to be doing and where the limits of their responsibilities lay. They could be freed, for one thing, from the anxieties which many of them presently feel about having to make decisions about the ends of education and the Good Society, which they know that they are in no position to make. It is an assumption of this fourth argument that the quality of teaching is high in an autonomous system. But is this assumption well founded?

These are, then four initial arguments against state control. As you see, I do not think any one of them will do – at least in the crude forms in which they have been expressed so far. Some of them have, however, more substance to them if we dig a little below the surface to the level of fundamental principles. This I shall do in a moment. First, though, I shall present an argument on the other side, in favour of state control.

Section 3: efficiency arguments for state control

This argument is that the educational system as a whole is likely to work more efficiently under state control. There are two ways, at least, in which this might be so. First, longitudinal co-ordination of courses could be improved. Under the autonomous system, the eleven-year period of compulsory schooling, from five to sixteen, need not be, and very often is not, planned as a whole, since each school makes its own arrangements. The problem is made worse for children moving to a school in a new area. State control could ensure that each child's total curriculum was planned as a whole. It could also, secondly, ensure a match between the schools' requirements and the colleges' or universities' supply of teachers in different content areas. As things are, colleges and University Departments of Education are themselves pretty autonomous in this respect. Of the 6,600 candidates for the London Teachers' Certificate in 1972, 1,123 offered art as a main course, 209 some form of physical science. Do the schools need five times as many teachers with a background in (largely practical) art as in physical science? This *may* be a good balance. But, if so, it is only an accident; it is not the result of deliberate and comprehensive matching.

How cogent are these efficiency arguments? Assuming these two kinds of co-ordination are desirable, it would have to be shown that either (i) the only way or (ii) the best way of bringing them about would be by state control. (i) would be difficult to establish, since an alternative is conceivable; the different institutions whose work had to be coordinated could autonomously get together for this purpose. A question would then be whether their systems of co-ordination would not be impossibly unwieldy and unmanageable. If so, co-ordination originating from a central body rather than from the periphery might well be preferable. I cannot, of course, give a verdict on this point, and it would be inappropriate in a philosophical paper to do so; but it is important to see what *kinds* of argument are relevant here and how much can be built on them. Suppose it *can* be shown that centrally originated co-ordination is (in some sense) preferable. Does this justify *state* control? Two further conditions would have to be satisfied for it to do so. It would have to be shown, first, that the only or best form of central control was state control; and, secondly, that there are no strong reasons against state control that would outweigh the state's advantage in efficiency. In each case it seems, *prima facie*, that these conditions cannot be met. There can be central curriculum control which is not *state* control – by an autonomous Teachers' General Council, for instance, whose regulations schools and colleges agreed to accept. And efficiency arguments could never be *sufficient* to justify state control since it would be irrational to agree to *any* form of state control – a Nazi system, for instance – provided only that it was efficient.

These two objections do not destroy the case for state control. In seeking to answer them, we are reminded that the strongest case for it has already been made, implicitly, in Section 2 above. The question – what should be the content of education – is a political one, undivorceable from the question – what is a good society? As such, it must be answered not at the professional, but at the political level. Hence, it is not enough to say that if central curriculum control is required, this can be left to a Teachers' General Council; for if an individual teacher is in no privileged position to determine content, then neither is a representative body of teachers. Hence, too, the case for state control cannot merely be based on efficiency, important though this is, but must be substantive as to content; it must, that is, include within it a picture of the good society and its curricular implications.

Section 4: curriculum control and the good society

At this point, the deeper difficulties begin. If I cannot conclude an argument in favour of state control without providing a picture of the good society, can any such argument be anything more than an expression of personal preferences? It would be tempting to write into the notion of the 'state', as T. H. Green did when he denied that the Tsar's Russia of his day was a state, that states necessarily promote the common good. Then it might not be difficult to argue that educational content should be left in the hands of the state, but there would clearly be a serious difficulty of application: to whom or what should one entrust the power to decide content? What we ordinarily understand as the apparatus of the state would be no answer, since there is no guarantee that this empirical state is a state in the ideal sense.

A specification of the good society seems inevitable. But is it possible? Martin Hollis (1971: 168) has stated that 'if we knew what would count as moral progress, in that we had a blueprint for a good society and knew how to achieve it, then a ruthless educational programme would be warranted'. He argues, however, that we lack such knowledge and hence have no blueprint. He therefore cautions us against radical change in education, arguing that it *may* be the best political strategy to leave the latter to 'men of good sense' who feel their way slowly forward from *the status quo*; but at the same time he is not entirely happy with this suggestion, since he recognizes that 'delay has its effects on the next generation and its price in opportunities foregone'.

Hollis' argument helps us to see the deeper strengths of the objections to state control summarily dismissed in Section 2. Reliance on traditional forms of curriculum control is recommendable, it may be said, not on the grounds that tradition is always right, but because our traditions (albeit our very recent tradition) has been *of a certain sort*, that is, one where control has been decentralized. Where we lack the knowledge to introduce a centralized system, it is politically sensible to continue in the old way.

What implications have Hollis' argument for the question whether the schools or the state should determine educational content? He speaks of leaving decisions to men of good sense, 'or at any rate to educationalists'. Possibly he would be in favour of school autonomy: it is hard to tell for sure. He in any case faces, in his reliance on 'men of good sense', very much the same kind of problem which Green faced over the 'state'. For if there *were* men on whose good judgment we could rely to let our society slowly evolve in the right direction, it would be sensible for us, perhaps, given that we discounted the problems of dilatoriness, to leave the decisions to them. But how do we identify them, if Hollis is right in claiming that we do not know what could count as moral progress? There is a dilemma here. If we cannot pick out the men of good sense, then we have no reason to believe that leaving decisions about content to the schools will be leaving them to men of good sense; the decision-makers may be leading us not forwards, but backwards, round in circles or up gumtrees. If, however, we *do* know who the men of good sense are, we must have some knowledge of what ought to be done; and if we have, then why could we not seek to ensure that the men of good sense used this knowledge in *central* planning rather than leaving everything to the periphery?

Hollis' argument for decentralized decisions rests on the premise that we do not know what would count as moral progress, in that we lack a blueprint for a good society. Now if we are *totally* ignorant of what a good society is like, then it is hard to see how *any* central decisions on *any* matter can be justifiable. This path leads quickly to anarchism. But is it true that we are totally ignorant? About many central decisions of the past there is now universal agreement that they helped to promote a good society – the decision no longer to hang sheep-stealers, for instance, or the decision to lay down minimum standards of domestic sanitation. As for educational policy, few would challenge the decision that all children should be legally bound to be educated. This, just as much as the previous examples, rests on a belief about a good society, in this case the belief that a good society is incompatible with widespread ignorance.

It may be objected that this rational agreement about a good society is not likely to get us very far when it comes to making decisions about curricula. We may indeed agree that the state should insist on every child's being educated, but when we go on to determine what we each mean by 'being educated', all kinds of disagreements begin to appear.

There are a number of points to make about this objection. First, it accepts that there can be *some* consensus about a good society. How extensive this is unspecified. Disagreements, it is claimed, will appear at some point, but where this point is we are not told. The area of agreement, then, might be broader than is commonly imagined. Second, disagreements at one level may be compatible with agreements at another. Abortion on demand may be excluded from one person's picture of a good society and included in another's. But both may agree that in a good society everyone ought to be intellectually equipped to reflect on the moral pros and cons of abortion. Similarly, one person's vision of a good society might be dominated by a religious *weltanschauung*, while another's is not. But both may agree that children should not be indoctrinated into any particular ideal of life but that they should all be introduced to as wide a range of ideals as possible. Quite fundamental disputes about the nature of a good society may go together, therefore, with solid agreement about curricular matters. Third, the objection under discussion fails to insist on the objectivity of a point of view. It argues that consensus about a good society is impossible once there is any disagreement. But people can disagree on this for all sorts of reasons. Some people may have fixed ideas about it indoctrinated into them in youth; others' ideas may be easily discounted because they are based on false premises; others' pictures of the good society may be askew because they see it from the standpoint of a sectional interest, and so on. In raising the question of what a good society is like we are assuming that all those whose views on the topic are to be taken into account are seeking an objective answer; they are ignoring, for instance, their present social station; and they are open to rational persuasion, being prepared to give up a point of view if it is shown to be false or ill-grounded.

In the light of these three points I see no grounds for pessimism about how much objective agreement there can be about a good society. Who knows what agreement there might be if only one got down to the job of assessing it? Certainly there is no *a priori* reason why the pessimist's view must automatically be preferred.

Section 5: towards an agreed content

This is not the place to go into a detailed discussion of the nature of a good society, important though this is. Instead I shall simply indicate two features of such a society which I am confident will be generally acceptable. My purpose is not only to show that curricular consequences of great importance may flow from virtual platitudes of this sort, but also to emphasize the fact that despite the ease with which they can be derived, these curricular consequences are not realized in most English secondary schools today.

(a) The first feature of a good society is that its members are not egoists but have a genuine regard for the well-being of others as well as of themselves. There are various ways in which this point would need elaboration in a fuller account. First, one would need to argue the case that no society (regardless of whether it is a good society) is reducible to a collection of atomic individuals. It is an implication of Wittgenstein's 'private language' argument that the notion of a pre-social individual is nonsense. Any form of individualistic social theory which is based on the atomic assumption is a non-starter; the members of a society must be bound together in some kind of organic unit. This does not, of course, preclude the possibility of some individuals' being egoists (whether or not it is possible for *all* to be egoists in the light of the organic nature of society is another question). But egoism is irrational, assuming that the egoist can give no good reasons for generally preferring the promotion of his own well-being to that of others'. Given, then, that the good society is a universally benevolent community, the next point which would have to be elaborated would be the double universality which is here involved. It would be double because, first, *all* would be benevolent, and, second, because this benevolence would not be restricted to certain classes of individuals, for example, family, friends, those with whom one has face-to-face relationships, but would include anyone whose well-being one was in a position to affect – including one's own. There would be no good reason to restrict one's benevolence in the former way. Since one's sympathies would extend beyond one's face-to-face contacts, one would necessarily be concerned with the well-being of others in the community who lived perhaps far away from oneself. One would be concerned that they all had the basic material necessities of life, that they were able to live in peace, that they were not deprived of an education, and so on. In other words, one would necessarily acquire an interest in *political* matters. Members of a good society would see themselves among other things as *citizens* of that society, working together for the common good. (At this point one would need to show how the impossibility of moral experts would necessitate a democratic political organization rather than any other sort.)

I mentioned above the double universality of benevolence. It would need to be explored how far it was, in fact, *trebly* universal. For if a man must be doubly benevolent at some times in his life, why should he be so at some times *only*? Why not at all times? We face the question: is there any purely private sphere in a man's life where he is justified in taking only his own interests into account and ignoring others'? If, as I would be inclined to argue, there is no such sphere, then members of a good society would see themselves *primarily* as citizens; private spheres would be created only within the framework of their public concerns.

All these arguments are deliberately impressionistic and incomplete. But I would hope that, when elaborated, most would be seen as reasonably uncontentious to an objective eye. Some points, especially those in the last paragraph, may seem less uncontentious than others. Even so, if we turn now to a curricular implication of this line of thought, we will see, I think, that even from the most uncontroversial of the claims, big consequences follow.

An important aim of education for a good society will be the creation of the citizen. (Whether this is the *most* important aim will depend on the resolution of the problems touched on in the last paragraph but one.) Pupils (not necessarily only schoolchildren: some form of continuation education may also be suitable) will have to have, among other things, considerable understanding of the nature of society in general and of the particular society in which they live. This understanding will have to be both of factual matters of various kinds and of moral values, including democratic principles. Political understanding, then, will become an important feature of the curriculum. Far from being an important, let alone the central, feature in our actual educational system today, it is often peripheral at most. This is one area where state control is necessary to enforce an evidently desirable curriculum ingredient. (It is odd that even in our actual society there is no insistence that all children be politically educated, since, if we seriously want a democratic form of government to continue, a necessary condition is that the citizens of that democracy know something about politics.)

(b) The second feature of a good society that I want to pick out is the importance it attaches to leaving the individual as free as possible to pursue his own concerns within an area of privacy and non-interference. This individualistic ideal is not necessarily linked with atomic individualism and does not sink in the wreck of that theory. It is compatible even with the extreme form of communitarianism mentioned in (a), that is with an individual's seeing himself primarily as a citizen and only secondarily as a private person. What it is *not* compatible with is a still more extreme communitarianism in which individuals have to spend *all* their time on cooperative projects with others. There is no good reason that I know why this latter way of life should be mandatory on all. (If each voluntarily decides to dispense with private pursuits, that is another matter.) Since a good society will aim at promoting the well-being of individuals and since, as I should want to argue in a fuller account, the individual is to a certain extent the final authority on that in which his well-being consists, he must be left as free as possible to develop his own preferred way of life within the framework of his moral, including political, commitments.

To be in a position to know in which his well-being may consist the individual will have to have some understanding of the various possible ingredients of that well-being, for example, of all kinds of activities which he may wish to pursue for their own sake, of all kinds of different ways of life, and of the means and hindrances to enjoying any of these. A narrowly specialized education, or an education which did not introduce pupils to whole areas of human endeavour – an education without musical understanding, for instance, or without physical science – would fail to meet this criterion of breadth. Again, as we all know, in our autonomous system there are many pupils, probably the majority, who have not had a broad enough curriculum, especially in the last few years of their schooling when so much could be done. State control would be able to oblige the schools to broaden their curricula and prevent them turning out the tens of thousands of mentally lopsided and mentally stunted individuals which they do at the moment.

Section 6: curriculum control – parents and local authorities

As I mentioned above, this is not the place to go any more fully into the nature of a good society. Some will, no doubt, think I have already gone too far. However, if anyone makes the further claim that objectivity on such matters is inconceivable, it is worth stating again that in so far as this constitutes an objection to *state* control of curricula, it also constitutes an objection *to school* control. The headmaster and staff of a school can no more than any central planner be relied on to provide a curriculum consonant with an objective picture of a good society. But if personal preferences must shape their decisions (assuming that they are not blind traditionalists), then why should they be allowed to impose them on generations of pupils?

It may be said that I have conducted this whole debate in too black-and-white a way, as if the only two agencies of control could be the state or the school. But there are other possibilities. I will conclude by a brief discussion on two of them. First, parental control. This could be understood in two ways, as (a) control over the curriculum of the parents' own child or as (b), for a school's curriculum policy to be determined by a committee of parents rather than the headmaster. But protagonists of parental rights in these matters usually have (a) in mind, and it is that that I shall discuss. A demand for parental control (sense (a)) is compatible with and usually goes together with school control. The demand often springs out of a denial that objectivity is possible about a good society. It goes like this. There are, and must be, widely differing views about a good society. Different schools can, and should, encapsulate these different views in the differing kinds of education, including differing kinds of curricula, they provide. Parents should have the power to choose to which kind of school they wish to send their child – a religious school, a school stressing community service, a school with a strong artistic and creative bent and so on.

This is an increasingly popular argument, especially with Conservative politicians. But is it a good one? Why should *parents* have this power? If objectivity is impossible, then what parents choose will be open to the same objection that they are imposing a personal preference on a pupil. I cannot see any feature of the relationship between parents and children which justifies them in this imposition.

Parental control (sense (a)) is sometimes supported on quite other grounds, grounds which presuppose the possibility of some kind of objective determination of the good society. The content of education, it is agreed on this view, is a political matter. But parents, like any other adult, are judged to be qualified in a democracy to make political decisions, for example, in general or local elections or in referenda. So parents are qualified, among other things, to make decisions about the content of education.

This argument is persuasive to a point, but it can be misleading. It may be true that parents *qua citizens* are in a position to make decisions about content (although, of course, parents are not the *only* citizens). This is to assume that they are looking at the education of children, including their own, from the point of view of the good of the community as well as (or including) the good of the children themselves. The argument is only valid if one writes in such a point of view into the notion of 'citizen'; it is less impressive if it is said that parents are qualified to make political decisions simply because they have the right to vote, *even if* they vote in their own interests or in other sectional interests. The argument can be misleading because it may seem to support parental control as this is normally understood. On this conception a parent is fully justified in favouring a curriculum which will enable his child to 'get on', to open the door to a well-paid job and a comfortable life. Here the parent's vision can be limited to the interests of his child as the parent conceives them. He is not obliged, as he is *qua* citizen, to look at the matter from a wider, community-oriented, point of view. If this wider point of view is important – and it is a premise of the present argument that it is – then we have a powerful argument *against* parental control: if parents are left to determine their children's curricula, what guarantee is there that they will not be directed in their judgment by purely selfish considerations?

Political control of education cannot, therefore, be eroded into parental control. But does it necessarily imply *state* control? A second alternative to the state vs. school control dichotomy might be that *local* government, not central, should control curricula. In one way, it might be said, that is in fact the *status quo*. Local authorities rarely, if ever, interfere with schools over curriculum policy, but technically they are in charge. But I am not here concerned with this technical point. The question is, rather, if content is a political matter, why should not *local* authorities work out a curriculum policy for all schools in their jurisdiction to follow. Why must it be the state?

There is an assumption in all this that the state excludes local government. I do not know how such an assumption would be justified and will leave it to its adherents to do so. But let us take it that the argument is over whether the curriculum should be directed centrally or locally. How should this be decided? One consideration is the following. If one argues for local control, one must show that there are local factors which might justifiably influence the shape of school curricula. In the nineteenth century, I believe, seaports like Portsmouth were allowed to include nautical subjects in the curricula of their elementary schools. Whether or not such a franchise is justifiable would depend on whether curricula in their vocational aspects should be tailored to suit particular industries as distinct from giving pupils the basic equipment for *any* vocation. In a geographically mobile society such as our own there is more reason for favouring the second alternative than in the Britain of a century ago. In any case, whatever good reason might be adduced for giving local authorities curricular franchises of this sort, this still would not show that the *overall framework of* school curricula should be left in their hands. If there is no reason why this overall framework should differ from child to child, there is every reason why it should be worked out centrally. How it is implemented in detail may well be a matter for the periphery not the centre. *That* domestic refuse should be collected may be a matter for central legislation; *how* it is done in detail is often best left to local authorities, since they are on the spot and so in the best position to decide. How curricula are implemented in detail is similarly a matter for the periphery. I express this point in this clumsy way because in the case of curricula 'the periphery', for reasons already given, are the *teachers*, not the local authorities. We have still no argument to support control by the latter. This is not to say that local authorities may not, simply because they are on the spot, ensure that their schools do keep to the curriculum framework laid down by the centre. They may well have such a monitoring role. But it has not been shown that they have any right to *determine* curriculum content.

If there is to be central control what does this imply? This remains to be worked out. What it does *not* imply, I am sure, is that the framework of school curricula is to be decided by central politicians *alone*. Much of the work may be done by others, perhaps not least educationalists. Whether this results in legislation, or a combination of legislation and non-mandatory guidelines as in Sweden, is also as yet undetermined. But whoever does the work must be doing it under the direction and control of the political authorities.

Further reading

The present paper is a slightly amended version of a paper originally entitled 'Teacher accountability and school autonomy: a reply to Hugh Sockett', which appeared in the *Proceedings of the Philosophy of Education Society*, Vol. X, July 1976.

For a pre-'Great Debate' picture of the powers that different powers had to control school curricula see the 'Tyndale Report' (Auld, 1976). A term-by-term account of what went on at William Tyndale Junior School, it forces one to reflect on the *then status quo* and ask whether any alternatives were preferable.

Among the philosophical contributions to the wealth of literature on curriculum control since the beginnings of the 'Great Debate' of 1976–7 is Dearden (1976, ch. 1). This is a judicious analysis of who should determine educational aims, coming down broadly on the side of teacher autonomy. Warnock (1977) is, like the present writer, more critical of the *status quo*.

For a historical account of the relaxation of state control of curricula in 1926 and 1944, see White (1975).

References

Auld, R. (1976) *William Tyndale Junior and Infants School Enquiry: Report*, London: ILEA.
Dearden, R. F. (1976) *Problems of Primary Education*, London: Routledge and Kegan Paul.
Hesse, H. (1970) *Magister Ludi*, London: Bantam.
Hollis, M. (1971) 'The pen and the purse', In *Proceedings of the Philosophy of Education Society of Great Britain*, Vol. V, No. 2.
Warnock, M. (1977) *Schools of Thought*, London: Faber and Faber.
White, J. (1975) 'The end of the compulsory curriculum', in *The Curriculum: The Doris Lee Lectures*, London: University of London Institute of Education.

CHAPTER 7

THE AIMS OF EDUCATION IN THE LIBERAL DEMOCRATIC STATE

Education and the Good Life (1990). London: Kogan Page

The aims of the 1988 national curriculum

It's amazing how wrong one can be. It is nearly 20 years since I first began to argue for a national curriculum. In all that time, I have been assuming that once the need for such a curriculum had been established and people began to think about its more determinate shape, they would be embarking on a pretty complex task. They would have to work out a coherent and defensible set of overall aims; examine what sub-aims, or intermediate aims, these might generate on logical, psychological and other grounds; bear in mind the wide variety of ways by which aims might be realized; and try to work out criteria delimiting the role of central government from that of local government, governing bodies and schools . . . all of which would be a long and massive undertaking, requiring the collaboration of professionals, civil servants, politicians and others in some kind of semi-independent but politically accountable national educational council.

When the British Government published its National Curriculum proposals in 1987, I felt a complete idiot. They showed that devising a national curriculum is simplicity itself. You pick ten foundation subjects to fill most of the school timetable, highlight three as of particular importance and arrange for tests at different ages. I could have worked out the national curriculum years ago. Anyone could have.

But perhaps things are more complicated than this. There must be some reason, surely, why the Secretaries of State picked out their ten foundation subjects and their three core subjects as particularly important. There must be some underlying ends to which they see these as means. What could they be?

Statements of rationale are sparse. The Act itself says merely that the school curriculum must be a 'balanced and broadly-based' one which:

> [a] promotes the spiritual, moral, cultural, mental and physical development of pupils at the school and of society; [b] prepares such pupils for the opportunities, responsibilities and experiences of adult life.

Apart from these few words, there is no indication of what sorts of people pupils are expected to become or of what kind of society they are expected to live in. The words themselves, moreover, are so general as to give no clue about these matters. What is meant by 'spiritual development', for instance? How does it differ from 'moral development'? What are 'cultural' and 'mental' development? And what sorts of opportunities, responsibilities and experiences of adult life are meant?

These bland phrases might mean virtually anything – or nothing. There is no obvious reason, for instance, why a tyrant like Hitler or Stalin should object to [a] and [b] as statements of *their* educational aims. And speaking of Stalin, it is instructive to see what kind of national curriculum *he* had. Leaving out tiny inputs on the USSR Constitution, astronomy and psychology, it consisted of: language and literature, mathematics, history, geography, the sciences of biology, physics and chemistry, a foreign language, physical education, drawing, singing and practical work in agriculture or industry. The list is almost identical to Mr Baker's ten foundation subjects. Not only that, three of Stalin's items were classified as 'important subjects' – language, mathematics and science. Today we call these 'core subjects'. Detailed syllabuses for every subject mentioned, covering the ten years of compulsory education, were laid down rigidly from the centre.

None of this implies that our government's policy is Stalinist or that there is an affinity between Russia's Man of Steel and our own Iron Lady. But it does prompt the question: in the light of the surprising similarities between the two curricula, what differentiates them?

We come back to the importance of providing a rationale for National Curriculum proposals – and a rationale, moreover, of some determinateness. In examining such a rationale we should take care to distinguish publicly avowed from covert intentions. In Stalin's case the task is pretty easy. Behind the Marxist–Leninist rhetoric about the making of the New Soviet Man lay Stalin's desire to harness the school system to the demands of his police-state autocracy. What about Mr Baker?

As we have seen, the Education Reform Act itself is not helpful. Will we do better to look at some of the earlier documentation? The 1987 Consultation Document on the National Curriculum contains just three pages of rationale. Most of it Stalin could have accepted. To equip pupils 'for the responsibilities of citizenship and for the challenges of employment in tomorrow's world'. No problem. To ensure that all pupils 'study a broad and balanced range of subjects throughout their compulsory education'. Ditto. To ensure that 'all pupils, regardless of sex, ethnic origin and geographical location, have access to the same good and relevant curriculum'. Da! To 'check on progress towards those objectives at different stages'; to 'enable schools to be more accountable'. Da again!

The only hint of distinctiveness comes not in the document itself but in its approving reference to the White Paper *Better Schools* (1985). This gave us a very brief list of aims, including such things as helping pupils to develop lively, enquiring minds and the ability to question and argue rationally; to acquire knowledge relevant to adult life and employment; to use language and number effectively; to develop personal moral values and acquire respect for religious values and tolerance of other races and ways of life; to understand the world in which they live; to appreciate human achievements.

Apart from the references to personal moral values, religion, tolerance of other ways of life and the ability to question, there is again nothing here to which Stalin need have objected. Agreed, though, these do give us something.

But how much? Three lines of text scarcely provide a fully worked out underpinning for a non-Stalinist National Curriculum. They are capable of innumerable interpretations. Not only this: we are not told how they are supposed to map on to the curriculum subjects. The most puzzling thing about this National Curriculum is that it includes no obvious vehicle whereby to develop personal values, including tolerance of other races and ways of life. True, some of the foundation subjects, especially English, history and geography, can play a part – not that the Baker curriculum says they should. But there is in any case only a limited amount the *academic subjects* can do to promote these aims – as compared, say, with whole-school policies on respect and tolerance within the classroom, the pastoral curriculum and non-authoritarian forms of school organization.

Mr Baker failed to explain why he said nothing about other means of realizing aims than traditional subjects. But this is only one instance of his more general reluctance to give us more than the glimmerings of a rationale. We simply don't know, on the information given so far, how un-Stalinesque the National Curriculum will turn out to be. Part of the problem is that the Act gives ministers very wide powers to determine the details of curricular programmes, all these being as yet unspecified. Since public statements about underlying aims are so meagre, the way is left open for Mr Baker and his successors to gear the syllabuses in different subject areas to virtually whatever purposes they think fit.

What is odd about the Baker proposals is that they *begin* by laying down the timetabled curriculum. They are not only vague about the wider aims which this subserves, but they also fail to explain why *this* way of realizing aims is singled out in preference to others. But the gaps in explanation do not end there. Even if one begins only with the formal curriculum, there are still various possible ways of proceeding. The most logical would seem to be to start with broad curriculum objectives and only then attend to the vehicles by which these might be attained, whether these be traditional school subjects, interdisciplinary courses, projects, or whatever. The Baker curriculum goes straight for subjects, as I have said, but does not say why. There is only one point in the Consultation Document at which its thinking goes momentarily beyond a subject framework. In paragraph 18, it acknowledges 'subjects or themes such as health education and the use of information technology'. However, it quickly makes it plain that 'such subjects or themes should be taught through the foundation subjects'. The wayward horse is soon reined in.

A final lacuna. As well as the question 'Why *subjects?*' one should also ask 'Why *these* subjects?' Why, for instance, are Latin and sociology excluded? (I am not necessarily advocating these.) No reason is given for choosing the ten foundation subjects. Unless, that is, one sees one in the statement in paragraph 16 of the Consultation Document that 'the foundation subjects commonly take up 80 per cent of the curriculum in schools where there is good practice. The Secretaries of State will take that as their starting point...'. But this does not get one very far. If good practice can be identified, of course it is a good idea to use it as a starting point. But how do you identify good practice? And what criteria, more particularly, are the Secretaries of State using to pick this out? We are not told.

One should not confuse favouring the principle of a national curriculum with favouring *this* National Curriculum. The main argument for shifting from professional to political control of the broad framework of the curriculum is that questions about the aims and content of education are intimately connected with views about the kind of society we wish to live in. They are as much political questions as issues of taxation policy or defence. Every citizen in a democracy – as we, but not Stalinists, understand these terms – should have an equal right to participate in the control or exercise of political power in these and other areas. The problem with leaving curricula in the hands of the teaching profession is that it is, after all, only one section of the citizenry and there is no reason why its opinions should be privileged over that of other people's.

This argument does not show that there should be *central* control of educational content, only that there should be political control. It is compatible with wholly local control. But there is nevertheless a good reason for *some* central control. If British people saw themselves only as citizens of Lincolnshire or Gwent, wholly local control might be in order. But we do not. The 'kind of society we wish to live in' is for us in large part our national community, and our educational planning needs to be premised on this. This is not at all to exclude some element of both local control and of supra-national, for example, European Community, control.

The case for political determination of aims and content does not rule out some element of professional control. Teachers may have no privileged status in setting the wider, political goals, but they do have a special expertise when it comes to applying general prescriptions to the complexities of actual schools and actual classrooms. Where the line should be drawn between political and professional responsibility is a further question.

The only defensible form of national curriculum is one that is genuinely committed to democratic principles, not least equality of political power. A minimum test of its commitment is whether it includes among its goals preparing all young people to become equal citizens of a democracy. There is nothing in the Baker curriculum about this – nothing about the prerequisite understanding of the socio-economic structure or the principles of democracy, about fostering the virtues necessary in democratic citizens, about equipping people for critical reflection on the status quo, or about building the imperfect democratic structures we have now into something more adequate, through extending democracy into the workplace, for instance.

All of which raises again the question: in what way does Mr Baker's National Curriculum diverge from Stalin's? If it does nothing to celebrate and nurture our democratic values, wherein lies the difference?

The state and the good life

The general argument for a national curriculum rests on the notion of democracy. This has been taken to be a form of government in which every citizen has an equal right to participate in the exercise and control of political power. Suppose now a democratically elected government decided to shape its educational and other institutions so as to promote a certain view of what human well-being consisted in and to discourage rival views. Suppose, for instance, it sought to set up some kind of theocracy in which the good life for the individual was premised on the love of God and obedience to His will. We can have in mind, perhaps, the religious communities of seventeenth-century New England for a partial parallel.

All of us, I would imagine, would reject such a polity. If we did so, we would be appealing, I suggest, to something like the principle that, in a *liberal* democracy, the state should not steer people towards determinate ideals of human well-being. In so far as we accepted some such principle, we would be implicitly accepting that it is not enough for a government to be democratically elected to be justified in imposing a national curriculum. That curriculum must also conform to this basic liberal principle: the government would be exceeding its powers if it steered pupils towards determinate pictures of the good life. These need not, of course, be religious.

It is important, I think, to look further into how we should formulate this basic liberal principle, of which we all have, I suggest, a rough intuitive idea.

A common way of expressing it among philosophers of liberalism is in terms *of neutrality*.[1] They hold that the state ought to be neutral with regard to different conceptions of the good life. Dworkin (1978: 127), for instance, starts off from the claim that:

> Each person follows a more-or-less articulate conception of what gives value to life. The scholar who values a life of contemplation has such a conception; so also does the television-watching, beer-drinking citizen who is fond of saying 'This is the life', though he has thought less about the issue and is less able to describe or defend his conception.

Dworkin argues that if the state is to treat its citizens equally it has not to prefer one conception of the good life to another. Rawls (1971) and Nozick (1974), who differ radically in other ways about the proper sphere of state action, nevertheless agree with Dworkin that conceptions of the good are not for the state to promote.

If one accepts this, then how is the state's proper sphere to be delimited? One argument might be that it should have a hand in trying to ensure that the necessary conditions are provided for everyone to lead his or her preferred way of life. These necessary conditions may take different forms.

There is first of all what we might call the 'moral framework' of the society.[2] This is a set of rules which protects or promotes the actions of individuals in pursuit of their own well-being. Examples might be prohibitions against murder, physical injury, stealing, breach of contract, lying, infringements of liberty, as well, perhaps, as positive injunctions like that of helping those in distress.

The state may also have a role in helping to provide other necessary conditions of the good life which we may label 'welfare'. Whatever one's particular view of the good life, one will need, among other things, food, clothing, shelter, good health, a secure and predictable environment, an income. (The list is not intended to be complete.)[3] The state can play a part in providing these goods, although people will differ about how far its powers should extend.

Educational implications

While it may be true, then, that educational aims carry with them some picture of the good society, it does not follow that the state must have a hand in determining them. On the neutralist liberal theory of politics just outlined, it would be debarred from laying down any aims which encapsulated a view of the good life.

On the other hand, it might be possible to distinguish among aims between those which carry with them a picture of the good life and those which have to do with necessary conditions for leading the good life, however that be conceived. If the state can legitimately be concerned with helping to supply those necessary conditions, then it could legitimately help to determine aims falling in this category.

Following the distinction made above, it could be involved in aims concerning the moral framework or aims to do with welfare.

This still leaves the state a broad territory. As to the moral framework, it might lay down aims to do with law, or aims regarding that part of morality not enshrined in law. It could, for instance, insist that everyone is brought up with some knowledge of what law is in general and its function in promoting individual well-being. To that aim it might add an acquaintance with major particular laws currently in force. Again, it might also think it important to build up dispositions in children not to want to break these laws and, more widely, dispositions to conform to moral rules that lie outside the legal framework. Some people would want state prescription under this heading to go still further – beyond law and order and conventional morality. Part of the moral framework within which we live is our democratic constitution. One can argue on neutralist grounds that the state should develop in future citizens the understandings and attitudes necessary to making democracy work. One might also want to argue that the state should not only promote conformity with moral rules but also a reflective attitude towards them.

Welfare aims might also be various. The state could lay down, for instance, that children should be acquainted with the different forms of welfare and their contribution to individual well-being: this might cover work on subjects such as peace, the police, health, the social services, and the economy. Preparation for roles within the economy might also fall under this heading: this might range from equipping pupils with useful general skills, dispositions and knowledge, in the areas of science and technology, for instance, to more specific training for particular types of job.

It is not difficult to find examples of state determination of moral and welfare aims in the recent history of education in Britain. Before the shift away from professional and towards political control of aims and curricula that has recently taken place, the only compulsory curriculum subject in state schools was religious education. One of the reasons why this was included in the 1944 Education Act was that it was felt that it would help to shore up moral values in the post-war period. There may be philosophical difficulties about basing moral values on religion, but, these aside, this looks like a particularly clear illustration of the neutralist liberal theory of state control in action.

More recently, since the 'Great Debate' of 1975–6, and more particularly since the Thatcher Government of 1979 to date, we have seen a marked emphasis on economically orientated aims. The balance of curriculum subjects in various national curriculum proposals has been tilted increasingly towards mathematics, computer studies, science and technology; and government initiatives like TVEI and proposed City Technology Colleges have been targeted at improving the economy.[4]

To return to more general considerations, suppose the state restricted itself to moral framework and/or welfare aims, who would be responsible for aims to do with the good life? Could these be justifiably left to schools and/or parents? A difficulty is that if those educators steered pupils towards some ways of life rather than others, they would be in the same position as a non-neutralist state and neutralist objections to the latter would also seem to apply to them. One alternative would be to exclude life-ideals from educational aims altogether, but this would seem to leave children without any guidance, except what they might pick up incidentally, about what goals in life they should follow – and this is especially hard to defend.

But is it clear, in any case, that a neutralist state must restrict itself to aims concerned with the moral framework and welfare? There is one further way in which it can help to provide the necessary conditions of the good life without favouring a particular version of it. It can aim at acquainting pupils impartially with a whole range of different ideals of the good life, without steering them towards any in particular. I had this principle very much in mind in writing *Towards a Compulsory Curriculum* (White, 1973).

Critique of neutralism

There is one major problem with this line of thought. Is it true, in fact, that being acquainted with different ideals of life is a necessary condition of personal well-being? A positive answer here presumably takes for granted that this knowledge is indispensable for *choice* of a way of life. But this itself embodies a particular view of the good life – namely one in which the individual chooses his or her way of life, rather than having this determined by others. Because this conception is so much a part of our cultural background, it is often difficult for us to see it for what it is. But it should be clear enough on reflection that the autonomous life, as just described, is not without its competitors. In more traditional societies than our own, there are many other versions of the good life which do not embrace personal autonomy: societies, for instance, in which life-goals are determined by caste, gender, fortune-telling or magic, parental profession, religious doctrine, or various combinations of these. In supporting autonomy, a state would be abandoning neutralism since it would be favouring one particular version of the good life.[5]

This means that a neutralist state cannot consistently lay down aims to do with acquainting pupils with different life-ideals. It also brings us back to the problem of what guidance any pupil can expect, on neutralist principles, about what kind of life he or she should lead. Nothing now seems to be available.

But this in its turn provokes further questions about the role of a neutralist state in laying down aims regarding the moral framework and/or welfare. The reason for doing this is to help to provide the necessary conditions for people to lead a life of well-being, yet if no guidance can be given on what such a life might consist in, one wonders what the point is of building a substructure where there is no superstructure to support.

The truth is, however, that there *is* a superstructure, after all. In the kind of society in which we live, that is a liberal democracy built around an advanced industrial economy, welfare provision and a moral framework only make sense if seen as necessary conditions for an autonomous way of life.

It is true that some version of a moral framework and some version of welfare will be necessary for *any* type of society, including those resting on non-autonomous forms of life. Every society will need prohibitions on murder, bodily injury, stealing, lying and promise-breaking; and in every society people will need food, clothing and shelter. But in a society such as ours, more is included in the above two areas than these very basic requirements. In particular, we see it as a vital function of the state to protect various individual liberties: there are, for instance, legal or moral prohibitions on interference with freedom of expression, freedom of movement, freedom from indoctrination or manipulation and freedom from intrusion into one's private affairs.

Why do we consider personal liberty important? One could take the view that this is an ultimate value which cannot be supported by reference to anything more basic,[6] but such a position would be hard to maintain. If it were true, then *any* form of liberty would be seen as valuable. It is noteworthy that the liberties we see as requiring protection, like those mentioned above, are of a particular kind. Charles Taylor (1985, Vol. 2: 219) has recently pointed out that although there are far fewer traffic lights per kilometre in the streets of the capital of Albania, Tirana, than in, say, London, we would not call the Albanians freer than the British because they are less constrained in this way. A liberal's attachment to negative liberty – that is, freedom from interference in doing what one wants – has to do with forms of interference which most seriously impede the kind of life one chooses to lead. Impediments to the realization of one's most important desires are of more moment than others. It is because people's desires to practise their religion, express their ideas, control their own lives and determine where they will live and what kind of work they will do, are seen as more important to them than the desire to drive unimpeded through city streets, that political liberty has to do with the former rather than the latter. If this is right, then negative liberty is desirable not in itself, but as a requirement of positive liberty – that is, of one's leading a life which one has autonomously chosen to lead.

All this means that neutralism is an untenable position: in refusing preference to some ideals of life over others, it overlooks the fact that it is tacitly presupposing the value of personal autonomy. This comes out not only in its commitment to negative liberty, but also in the underlying reasons for advocating neutralism in the first place. Why, after all, should it be thought desirable to avoid entanglement in different conceptions of the good? Why should one try to ensure that one conception is not favoured over another? The root anxiety here seems to be that non-neutrality brings with it the danger of *imposing* one way of life rather than another. But this is only an anxiety for someone who is already wedded to the view that individuals should freely determine their own way of life, ie for someone who already places a high value on autonomy.

The state, education and personal autonomy

All this has important implications for the conduct of government in a liberal democracy like our own. Political battle lines tend to be drawn between those on the right, who advocate freedom from state control in sphere after sphere and left-wingers, who call for an extension of state welfare provision. Insofar as negative freedom derives its value from positive freedom, or autonomy, and insofar as welfare provision likewise subserves autonomy, then left and right could well be united in a common goal: the promotion of general autonomy.

I shall take it henceforth that a *justifiable* government policy is one which seeks to promote the autonomy of all its citizens and does not favour some at the expense of others.

How does education fit into this picture? We have seen that the autonomous life has many prerequisites, covering both what we have called the 'moral framework' and 'welfare'. The state has a role in both areas. Some of its work has to do with trying to ensure that its citizens' autonomy can be *exercised*. To this end it maintains a framework of protective laws, provides health and other social services and endeavours to keep internal and external peace. But one cannot talk about individuals' exercising their autonomy unless they have become autonomous in the first place. The state can help in this task, too. Of course, many of the institutions needed in order to protect the exercise of autonomy are also necessary for its formation: if children were brought up without health care, or in a society in which law and order had broken down completely, then their chances of growing into self-determining adults would be severely reduced. But other policies and institutions are needed, too. In order to become autonomous, there has to exist a range of options from which one can choose preferred alternatives. How extensive this range should be is a further question, but, whatever its extent, the state can and should have some hand in ensuring that it exists.

It is not enough, however, that a wide range of options *exists*; those who are to choose them must also *know* that they exist. This is where education begins to enter the picture. More generally, in order to become autonomous one needs to have acquired various capacities, dispositions and types of understanding. If a government is committed to the promotion of autonomy for everyone, its aim must be that everyone should be educated to enable them to exercise it. To become self-determined, one needs, as we have seen, an understanding of the various options that are open. Some of the available choices are more important to one as an autonomous person than others. Knowing the differences between the types of socks, or baked beans, or television sets from which one can choose is normally less important than understanding what differentiates the life of a religious believer from that of a sceptic, or being a trade union official from being a manager, or voting for the policies of one political party over another. Behind such more specific knowledge will be knowledge of a more general sort – about religion, for instance, about the structure of one's society, or about the physical sciences. But autonomous persons need more than knowledge or understanding. They also have to have certain dispositions of character. If they are to withstand possible manipulation or coercion by others they need independence of mind, resoluteness and courage. If they are to be free from obstacles arising from their own psyches, they need to be clear on where their major priorities lie and firmly committed to those priorities over values of lesser importance. More needs to be said elsewhere about the virtues necessary for autonomy. In particular, nothing has yet been said about attitudes towards other people. But even this brief introduction should be enough to underline the point that a state committed to autonomy must see to it that certain educational aims are met which go beyond those to do with welfare and with the moral framework that we earlier described. To these – which are concerned with knowledge and dispositions pertaining to the necessary conditions of personal well-being – are now added aims to do with the nature of that well-being itself. How all these various aims are to be related each to the other is again a topic for another occasion. The main conclusion at this point is the extensive responsibility that liberal democratic states should have for laying down educational aims which prepare their citizens for autonomy.

The value of personal autonomy

All this, however, is to presuppose the value of autonomy itself. This has seemed legitimate enough, working as *we* have been within the framework of liberal democracy. We have shown how neutralism collapses into a hidden perfectionism in favour of autonomy; and we have shown how the value which is central to liberalism, liberty itself, also rests on a prior attachment to autonomy. But we have still done nothing to show that autonomy itself is to be desired. Even if convincing grounds have been given by the above arguments as to why a liberal-democratic state should lay down autonomy-supporting educational aims, it could be said that these grounds don't go deep enough: further reasons have to be put forward as to why autonomy is a good thing.

This is a large topic, which really needs another essay to itself (see White, 1990, ch. 6). Here, I have just one point to make. It is about a particularly powerful obstacle which any justification of autonomy will have to face. As we shall see, this is not purely theoretical, but intimately touches our living together within a multi-cultural society.

We have already referred to the point that conceptions of personal well-being do not all incorporate a high regard for autonomy. In traditional societies one's main goals in life are laid down for one by custom; and for many religious people the ideal of self-determination is anathema, since one's task in life is to subjugate oneself to the will of God. This raises a problem within the theory of liberal democracy itself, since societies like our own contain certain ethnic or religious minorities for whom autonomy is not a value. This means that one cannot make the straightforward claim that liberal democracy is committed to autonomy. If certain strands in it lead us in that direction, others, notably the freedom accorded to religious and ethnic minority groups to disvalue autonomy, are at odds with it. From an educational point of view, the conclusion at the end of the last section, that the liberal democratic state ought to lay down autonomy-supporting aims for all its citizens, is now open to challenge. If certain minority groups disassociate themselves from this value, is there any good reason why young people being brought up within those communities should be educated in accordance with it?

If it could be shown that all other conceptions of personal well-being were in some way *mistaken* and that the autonomy ideal were not, one would have the makings of a strong argument in its favour. Can this be shown? On the face of it this would be a hard task, since however many alternatives one managed to exclude, there might always be others, as yet unexamined, which passed the test. One could, it is true, restrict oneself to examining the credentials of those alternatives which are found in our own society. One could look at what is presupposed in the values held by those Islamic or Christian believers, for instance, who reject autonomy. Incoherencies, or unsupported assumptions, might be found in the metaphysical doctrines which they embrace. On the other hand, it is notoriously difficult to produce cast-iron refutations of religious positions, since all kinds of countermoves have been assembled over the centuries in their defence.

In any case, there do seem to be *positive* grounds in favour of some non-autonomous conceptions of well-being. Suppose, we take a traditional society from another time and place, say a North American Indian community or an African tribal community before the coming of the Europeans. Personal well-being, let us accept for the moment – although this needs further discussion – consists in the overall satisfaction of one's most important informed desires or goals, taking one's life as a whole. A person who has had most of his or her major desires fulfilled can be said to have had a life of greater well-being than someone whose major desires have been checked and thwarted at every point. Given this, then if a member of a traditional society lives a broadly fulfilled life in this sense, then he or she has achieved a high measure of well-being. Would that well-being have been increased still further, or indeed shown to be illusory, if that person had been an autonomous agent? There are difficulties about conceiving what it would be like for him (or her) to be autonomous. For one thing, there would have to be a range of options among which he could choose, but this would be by definition unavailable in the traditional society. For another, he would have to have been educated in the ways of autonomy and this, too, is ruled out. But if we try to ignore these problems and imagine someone who had somehow acquired some of the cognitive requirements of autonomy – independence of thought, some arrangement of preferences in a hierarchy of importance, or whatever – even though he were still unable to make the choices which he envisaged owing to the tradition-bound nature of his community, there are good reasons, perhaps, for thinking that this frustrated autonome would lead a life of less overall satisfaction than the unimpeded heteronome.

The autonomous way of life is not the best way of life in *every* set of circumstances. Nearly all human beings who have ever lived have belonged to traditional societies. *Their* well-being has consisted in living, as far as good fortune has permitted them, a broadly fulfilled life according to the mores and expectations of those societies. How, then, can the autonomous version of the good life be justified? And how far does the fact that non-autonomous versions exist bear on the question of whether a liberal-democratic government can legitimately lay down the educational aim of promoting autonomy for all, in view of the fact that some ethnic and religious minority communities do not value this? The deeper problem remains.

Notes

1   See Raz (1986) ch. 5. I have found Raz's book invaluable for the argument of this chapter and have drawn on it at several points.
2   I here follow a suggestion in Raz (1986: 136).
3   The categories 'moral framework' and 'welfare' are only very rough. They may overlap.
4   As far as I am aware, the Thatcher moves towards a national curriculum owe no explicit allegiance to neutralist liberal principles. I leave on one side Conservative onslaughts on peace education. Since security against external attack is one of the deepest foundations on which personal well-being is built, it would be entirely consonant with the welfare aims permitted by neutralism to urge that the government should include work on this topic in its national curriculum proposals.

   I would suggest that present Conservative thinking about education is *not* based on liberal principles at all but has quite another basis. At present there are two strands in Conservative thinking – the 'Scrutonian' strand which emphasizes traditional academic subjects, and the 'Keith Joseph' strand which stresses the demands of the economy. What both views have in common is élitism. The first group would like the country to be run by an intellectual élite, the second by businessmen. Élitism of these sorts or any other sort offends against liberalism in privileging a certain view of the good life over others – that is, the conception of the good life favoured by the élite.
5   On the disconnexion between autonomy and personal well-being, see Raz (1986: 369). He makes it clear that the ideal of personal autonomy belongs to 'a particular conception' of individual well-being.
6   For an example of an ethical theory where liberty is taken as a fundamental principle, see Peters (1966).

References

Dworkin, R. (1978) 'Liberalism' in Hampshire, S. (ed.) *Public and Private Morality*, Cambridge: Cambridge University Press.
HMSO (1985) *Better Schools*, London: HMSO, Cmnd.9469.
Nozick, R. (1974) *Anarchy, State and Utopia*, Oxford: Blackwell.
Peters, R. S. (1966) *Ethics and Education*, London: Allen and Unwin.
Rawls, J. (1971) *A Theory of Justice*, Oxford: Clarendon Press.
Raz, J. (1986) *The Morality of Freedom*, Oxford: Clarendon Press.
Taylor, C. (1985) *Philosophical Papers, Vols. 1 and 2*, Cambridge: Cambridge University Press.
White, J. (1973) *Towards a Compulsory Curriculum*, London: Routledge and Kegan Paul.
White, J. (1990) *Education and the Good Life*, London: Kogan Page.

CHAPTER 8

RETHINKING THE SCHOOL CURRICULUM

Rethinking the School Curriculum (2003). London: RoutledgeFalmer

The year 2000 was revolutionary for education in England. For the first time in the country's history, all state schools were given a common framework of curricular aims. What are the implications of this revolution for the school curriculum itself – not least for the subjects that make it up? Nearly all of these were part of the curriculum before 2000. At that time they were not directed by a national framework because there was no such framework. How closely have the new overall aims matched the aims of the subjects? How far should the latter now evolve so as to improve the match? How far indeed should the curriculum be planned on a subject basis at all? School subjects are, after all, only vehicles to achieve certain ends: they are not self-justifying entities. Now that we have a set of overarching aims, could these be realised by other kinds of curricular vehicle?

Further questions arise about the validity of the new aims themselves. However close the fit may be between subjects and overall aims, nothing is gained if the aims themselves are faulty. The question 'What should be the aims of school education?' is now in the spotlight in post-2000 England. But really it is fundamental to *any* system. So are the questions 'By what means may aims be best realised?' and 'How good is the match between system-wide aims and the specifics of different curriculum subjects?'. Many, if not most, countries have official statements of aims. Many, if not most, also build their curriculum around a familiar set of subjects, including native language and literature, mathematics, science, history, geography, one or more foreign languages, music, art and physical education. What links are there between recommendations about general aims on the one hand and requirements in the different subjects on the other? Are the latter explicitly derived from and justified by the former? Or are the overall aims more like high-sounding national mission statements which can be ignored in practice? Are the familiar subjects included because it is *taken as read* that these are what the school curriculum must consist of?

At one level, the book from which this chapter is taken concentrates on fundamental issues of this sort. At another, it is intended as a contribution to the next stage of curriculum reform in England. Global and national themes interconnect and illuminate each other throughout its length. England is unusual among countries due to its belated adoption of overall aims. This means that its recent and continuing experience of curriculum reform allows globally important issues to be raised in unusual starkness.

The new aims for the school curriculum

Before 1988, maintained schools in England were responsible for their own curricula and the aims underlying them. That year saw the introduction of the National Curriculum. This was based on ten foundation subjects – English, mathematics, science, technology, history, geography, a modern foreign language, music, art and physical education.

It is hard to say for certain why these were chosen, since no rationale was provided for them. Richard Aldrich has drawn attention to the very close similarity between the 1988 list and the subjects prescribed for the newly introduced state secondary (later grammar) schools in 1904 (Aldrich, 1988: 22). The National Curriculum gives every appearance of having been lifted from what was originally traditional grammar school practice.

Whatever its origin, it was *not* derived from a set of underlying aims – not that it was entirely bereft of aims. After 1988, it had two:

- [to] promote the spiritual, moral, cultural, mental and physical development of pupils at the school and of society;
- [to] prepare such pupils for the opportunities, responsibilities and experiences of adult life.

Uncharitable commentators may find these a trifle on the thin side. Certainly it is impossible to read into these bland truisms anything like a justifying rationale for the ten foundation subjects.

In the late 1990s, pressure grew for the purposes of the National Curriculum to be more clearly spelt out. The discussions which the Qualifications and Curriculum Authority (QCA) had around this time with teachers, teaching organisations, local authorities and researchers showed that many believed that current statutory arrangements, including the National Curriculum, lacked a clear vision of what the parts, individually and collectively, were designed to achieve. This reinforced the QCA's view, and that of its predecessor the School Curriculum and Assessment Authority (SCAA), that there needed to be 'a much clearer statement about the aims and priorities of the school curriculum' (SCAA, 1997).

This statement materialised in the opening pages of the *Handbook* for teachers on the National Curriculum post-2000. This comes in two volumes, one for primary teachers, the other secondary teachers. I shall call these HPT and HST respectively. The main section is called 'The school curriculum and the National Curriculum: values, aims and purposes'.

Values, aims and purposes

Values and purposes underpinning the school curriculum

> Education influences and reflects the values of society and the kind of society we want to be. It is important, therefore, to recognise a broad set of common values and purposes that underpin the school curriculum and the work of schools.
>
> Foremost is a belief in education, at home and at school, as a route to the spiritual, moral, social, cultural, physical and mental development, and thus the well-being, of the individual. Education is also a route to equality of

opportunity for all, a healthy and just democracy, a productive economy and sustainable development. Education should reflect the enduring values that contribute to these ends. These include valuing ourselves, our families and other relationships, the wider groups to which we belong, the diversity in our society and the environment in which we live. Education should also reaffirm our commitment to the virtues of truth, justice, honesty, trust and a sense of duty.

At the same time, education must enable us to respond positively to the opportunities and challenges of the rapidly changing world in which we live and work. In particular, we need to be prepared to engage as individuals, parents, workers and citizens with economic, social and cultural change, including the continued globalisation of the economy ahd society, with new work and leisure patterns and with the rapid expansion of communication technologies.

Aims for the school curriculum

If schools are to respond effectively to these values and purposes, they need to work in collaboration with families and the local community, including church and voluntary groups, local agencies and business, in seeking to achieve two broad aims through the curriculum. These aims provide an essential context within which schools develop their own curriculum.

AIM 1: THE SCHOOL CURRICULUM SHOULD AIM TO PROVIDE OPPORTUNITIES
FOR ALL PUPILS TO LEARN AND TO ACHIEVE

The school curriculum should develop enjoyment of, and commitment to, learning as a means of encouraging and stimulating the best possible progress and the highest attainment for all pupils. It should build on pupils' strengths, interests and experiences and develop their confidence in their capacity to learn and work independently and collaboratively. It should equip them with the essential learning skills of literacy, numeracy and information and communication technology and promote an enquiring mind and capacity to think rationally.

The school curriculum should contribute to the development of pupils' sense of identity through knowledge and understanding of the spiritual, moral, social and cultural heritages of Britain's diverse society and of the local, national, European, Commonwealth and global dimensions of their lives. It should encourage pupils to appreciate human aspirations and achievements in aesthetic, scientific, technological and social fields and prompt a personal response to a range of experiences and ideas.

By providing rich and varied contexts for pupils to acquire, develop and apply a broad range of knowledge, understanding and skills, the curriculum should enable pupils to think creatively and critically, to solve problems and to make a difference for the better. It should give them the opportunity to become creative, innovative, enterprising and capable of leadership to equip them for their future lives as workers and citizens. It should also develop their physical skills and encourage them to recognise the importance of pursuing a healthy lifestyle and keeping themselves and others safe.

AIM 2: THE SCHOOL CURRICULUM SHOULD AIM TO PROMOTE PUPILS'
SPIRITUAL, MORAL, SOCIAL AND CULTURAL DEVELOPMENT AND PREPARE ALL
PUPILS FOR THE OPPORTUNITIES, RESPONSIBILITIES AND EXPERIENCES OF LIFE

The school curriculum should promote pupils' spiritual, moral, social and cultural development and, in particular, develop principles for distinguishing between right and wrong. It should develop their knowledge, understanding and appreciation of their own and different beliefs and cultures and how these influence individuals and societies. The school curriculum should pass on enduring values, develop pupils' integrity and autonomy and help them to be responsible and caring citizens capable of contributing to the development of a just society. It should promote equal opportunities and enable pupils to challenge discrimination and stereotyping. It should develop their awareness and understanding of and respect for, the environments in which they live, and secure their commitment to sustainable development at a personal, local, national and global level. It should also equip pupils as consumers to make informed judgements and independent decisions and to understand their responsibilities and rights.

The school curriculum should promote pupils' self-esteem and emotional well-being and help them to form and maintain worthwhile and satisfying relationships, based on respect for themselves and for others, at home, school, work and in the community. It should develop their ability to relate to others and work for the common good. It should enable pupils to respond positively to opportunities, challenges and responsibilities, to manage risk and to cope with change and adversity. It should prepare pupils for the next steps in their education, training and employment and equip them to make informed choices at school and throughout their lives, enabling them to appreciate the relevance of their achievements to life and society outside school, including leisure, community engagement and employment.

The interdependence of the two aims

These two aims reinforce each other. The personal development of pupils, spiritually, morally, socially and culturally, plays a significant part in their ability to learn and to achieve. Development in both areas is essential to raising standards of attainment for all pupils.

(DfEE/QCA, 1999: 10–12)

It should be apparent from this how much more determinate are these aims than the platitudinous ones of 1988. True, some of the 2000 aims need further precision, but overall they do present a picture of the kind of pupil that the school curriculum can ideally help to foster. They draw attention to the personal qualities pupils require, as well as intellectual equipment in the shape of knowledge and skills. Broadly speaking, the ideal pupil is an informed, caring citizen of a liberal democratic society. He or she is an enterprising, independent-minded, contributor to the well-being of the national community and all its members, respectful of differences of culture and belief, aware of transnational and global concerns and with an understanding of major human achievements in different fields.

Some 60 per cent of the specific aims mentioned are about the pupil's personal qualities, as distinct from skills or types of knowledge or understanding. The detailed items in these three categories are:

Personal qualities: valuing ourselves, our families and other relationships, the wider groups to which we belong, the diversity in our society and the environment in which we live; the virtues of truth, justice, honesty, trust and a sense of duty; enjoyment of and commitment to learning; confidence in one's capacity to learn; an enquiring mind; capacity to think rationally; sense of identity; appreciation of human aspirations and achievements; thinking creatively and critically;

being innovative and enterprising; integrity and autonomy; responsible and caring citizens; challenging discrimination; respect for the environment; commitment to sustainable development; making informed judgements as consumers; self-esteem; emotional well-being; respect for oneself; respect for others; being able to relate to others; being able to manage risk, cope with change and adversity; making informed choices at school and throughout pupils' lives; having the will to achieve; curiosity about themselves and their place in the world; attitudes needed to foster the inner life; willingness to participate, work with others for the common good; financial capability; Qualities associated with enterprise education (confidence, self-reliance, learning from mistakes); entrepreneurial characteristics of tenacity, independence.

Skills: essential learning skills of literacy, numeracy and ICT; physical skills; six key skills; five thinking skills.

Knowledge and understanding: knowledge and understanding of the spiritual, moral, social and cultural heritages of Britain's diverse society and of the local, national, European, Commonwealth and global dimensions of pupils' lives; acquiring a broad range of knowledge and understanding (so as to enable pupils to think creatively and critically); knowledge and understanding of pupils' own beliefs and cultures; recognising the importance of pursuing a healthy lifestyle; understanding the environments within which one lives; self-understanding; understanding necessary to making moral judgements; understanding relevant to making financial decisions, running mini-enterprises, sustainable development.

It should not be surprising that personal qualities are so prominent in this scheme. Since the view of education in the document is about promoting a certain kind of society, it is understandable that it should concentrate on cultivating citizens of an appropriate sort. This means delineating the type of people these citizens will be.

The skills, knowledge and understanding these citizens will need is a further matter. To some extent these can be derived from the personal qualities themselves. One example in the document is the claim that developing a sense of identity requires one to have knowledge and understanding of diverse cultural heritages. Another, not explicitly mentioned in the document, but in line with it, is that autonomy, which has to do with making informed choices about important goals in one's life, requires knowledge and understanding of the various options among which one is to choose.

One further preliminary point: the section on 'Values, aims and purposes' at the beginning of the *Handbook* is not the only place in it where overall aims are mentioned. They also appear a few pages further on in the section called 'Learning across the National Curriculum' (DfEE/QCA, 1999, HPT: 19–23, HST: 21–5). This consists of a heterogeneous collection of general objectives which the different curriculum subjects are intended to serve. Here is an indication in note form of the aims covered in these four pages.

> growth of a sense of self; curiosity about oneself and one's place in the world; fostering the inner life; concern for others; making responsible moral decisions; responsibilities and rights of being members of families and communities; making an active contribution to the democratic process; understanding and respecting cultural traditions, one's own and others; appreciating and responding to a variety of aesthetic experiences; acquiring 'key skills' of

communication, application of number, information technology, working with others, improving own learning and performance, problem solving; acquiring 'thinking skills' of information-processing, reasoning, enquiry, creative thinking, evaluation; learning to make sensible choices about managing money; in the context of enterprise education, developing confidence, self-reliance and willingness to embrace change; acquiring the understanding, skills and attitudes required to participate in decisions to do with sustainable development.

A fuller discussion of the overall aims comes in Chapter 2. As has been made clear, the aims are set out in lists of items. No rationale for these is given. In the next chapter we explore how well the items hang together in a coherent pattern and whether any adequate justification can be provided for them. For the moment they will be taken as read. This is not a wholly arbitrary decision. Intuitively at least, they appear to be on the right lines, at least if one is working within a broad liberal democratic compass. Although we have to go beyond intuitions into more rigorous assessment, the aims as stated will be taken as baseline for the rest of this chapter.

From aims to curriculum

Having discussed the aims themselves, I now turn to how schools are to realise them. Here it is crucial to bear in mind that the aims are for the whole school curriculum, not just the National Curriculum. The *Handbook* states that 'the school curriculum comprises all learning and other experiences that each school plans for its pupils' (DfEE/QCA, 1999: 10). As far as school subjects are concerned, this covers work in religious education as well as in the National Curriculum areas (religious education has been a compulsory subject in state schools since 1944). The *Handbook* definition also transcends the 'timetabled' curriculum. It can cover what a school plans through the way it structures its 'ethos': its encouragement, for instance, of respect for others in the class room and in the playground. In sum we can distinguish between general aims and the school curriculum (in this wide sense) as the vehicle intended to realise them.

Curriculum planning cannot sensibly start with the curriculum. Given that the curriculum is a vehicle, or collection of vehicles, intended to reach a certain set of destinations, we have to begin with the destinations themselves. Once we have these, we have at some point to work out what kind of vehicles are best to help us attain them in particular circumstances.

Suppose, as suggested, we take as read the overall aims. How is it best to try to realise them? Can we go straight to the curriculum, in its broad sense? The curriculum consists of *experiences*, the planned pupil experiences intended to realise the aims. Possible examples of these – generated both via timetabled activities and via whole school processes (school ethos) – are as follows:

Pupils are encouraged to:

- listen to things (stories, instructions, others' views);
- look at things (diagrams in books, writing on the board, videos);
- reason things out (how to solve a problem in maths);
- how to create more interest in the School Council;
- imagine things (what it is like to be in someone else's shoes);

- contemplate things (poems, paintings, aesthetic features of the school environment);
- feel various emotions (compassion, suspense, delight, imagination-mediated fear);
- try to remember things (past feelings, geographical facts);
- exercise their bodies.

These and other types of experience constitute the school curriculum as the *Handbook* defines it. What connection is there between things like these and the overall aims? Well, why do we want students to look at things, think about things, feel things and so on? Sometimes, these have a partly intrinsic justification: the delight that young children feel in listening to a story is an end in itself. But teachers also have intentions for their pupils which go beyond immediate experience. They are interested in more long-lasting mental states: they want the children to come to believe, know and understand things; to acquire mental or physical skills, like reasoning historically or climbing ropes; to acquire or deepen dispositions or habitual ways of behaving, like controlling fears or resentments, being cautious in their thinking, having an appropriate kind of confidence or self-esteem.

This brings out the fact that there are two importantly different kinds of ingredient in the mental life of the child (or, indeed, of anyone) (see also White, 2002, ch. 1). On the one hand there are conscious occurrences, (experiences of listening, thinking, moving one's limbs); and on the other continuing mental states (understanding, knowing how to swim, being kind). The continuing mental states exist even when there are no present conscious occurrences. A child can understand fractions without having anything to do with fractions at the moment. She still understands them when she is having her tea, perhaps even when she is asleep. The same goes for skills and for personal qualities. A child can know how to dive without actually diving; and is still a kind person when she is on her own and there is no one around to be kind to.

The experiences – the conscious occurrences – which constitute the school curriculum are vehicles intended to bring about continuing mental states such as knowledge and understanding, skills and dispositions (personal qualities). These are the curriculum's aims. Indeed, as we have already seen, the overall aims in the *Handbook* fall under these headings. General aims take more and more determinate forms, the closer one gets to the pupil's experience. At the experiential end they are maximally determinate. Take the class of young children delightedly listening to a story. What does their teacher plan that they learn, over and above, that is, intending them to have an experience enjoyable in itself? One of the things she wants is for them to enjoy experiences *of this sort*, that is to get into the habit of wanting to hear simple stories like this. We can call this an 'immediate' aim – the aim a teacher (or whole school) has in engaging learners in a particular activity. Behind the immediate aim lie aims of increasing generality. She wants them to enjoy simple stories of this sort not only through hearing them, but also through reading them. She wants them to enjoy literature in general. She wants them to develop a deeper understanding of human nature or a more refined aesthetic sense. Of course she is also likely to have other aims in reading the story – to do, for instance, with sharing enjoyable experiences with others or introducing more advanced vocabulary.

These aims also fit in a range from immediate to very general. In addition, all the aims mentioned interconnect and are inextricable from each other in practice.

At the more general end of the continuum we reach the kind of overall aim that we find in the *Handbook* or similar documents. In between the highly general aims and the teacher's immediate aims are aims of varying levels of generality or specificity. Curriculum planning consists in mapping out, and relating to each other, aims across the whole range, from the most general to the most immediate. At the immediate end, the teacher's, it also includes working out experiences – specific forms of listening, looking, thinking and so on – designed to realise these aims.

Curriculum planning, therefore, is a collaborative enterprise at different levels. As is often the case, not least in post-1988 England, governments lay down overall aims (e.g. developing self-understanding). They also lay down aims at the next levels of specificity, aims for and within particular curriculum areas (e.g. understanding aspects of one's own society's history which help one to understand oneself; more specifically again, understanding the significance of the rapid rise in the population since the late eighteenth century). Teachers specify these further at the level of the school and the classroom.

In Chapter 2, I will be saying more about curriculum planning, both in general and in relation to developments in England. As well as looking more closely at the justification of overall aims, I will go further into ways in which they may be realised, concentrating especially on what can and should be done via whole school processes and, within timetabled activities, what can be done without using school subjects as a framework.

Matching school subjects to overall aims

I now narrow the focus on to the curriculum subjects themselves, specifically the subjects of the English National Curriculum plus religious education (RE).

The *Handbook* on the National Curriculum, separate booklets on all the National Curriculum subjects (which cover most of the same ground as the *Handbook*), and a booklet on the RE curriculum are constructed on a subject basis. As we have seen, the overall aims at the beginning of the *Handbook* in principle cover non-subject-based learning. In actuality, however, virtually the whole of the government documentation just mentioned is about the aims of the different *subjects*, their programmes of study, their contribution to learning across the curriculum and their attainment targets.

The explanation for this is obvious enough. When the *Handbook* appeared in 1999, nearly all the curriculum subjects with which it deals (with the exception of personal, social and health education (PSHE) and citizenship) had already been compulsory elements since 1988. The government had to work with what was already in place.

This is understandable, but it does give rise to a question. The *Handbook* introduced a set of overall curricular aims. Presumably some coherence is intended between these new aims and the documentation on the aims, programmes and attainment targets of the various subjects. Presumably these latter features are seen as ways in which the overall aims are to be made more determinate in the way described in section 3. The question is whether these presumptions are justified. To what extent do we find a good match between the overall aims and the specific requirements laid down for the different subjects?

I explored this question in detail in a project, so far unpublished, undertaken in 2001 for a national educational agency. I took all thirteen current subjects, including RE and the two newcomers PSHE and citizenship, looked at their aims,

Table 8.1 Compulsory subjects of the English school curriculum, including the National Curriculum, from 2003

	Key stage 1	Key stage 2	Key stage 3	Key stage 4
Age	5–7	7–11	11–14	14–16
Year groups	1–2	3–6	7–9	10–11
National Curriculum subjects				
Core subjects				
English	*	*	*	*
Mathematics	*	*	*	*
Science	*	*	*	*
Other subjects				
Design and technology	*	*	*	
Information and communication technology	*	*	*	*
History	*	*	*	
Geography	*	*	*	
Modern foreign languages			*	
Art and design	*	*	*	
Music	*	*	*	
Physical education	*	*	*	*
Citizenship			*	*
Religious education	*	*	*	*

programmes of study, attainment targets and contribution to learning across the curriculum and tried to establish how far there is a match or mismatch between these specific items and the overall aims. To what extent are the subjects, as officially conceived, suitable instruments for realising the general aims?

The short answer is that the results are patchy. Very broadly speaking, the best match tends to be found in subjects only recently introduced into the curriculum: design and technology, ICT, citizenship and PSHE. Many longer established subjects tend to be problematic in various ways. These include art and design, English, geography, history, mathematics, modern foreign languages, music, physical education, RE and science.

There is not space to run through all the results, but below are some examples. In citizenship there is a good match. Its aims are stated as follows:

> **Citizenship** gives pupils the knowledge, skills and understanding to play an effective role in society at local, national and international levels. It helps them to become informed, thoughtful and responsible citizens who are aware of their duties and rights. It promotes their spiritual, moral, social and cultural development, making them more self-confident and responsible both in and beyond the classroom. It encourages pupils to play a helpful part in the life of their schools, neighbourhoods and communities and the wider world. It also teaches them about our economy and democratic institutions and values; encourages respect for different national, religious and ethnic identities; and develops pupils' ability to reflect on issues and take part in discussions.
>
> (DfEE/QCA, 1999, HST: 183)

If we compare these with the overall aims, we see close links between them. There is the same concern with personal qualities like self-confidence, responsiveness to others' needs, civic involvement, respect for cultural differences, reflectiveness, as well as with the knowledge and skills needed to sustain them. The programme of study for citizenship is also in sync. It is not difficult to see how the overall aims map on to such randomly selected items as learning about the criminal justice system or the significance of the media in society, learning to 'negotiate, decide and take part responsibly in both school and community-based activities' (KS 3 HST: 184–5). The whole tone of the citizenship documentation is pupil-centred, in that, like the overall aims, it keeps firmly in mind the ideal of acertain kind of person and the skills and understanding which such a person must have.

The same is true of design and technology. As with citizenship its own aims look outwards, beyond its own confines, towards wider personal and social horizons picked out in the overall aims:

> **Design and technology** prepares pupils to participate in tomorrow's rapidly changing technologies. They learn to think and intervene creatively to improve quality of life. The subject calls for pupils to become autonomous and creative problem solvers, as individuals and members of a team. They must look for needs, wants and opportunities and respond to them by developing a range of ideas and making products and systems. They combine practical skills with an understanding of aesthetics, social and environmental issues, function and industrial practices. As they do so, they reflect on and evaluate present and past design and technology, its uses and effects. Through design and technology, all pupils can become discriminating and informed users of products, and become innovators.
>
> (DfEE/QCA, 1999, HPT: 90, HST: 134)

Further specification is given to these aims in the programme of study. This includes such items as learning 'to generate ideas for products after thinking about who will use them and what they will be used for' (KS 2 HPT: 94); learning 'to select appropriate tools and techniques for making their product' (KS 2 HPT: 94), learning 'to identify and use criteria to judge the quality of other people's products' (KS 3 HST: 136–7).

Gaps in matching

With most of the longer-established subjects, there is much less room for confidence about a good match with the overall aims. Subjects where the match is – to different degrees – problematic include art and design, English, geography, history, mathematics, modern foreign languages, music, physical education, RE and science. These problems are discussed below.

Art and design

Similar points, as for Music (see below), could be made about art and design, except that there is more weight here on pupils' making works of art (the musical equivalent being composition). The justification of both subjects in terms of larger aims is unclear both from the documentation and more generally. Both subjects have appeared in curricula for maintained schools since the late nineteenth century. Music grew out of 'singing' and art and design out of 'drawing', the latter included originally for 'the great mass of our working population' as 'likely to be useful to them in their future occupations as workmen and artisans' (Selleck, 1968: 121). Today, they are both multi-faceted, sophisticated subjects, assured of a place in the curriculum, but unclear as to their over-arching purposes.

English

One of the overall aims states that the school curriculum: 'should encourage pupils to appreciate human aspirations and achievements in aesthetic, and.... social fields, and prompt a personal response to a range of experiences and ideas' (DfEE/QCA, 1999: 11). This would suggest, among other things, acquaintance with literature on a human scale, not necessarily literature written in English. There is no need to dwell on the extraordinary richness of world literature, which nearly all of us access only in translation. It is not only absorbing for its own sake, but affords us the best insights we often have into other cultures and countries.

Yet because the school subject responsible for literature is called 'English', it has traditionally been taken as read that the texts it studies are those written originally in English. This tradition has come through to the 2000 curriculum, with its long statutory and non-statutory lists of works to be read at Key stages 3 and 4. All these are texts written originally in English.

If, as seems sensible, we need to create room for world literature in schools, how should this be done? Should we stretch the label 'English' to cover it? Or should the title of the subject be changed to 'language and literature'?

Film is among the most important forms of dramatic art of the twentieth century. There is no clear place for it in the school curriculum, although it is mentioned in odd places under English. It is a visual art, but not included with other visual arts under art and design. All this may reflect the fact that the categories under which education in the arts is delivered – art and design, English, and music – date back to the nineteenth century and so do not well reflect twentieth century developments.

Geography

Unlike some other subjects, most of geography's aims closely match overall aims statements, for instance, geography:

> prepares pupils for adult life and employment. It is a focus within the curriculum for understanding and resolving issues about the environment and sustainable development. It links the natural and social sciences. Through geography pupils encounter different societies and cultures. This helps them realise how nations rely on each other. Geography can inspire them to think about their own place in the world, their values, rights and responsibilities to others and the environment.

> (DfEE/QCA, 1999, HPT: 108, HST: 154)

But with the exception of work on the environment and sustainable development, the programmes of study and attainment targets tend to focus largely on intra-subject material to do with geographical enquiry and skills. There is less than might have been expected about cultural matters; but much about repeatable features found across different countries, in other words, about subject matter approached scientifically and in abstraction from the child's own perspective.

History

So many of the overall aims are about pupils' roles as national and global citizens in rapidly changing cultural, political economic, technological and social conditions. This requires a background of understanding of recent and contemporary history. Yet the history curriculum contains very little work on the twentieth century.

Mathematics

The first reason given for mathematics' importance is that it equips pupils with powerful tools of logical reasoning and problem-solving (DfEE/QCA, 1999, HPT: 60, HST: 57). This is an ancient argument for the subject, and it assumes the existence of general thinking skills. However, there are problems about this – akin to problems raised, incidentally, more than a hundred years ago when faculty psychology provided a rationalising theory for the elementary school curriculum (Selleck, 1968: 45–58), For instance, the reasoning and enquiring acquired in history classes seems very different from the reasoning and enquiring involved in planning a family holiday. There *may* be general skills which cover widely diverse fields, but it should not be assumed that they exist before evidence – at present non-existent – is provided for this.

Statutory requirements in mathematics are laid down in great detail. Fourteen pages are devoted to its programmes of study, as compared with an average of four pages for all subjects. From the standpoint of the overall aims, just how important are all these statutorily required items? Students at Key stage 3 have to recall the essential properties of quadrilaterals like the trapezium and rhombus. When was the last occasion that any reader of this book made use of these notions?

Modern foreign languages

The importance of MFL is said to lie in helping pupils to understand and appreciate different cultures and countries; and to think of themselves as citizens of the world (DfEE/QCA, 1999, HST: 162). These are goals wholly in line with the overall aims. Yet virtually all the material in the attainment targets and programmes of study has to do with learning linguistic skills. No attempt is made to show why the latter should be thought an especially good means of attaining the goals just mentioned. If promoting the understanding of other cultures is what one is after, other vehicles look much better bets for the non-specialist: accounts of them in English, literature in translation, foreign films with subtitles or dubbing.

Music

The attainment targets and programmes of study are inward-looking. They provide structured progression in acquiring the various sub-skills and forms, of understanding and appreciation found within the subject – that is, as performers, composers, listeners and judges. Pupils are thus led into the foothills of various related specialisms, yet the overall point of this for those children who will not become specialist musicians is not clear.

Physical education

For most people good physical health is a basic need for whatever activities they wish to undertake. The overall aims acknowledge this in their reference to encouraging pupils to 'recognise the importance of pursuing a healthy lifestyle'. Sub-aims covered by this may be taken to refer to understanding how the body works, diet, sensible habits of eating and drinking, work on body image, the need for adequate exercise, care in avoiding damage to one's body, drugs education and aspects of sex education. School dinner policy can play a part in this, along with timetabled classes in various areas.

In addition some children have a more specialised interest in developing their physical skills in some more particular direction – through dance, gymnastics, games, swimming and athletics. Physical education as a curriculum subject is almost totally orientated towards such specialisms. Its contribution to more general health aims is not well worked out.

Religious education

This subject presents a quite different matching problem. No problem here of links between the aims of RE and overarching aims. The RE material is full of statements such as: 'Pupils learn about religious and ethical teaching, enabling them to make reasoned and informed judgements on religious, moral and social issues' (QCA, 2000, inside front cover).

The most natural way of taking such comments is that RE deals with ethical and moral issues as part of children's general moral education. This is in line with the tradition of religious education in this country. There was a tight link between religious instruction and moral instruction in the elementary schools of the late nineteenth century (Selleck, 1968: 59). Closer to home, the introduction of RE as the only compulsory subject in maintained schools after 1944 had much to do with the belief that Britain needed to 'revive the spiritual and personal values in our society and in our national tradition' (Niblett, 1966: 15).

The civic significance of RE may well have dwindled between 1944 and 2000, but the more general association between religious and moral education has persisted more tenaciously. Until 2000 RE was seen in many quarters as *the* locus for moral education in the curriculum. In 2000 PSHE and citizenship were added to the National Curriculum subjects. In addition to these two new subjects in the ethical/moral/civic field, *every* subject has now to declare – in its *Learning across the National Curriculum* statement – how it contributes to learning in this area.

There are thus two sources of ethical and moral education now flowing into the new curriculum, one associated with religion, the other not. How far may this lead to a confusion in pupils' minds at odds with the insistence on clear, rational thinking prominent among the new overall aims? Recent statistics suggest that Britain is now a country where organised religions play little or no part in the great majority (perhaps 80 per cent) of people's lives. If present trends continue, this majority can be expected to increase (HMSO, 2000, 13.19, 13.20).

The points just made suggest that the whole area of how ethical/moral/civic aims are to be delivered calls out for review. In particular, it needs to be asked if this area of learning should now fall outside RE's remit altogether.

Science

The documentation on this rightly makes much of such aims as understanding the impact of science on industry and the quality of life; and discussing science-based issues that may affect the future of the world. But these are not reflected in the attainment targets. Virtually all the level statements here are about mastering specific areas of knowledge and techniques of enquiry within science.

Jenner, Lavoisier and Darwin are the only names of scientists mentioned, and their theories appear only as non-statutory examples to illustrate more general points. There is almost no work on the great turning points in the history of science, for example, the impact of Copernicus and Galileo, the scientific revolution and the enlightenment, the impact of geology and evolution theory on views about man's place in the universe, the harnessing of science in the last two hundred plus years to industrial production, military affairs, medicine, social improvement etc. There is nothing about the impact of science on religion over the past five hundred years. There is no reference to any of the human sciences.

Inward-looking tendencies

Judging by the documentation, all the subjects we have considered, with the partial exception of English and RE, have an intra-subject orientation. In other words, their main preoccupation is with helping pupils to acquire knowledge, understanding and skills in their specialised area. Thus history aims at equipping pupils with a degree of historical knowledge and understanding, as well as reasoning and enquiry skills pertinent to the discipline. The same is true, *mutatis mutandum*, for other intellectual subjects, that is, mathematics, geography and science. In MFL, art, music and RE the emphasis is more on skills of performance and production informed by relevant knowledge and understanding.

Learning in these subjects has to do with inducting novices into their *modi operandi*. The model at work seems to be something like apprenticeship in acquiring the rudiments of competence as a geographer, historian, mathematician, scientist, musician, visual artist and linguist.

It would be quite unfair to say that these subjects profess no links with overall aims. Geography, for instance, mentions its contribution to understanding other societies and sustainable development; mathematics its application to everyday life; science its role in understanding technological aspects of industrial and social life. Despite this, the attainment targets, programmes of study, and aims statements show a marked intra-subject emphasis.

Does this matter? It may seem odd to upbraid these subjects for concentrating on their own special ways of thinking, their own special skills and facts. What could be wrong with that? In another context, specialist courses at university, might be unremarkable. But in the new school curriculum, overall aims come first, subjects second. Schools' first duty is not in the preparation of specialists, but with providing a sound general education in line with subject-transcending aims.

That does not necessarily mean that an intra-subject orientation is wholly to be ruled out. Among the new overall aims we find 'developing...pupils' autonomy' and 'equipping them to make informed choices at school and throughout their lives'. There is a powerful argument that in order to choose options which include science-based or music-based careers, or indeed science or music pursued as ends in themselves, pupils have to have an appropriate understanding *of* the nature of science or music. The knotty question then becomes: what counts as *appropriate* understanding? How much acquaintance with science or music does one need as a basis for choice, and of what kind? Is the apprenticeship model adequate for this, or should one look for one with wider horizons? This kind of justification in terms of equipment for choice is scarcely, if at all, found in the new *Handbook*.

The most striking finding from the survey I carried out was the intra-subject orientation of so many curriculum subjects. However, in the light of the history of school subjects, this is perhaps not so surprising. The intra-orientated subjects have been statutory elements in the National Curriculum since 1988, that is more than a decade before the new aims appeared on the scene. As noted earlier, the list of subjects included in 1988 is remarkably similar to the list included in the secondary regulations of 1904. In those eighty-four years the internal strength of these subjects increased and was consolidated via their statutory – and later non-statutory but by then entrenched – place in the school curriculum, via their subject-associations, and via their links with higher education. Most of them originated as school subjects in the late nineteenth century and were not then taught in universities. Promoters of these subjects sought to enhance their status by emphasising their academic rigour. This process developed further in the twentieth century via links between secondary school teachers, university teachers, subject associations and examining boards (Goodson and Marsh, 1996: an overview drawing on subject-specific works by Ball, S., Jenkins, E., Layton, D. and others). Over the years subjects which had a lowly place or no place in the 1904 curriculum joined the others on the escalator of respectability and professionalism: as mentioned already, 'drawing' was elevated into 'art and design', while music, absent in 1904 but common in elementary schools as 'singing', grew into the sophisticated, many-sided subject we know today. Achieving the status of a 'foundation' or 'core' subject in 1988 strengthened still further the power of these subjects and of their institutional links.

In 1993 Duncan Graham, the first Chairman and Chief Executive of the National Curriculum Council which preceded QCA, wrote: 'Do subjects exist to enable learning or as a vehicle for vested interests, lobbies, and departmental baronies?' (Graham and Tytler, 1993: 120).

The inward-looking nature of many of the subjects, their attachment to the apprenticeship model and the demands of specialisation raise questions about how far they should be allowed to continue in their present form. The arrival of the new overall aims has given us a touchstone, previously lacking, for assessing their suitability, as presently constituted, for delivering the pupil- and civic-centred education now required.

References

Aldrich, R. (1988) 'The national curriculum: an historical perspective', in Lawton, D. and Chitty, C. (eds) *The National Curriculum*, Bedford Way Paper 33, London: Institute of Education, University of London.

DfEE/QCA (1999) *The National Curriculum Handbook for Primary/Secondary Teachers in England* (two versions, labelled here HPT/HST).

Goodson, I. F. and Marsh, C. J. (eds) (1996) *Studying School Subjects; a Guide*, London: Falmer.

Graham, D. and Tytler, D. (1993) *A Lesson for Us All*, London and New York: Routledge.

HMSO (2000) *Social Trends 30*, London: HMSO.

Niblett, W. R. (1966) 'The Religious Education clauses of the 1944 Act: aims, hopes and fulfilment', in Wedderspoon, A. G. (ed.) *Religious Education 1944–1984*, London: Allen and Unwin.

QCA (2000) *Religious Education: Non-statutory Guidance on RE*, London: Qualifications and Curriculum Authority.

SCAA (1997) *Second Annual Report on Monitoring the School Curriculum 1996–7*, London: School Curriculum and Assessment Authority.

Selleck, R. J. W (1968) *The New Education: The English Background 1870–1914*, Melbourne: Pitman.

White, J. (2002) *The Child's Mind*, London: RoutledgeFalmer.

PART 3

WELL-BEING AIMS

CHAPTER 9

THE PROBLEM OF SELF-INTEREST
The educator's perspective

Journal of Philosophy of Education (1986), 20(2): 163–75

I

There are many problems to do with self-interest, but the one I have in mind here is whether what is good or bad for people depends on what they want. Some writers hold a version of what Derek Parfit (1984: 499) calls the 'objective list' theory. In this view,

> certain things are good or bad for people, whether or not these people would want to have the good things, or to avoid the bad things. The good things might include moral goodness, rational activity, the development of one's abilities, having children and being a good parent, knowledge, and the awareness of true beauty. The bad things might include being betrayed, manipulated, slandered, deceived, being deprived of liberty or dignity, and enjoying either sadistic pleasure, or aesthetic pleasure in what is in fact ugly.

Other writers see what is good or bad for one as dependent on one's desires. A common view is that the good life for the individual is one in which one's major preferences in one's life as a whole, given that one knows the alternatives open to one, are by and large fulfilled. On this view, items on a theorist's objective list, like moral goodness, for instance, or the pursuit of knowledge, may or may not form a part of the good life for any particular individual: if such items are not part of one's preference-hierarchy, they are not included in one's well-being.

Let us call the two broad theories the 'objective list' view and the 'desire satisfaction' view. Both theories are currently influential. Neither, it seems to me, clearly scores over the other. Attempts I have read to combine the two in a single theory also seem to me to be inconclusive.

Each theory has its characteristic difficulties. The 'objective list' view depends on the possibility of what have been called 'external reasons' for action. If, as has been claimed, there are no such reasons, then all reasons for action depend on one's desires. Leaving on one side *this* issue, 'objective list' theorists have *to justify* the inclusion of items in their lists as belonging to anyone's good. The trouble is that these theorists seem always either not to attempt such a justification or to attempt a justification which is patently inadequate. Among recent writers in the former category, I would place E. J. Bond, who states, but without argument, that moral virtues and the development of various talents and abilities, including taste and aesthetic perception, are such as to make our lives worth living (Bond, 1983: 160).

Among those in the latter is A. MacIntyre. He argues on Aristotelian lines that an individual's well-being must consist predominantly in the pursuit of the shared ends of 'practices' and in possessing the virtues required both by the latter and by the demands of a unified life. Against the Nietzschean sceptic, however, MacIntyre (1981: 242), it seems, has as yet no answer: he admits that his theory presupposes an account of rationality which he has not yet supplied.

'Objective list' theorists in philosophy of education also typically divide into intuitionists (like Downie *et al.* 1974: 50) and perhaps R. Haack (1981) and those who have attempted, but failed, to put up a convincing case (like R. S. Peters 1966: ch. 5).

The trouble with the 'desire satisfaction' view is that it seems to allow too much. Rawls' (1971: 432) example of the man who, having reflected on alternatives, prefers to spend as much time as possible counting blades of grass in city squares typically provokes the reaction that a person's well-being cannot consist in satisfying *that* desire.... And here the objector seems to be relying on some version of an objective list, even if he has not articulated this to himself. (Similar reactions occur to hypothetical cases of individuals' autonomously choosing to become non-autonomous.)

Each of our two theories, the 'objective list' and the 'desire-satisfaction' theories, derives its chief support from the weakness of the other. The former lacks arguments against the determined sceptic. Whatever item *x* is included in the list, the sceptic can always say, 'But *x* does not attract me. It may be good for *you*. Are you sure you are not simply foisting your preferences on others?' The latter, as we have seen, allows in examples which many people would see as counterintuitive.

This may make one wonder whether the solution does not lie in a *combination* of the two theories. There are problems here, too, however. Frankena and, more recently, Parfit have been attracted by this move.

In his *Ethics* Frankena (1973: ch. 5) provides us with a long list of what he takes to be necessary elements in the good life. These include such things as life, health, happiness, truth, beauty, aesthetic experience, morally good dispositions, self-expression, peace, adventure, good reputation.... What makes these elements good is 'the presence in them of one or both of two factors: pleasure or satisfaction or some kind of excellence' (p. 91). As far as I can see, however, Frankena's argument is no proof against the objector whose conception of the good life is very different from his own and who sees Frankena's list as reflecting no more than the latter's personal values.

Parfit (1984: 502) writes:

> We might claim, for example, that what is good or bad for someone is to have knowledge, to be engaged in rational activity, to experience mutual love, and to be aware of beauty, while strongly wanting just these things. On this view, each side in this disagreement saw only half of the truth. Each put forward as sufficient something that was only necessary.

Parfit produces no arguments for this 'mixed' theory. His intention is only to mention it as a further possibility, although he seems to find it appealing. The question remains: what arguments *could* support it? If possessing knowledge, experiencing mutual love and so on are *necessary* components of one's well-being, then *why* should this be so? Why possessing knowledge and not watching TV sit-coms? Why poetry and not push-pin? Why exclude the grass-counter?

I suspect that we will not get much further if we stick to the two traditional approaches, either separately or in combination. One way of moving forward may be to look more closely at the *point of view* from which these and other theories of self-interest are or might be formulated. The 'desire-satisfaction' theorist adopts the standpoint of a mature individual looking impartially at the well-being of himself and other mature individuals, real or imaginary. When he raises sceptical doubts about objective lists ('But suppose I don't (or somebody doesn't) enjoy *x*?'), he is operating from this standpoint. Where the 'objective list' theorist is operating from is less clear. Sometimes he adopts something like God's perspective. (This may also be true if he is an intuitionist.) Some, like Mackie (1977, ch. 1), would claim that he is *in fact* looking at things from his own perspective, erecting his own preferences into universal values via an illicit 'objectification'.

The greater clarity about the 'desire-satisfaction' theorist's standpoint is perhaps one reason why some have found this theory more attractive. It has its own difficulties, as we have seen, which tempt one back towards an objective list. The latter theory, it seems to many, won't do either. But is this because it is formulated from the wrong point of view? For those who reject God's (or the intuitionist's), is there any other which they can adopt? If we change the perspective, does the 'objective list' theory suddenly begin to seem more plausible?

II

Philosophers of education have their own, very practical, reasons for being especially engrossed by the problem of self-interest. Starting, perhaps, from teachers' questions about what the content of the school curriculum should be, they are soon led into reflecting on what the aims of education should be, and this leads them, among other things, into questions about what the well-being of the pupil consists in. At this point, they have been drawn into mainstream philosophical debates about the good life for individuals, with all its inconclusiveness to which I have drawn attention. This has not only been intrinsically unsatisfying: it has also meant that philosophers of education cannot be of much practical help to schools and teachers.

But perhaps philosophers of education are better placed to tackle the problem of self-interest than 'pure' philosophers. For among the points of view on it – the mature and impartial individual's, God's, etc. – we have not included that of the *educator*. I mean by that term someone responsible (wholly or partly) for the upbringing of a child: educators include parents as well as schoolteachers and no doubt others as well. Now educators are vitally interested in the well-being of individuals, not least the well-being of the particular children in their charge. The question is: when the educator thinks about what the well-being of his pupil consists in, does he arrive at any different conclusions from those of the mature, impartial individual found in 'desire-satisfaction' theory? Does he, that is, find himself drawn – by rational argument and not simply by his preferences – towards some sort of objective list? If so, then the philosopher of education may have got the relationship between his branch of applied philosophy and 'pure' ethics the wrong way round. It may be not that philosophers of education have to have recourse to pure ethics to throw light on the problem of self-interest; it may rather be that only by shifting to the educator's perspective and examining it philosophically can pure moral philosophers get beyond their present impasse.

Of course, the fact, if it is a fact, that the educator would reach different conclusions from those of the mature, impartial individual does nothing to show, as yet, that the conclusions would be any sounder. Whether he *does* come up with sounder conclusions, we shall have to examine as we go.

Certain items recur time and again on different objective lists: altruism, rational activity, knowledge and the awareness of beauty are typical examples. In turning to the educator's perspective, we shall have to look at these and other candidates one by one. In the rest of this paper, I cannot deal with all of these, but will concentrate on altruism.

The first question, then, is whether altruism is a necessary feature of an individual's well-being. This is an ancient problem in general moral philosophy and, as far as I can see, no argument to a positive conclusion has yet been produced which a determined sceptic cannot answer. Idealists and Wittgensteinians have attempted such arguments, based on the inalienably social nature of the individual; but the sceptic can without difficulty accept this premise in some (not necessarily every) form, but point out that even though a person may need to be brought up in a network of social relationships, that does not stop him living a selfish life. MacIntyre's recent attempt to show that it is good for anyone to possess a range of virtues (where moral virtues are deliberately not differentiated from prudential ones) depends, as has been pointed out, on a theory of rationality not yet provided. Parfit's many-pronged attack on the 'S-theorist', who holds that the most rational aim is that his life go, for him, as well as possible, is more complex to assess; but first thoughts suggest that the S-theorist can stand his ground both against that part of Parfit's argument which depends on his theory of personal identity, by challenging that theory; and against the 'pincer' argument that the S-theorist goes down under a double attack from both morality and present-aim theory, by denying any inconsistency in adopting the hybrid position of temporal neutrality but not personal neutrality.

R. M. Hare has been noteworthy among moral philosophers in arguing over three decades that light can be thrown on philosophical problems of morality by adopting the educator's (and, more specifically, the parent's) point of view. In *Moral Thinking* he claims that the clearest way of seeing this (i.e. that 'what we morally ought to do is always in our prudential interest') is to consider what our position would be if we were bringing up some child, and had *only* the child's interests at heart (Hare, 1981: 191). It would be his preference-satisfactions alone, over his life as a whole, that we were seeking to maximise. He bypasses Plato's argument based on the supposition of a ring of Gyges by pointing out that rings of Gyges do not exist in the world in which the child will grow up; and he pursues this 'realistic' line in claiming both that this world is generally such that immorality does not pay, and that since all but a very few are unlikely to have the capacities required consistently to do immoral things if they think they can get away with it, it is not sensible to bring up one's child (who may be presumed to lack these capacities) in this way of behaving.

Hare (1981: 196) then asks:

> Why not bring up the child to conform to the accepted mores for the most part, but to transgress them cynically when he can escape detection or at least retribution?

He repeats his claim that 'successful crime is for nearly everyone an impossibly difficult game', and continues,

> If it is alleged against this that in the past people have amassed large fortunes in business careers which were far from unspotted, I reply that the money did not on the whole bring them happiness, and that with their talents they could have done better for themselves by making less money in a socially beneficial career. If there are exceptions, they are rare enough to be unpredictable by an educator.

It is clear from the quotation given above that Hare understands by 'happiness' the maximisation of one's preference-satisfactions over one's life as a whole, and that 'doing better for oneself is doing what brings a greater amount of such preference-satisfaction. Given this, his argument rests on empirical claims that are left unjustified. Not only are they unjustified: they seem prima facie most implausible. Money is by its nature something which can help to satisfy all sorts of different desires. If I have £10, I can spend it on food, or drink, or clothing, on the theatre, on a train ticket, or any combination of these. If I have a lot of desires I want to satisfy, having a comfortable income is likely to help; and if I have a lot of expensive desires, a really large income is a necessity.

Hare's version of the 'educator's argument' is unconvincing. If I were to bring up my daughter with 'only her interests at heart' (in Hare's sense), it would seem to me sensible to encourage her to cut moral corners on occasion. I might well bring her up to follow, by and large, a range of negative moral injunctions: it would be better for her generally not to kill or injure other people, not to cheat, break her promises, lie, etc. Sometimes, however, if she could get away with it, it *would* be better to do so. I might encourage her, for instance, not to be too scrupulous, later on, in declaring all her income to the Inland Revenue and to get paid in cash wherever possible. As for *positive* obligations of beneficence, I might well bring her up to believe that there are no such things: if she feels *drawn* towards helping others to flourish, the starving of the Third World perhaps, or, as is most probable, her friends and family, then that is up to her; and if her ambitions are more self-centred, that, too, is her business.

Advanced industrial societies make this kind of combination of a minimal morality with occasional free-riding in the moral area an attractive option from a self-interested point of view. Hare may well be right that there are no rings of Gyges around today. But we have in our large-scale, amorphous kind of society, in which it is so easy to slip through the moral net, a modern equivalent of a ring of Gyges undreamed of by the Greeks. Hare's 'realistic' approach, referred to above, is not realistic enough. I suspect – and this is admittedly only speculation – that the sort of moral upbringing I was hypothesising for my daughter is becoming increasingly common in our increasingly egoistic social world. This is not to suggest that many parents who incline in this direction would begin from Hare's wholly prudentialist education aim. See later.

III

Hare first drew attention to the philosophical importance of asking 'How shall I bring up my children?' in *The Language of Morals* (Hare, 1952: 74). His interest in the question has persisted, as we have seen, into *Moral Thinking*. Whatever one may say of his earlier work, it seems clear that in the relevant chapter (ch. 11) of *Moral Thinking* he has not gone far enough towards getting inside the educator's point of view. Not, I think, that he has wholly intended to get inside it. His interest has been focused principally on certain traditional problems in ethics, and his approach, despite the educational orientation, has also followed familiar lines. Hare takes as given, as far as I can judge, that an individual's well-being consists in the maximisation of his preference-satisfaction over his life as a whole. He seems firmly in the 'desire-satisfaction' camp on this issue. At the same time, just as Rawls moved away from the pure 'desire-satisfaction' position nearer the 'objective list' alternative in adopting his 'Aristotelian principle', so Hare has done the same by his 'educator's' argument. Both writers end up, it seems, with a form of the theory which combines the two major positions on the good life for the individual mentioned in a quotation from Parfit earlier (p. 164). As with Rawls's, Hare's is an uneasy combination: the 'educator's' argument is not sufficient to dislodge the theorist who both adheres closely to Hare's basic assumption about well-being and is also resolved to withstand, as far as rational argument will permit, any attack from the 'objective list' side. Hare's mode of argument is a familiar one in the history of philosophy: it is one more breaker beating against, but failing to destroy, the moral sceptic's defences.

I said above that Hare's 'realistic' approach to the problem was not realistic enough. This applies, too, to his initial characterisation of the educator's point of view. He asks us 'to consider what our position would be if we were bringing up some child, and had *only* the child's interests at heart'. Hare is more interested in using this hypothetical educational orientation to help get to grips with his pure philosopher's problem than in seeing what the real, flesh-and-blood, *educator's* problem is when he thinks about the well-being of his pupil. For actual educators – parents and teachers – do not, with I suggest the rarest of exceptions, bring up their children with *only* the latters' interests at heart. They take into account from the beginning that they are bringing them up as members of society and have also at heart the interests of other members of society.

I have talked about what real educators actually do and this is, of course, an empirical claim. But I would prefer, if possible, not to anchor my positive argument, towards which I am now working, in this alone, or, indeed, at all. To discover 'the educator's point of view', which I have suggested as an alternative to those of the mature, impartial individual and of God or the intuitionist, we would have to look at how the educator *ought* to look at the child's well-being, regardless of what views actual educators had about this. This, after all, would put the educator's point of view on all fours with the others. 'Desire-satisfaction' theorists do not begin with the views of just *any* grown-up people, however biased, mentally disturbed or feeble-minded they might be. They assume agents who are knowledgeable and impartial, who in short are prepared to follow reason as far as reason goes. God and intuitionists may be expected to lack the defects and possess the qualities just mentioned.

What, then, would it be reasonable for the educator to take as considerations bearing on the good of his child? Would it, in particular, be more reasonable to limit himself to Hare's framework, taking into account *only* what is in the child's interests, or to bear in mind also the interests of others in the society into which the child will grow up?

One reason in favour of the second alternative is that the interests of these others are (or will be) every bit as real as the child's own interests and if the latter are taken account of, why should not the former also be? The amoralist, when asked why he does not give others' interests any weight compared with his own, simply rejects the question: his own good is all that concerns him. But the educator, very importantly, is *not* an amoralist. He is attentive to the interests of at least one other person than himself, namely the child. Altruistic reasons count for the educator, even if they do not for the amoralist. So the traditional problem of getting the determined amoralist to adopt the altruistic point of view – the problem that Hare grapples with – evaporates when we turn to the educator. For the latter is at least some way inside the moral world by virtue of his concern for his pupil. Given that he *is* inside it, and his openness to rational argument, he has no reason, it would seem, to restrict his altruism to the child's interests alone.

It might be objected that this argument assumes a prescriptive picture of the educator which is not without alternatives. There are at least two of these which do not entail that the educator have a wider concern for people's interests. First, why can't he see the pupil merely as a means to his own ends? If he is a parent, he may, for instance, see his child only as a future worker and so a source of income for him; if a teacher, he may do so too (cf. Wackford Squeers), or he may be totally uninterested in what the child may become, seeing his job only as leading to a pay packet. Second, why can't his non-instrumental concern for his children be based on a prudential preference on his part? Caring for them is something which he has chosen to put high in the preference-hierarchy embedded in his life-plan: his is a deliberately limited altruism which he sees no reason to extend further.

Can these two objections be answered? To the first, one might reply that although actual parents and teachers may in some cases have a purely instrumental attitude towards their children, it is doubtful whether they can then be said to be 'educating' them. One has to be careful here: it is all too easy for people, not least for philosophers of education, to write their own, subjective value-judgements into their concept of education. On the other hand, there must be *some* limits around the concept, even in the very broad 'upbringing' sense which this paper is assuming throughout. Can one be said to be bringing a child up if one treats him merely as a means – as an object replaceable in principle by something that could achieve one's purposes better: for the parent who wants a worker, a slave perhaps, or a machine that can do the work, or a large gift of money? Perhaps there is no definitive answer to this question. If people want to use the term 'upbringing' to include such treatment, who am I to stop them? The best I can do here, I think, is to say that the term is also, and more commonly, understood in such a way as to exclude this. It is 'education' or 'upbringing' in the more restrictive sense on which my positive argument will rely.

I don't think I can refute the second objection entirely, either. Wackford Squeers cared for young Wackford in a non-instrumental way quite unlike his treatment of his paying pupils, but his altruism went no further than his family. On the other hand, if we are being 'realistic', few parents have as limited an altruism as this; and even fewer schoolteachers, seeing the large numbers of pupils passing through their hands, are likely to be so attached to just these children (and perhaps other particular individuals and groups beyond them) that they draw the boundaries of their beneficence just at this point.

I shall have to start my positive argument further in, then, as it were, with the assumption that the educator I have in mind when talking about the 'educator's point of view' *is* bringing his charges up as members of society and *does* have at heart the interests of other members of society as well as those of the child. I don't think it is very damaging to my argument that I shall be working within this framework. It is hardly a daring move. Virtually all education, at home or school, presupposes it to some degree or other. Those who reject the framework will reject what follows. But that is of little concern. The problem of self-interest with which we began faces those, and not least those educators, who accept the framework. For many of them it is a problem of great practical importance. If the ensuing argument goes any way towards helping them to solve it, it will have partially served its purpose.

IV

How, then, is it rational for an educator concerned for the interests of others in society as well as for the interests of the child, to perceive the latter?

If it could be shown that from the educator's perspective it would be rational to see the pupil's well-being as including altruism, then we would be lending support to the central hypothesis of this paper, that a shift to this educational perspective helps to avoid the impasse in the problem of self-interest.

At first sight the shift does *not* look particularly helpful, since the educator, it seems, could quite easily avoid seeing the pupil's good as embracing altruism.

The educator could reject all 'objective list' accounts of the good. He could hold, with some 'desire-satisfaction' theorists, that the good life for the pupil, as for any-one else, is one in which, given that he knows the alternatives open to him, his major preferences in his life as a whole are by and large satisfied. As for the educa-tor's concern for the interests of others in society, is there any reason, he may ask, why this should put any restrictions on his view of the pupil's good, just given?

There are two different ways in which the educator can be concerned with the interests of others than the pupil. He might try to build up dispositions in the pupil of an other-regarding sort; or he may think that he, the educator, can help to promote others' interests without building up such dispositions: he might hold, for instance, that it is in the general social interest if pupils are equipped to fill jobs 'required by the economy', and whether this shapes his educational aims more towards specific vocational training or more towards a general preparation for working life, he need not in either case see this as involving any kind of education in altruism.

These two ways of proceeding – via education in altruism and via other routes – can, of course, be pursued together, as part of any one pupil's education. Where the child comes to have many educators, say at secondary school, functions can become more specialised. A science teacher, say, may see herself as engaged in vocational preparation without seeing educating in altruism as her business, except, perhaps, incidentally. (Whether science teachers *should* take this attitude is another matter.)

Must every child be brought up, as part of his or her education, to acquire other-regarding dispositions? If so, we can ignore the second way (e.g. via voca-tional preparation) in which the educator can seek to promote the interests of others than the pupil: even if some particular educators have no hand in altruistic education, this could not then be true of all of them.

To avoid complicating things unduly, let us assume henceforth that when we talk of the 'educator' and the 'educator's perspective', we are imagining the educator as *one person* responsible for the whole upbringing of the child. In practice there may well be many people responsible – parents, teachers, perhaps also school governors, councillors, ministers, TV producers and others. These may vary widely in their views on educational aims. But for our present purposes in this paper we may treat them all as sharing a common point of view, at least to some extent. This is because, in shifting our perspective on the problem of self-interest to the 'educator's point of view', we are assuming a *rational* educator. We may assume, therefore, that insofar as a pupil has many educators rather than one, there will be a minimum consensus among them that one should proceed rationally. This is not to get us very far, of course, but it enables us, perhaps to speak of *the* educator of a child, abstracting the minimum consensus from what might in fact be a number of different standpoints.

To come back to the issue again, then: *must* the rational educator seek to build up other-regarding dispositions in the pupil? There would be a certain inconsis-tency in his position if he did not. We are taking it as read that the educator him-self is concerned to promote the interest of others than himself, both those of the pupil and those of others than the pupil. If he were to bring the pupil up without any altruistic dispositions, it is hard to see what reason he could have for this. If altruism is right for himself, why is it not right for the pupil? More importantly, perhaps, a pupil brought up wholly without altruism would be a psychopath and, given the educator's own concern for others' well-being, it would be irrational for him to bring the pupil up in such a way as to constitute such a threat to that well-being. We can take it, then, that the educator must include altruism in his educa-tion. He wishes to bring the child up as 'a member of society', not in the sense that a psychopath or a moral reprobate lives a non-hermit-like life among other people, but in the sense that the child shows some concern for others' welfare. The educator will no doubt want to bring the child up not, *ceteris paribus*, to lie, injure, kill, steal or break promises, since all these things are generally damaging to others' interests. What further the content of the altruistic side of his education will include is something that can be left open at this point.

This account of the rational educator fits empirical reality. I know of no parent, teacher, politician or other educator who advocates bringing children up as psychopaths. Perhaps for the reasons already given, every actual educator, I would hypothesise, would be in favour of some kind of education in altruism.

Given this, though, must the educator see the altruistic dispositions which he is nurturing in the pupil as in any way included within the latter's well-being? We come back to the central question raised, but not yet answered, on p. 137.

V

Let us assume, as we did there, that we are faced with an educator who is sceptical on this issue and who adopts the 'desire-satisfaction' view of interests as described there. How might he proceed?

He might argue that his educational aims bifurcate: 'altruistic' aims to do with good of others than the pupil on the one side, aims to do with the pupil's on the other (I shall call these 'personal aims'). These can be kept apart from one another. It is true that the altruistic aims will limit the personal aims. If there were no altruistic aims, then the educator's personal aims would involve promoting the pupil's overall desire-satisfaction, whatever form the latter took. The altruistic aims rule out types of desire-satisfaction deleterious to others' interests. But this does not make altruism *part* of the pupil's well-being, even though in some sense the pupil grows up concerned for others' well-being (in that he does not cheat, kill, steal, ignore others in distress, or whatever). The pupil can, of course, *choose* to build further altruistic ends into his conception of his well-being, but there is no obligation on him to do so.

This is the sceptic's case. Can it be answered? As a first move, we might claim that the fact, if it is a fact, that the sceptic *can* keep the two aims apart does not show that it is *rational* for him to do so. What considerations might bear on this?

Let us contrast two ways in which altruistic aims and personal aims may enter into someone's education. In both cases the pupil is to grow up altruistic in *some* sense. The first is the way of the sceptic: the child is to become altruistic but altruism is not part of his well-being. In the second way it *is* part of it. Faced with these two patterns, which, if either, does the educator see it as more rational to follow?

Let us see what kind of a case can be made for the second pattern and then see if adherents of the first can show theirs to be more rational. It will be convenient to label the second pattern the 'monist' view, and the first the 'dualist' view.

The dualist view may be represented thus:

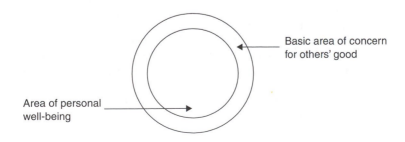

Basic area of concern for others' good

Area of personal well-being

Personal well-being here is the overall satisfaction of preferred desires. Not any preference is acceptable, since some (e.g. wanting to inflict physical injury on others) are ruled out as they fail to conform to the altruistic constraints found in the outer ring. The latter is labelled 'basic', because some people may choose to include *further* altruistic ends among personal preferences within the inner circle.

For the dualist educator the inner circle does not necessarily include any of the outer ring. Individual pupils of his may choose to make basic altruism part of their personal life-plan,[1] but these apart, for other pupils the two parts of the diagram must be kept separate. If the educator held that in *no* case could the inner circle exclude any of the outer ring, then he would not be a dualist at all, but a monist, since altruism would then necessarily be included in his concept of personal well-being. Even as concerns those pupils who make basic altruism part of their life-plan, *in a sense* the two areas must be kept separate: the pupil must be brought up at least to believe that they are in general separable and that his bringing them together in the way that he does is a personal preference and nothing more.

The question now is: given that the dualist is committed to keeping the two areas apart, how rational is it for him to do this? There are at least three kinds of considerations which cast doubts on this.

(1) First, the onus is on the dualist to provide criteria demarcating the two areas. What sorts of personal preference within the inner circle are permissible? We can take it, as we have done, that desires for physical injury are ruled out, but what, for instance, of a life-plan woven around physical enjoyments like food, drink, sex and holidays in the sun or around getting to the top in one's career? Both these life-plans, together with a third which amalgamates the two, are commonplace in contemporary Western society. They are likewise commonly taken to be within one's legitimate area of personal choice. But are they, in fact? The first, 'hedonistic', ideal requires time and money. Some would say that others' demands on us are so great – think of the poor in our own community, and of the poor and hungry in the Third World – that one has no right to be so self-indulgent. The same attitude could be taken towards the desire to get to the top; in addition, one has to ask how far it is possible to be a careerist without selfishly putting oneself first, doing down one's rivals, diminishing the moral autonomy of one's underlings, manipulating those who may be of use to one. Suppose one of our dualist educator's pupils became attracted by the 'careerist' ideal: what guidance could the dualist give him about where he should draw the line between one's own and others' interests? The answer, I suggest, as with the hedonistic ideal, is not at all clear.

The basic difficulty is that the extent of the outer circle is indeterminate. Many moral prohibitions are easy enough for the dualist to deal with. He can bring up his children not to lie, kill, physically injure, break promises, steal, frustrate or be rude. Refraining from doing things like these leaves the inner circle intact: it constitutes no threat to either the hedonist or the careerist, for instance. But *beneficence* is a different matter. *How* beneficent one ought to be in general, and how beneficent to different kinds of beneficiaries, are questions to which moral philosophers have given different answers. Peter Singer (1972), along with many utilitarians, would argue that most people in Western societies are morally obliged in a world of acute poverty to devote a large part of their income to its relief, while other views would be less demanding. What for some writers is supererogatory is for others – merely what should be normally expected.

This is not the place to adjudicate on how far beneficence should go. The only point is that the existence of serious differences of opinion on this matter poses a problem for the dualist, since he is committed to keeping the personal and the altruistic areas apart. He faces a dilemma: if he has criteria determining how much beneficence belongs to the outer ring, he faces the charge of arbitrariness ('Why stop there?'); while if he has no cut-off point, he leaves his pupils with insufficient guidance about what sorts of personal life-plans are and are not permitted.

(2) A second difficulty for the dualist educator concerns motivation. When his pupils are brought up to follow the altruistic rules in the outer ring, why do they do so? Certain possibilities are ruled out, given that the educator is both a dualist and is looking for what it is most rational for him to do. Egoistic forms of motivation depending on fear of punishment and hope of reward are ruled out, since dualism would thus disappear. (We have already appropriated the term 'the monist view' for the theory that sees altruism as a *part of* one's well-being. The present suggestion, which sees it as *instrumental to* one's well-being, is really another variety of monism.) Appeals to authority, in so far as they do not depend on egoistic motivation, are ruled out by the criterion of rationality. The idea of bringing children up not to lie, etc. in such a way that their awareness of these rules itself motivates them to obey them – an intuitionist solution – is obscure: how can this mere awareness motivate?

What is left? The obvious answer is that children are brought up to want to promote others' well-being, just as, within the inner circle, they are brought up to want to promote their own. But how can these altruistic desires be nurtured? One way is by beginning very locally with children's attachments to their immediate family and to their dolls and pets and gradually widening the circle of their altruistic concerns to embrace others in their family, friends, the members of various groups to which they belong, those in need in their own and other communities, etc. In this way they can come to acquire that more impersonal concern for the well-being of others that the outer framework demands.

Why should this constitute a difficulty for dualism? The problem is that the most local attachments, those at the centre of the widening circle, are, empirically speaking, not clearly altruistic *rather than* self-interested. Young children see their own well-being as intimately bound up with the well-being of others (including pets and dolls) within the household: an injury to a favourite cat is felt as if it were the child's own. As the circle widens, the intimateness, just mentioned, grows weaker, but even so there is no clear-cut division between my concern for my interests and my general concern for the interests of others that the dualist view requires.

Could education in altruism proceed differently? If there were some way in which children could come to feel a general altruistic concern without starting at the centre of an expanding circle, then the dualist might still be able to keep the two parts of his diagram distinct. Perhaps it is best to leave this as an onus on the dualist at this point.

(3) The dualist's third problem has to do with the unity of the pupil's personality. The more he stresses the division between the personal and the altruistic areas, the greater task he has of holding them together. The monistic view avoids this difficulty.

The dualist may reply that the monist will have to bring pupils up to be able to face and try to resolve all sorts of conflicts – for example, between competing desires, demands or ideals (or combinations of these) – and that the division between the two areas is a form of what is, after all, only another source of conflict.

The monist's reply will be that it is true that he does indeed recognise the ineluctably conflict-ridden nature of human life, and that he has ways of bringing children up to cope with it. Getting them to acquire virtues is one way, and perhaps the most important one. Coming to be courageous, for instance, involves coming to strike the right balance between satisfying one's immediate inclination to flee from a fearful situation and one's desire to stand one's ground. It is a matter, as Aristotle saw, of acquiring practical judgement. If the dualist claims that conflicts between self-interest and morality are on a par with any other, then on which educational devices can *he* rely – parallel to inculcating the virtues – for helping pupils to resolve them?

How can one learn to 'strike the right balance' between the claims of self-interest and the basic altruistic claims on one? Part of the problem here is, of course, the indeterminateness of the latter area, described under (1). But even if a line *were* clearly drawn around it, the question about learning to strike a balance would still remain. From what point of view would this balance be sought? Other conflicts can be resolved from the point of view of one's own good, like the conflict involved in becoming courageous, for instance. Some sort of rational procedures can be followed once one has such a standard. But what standard, or point of view, can the dualist adopt?

An obvious answer, it would seem, is the 'moral point of view'. Here, like Butler's 'conscience', one judges impartially between the claims of one's own well-being and the basic altruistic claims, from a standpoint beyond both. But there are further difficulties here. First, it is not clear what an impartial judgement would imply. If it means that each person whose interests are in question is to count for one and not more than one, then if my interests are weighed against those of all other human (or sentient beings), they become so infinitesimal in moral importance that they might as well not exist at all. Yet if my interests are to be given any extra weight than this, there seems no non-arbitrary way of determining what this weight shall be.

A second problem is: what is going to induce the agent to adopt this moral point of view? If motivation depends on desires, then the dualist educator must bring pupils up to want to judge things from the moral point of view. But how does he go about nurturing this desire? It is not enough to talk about building up self-interested desires on the one hand and altruistic ones on the other, since the desire to look at things from the moral perspective transcends these. What, then, could induce the pupil to adopt the latter?

The only plausible answer then I can think of is: the desire to prevent the two parts of his personality from being totally disconnected from each other. Part of his education has been directed towards his personal development; and part towards a basic altruism. If he is to remain an integrated person he has to bring these parts into some sort of relation with each other.

Not only is the need to inculcate this extra, unity-directed, desire avoidable by adopting monism rather than dualism, but also, once it is introduced, it is hard to make sense of it except as a higher order kind of self-interested desire. What more self-interested desire could there be than to preserve the unity of the self?

If this line of thought is correct, then the dualist pupil who takes this route finds himself a kind of monist, after all – not in the original sense of incorporating altruism with one's own well-being, but in that his master-desire is for his own unity. He is not an Aristotelian pupil brought up from the start as a unified being; but more (but loosely) like a Hegelian one, as portrayed in the *Phenomenology*, with the monistic drive towards unity at the very centre of his concerns.

These difficulties in the educator's adopting the dualist view can be overcome if he adopts monism instead. There is no problem about demarcating the personal and the altruistic area since the latter is now included in the former. There is no need now to keep the altruistic and the personal strictly apart: the fact that in more local attachments one cannot disentangle the two, causes no embarrassment to the monist. There is, as we have seen, no problem of unification, since nothing has been sundered.

Faced with a rational choice between dualism and monism, the educator, it seems so far, has more reason to choose monism. Are there any considerations which challenge this conclusion?

There may be worries about paternalism. In choosing monism, the educator is shaping the child's character in such a way that he will come to possess a particular, and highly controversial, view of what his well-being consists in. It is not a view that he will easily, if at all, be able to give up: the more successful his education has been, the firmer will be the dispositions which make up his character, and in which this view is embedded. Since this is only *one* view of human well-being – as it is opposed by various forms of unrestricted desire-satisfaction theory into which altruism does not necessarily enter – the question arises by what right the educator imposes his preferred form of upbringing rather than another.

The monist can answer this objection by pointing out that, as educator, there are only two choices before him – to bring up the pupil either with altruism incorporated into the conception of his well-being, or without this. If he chooses the latter, his choice is less rational. Since there is no point in going for what is less rational, there is no alternative left but monism.

The paternalistic objection may also be suggesting that the pupil has been *indoctrinated* into this monist conception of his well-being. What is meant by 'indoctrination' in such a context would have to be made explicit. If it is taken to imply preventing reflection on a belief or set of beliefs, then I see no reason why the child has necessarily been indoctrinated: he could, after all, have been brought up able, perhaps even disposed at an appropriate stage, to reflect on the credentials of monism and alternatives to it. But if what is meant, rather, is that relatively permanent dispositions have been built into his character, then indoctrination is unavoidable in any form of upbringing and not necessarily harmful: it would be indoctrination, for instance, to bring children up to use their native language correctly.

I have tried in this paper to throw some light on the seemingly interminable dispute between those who hold an 'objective list' account of individual well-being and those who hold some sort of 'preference satisfaction' account. I suggested that as long as we remain with the point of view of the mature individual, there seems to be no foolproof argument in favour of the objectivist view that the sceptic cannot refute. In shifting to the educator's point of view, I went on to try to show that there are good reasons for seeing altruism as part of any individual's well-being. I have not tried to say how large a part it should play or what its more detailed content might be. No doubt there may be room for all sorts of individual differences here. All I have tried to clinch is the minimal case that, from the educator's perspective, it would not be rational to exclude altruism altogether from individual well-being. This should be enough, if sound, to undermine the mere preference-satisfaction account and to support the objective list view.

Altruism is only one of the items typically found in objective lists. If there is anything in the argument of this paper, it would be interesting to see how far a shift to the educator's perspective would provide us with good reasons for including other such items – the pursuit of knowledge, for instance, or aesthetic awareness – as constituents of individual well-being in general. I hope to turn to this problem in another paper.

Note

1   These pupils differ from the 'supererogatory' pupils of the previous paragraph.

References

Bond, E. J. (1983) *Reason and Value*, Cambridge: University Press, p. 160.
Downie, R. S., Loudfoot, E. and Telfer, E. (1974) *Education and Personal Relationships*, London: Methuen, p. 50.
Frankena, W. K. (1973) *Ethics*, ch. 5, Englewood Cliffs, NJ: Prentice-Hall.
Haack, R. (1981) 'Education and the good life', *Philosophy*, 56, pp. 289–302.
Hare, R. M. (1952) *The Language of Morals*, Oxford: Oxford University Press, p. 74.
Hare, R. M. (1981) *Moral Thinking*, Oxford: Oxford University Press, p. 191.
MacIntyre, A. C. (1981) *After Virtue*, London: Duckworth, p. 242.
Mackie, J. (1977) *Ethics*, ch. 1, London: Penguin.
Parfit, D. (1984) *Reasons and Persons*, Oxford: Clarendon Press, p. 499.
Peters, R. S. (1966) *Ethics and Education*, ch. 5, London: Allen & Unwin.
Rawls, J. (1971) *A Theory of Justice*, Oxford: University Press, p. 432.
Singer, P. (1972) 'Famine, affluence, and morality', *Philosophy and Public Affairs*, 1, pp. 229–43.

CHAPTER 10

EDUCATION AND PERSONAL WELL-BEING IN A SECULAR UNIVERSE

Inaugural Lecture (1995), published under this name by Institute of Education, University of London

Since this lecture arises from a personal, not an established Chair, I cannot in all logic follow the common tradition of beginning with appreciative remarks about my predecessor. There is no predecessor! But perhaps, I might be allowed to say a few words about Richard Peters, who was the last holder of the established Chair in Philosophy of Education. It was through Richard's inspirational qualities as my first teacher of philosophy at Birkbeck College in the early 1960s that I became hooked beyond redemption on the subject. You can imagine my delight when I was appointed to work with Richard at the Institute of Education and collaborate with him in the new and exhilarating task of applying philosophical skills and under-standing to clarify some of the murky ideas about education which then domi-nated the world of teacher education. Since then I consider myself to have been very fortunate, and in several ways. First, to have worked in this Institute with a whole host of stimulating colleagues, all odd hybrids, like myself, too practically concerned to be able to contemplate a purely academic life. The Institute has provided a splendid environment in which to think freely and independently about fundamental educational issues – even, if I may say so, over the last 15 years when national resources for doing so have been increasingly hard to find. When he was Director, Denis Lawton worked fearlessly to keep this tradition alive and we are all very much in his debt for that. I also consider myself very lucky to have known *two* periods of intense intellectual activity within the history of my own discipline. The first was initiated largely by Richard Peters himself in partnership with Paul Hirst. It consisted in bringing the linguistic and other techniques of post-war philosophy to the study of education. The second – which is still very much in full flow – has been the new interest in normative and applied ethics which has been with us since the late 1970s. This has been immensely fruitful for the philosophy of education, which, thanks to the earlier work of Peters and Hirst, may justly be called the first of the applied philosophies.

It is often said these days, and rightly, that we in this country need to redefine what it is to be British. This is seen partly as a matter of ridding ourselves of ideas of imperialism and global commercial domination (the latter is not too difficult), but partly also as breaking the strong link between Britishness and Christianity, forged after the 1707 Act of Union between the three Protestant countries of England, Wales and Scotland and strengthened in the following hundred-odd years of wars with Catholic France. In the last year the government seems to have wished to re-weld this ancient link although not with its Protestant bias, via new guidelines on collective worship in state schools, which lay down that daily acts of worship in all schools shall be of a broadly Christian character, according a special status to Jesus Christ and showing 'reverence or veneration...to a divine being or power'. Of 900 secondary schools recently inspected, 95 per cent have been shown to be breaking this law on collective worship.[1]

It is also often said these days that our new notion of Britain should be of a multicultural, or plural, rather than a Christian country. I am sure there is some truth in this; but this may, even so, be putting too much weight on a plurality of beliefs. Tying Britishness to this still links our nationality too closely to religious notions, if no longer in a Christian, let alone a Protestant, form. But for me, the most striking thing about our present national community is its overwhelming unreligiousness – a fact reflected, perhaps, in the attitude of those 900 schools. In 1990, the proportion of active church members in the UK population was 15 per cent, the smallest for all West European countries and massively below the 52 per cent recorded for the Netherlands, to say nothing of the 81 per cent for the Irish Republic.[2] And the UK proportion has been steadily decreasing. On one extrapolation I have made, on present trends active church membership in the UK should be approaching zero some halfway through the next century.[3]

Whatever the precise truth about this, just how the government's attempt to involve a by-and-large godless school population in the rites of a dwindling religious cult will do anything for the students' own or that of other people's flourishing is not exactly clear. I shall be arguing for an alternative picture of personal flourishing suitable for a non-religious society. My basic thought is that non-religious citizens need frameworks within which to make sense of their existence, both at the social and at the cosmic level. Children brought up within religions, Moslem, Christian or other, are provided with such frameworks (I ignore problems about their logical and epistemological adequacy). With secular children it is more hit-and-miss, especially as regards any cosmic framework. They deserve, in my view, clearer bearings.

I begin with some comments about the tradition of thinking about personal well-being in which I have developed philosophically and against which I have been reacting in the last half of my career to date. I hope, as I go through, you will see the importance of these remarks in connexion with the point just made about the education of non-religious youngsters. The concept of personal well-being is central to thought about the aims of education. In bringing up children, the skills, attitudes and kinds of knowledge which we are transmitting to them are intended, among other things, to help them to lead flourishing, fulfilling lives. So it is essential to be as clear as we can about what it is to lead a flourishing life, or, to put the same thing another way, about what the concept of personal well-being involves. This is one major way in which my own discipline, the philosophy of education, can contribute to thought about the aims of education. I myself have been exploring the notion of personal well-being for this purpose since the 1960s. As I implied, I have gradually come to detach myself from the tradition in which my early thinking about this was formed. Let me say a few words about this tradition, bearing in mind our main topic about the place of frameworks, especially a cosmic framework, in the education of non-religious children.

I shall begin, then, by looking at the place that modern British philosophers have accorded to frameworks, social or cosmic, in their accounts of personal flourishing.

In Benthamite utilitarianism, a framework scarcely, if at all, exists. Here flourishing is seen in terms of the maximisation of pleasurable experiences. It takes into account nothing outside these, no wider background.

This conception of personal well-being is, it seems to me, a secular version of a Christian account. While Christianity has stressed a state of blessedness beyond our mortal life, utilitarians have typically been thoroughly this-worldly. Yet in one way, the utilitarian conception remains close – too close – to the Christian, at least in one of its versions.

Christianity has often located human beings in two worlds, the natural world in which they exist as animals of a certain sort, and the eternal world in which they exist as immortal-souls. One finds a classic account of this, for instance, in Descartes' philosophy. It has echoes in Kant's moral theory. In this view one can distinguish between two conceptions of human happiness – an illusory conception which looks only at the pleasures of our animal nature, and a deeper, more objective, account that stresses the joys of eternity. Christian preachers through the centuries have sought to wean people from a false picture of their flourishing founded on this-worldly pleasures towards a more exalted, other-worldly, idea of this.

A common feature of both the allegedly false and true pictures has been their thinness, their inattention to detailed content, to any form of complexity. The illusory happiness of this world revolves, so it was held, around physical pleasures, around treasure corruptible by moth and rust. The contours of eternal blessedness are not for human beings to delineate: they belong to the divine mystery. In this story far more important than the pursuit of well-being of either sort has been the meeting of our moral obligations as enshrined in God's law: it is this that through God's grace may earn us eternal happiness, whatever form this might take.

The replacement of a Christian by a secular, utilitarian ethic by the end of the eighteenth century meant abandoning all notions of other-worldly felicity. The only true happiness is to be found in our animal nature: old appearances become the new realities. It is not surprising, then, that this earliest account of human well-being in the new secular world should have been so conceptually meagre. In going no further than pleasurable sensations, bereft of any wider setting, it simply took over the thinness of the Christian notion of the illusory form of happiness.

Benthamite utilitarianism was soon challenged in this respect by J. S. Mill's attempt to distance himself from an ethics of swinishness via his doctrine of the superior pleasures of intellectual and aesthetic activities. If Mill's argument was sound, it would be of immense importance to educators, since they could confidently steer pupils towards a life in which academic or artistic activities loomed large – without the usual anxiety about whether they have the right to impose what, after all, might only be a minority preference on every student. Unfortunately, for reasons which are well known. Mill's argument was soon seen to be flawed. But even though it failed, at least the notion of personal well-being now became more differentiated, less simplistic and one-dimensional. Yet it still lacked a framework. Personal well-being was still seen in terms of the subject's activities and experiences alone.

This remained true of most major treatments of the topic in mainstream British philosophy for the next hundred years and more – until very recently, in fact. Not that personal well-being was a topic to which mainstream moral philosophers paid much attention over that period. This is because, living among the shadows left by a receding Christianity, they were preoccupied with morality and moral obligation. There were some exceptions. Sidgwick's account of personal happiness in 1874 followed Bentham in basing this on pleasures and pains. For Moore 30 years later the *summum bonum* consisted in 'the pleasures of human intercourse and the enjoyment of beautiful objects'; while in our own field Richard Peters in the 1960s put most weight on theoretical – that is, truth-seeking-pursuits like history, science or philosophy which he saw as essential features of the rational life and hence of the content of education.

These writers thus preserved the assumption, found in Bentham and Mill, that personal flourishing has to do exclusively with atomic activities and experiences. Outside the mainstream, only the British Hegelian idealists, influential in the decades before the First World War, had viewed personal flourishing non-atomically. For F. H. Bradley, as for T. H. Green, 'self- realisation' was inseparable from the wider well-being of the communities, national as well as local, to which one belonged. Beyond these, it was tied in, too, into the unfolding development of reality as a whole. With each human being located within a series of concentric circles stretching out into eternity, absence of a framework was the very last charge that could be brought against the idealists.

Idealists apart, the mainstream of British moral philosophy had no truck with such metaphysical excesses. When it thought at all about personal well-being, it continued the thin, frameworkless treatment of it which it had inherited from Mill, Bentham, Kant and behind these, Christianity. This is true even in part of James Griffin's *Well-being*, the first full-length discussion of the subject, published in 1986. For him well-being, embraces such factors as accomplishment, autonomy, understanding oneself and the world, pleasures, the perception of beauty, appreciation of nature, deep personal relationships. No overarching rationale is given for the inclusion of these rather than other values. As in many other writers who have discussed well-being, all we have is a list.

In the last 15 years, philosophical accounts of well-being, including to some extent Griffin's own, have become incomparably richer in two ways. What might be called the internal structure of well-being has been more finely delineated, with attention broadening beyond the issue of worthwhile goals to questions of hierarchies and conflicts among goals, as well as to basic needs. Secondly, and this is closer to our theme, philosophers have focused, externally as it were, on relations between the individual's flourishing and that of other people or communities.

Alasdair MacIntyre, Joseph Raz, Charles Taylor, Martha Nussbaum and others have converged in different ways on the view that personal well-being is to be understood against a larger, social, framework. Fulfilment lies not only in achieving more determinate goals, but also in more global commitments to the various social groups to which we belong. Aristotle's assumption that one's own flourishing cannot be detached from the flourishing of one's family, friends and political community has been a powerful influence here. One of the most interesting developments of recent years, for instance, has been the new interest shown by thinkers in the left-liberal tradition – as well as the right wing – in the nation as one such social framework. This is not, of course, to say that these communitarian perspectives are all unproblematic, and indeed a great deal of research in philosophy of education in this Institute and elsewhere in Britain and the world is at present hard at work sifting through the complicated claims in this area and their relevance to how education should be conceived.

At all events, this uncovering of the social horizons of personal well-being reconnects current Anglo-American ethics with British idealism. But what of the cosmic framework, underlying the social, also found in Idealism? There is little of this in such influential writers as Raz, Nussbaum. What we *do* find in them is an awareness of unchanging features of human nature against which aspects of our well-being must be understood – for example, innately given passions and desires, including those we have as social animals, which make possible the virtues, or biological needs whose satisfaction is one facet of personal well-being. But human nature is as far as they go: they do not tangle with reality as such.

My main question in this lecture is whether we need to go further, whether, personal well-being needs to be understood against some kind of cosmic framework. If it does, the educational consequences are likely to be considerable. Religious educators have long thought in these terms, but the idea that the secular population could benefit by being brought up more explicitly within a cosmic framework, has been little explored.

But what kind of cosmic framework? Christianity, like other religions, has looked to such a framework for the *source* of ethical values. What is right and good depends not on human needs and desires, but on the will of God. The Catholic philosophers Alasdair MacIntyre and Charles Taylor move in this direction – most explicitly perhaps Taylor in his insistence on an ontological foundation for ethics in his *Sources of the Self*. Another recent work, Iris Murdoch's *Metaphysics as a Guide to Morals*, like her earlier *The Sovereignty of Good*, seems to posit a non-theistic stand-in for God in the shape of something close to a Platonic Form of the Good which irradiates our value-world.

I find it hard to attach sense to the notion of a source of value located in the universe, whether this is a religious source or a quasi-religious one as in Murdoch. There is also a non-religious version, but this is no more satisfactory. I am thinking of the view that ethical values are rooted in human nature – as in ideas of innate goodness underpinning theories of child development in the West and the ethical tradition deriving from Mencius in the East (*Mencius*, especially Book 6).

What would it mean to say that the source of personal flourishing is found in Reality, natural or supernatural? It would mean that to understand what flourishing is, we would have to leave our ordinary human world and go back to the source in question – to interrogate nature, including human nature, or to find out God's will or the nature of the form of the good. But supposing we could do any of these things, how could any discovery about what is the case reveal anything to do with what is good or valuable, for example, to do with human flourishing? We come back to the seemingly impassable gulf between statements about the natural or supernatural world and ethical values.

There may be some way of bridging the gulf, but I do not know what it is. If religious or, for that matter, developmentalist ethical theorists claim otherwise, they should be constrained to spell out their arguments. This is especially important in Britain at the moment, where it is taken as read – as no more than common sense – in some quarters that moral education must have its basis in religion. Yet just how this could conceivably be so, is deeply problematic. If only this point, so obvious and familiar to most philosophers, could penetrate current government thinking about the moral needs of the nation!

Ethical values, including values associated with personal well-being, are, as far as I can see, through and through a product of our human world. They have been developed across human time in response to our needs and desires as biological creatures and our interest as social beings in creating congenial forms of communal life. If you ask me why friendship, or sexual pleasure, or concern for the needy, or personal autonomy are good things, my answer will have to be in those terms. There is no need to appeal to a deeper basis in the ultimate nature of things – and neither, as I say, is it clear what any such appeal would mean. Collectively, we are not given ethical direction by forces outside ourselves, whether these are natural or transcendental: we have worked this out over millennia from our own resources.

But if the cosmos is not the source of our values, especially those to do with personal well-being, it is still surely connected with them in some way. One very obvious way is that it provides the ultimate framework within which values exist. We would not have values at all unless we were biological organisms, part of a larger framework of living nature, and behind that the natural world more generally – the world of animals, plants, rocks, seas, clouds, planets, stars. Part of our understanding of personal well-being is that it is located within such a natural framework. So much should be obvious, although it is not often mentioned in philosophers' accounts of well-being.

As well as providing the ultimate framework, nature, globally or in its particular manifestations, can also be the *object* of many of our values. There seems to be a range of different, though interconnected, values here. I begin with some values directed towards particular phenomena rather than nature as a whole.

First, at a very basic level, we enjoy and value such things as feeling the sunshine and the wind on our bodies, smelling the scents of flowers and grasses, or walking in the countryside. This must have its roots – as a matter of explanation, rather than justification – in our animal nature. Cats, too, enjoy lying in the sun and running up and down trees – although in their case there is no object, as there is in ours, towards which their enjoyment is consciously directed.

A second value, which takes us beyond feelings of bodily well-being, is a feeling of attachment to nature as our dwelling place. Again, this is surely rooted in the attachments that other animals have to their nests and lairs and wider habitat. Mention of it also reminds us that, for us, there is no sharp divide between the natural framework and the social framework within which we live. We cannot – as yet – change the course of the planets or stars; but we can and do shape the more local features of the natural world around us so that they become an inextricable part of our social world. This is true at an instrumental level in our use of all kinds of natural products. But it is also true non-instrumentally. The most obvious example is what we do to ourselves – the ways in which we cultivate our minds and characters and adorn our bodies. But we also surround our dwellings with flowers and gardens, share our lives with non-human animals, collectively and over the longer term, tame and fashion our local landscapes.

This merging of the social and the natural must help to explain the sense of attachment which we come to have towards the latter. Our bonds of sentiment with family, local community, national group, humanity as a whole embrace also the natural settings in which these communities exist – gardens, parks, woods, rivers, and behind everything, skies, clouds, moonlight, starlight. Natural phenomena constitute our dwelling-place in the widest sense; we languish when we are deprived of them.

Closely connected with this feeling of attachment is our delight in the beauty of the natural world. Just how these two values – one linked backed to ethical values of community, the other purely aesthetic – are connected, is worthy of further investigation.

Delight in beauty merges in its turn with feelings of sublimity evoked by grander, wilder, more terrifying parts of nature like storms, mountains, seascapes, starry skies.

This leads us towards a fifth value. This one is orientated to the natural world as a whole, rather than to particular parts of it as often with the four earlier values – a sense of wonder at its very existence. I think this has to be distinguished from two further emotions, with which it may become confused. It is not the same as awe, where this implies some object of reverence, some spiritual entity infusing or beyond the natural world. Wonder, as I am using the term in a secular context, is not to be conflated with this religious emotion. Neither has it to do with the kind of wonder that the scientist may experience in trying to 'unravel the mysteries of the universe'. The latter is connected with the thought of some solution. Wonder as I am using the term here stops short of answers: it is a wholly contemplative emotion where one is amazed at, nonplussed by the existence of anything at all.

I have just distinguished wonder in my sense from awe at the natural world. I have labelled the latter, a religious emotion. But there is a sense in which this can be experienced by a non-religious person. A secular reader of Wordsworth's poetry, for instance, can in imagination experience nature as if it were animated – as if it were a source and not merely an object of value. For many non-religious people this imaginative type of awe is an important element in their flourishing. Given humanity's long history of seeing the world in a religious light, it is not surprising that some of the attitudes we have learned to cherish over these millennia should still be a valued part of the secular consciousness, if only in an 'as if' way.

Next along my range of values, and overlapping with a sense of wonder at the existence of things, is respect for the natural world, the desire to leave it as it is and to preserve it from human depredations. We wish to preserve wilderness, to save endangered species. This stand-off value shades into a more positive desire to help natural things to flourish, often in association with our social environment – through forestry, for instance, gardening and landscaping. National Parks. Respect for nature of either type can be directed to particular features or to nature as a whole more globally. At the back of the latter can be a value to do with the harmonisation of the natural world with the social world – a value prominent in traditional Chinese culture. Talk of links between nature and society brings us back to values associated with attachment which came earlier on my list: they seem inextricable from these.

These, then, are some of the secular values which take the natural world in some way as object, overlapping and interrelated with each other as they proceed from physical feelings of well-being, through attachment, delight in beauty, a sense of the sublime, wonder, imaginatively mediated awe, respect, care and harmony with the human world. Of course this is not meant to be an exhaustive list. I see it only as a starting point for a fuller investigation.

How do all this bear on the philosophical problem of the nature of personal well-being and thereby on educational issues? It provokes the thought: how far is adhering to any or all of these values an *ineliminable feature* of human flourishing? It is obvious that in the lives of some individuals one or other of these values can be important, but can we go further than this to say that *anyone's* flourishing is diminished if these values are not realised?

The question is important both conceptually and educationally. Conceptually, since it bears on our understanding of well-being; educationally, because if they are ineliminable features of our well-being we have a good reason to bring up all children to adhere to them, while if they are not, we may run the danger of imposing on them values which may only be important to us subjectively: at most we would seem to be justified in *opening up* such things as enjoying natural beauty and experiencing primal wonder as options for them to accept or reject.

I shall not offer a definitive answer to this question, only some provisional speculations about whether living by these nature-directed values is essential to well-being, or merely a matter of different individuals' preferences.

First, enjoying nature-orientated feelings of physical well-being may well be as ineliminable as enjoying food or rest, we being the kind of animals that we are.

Second, if we cannot flourish well without social attachments – to friends, family, larger communities – then, given the overlap between the social and the natural, attachments to the natural world as our larger dwelling-place may also be indispensable to us.

If so, perhaps one can also build in, thirdly, a love of natural beauty. I don't know whether trees, flowers and mountains seemed beautiful to the very first human beings, but I rather doubt it: perhaps our attachment to the beauty of the natural world derives, historically, from our attachment to beauty in art. The fact is that we are all now born into a form of life in which attachment to nature and its beauty is taken as read as an important, perhaps indispensable, part of our life, just as attachment to one's friends is. It is hard for us to credit that anyone could be personally better off if unconcerned with the lovelinesses of flowers, mountains, water, sky, animal and human bodies. Why should this be? Kant maintained 'that to take an immediate interest in the beauty of nature . . . is always a mark of a good soul' (*Critique of Judgment*, para 42). Anthony Savile (1982) gives his own interpretation of this without commitment to Kant's theory of moral goodness underlying this quotation. He says that it is a truth about human beings that attachments to the world via appreciation of its beauties 'encourage reverence for it and a respect for the claims that it makes against ourselves' (p. 182). Becoming disinterestedly attached in this way helps to free us from 'the tyranny of self'. If Savile is right, does this connect the love of natural beauty to personal well-being which is what I am seeking – rather than, as with Kant, to moral goodness? The answer is not clear to me, neither is whether Savile's account is on the right lines. Is Bernard Williams (1992) perhaps nearer the mark in connecting our delight in natural beauty with feelings of gratitude towards nature and a sense of peace? I am not sure, although his account seems truer to our experience than Savile's more austere theory. I am merely left with an as yet ungrounded intuition that love of natural beauty is a vital part of our flourishing – where 'we' may not refer to all human beings in general, as in Savile's argument, but only, perhaps, to people in a society living at a certain level of reflectiveness. Here as elsewhere, what this inaugural lecture is inaugurating, above all, is a personal quest to get a little clearer over the years to come on such matters.

To return to my list of values. If one can build in attachments to nature as our home as a vital part of our well-being, this may well be one route for also including the ecological values of respect, care and harmony.

One route, but perhaps not the only one. It has become clearer in recent discussions of personal well-being, especially by Joseph Raz, that in a society like our own, personal autonomy has come to be, for nearly all of us, an essential element in our well-being. I mean by 'personal autonomy', the idea that one should be a self-directed person in the conduct of one's life – that one should determine one's major goals oneself and not have these decided by God, social custom or pressure from one's peer group. Personal autonomy is not a necessary feature of human well-being in general, since the contrast between better and worse flourishing is applicable to members of, say, religious communities in which life is seen as God-directed rather than self-directed. But if we work for the moment within that conception of autonomous well-being which most of us these days take for granted, this may bring in its train further nature-orientated values not applicable in a non-autonomous framework. I am thinking particularly of the sense of wonder at the world being there at all. As a self-directed person, one cannot blindly accept the frameworks within which one has grown up. This applies to social frameworks of family and wider communities: one learns not automatically to do what one's father, or one's priest, or some political leader demands. But it cannot end with society. The autonomous person will want to reflect on wider frameworks, to see what if any constraints are laid on him or her by nature or the supernatural. It is via a rejection of these as the source of values, as outlined earlier, that autonomous thinkers come to see themselves as living in a world with no apparent meaning or purpose, yet which is palpably *there*. It is perhaps in something of this way that the value of wonder comes to play such a pivotal role in the lives of many of us in this secular age. Insofar as ecological values of respect and responsibility for nature emanate from this sense of wonder, these, too, may be peculiarly associated with the value of autonomy. (As stated earlier, they can also be traced back to attachment to nature, a value not necessarily associated with autonomy as it is found in non- autonomous communities.) Finally, to come back to natural beauty, how far is this valuable to us in part because our attachment to it reinforces this sense of wonder? Are these two values inextricable, at least for an autonomous person? Again, these are questions to which I do not yet have answers.

I have not said anything about the value we attach to the sublimer elements of nature – storms, mountain-tops, the infinity of stars. Bernard Williams (1992: 66–7) has recently linked the sublime to what he has called 'Promethean fear', that is, 'a fear of taking too lightly or inconsiderately our relations to nature'. He sees this as 'based on a sense of an opposition between ourselves and nature, an old, unbounded and potentially dangerous enemy, which requires respect' – a respect which he sees as the root of many of our environmental concerns. While his account seems to make sense for such phenomena as treacherous seas, storms, floods or mountains, it applies less aptly to the starry skies that for Kant were the supreme example of the sublime. Here, I think, we come back, simply, to wonder: for many of us, I suspect, our experience of these boundless expanses has elicited this feeling in us rather than some kind of fear.

If these speculations have anything in them, there may be ways of showing that nature-directed values of these different sorts play an ineliminable role in personal well-being, perhaps not in general, but at least in that autonomous form of well-being now so familiar to us.

I shall turn in a moment to the educational upshot of all this; but, first, a few words about a more purely philosophical point. This brings us back to mainstream British philosophising about personal well-being. I argued earlier that Mill, Moore, Griffin and others did without the notion of a cosmic framework. This claim now needs qualification. If we look at the kinds of activity and experience that these thinkers have listed as ingredients of well-being, we find aesthetic experiences occurring again and again. Given the prominence with which aesthetic reactions figured in the account just given of values directed towards the natural framework – experiences of wonder at the existence of things, delight in the world's beauty, responses to the sublime, imaginative involvement in religious perspectives – it is hard to make sense of the philosophers' claim that aesthetic experience is on a list of universal ingredients of well-being without interpreting it in terms of orientations towards such a framework, even though there is nothing explicitly about this in the theories.

If these thoughts are on the right lines, what follows about education? We have been hampered in our thought about this by the lack of an adequate conception of human well-being. The developmentalist child-centred school rightly placed the child's flourishing at the centre of education; but it made the same mistake as the religiously based educational theory in which it often saw itself in competition. It looked for the *source* of this flourishing in the natural order – in innate seeds of natural development, in its case, rather than in God's dispensation. We would do well to reject such a notion. Parents, teachers and policy-makers need to be at home with a notion of well-being rooted wholly in our human world and broad enough in scope to help children to maintain their bearings in both the social world and a world beyond the social.

This is an unfamiliar notion as far as secular education goes. Religious educators have long emphasised the last aspect just mentioned – helping children to locate themselves in the universe as a whole. But children from non-religious homes – in Britain by far the majority – have often been bereft of guidance from their schools. After a promising envelopment – for some – in the world of catkins and frogspawn at primary level, too many are then left to sort out on their own, with what intellectual resources it is wholly unclear, what relationships they need with the cosmos – as if the proper business of their education had all to do with academic enterprises like French and mathematics and other subjects befitting inclusion in a national curriculum.

This is not to say that non-religious children are brought up without *any* kind of wider framework to their existence. Max Weber in *The Protestant Ethic* claimed that 'the capitalistic economy of the present day is an immense cosmos into which the individual is born, and which presents itself to him, at least as an individual, as an unalterable order of things in which he must live' (1976: 54). At one time, in the culture of the puritans, the everyday world of work and business was invested with religious significance: it was through success in business that human beings made themselves candidates for eternal salvation. The old rationale for the economic framework has now gone. Yet the framework is still 'too much with us', in Wordsworth's words.

In education, as in life in general, a view fostered by the present government over the last 15 years is that schools should be preparing pupils for the 'world of work', with cosmic horizons left to religious education or, since the arrival of the National Curriculum, to work on the development of 'spirituality'. (Whatever that might be: schools have a statutory obligation to promote it, but nobody, despite all the conferences and colloquia held on it in the last couple of years, has come up with any defensible account of what it might mean. The whole area is a conceptual morass, needing at least two research theses in philosophy of education to find some firm ground (fortunately, they are under way here at the Institute). I would advocate an absolute embargo on the use of the terms 'spirituality' or 'spiritual development' in all official documents on education, all conferences on education, all in-service courses for teachers, all inaugural lectures. The words simply hamper the way of thinking.)

At all events, the combination of education for work and religious education that might have made coherent sense for puritan businessmen is now, for more and more of us, meaningless. In our country Christianity is crumbling everywhere except on the radio; and there is serious reflection these days about the significance of economic activity in human flourishing.

Families and schools across the world need to pay more attention to the frameworks of well-being into which they induct children. All of us – in long-standing liberal communities like Britain as much as in countries nearer the edge of social chaos like Russia – need to create an orderly as well as a free society. Order is partly a matter of institutions; but more basically it is a feature of the individual's mind. As part of their conceptual apparatus, children need frameworks of reference within which to place the more particular elements of their well-being. Among social frameworks, the economic framework of work and consumption is undoubtedly important, but just *how* important it should be needs reconsideration. So does a framework provided by a national community, as I hinted earlier.

But social frameworks like the family, the economy and the nation need to find their due place within a larger, natural framework. (We can adopt this as a modest insight from the Hegelian idealist tradition, without all its metaphysical luggage.) Families and schools need more systematically to induct children into the various nature-directed values outlined earlier, certainly at least as options which students can autonomously accept or reject, but perhaps also – if the speculative lines of thought sketched in above can be made to work – as unrejectable, vital constituents of their well-being. Whichever of these views one adopts, here as in other spheres, children from more affluent families often start with an advantage. I am thinking of children brought up in up-market villages in the countryside or in so-called leafy suburbia. Contrast these with young people from flats in inner cities whose contact with the natural world is minimal, whose experience of natural beauty may become confined to little more than seeing attractive people on the streets or in the media. As for schools, how far should there be whole school policies on a secular cosmic framework? Many of the elements are already there, of course – in outings and field trips, ecological or environmental education, work in the biological sciences, geography, the visual arts and literature. But what is done is piecemeal and could benefit from a more coherent approach. Perhaps, too, there could be more coherence in educational thinking about the overlap between social and natural frameworks. How far, for instance, in any reconceptualisation of British nationality, should we take more conscious account of the British landscape and its place in our conception of ourselves – both at first hand and as mediated through art and photography?

Mention of art allows me to introduce the further remark that it is sometimes said that in our secular age, art has replaced religion as the repository of our fundamental values. This is too general a claim as it stands, but at least, as far as schools go, in the revaluation of values I am proposing, aesthetic education would be given greater prominence. If the speculative claims about well-being proved well-founded, children would become attached to the natural world partly by threads of beauty, this aesthetic love of the world merging with a concern for its continued flourishing. Just as moral education fosters an array of virtues of attachment to people and communities, so one function of aesthetic education is to cultivate a range of similar dispositions directed towards nature. 'Aesthetic education' in this context is to be distinguished from 'education in the arts'. Bringing children to see the beauty of the world need not rely wholly, if at all, on art at all: it can be done by direct experience. Equally, much of what we value in the arts is not to do with enhancing our responses to nature: most music, for instance, does not seem to be to have this potentiality; and most fiction is about the social rather than the trans-social. This said, *one* thing we value in *some* of the arts is that they do heighten, or revivify, our aesthetic responses to nature. The part played in this by landscape art, by some architecture and sculpture and by much literature is evident. In addition, it is through the arts that we can come to experience again that primal wonder at the existence of things at all, even where there is no depiction of natural beauty – the aesthetic experience of contemplating, for instance, a painting by Van Gogh of a yellow chair or a pair of peasant boots. Ray Elliott (1993) has described this function of art more eloquently than I ever could in his article on Wittgenstein's aesthetics in the recent Festschrift for Paul Hirst.

Education's task here is not only to *reveal* to children the beauty and wondrousness of the world – for if this were all there were to it, there would be no reason why the children should not forget all this and pass on to other things.

Aesthetic education of this sort has not to do with momentary insight, but with building up habitual responses. If they are indeed permanent constituents of our well-being, we need to be kept in touch with beauty and wonder. Just as religions have rituals, services, prayer and other devices to keep people attached to God, so the secular world, too, needs its bulwarks against ontological forgetting. The arts mentioned can help in this project – and not least when our everyday paths lead, as so many of ours do for so long, through the nature-less expanses of Weber's 'disenchanted' world of economic activity. Neither is this aesthetic education to be conceived individualistically – as if its aim were to bring about aesthetic responses in pupils confronting the universe wholly on their own, like existentialist heroes. We face our world together; and our delight in it is shared. Works of art, as public, sharable, objects, are peculiarly well-fitted to heighten this communal aspect of our experience.

There is much more to be said than this, of course, about that part of a secular education which attends to the widest horizons of our being. And most of it will be said not by philosophers, who perforce work at a certain level of abstraction from practical circumstances. If I have said little about institutional arrangements in this lecture, it is because these are not the central part of the philosophical task in this area. What philosophers can do, first and foremost, is to look more globally at the whole enterprise of education and its aims and the values on which these should rest. I hope at least that I have indicated one direction in which our thought should now go. We need a vision of education in which our attachment to the experienced world is placed centre-stage. Philosophy of education has an irreplaceable role in illuminating the place of a non-religious, non-relative – and, as far as I can make sense of this fashionable term non-post-modernist – cosmic framework in the education of our children. This means in the education of *all* our children.

Notes

1   *The Independent* 6.10.1994.
2   *Social Trends 24* (London: HMSO, 1994), p. 145.
3   Membership of trinitarian churches was 18.6 per cent of the adult UK population in 1975 and 15 per cent in 1987 (*Social Trends 19*, London: HMSO, 1989, p. 178). Extrapolating forwards, this trend would reach zero around 2037. There were 8.063 million members of trinitarian churches in 1975 and 6.72 million in 1992 (Ibid. and *Social Trends 24* (London: HMSO, 1994, p. 145). At a constant rate of decline, there would be no church members by about 2076.

References

Elliott, R. K. (1993) 'Wittgenstein's speculative aesthetics in its ethical context', in R. Barrow and P. White (eds) *Beyond Liberal Education: A Festschrift for Paul H. Hirst*, London: Routledge.
Griffin, J. (1986) *Well-being*, Oxford: Oxford University Press.
Kant, I. (1790) *Critique of Judgment*, Translated by J. H. Bernard (1951), New York: Hafner.
Mencius (1970) *Mencius*, Harmondsworth: Penguin.
Murdoch, I. (1992) *Metaphysics as a Guide to Morals*, London: Chatto & Windus.
Savile, A. (1982) *The Test of Time*, Oxford: Clarendon Press.
Taylor, C. (1989) *Sources of the Self*, Cambridge: Cambridge University Press.
Weber, M. (1976) *The Protestant Ethic and the Spirit of Capitalism*, London: George Allen & Unwin.
Williams, B. (1992) 'Must a concern for the environment be centred on human beings?', in C. C. W. Taylor (ed.) *Ethics and the Environment*, Oxford: Corpus Christi College.

CHAPTER 11

EDUCATION, WORK AND WELL-BEING

Journal of Philosophy of Education (1997), 31(2): 233–47

The 'work-society' that has existed in Britain and comparable countries for the last two centuries is now in crisis: in Ralf Dahrendorf's words, following Hannah Arendt, 'the work-society is running out of work' (Dahrendorf, 1982: 182). With thirty per cent of the British working population now economically inactive, the future of work, its place in personal fulfilment and its distribution are bound to be key issues in general politics and in educational policy well into the next century. Backing practical proposals there needs to be a well thought-out theoretical rationale of a philosophical rather than an empirical kind. What is work? Just how important is it to our well-being? *Is* it a basic human need? What consequences might answers to these questions have for education?

The meaning of work

We need to start with some kind of definition of 'work'. As I shall be using the term, work is a kind of activity. Doing nothing is not working. Doctors may be paid for being on call even though they are inactive, but we think of this as part of their work because of the readiness for activity if required implicit in the notion of being on call. Similarly, passive enjoyment like lying out in the sun is not work.

If work is a form of activity, not all forms of activity are work. Strolling in the countryside is not; and neither need listening to a string quartet be. In neither case does the agent have to intend the activity to produce some end product outside the activity itself. In this the activities are unlike making horseshoes or teaching children. One might, of course, say that one strolls in the woods in order to bring about the end product of an enjoyable stroll, but this is only a restatement of what the activity is and does not introduce an end product outside it. Listening to quartets may be undertaken so as to enlarge one's musical understanding and sensibility – and this does sound like an end product. But one may listen to them also for more intrinsic delights, and if one does so any thought that this is a form of work drops away.

It should be plain that, as I am using the term, 'work' is activity which the agent intends to lead to some end product outside the activity itself. Not all work is paid employment. One can plant a row of beans in one's garden to get a good crop; housewives – and house-husbands too – wash clothes and clean the flat; schoolchildren write essays and do arithmetic. All this is work.

Work can be either autonomous or heteronomous. It is autonomous if its end product constitutes one of your more important goals in life and if you have chosen to do it. Novelists and composers engage in autonomous work; so do many – not all – teachers or health-care workers. Heteronomous work is work whose end product has not been chosen as a major goal. It is work which for some reason one has to do, is constrained to do. The constraints may be of various sorts: God may have urged or driven you to it; you may have to do it as a slave; you may have to do it to earn money to survive; as a pupil at school you may work because your teacher expects this. If you work as a teacher not because teaching people is important among your life goals, but only for the money, your work is heteronomous. If you do it partly for the money, but would do it anyhow even if the money came from a different source, you work autonomously.

Most work that is done in the world is heteronomous. I shall take this as read. The fact that it is does not imply that people do not enjoy doing it. Slaves, some factory workers, even some teachers may hate what they do. But others in this category might work willingly – the priest carrying out God's work, the business person with a high income and all kinds of fringe-benefits, the secretary who likes the company and busyness of the office.

The centrality of work

Heteronomous work takes many forms. It covers virtually all paid employment – all, that is, except that which a person would take on even if unpaid, much housework and house maintenance, shopping, childcare, schoolwork and even activities flowing from being unemployed like filling in forms to claim benefit. Until very recently the striking fact about such work has been that it has filled nearly all our lives. Only pre-school children and retired adults have escaped its demands. Broadly speaking, we have lived to work. This has been so both over a lifetime and, more microscopically, from day to day. For virtually all of us each day has been nearly completely taken up either with work or with what is necessary to work effectively – sleep, eating, washing, eliminating, relaxation, recreation.

The centrality of work in our lives has become, over the centuries, a prominent feature of British culture as well as of others. In the British case it has its roots in the Puritanism of the seventeenth century with its rejection of the contemplative, or monastic, ideal of the religious life and its revolutionary notion that true Christianity lies in the proper performance of one's daily work and (as a woman) domestic duties. A life of hard, unremitting work was seen as a sign that one belonged amongst God's elect – as a token of salvation. As Tawney (1926) and Weber (1976) have both shown, from English and from German sources respectively, the Protestant work ethic was closely connected with the early development of capitalism. Religious and economic motives joined forces to help weave the new gospel of work into the social fabric.

Socialist critics of the new capitalist order, beginning with Marx and extending into the present day, tended to operate within the framework already created. Although Marx criticised the alienated work which capitalism brought with it, he still saw work – unalienated work – as an essential feature of human nature. For the most part, socialist philosophers have gone along with the idea that work, or meaningful work, is a basic human need. Some among them have been more sceptical, notably Bertrand Russell, who saw the origins of the modern cult of work in a pre-industrial serf/slave economy where it was in the interests of the elite to have others labouring for them, and who famously defined 'work' as being: 'of two kinds: first, altering the position of matter at or near the earth's surface relatively to other matter; second, telling other people to do so' (Russell, 1960: 11). Such sceptics and their successors apart, what is remarkable about our culture is the great attachment to the centrality of work shown on all ideological sides – religious, capitalist, socialist.

Schools and schoolwork

What place does the education system have in a society premised, like the British, on the centrality of (largely heteronomous) work? We should reject one familiar way of thinking about this. It is misleading to see the school system as autonomous vis-à-vis 'the world of work' in the sense that it is still an open question whether or not schools should be preparing pupils for this or for something else, for example, for leisure or for personal fulfilment. As soon as they begin compulsory schooling, pupils are as much involved in work as lorry-drivers or mothers looking after children. They are constrained to engage in activities directed to some end product or other whether they want this or not. For them as much as for adults, heteronomous work comes to be the central feature of their lives, the arrival of homework in increasing amounts with the transition to secondary school and the preparation for public examinations hard on its heels powerfully reinforcing this.

If I am right in claiming that, as things are now, work is central to most people's lives as a day-to-day reality, and to nearly everybody's life as a social ideal, it would not be surprising if schools and those who control their curricula made work-related aims central to their thinking: on any reasonable account of education, its aims should fit rather than unfit young people for adult life. Perhaps schools' greatest contribution is in habituation – in involving pupils in work from the age of five and making this progressively more dominant in their lives until sixteen or eighteen. When they leave school, their minds are – ideally, at least – set firm in the work ethos. More than that: since schoolwork is often to do with subject-matter taught in a way remote from young people's lives and interests, it can be a particularly useful device to prepare them for the personally non-significant work which most will be doing as adults.

A second form of preparation is in equipping students, where suitable, with the qualifications needed for entry into 'better' jobs. A third is in arranging the curriculum, and priorities within it, to fit the demands of adult work, highlighting literacy, numeracy, science and technology.

The need to work

I have said something about the meaning of work, its central place in our lives and its central place in schools. I now want to turn to the ethical question about what place work *should have* in human life. Is it, as many socialists and others have argued, a basic human need? I shall proceed by a critical assessment of the views of two socialist philosophers, Richard Norman (1983) and Sean Sayers (1988), who claim that it is.

Other philosophers have written about work in recent times – for example, Arendt (1958), Arneson (1987), Schwartz (1982), and Weil (1977). Elsewhere (White, 1997) I examine their views in some detail. Norman and Sayers stand out among this group in tackling head-on the question of how valuable work is in human lives. It is because this question is central to my present paper that I concentrate on their positions here.

Richard Norman's argument is part of a larger project in ethical naturalism which seeks to base ethical values in human nature. It is through reflection on what we are like as human beings that we quickly light on our biological needs for food, water, air, shelter and so on, whose satisfaction is so central to our flourishing. Norman extends this list of needs beyond the physical to such things as psychic harmony, sexual fulfilment, being treated as persons, not objects, creativeness and rootedness (Norman, 1983: 239). Included in the extended list is 'meaningful, unalienated work'.

What is work of this kind necessary for? Norman makes a general distinction, applicable to the whole range of needs, between what is necessary for mental health, 'understood as that harmony of the personality which enables a person to function effectively' (p. 240), and what is needed for a life of happiness and fulfilment. He further suggests: 'that those needs which have to be satisfied in order for one to be able to function effectively are the same needs whose fuller satisfaction makes for a richly happy life' (p. 241).

As regards the first level of needs, that of effective functioning, Norman states that human beings need among other things to engage in activities which are not totally mindless and mechanical (ibid.). He goes on to say that:

> it is also the case that the richest enjoyments and satisfactions of human life are to be found in the further meeting of these same needs – in work which uses to the full one's creative capacities, and in the life of the emotions, and the many different kinds of human love and solidarity.
>
> (ibid.)

It might well be true that if people engaged in no activities other than mindless and mechanical ones their mental health would suffer. But it does not follow that *work* of some sort is a need at some higher level: it merely follows that activity which uses one's intelligence to a high degree is such a need. The point here is that there are many kinds of intelligent activities and only some of them have to do with producing things. Enjoying rather than creating works of art, playing games, witty conversation – these and other things can be undertaken with great finesse and judgement, but none of them need to be undertaken as work. What Norman would have to show is that if work is indeed a human need, it must itself be necessary for some further end, for example, personal well-being, and not merely a member of a class of things (e.g. highly intelligent activities) which are necessary for it.

I conclude that Norman has not made out a valid case here for meaningful work as a human need. Elsewhere in his book, in the course of a discussion of Marx's ethical views on work, he produces further arguments 'for the claim that work is so important for self-realisation' (p. 177). He writes:

> There is, first, the sheer quantitative dominance of work in relation to other activities. The work which people do to maintain themselves and their dependents engages a great deal of their time, and because it bulks so large it does more than anything else to shape the general character of their lives. Then there is its inescapability. Other activities which people perform are largely a matter of individual choice, but work is the one activity which almost all human beings (other than the young, the old, or the excessively privileged) have to perform in order to maintain themselves. For this reason it forms the common core of people's lives, which sets the pattern for their general character. Finally, there is the fact that people's work is the most clearly public aspect of their lives. It is their work above all that defines them in the eyes of others – and I have stressed previously the importance of being recognised by

others as an aspect of self-realisation. Putting all of this together, we can say that what you are is primarily a matter of what you do, and what you do is primarily a matter of what work you perform.

(pp. 177–8)

This passage lucidly shows the central place that work has – as a matter of fact – in our lives. If it is not only an empirical fact but also a good thing that work should be so central, one could then go on to ask which kinds of work are desirable and which undesirable, and it is not difficult to see how one might make out a case for meaningful rather than mindless work. But how does one get from the empirical fact to the positive value judgement? If work is indeed so quantitatively dominant over other activities in our lives that is not necessarily to be welcomed. It might be something we should have less of. Norman comes near this point in his answer to the objection:

that the reasons just given for making work so central are, in fact, historically transitory. It may be argued that with increasing automation the production of material necessities requires less and less labour time, and that there is a real prospect that in the future people may need to devote only a small portion of their time to work.

(p. 178)

He is inclined to think that even if the average working day were halved (in his eyes a Utopian idea) 'work would still play a large part in people's organisation of their time' (ibid.), although he gives no reasons in support. He is also inclined to think that there may be truth in the objection that 'work has been given its present quantitative and qualitative importance only in modern industrial societies' (ibid.), concluding from this that perhaps:

the need for self-realisation through work is indeed historically and culturally specific. Even so it can still be maintained, at the very least, that within our own society the need is a real and objective one. The idea that one's work determined one's identity, and the stimulus to invest one's energies in that work, are so deeply embedded in our culture that no one could now find full satisfaction in a life which did not contain its component of meaningful work.

(p. 179)

This final position seems to me decidedly shaky. In fact, we have been here before – a couple of paragraphs ago. The centrality of work is certainly deeply embedded in the culture. But this fact does nothing to shore up the evaluative conclusion that in our society work is a well-being (or self-realisation) need. For all we know, people's well-being in that society may be best served by challenging and undermining work's hegemony. We may, for all we know, do well to reject the view that work determines our identity: perhaps we would flourish better if attachment to work were not so indelibly a part of us.

Sean Sayers (1988) defends the central contention in Marxist socialism 'that socially productive labour is, in Marx's words, man's essential activity' (p. 722). Like Norman, whose views are also in the Marxist tradition, if less tied to Marx's writings themselves, Sayers believes there is a human need to work. 'Work' he defines as a form of productive activity directed towards useful ends. It is also for the most part a social activity (pp. 726–7). He seems ambivalent on whether or not 'work' should be equated with 'a job', with 'paid employment'. On the one hand, he states that there are many kinds of work which do not take the form of a job, not least domestic work traditionally performed by women (p. 727). On the other hand, we find statements like 'women feel a need – an inner need – for work: a need for a job as an end in itself...' (p. 728); or 'the socialist principle of the "right to work" is a demand for jobs' (p. 729).

Leaving this last discrepancy on one side, we can see that Sayers's definition is narrower than the one I proposed at the beginning of the paper. He wants to restrict 'work' to activity aimed at useful ends, whereas I treated it only as activity directed towards some kind of end product, not necessarily a useful one. If something is useful, it is a means to some end. But, following my account, producing a work of art counts as work even though one's symphony or poem is created as an object of intrinsic interest. There might also be 'useless work' in another sense – as in the case of soldiers on basic training kept busy by cutting grass with scissors. In this case, the work might still be useful to their superiors as a form of obedience-training. But even if it falls as a counter-example to the claim that work is necessarily directed towards useful ends, the art example still stands.

How does Sayers support his claim that there is a human need to work? He distances himself from the view, which he locates in Norman, that this is rooted in the unique creativity to be found in human nature 'which distinguishes us from the rest of animal creation' (p. 732). The socialist view of work 'rejects the idea of a universal and eternal human nature'. Human nature changes historically: 'Through the activity of labour, people develop their powers and capacities and create new needs – including the need to work.'

This has not always been so. In hunter-gatherer societies, indeed in many other pre-industrial societies, this need has not yet developed. Industrialism has brought with it a new emphasis on work and the virtues of work:

> Thus the modern need to work, although it is undoubtedly a historically developed need, should not be judged 'false' or 'artificial' simply for that reason. On the contrary, it is a real and ineliminable feature of contemporary psychology. For in the course of the historical developments I have been outlining, new habits, new attitudes, new needs have been created and old ones relinquished. Human nature itself has been transformed.
>
> (p. 736)

My difficulty with this argument is the same as that I have with Norman's. Facts about the emphasis industrial societies have placed on work or about individuals' attachment to the work ethic are one thing, the contention that we have a need to work another. One simply cannot derive the latter from the former.

So we are still left wondering why Sayers insists on this need. What does he see work as necessary for? He does not go into this so we can only speculate. Is it necessary to individual flourishing? Perhaps as a Marxist he would reject the 'individualism' embedded in this notion. Is it necessary (in contemporary industrial societies) not to individuals but to humanity in general as part of its historical development? I do not know whether Sayers would want to say this. If he did, we would have to tackle the credentials of Marxist theory as a whole, which is beyond my present remit.

Although it is not surprising that a Marxist writer like Sayers should wish to defend solidly the alleged human need to work, given the centrality which Marx attached to productive work as 'the first premise of all human existence' (Marx and Engels, 1965, Part 1: 48), it is disappointing at the same time that he sees so little virtue in the idea of liberating people, at least to some degree, from work's constraints, especially the time it takes up in and dominance over people's lives. For him, socialism demands 'not the liberation of people from work...but rather the liberation of work...from the stultifying confines of the capitalist system' (p. 740). I do not see why there need be an either/or. If personal autonomy is an important value, some kind of diminution of the power of the work ethic over our lives would seem reasonable. But here, perhaps, the cast of mind of Marxist socialism is at odds with that of a more liberal-democratic version. As will become clear, if it is insufficiently clear already, my own alignment is with the latter.

Why work?

I conclude that it has not been shown – at least, so far – that work is a basic human need for any individual. What place, then, does it have in personal flourishing? There is a lot that one could and perhaps should say about this. Here, to simplify matters, I shall assume that the more a person flourishes, the more he or she attains what for him or her are among the more important goals or ends in their lives. Of two people, equally set on a life of philosophising, intimate relationships and watching rugby, the one who fails his philosophy degree, whose friends all drift away and who then goes blind is likely to lead a life of lesser well-being than someone who successfully achieves these aims.

In modern industrial societies one widespread conception of personal flourishing brings with it the notion of personal autonomy. This adds to the idea of the satisfaction of one's major goals the further thought that these are goals one has chosen oneself, as a self-directed person – as distinct from goals laid down by custom or some religious or political authority. All of us these days, except those of us living in some strict religious community where we see our lives as directed by God's will rather than our own, would subscribe to the ideal of autonomy. I shall take it as read henceforth in what I say about the place of work in individual well-being. As before, I shall distinguish between autonomous and heteronomous work.

The place of autonomous work in personal well-being

Autonomous work is one possible ingredient in the good life, but it has its legitimate competitors. To put all or most of the emphasis on such things as artistic creation, craft activity or social service is to downplay activities like cycling, religious contemplation, walking on the downs, listening to music, eating out. None of these need involve producing any kind of end product; all of them could be among a person's major commitments. In addition to activities, major goals may also include desires to be a certain sort of person – to be friendly, fair-minded, a person of principle. If not all major goals are work-goals, must the latter figure among any particular person's major goals? Could one autonomously build a life around non-work?

Many, perhaps most, of us, given the power to choose, probably would go for end product goals, at least as part of the total package. But there is, as far as I can see, no necessity for us to do so: what mix we adopt is – within limits, to exclude the ethically suspect – up to us. G. E. Moore's ideal of life, as described in *Principia Ethica*, revolved around the enjoyment of beauty and intimate personal relationships (Moore, 1903). Work, even autonomous work, had no place in it. In some versions of the spiritual life, everything is subordinated to contemplation of the divine. Autonomous work may be something many of us would want to include in our lives in some way; but it does not seem to be strictly a need, a necessity.

A possible objection here might be that although one can imagine lives which are both workless and flourishing, this could only be on some restricted notion of flourishing which did not require much if any concern for the well-being of others. Rich self-centred fainéants may find fulfilment in a round of pleasures. The Bloomsbury ideal insists at least on intimate relationships, but its altruistic sensitivities evaporate beyond the salon and the sitting room. If we are working with a notion of autonomous well-being, which has written into it a responsiveness to the needs and aspirations of others across the national community and beyond, will this not necessarily include among its major goals wanting to serve others in some way – attending to their physical or other needs, or helping them to realise important goals? If so, will not autonomous well-being embrace within it autonomous work?

Not necessarily. Even if one spends part of one's life working for others, this need not be autonomous work – even if one is an autonomous agent. One may autonomously choose to make supermarket trolleys or paperclips where these products have no personal significance, but where the money one earns enables one to lead a decent life, attentive to others' needs and wants as well as one's own.

Pressing for autonomous work to be an indispensable element of the good life ignores the elasticity of the latter concept, the very many forms it can take. This is important educationally, as insisting to younger people on the indispensability of autonomous work limits their possibilities. There is even less reason to believe that autonomous work must be *central* to a human life. Some people will want it to be in their own case, but others will prefer a variety of types of major goal. Social policy should reflect this and encourage the availability of a wide variety of ways of life in which autonomous work might – or might not – find a place.

The place of heteronomous work in personal well-being

For many it would be an ideal world if the only work anyone ever did were autonomous. But the real world is not like that. Drains have to be laid, buses driven, carpets hoovered. In any modern society all sorts of jobs have to be done which few would wish to do unless they had to. Some heteronomous work is unavoidable. But if the social ideal is that every individual should lead a flourishing life, there, is a good reason for making whatever heteronomous work there has to be as compatible as possible with this. How?

Heteronomous work, as constrained, is *prima facie* in conflict with the ideal of an autonomous life and would seem to diminish one's well-being rather than promote it. Is the way forward, then, to try to reduce it to a minimum? This does not strictly follow, because a job's *prima facie* disbenefits might be outweighed by financial or psychological advantages – if, for instance, an otherwise unattractive job earned one extremely high wages for two or three hours work a day. But it would seem desirable, if not to reduce heteronomous work to a minimum, at least to reduce it, especially because the *prima facie* drawbacks are unlikely to be countered in this way in very many cases.

How this reduction might come about is for the most part a practical rather than a philosophical matter, about scope for further automation, for instance. But there are ethical dimensions too. I am thinking of the interconnections between work, the worker's character and the character and general well-being of those affected by the work.

Some work is ethically repellent and cannot be undertaken without threat to one's moral integrity. Extorting money from shopkeepers for protection is an extreme example, but any work which treats others merely as means to ends also falls into this category. As well as endangering one's own integrity, it is likely to harm these other people in various ways. The business world of making money, managing, selling, advertising, is always at ethical risk here – which is not to say that codes of good practice and other controls cannot redeem it. If there is a case for reducing the volume of heteronomous work on ethical grounds, perhaps this is the place to start.

I turn from the powerful to the powerless, from managers to managed. The case for reducing unpleasant work – work which is mechanical, exhausting, dangerous or boring – in the interests of personal well-being is overwhelming. There is no need to press the familiar point that in a society like ours a lot of work like this goes into producing goods and services which are superfluous to people's basic needs and uncoerced preferences, and which depend on mass advertising to get us to want them. The wastefulness of our consumer society heaps up behind it a quite unnecessary mountain of heteronomous work. Individual well-being can be dealt a double blow: the temptations and pressures of consumerism can knock *consumers'* value-hierarchy out of kilter, and can oblige themselves or others as *producers* to spend too much of their lives in thrall to labouring.

What do I mean by 'knock their value-hierarchy out of kilter'? Our consumerist society is a culture of temptation. Newspapers, magazines, television and advertisements fill our value-horizons with the imagined delights of status, sex, food and drink, as goods either in their own right or associated with some other product. More general than these temptations is the temptation to acquire goods as such – as when we feel that we cannot leave *Our Price* or *Next* empty-handed, even though so far we have seen nothing that we want. The upshot is that people buy masses of goods and services not because they need them, but out of temptation. If we were better equipped to understand and withstand these temptations, we would be less likely to want to buy things. If so, less unattractive heteronomous work might have to be engaged in to produce them.

Underlying the consumer society is a utilitarianism which emphasises the maximisation of welfare and is manifested in the efforts of companies and governments to increase output, growth, profits, GNP without limit. Over the last twenty years philosophers have subjected utilitarian ethics to radical criticism. Its maximising assumption that the supreme ethical principle is that the greatest happiness ought to be produced has been shown to be without foundation; thinkers like Michael Slote (1989) argue for 'satisficing' policies – which call for people having enough of life's goods – rather than 'optimising' approaches which demand the best possible. If one follows this line of thought in the present context, the centrality of work in individuals' lives and in social policy may with luck be replaced in both spheres by a different ideal: the centrality of a satisfactory life for all.

Education and the future of work

In previous sections I have only begun to sketch out the place that work should have in personal well-being. There is much more to be said. I concluded that (a) assuming personal well-being is that of autonomous persons, the latter may well wish to include autonomous work among their major goals, although, because these could also embrace non-work activities, there seems no *necessity* for them to do so: it has not been shown that autonomous work is a human need; (b) there is no good reason why we should remain attached to the traditional doctrine that work should be central to our lives; and (c) there is a strong case for reducing the amount of heteronomous work.

It would be too bold to believe that Britain and comparable societies *will* be moving in these desirable directions. Indeed, the ex-Secretary for Education John Patten's statement (*Times Educational Supplement*, 9.6.1995) that: 'We need the help of religious education in order to underpin a re-born theology of work which in its turn can be a foundation for the moral legitimacy of the free market' reminds us that not everyone would want to put work's centrality behind them. Support for it is still strong in official thinking across the left-right spectrum and across the secular–religious divide especially on the right-hand sides of these phrases.

But suppose that the work ethic *does* weaken, what role might schools play in the new order? As far as their aims are concerned, one would expect all schools to concentrate on preparing people for autonomous well-being rather than a life at work. Among other things, this preparation would open up horizons on possible major goals which pupils might wish to pursue. These would include all sorts of activities and other ends, among them forms of autonomous work. They would also embrace types of heteronomous work – for example, kinds of paid employment or housework – which might still play a part in a flourishing life, given that their disadvantages were sufficiently outweighed by other considerations. The school's task in opening up these various options would be partly informative – to make pupils aware of possibilities, and partly reflective – to encourage them to think of benefits and disbenefits, so that they were adequately equipped to give their preferences appropriate status within their system of goals. It should go without saying that the range of activities, both work activities and non-work ones, to which children would be introduced should not be confined by social class. Making children aware of work-related options is a task that the school could and should share with the family, the more sophisticated part of it being left to schools.

As well as an understanding of specific forms of work and non-work – those selectable as options – pupils would also need an understanding of the operations of the economy as a whole, as well as of its technological – scientific basis. This would be essential background knowledge both for their own self-directed choices and for their developing interests in helping to satisfy the needs and preferences of other people.

Pupils should also be encouraged to reflect on the place of work in their own and other cultures and in human life more generally. For British children this would mean becoming aware of the traditional work ethic and the centrality assumption which has emanated from it. Schools should no longer unquestioningly induct them into this.

Personal qualities, as well as intellectual achievements, would also need to be fostered. An account of these could be a study in its own right. Here let me just mention the virtues necessary to withstand consumerist temptations, the salesman's appeals to one's bodily appetites, acquisitive instincts and desires for status and recognition that both generate superfluous work and threaten the consumer's psychic harmony. Families would be the first site for such withstanding, but schools could and should support what they do.

I conclude this section and the paper as a whole with a comment not on the school's aims but on its procedures. We saw earlier that, as things are, schools mirror in their own arrangements the centrality of work in the larger culture. Pupils are constrained, whether they like it or not, to come to school and to engage in various kinds of productive activity, homework as well as schoolwork, for most of their waking day. If work patterns changed in the wider society and the work ethic lost its old authority, schools would no longer have to socialise children in these ways into accepting work's centrality. To do this would be counter-productive.

A new kind of socialisation, based on a new kind of mirroring, would become appropriate.

I have two suggestions here:

(a) Non-work-based forms of learning as well as work-based forms of it should be consciously promoted. Some people, like Dewey, have wanted to base learning on the occupations of the outside world. But even in ordinary, non-Deweyan schools most learning that actually goes on is work-related. Pupils are set tasks, pieces of work to do: they do sums, write stories, draw, conduct experiments. I by no means wish to decry this, but would only make two points.

First, the fact that work is going on in schools in all these kinds of ways does not necessarily imply that learning is also taking place. As we know, teachers can, and some do, keep children's heads down doing fraction-sums with which they are already thoroughly familiar, or, worse, copying out material from textbooks in a mindless way. If schools are to become learning-places rather than mere work-places, teachers need to bear this conceptual distinction in mind.

My second point is that not all forms of learning are work-related. In the home a young child learns to talk through interaction with parents and siblings, rather than by being given tasks which are to emanate in some end product. Children learn by example and through the persistent correction and shaping of their behaviour to be truthful, thoughtful, self-controlled, appropriately confident: again, they do not, as a rule, engage in activities intentionally designed to lead to such end products. (Deliberate attempts at self-creation on the part of older children and adults are perhaps another story.) Think, finally, of everything people learn from books that they have really enjoyed, books not picked up with productive goals in view, but more for pleasure, or out of curiosity – novels, biographies, history books and others. There are no doubt other types of learning which do not involve the learner in working, but the examples just given are enough to suggest that, if we want schools to mirror a societal shift from the centrality of work to the centrality of activity, teachers can begin to alter conventional practice by consciously tilting the balance from work-based to non-work-based forms of learning. This might also become part of the agenda of teacher education. It might involve, among other things, encouraging reflection on such concrete phenomena as classroom furniture and design: as things are now, many classrooms are so set up that work-activities are the only ones that could take place in them.

(b) There is another way in which teachers and schools can challenge the centrality of work. That is by rethinking the shape of the school day. At present, in Britain pupils work through from nine in the morning to half-past three or four in the afternoon. This already earmarks most of their waking day as work-related. With homework added to this, the doctrine of work's centrality is further reinforced. So why not challenge the doctrine – and its daily reinforcement – by reducing the time students at school spend on compulsory curriculum activities?

In my first book (White, 1973) I argued for a shorter compulsory school day coupled with a system of voluntary after-school optional activities modelled on a de-ideologised version of the Soviet system of Pioneer circles. Pupils would be able to choose from a wide range of activities – academic, creative, practical, recreational, athletic. My grounds for a divided school day were partly libertarian: it seemed to me *prima facie* an infringement of children's freedom to compel them to come to school and then compel them to attend classes in a whole range of mandatory subjects. If compulsion were to be justified at all, it had to be clearly in the interests of the child. Only some of the school's traditional areas of study seemed to me to pass this test; these, I suggested, could well be covered in a shortened school day. Other school activities – for example, team games, creative activities in the arts, even foreign languages – could well be transferred to the options system.

I think now that there were problems about basing the argument on libertarian foundations, but the notion of a divided school day is still appealing for another reason. It can help supply us with the new mirror mentioned earlier. Life should not be all (largely constrained) work, and neither should school. At the centre of both should be the autonomous life of self-chosen major goals. In adult life some heteronomous work would be unavoidable for most people – they would still have to work to eat and not all would be lucky enough to do autonomous work. Most school children would find the work they were asked to do in the compulsory part of the day more constraining than the self-chosen activities; although in their case the compulsory work would be necessary not for survival but as a necessary condition of autonomous personhood in later life.

Under this new system, teachers dealing with the compulsory curriculum would also be working a short school day. As well as having more opportunities in their free time for the autonomous activities of intellectual, recreational and artistic kinds which so many actual teachers would welcome, they would serve as models for their pupils of what adult life and work could be like and of the enthusiasm with which one could engage in them.

Teachers are vocational models today of course – daily reminders to their pupils of unremitting busyness. But their impact could be quite otherwise.

References

Arendt, H. (1958) *The Human Condition*, New York: Doubleday Anchor.
Arneson, R. (1987) 'Meaningful work and market socialism', *Ethics*, 97.
Dahrendorf, R. (1982) *On Britain*, London: British Broadcasting Corporation.
Marx, K. and Engels, F. (1965) *The German Ideology*, London: Lawrence and Wishart.
Moore, G. E. (1903) *Principia Elhica*, Cambridge: Cambridge University Press.
Norman, R. (1983) *The Moral Philosophers*, Oxford: Clarendon Press
Pahl, R. E. (ed.) (1988) *On Work: Historical, Comparative and Theoretical Approaches*, Oxford: Blackwell.
Russell, B. (1960) *In Praise of Idleness*, London: Unwin Books.
Sayers, S. (1988) 'The need to work: a perspective from philosophy', in R. E. Pahl (ed.), *On Work: Historical, Comparative and Theoretical Approaches*, Oxford: Blackwell.
Schwartz, A. (1982) 'Meaningful work', *Ethics*, 92.
Slote, M. (1989) *Beyond Optimising*, Cambridge, MA: Harvard University Press.
Tawney, R. H. (1926) *Religion and the Rise of Capitalism*, West Drayton: Penguin.
Weber, M. (1976) *The Protestant Ethic and the Spirit of Capitalism*, London: Allen and Unwin.
Weil, S. (1977) 'Factory work', in G. Panichas (ed.), *Simone Weil Reader*, New York: Moyer Bell.
White, J. (1973) *Towards a Compulsory Curriculum*, London: Routledge and Kegan Paul.
White, J. (1997) *Education and the End of Work: A New Philosophy of Work and Learning*, London: Cassell.

CHAPTER 12

EDUCATION, THE MARKET AND THE NATURE OF PERSONAL WELL-BEING

British Journal of Educational Studies (2002), 50(4): 442–56

A key aim of education is to help students to lead personally fulfilling lives. The aim has to do with *the pupil's* well-being, not – at least, not initially – with his or her moral responsibilities towards other people.

The moral aims of education also have personal well-being at their core. If children are brought up to be morally sensitive to others' needs and interests, it is the well-being of these others to which they must attend. So at the heart of both the prudential and the moral aspects of education is the notion of individual flourishing.

In this paper I will be focusing on the former – on education insofar as it aims to help those being educated to lead flourishing lives. (I am not assuming that this aim is entirely separate from education's moral aims. Whether a flourishing life from a prudential point of view must contain an altruistic element is an issue I shall leave open at this point.)

In England and Wales it is only since 2000 that the government has laid down for schools, in any detailed way, what their aims should be. These include 'personal' aims to do with helping the pupil to lead a flourishing life. Before 1988, aims were in the hands of schools and teachers. The year 1988 saw the introduction of the National Curriculum, but despite its complicated programmes in specific subjects it came with next to nothing in the way of overall aims attached to it – a mere two lines. The post-2000 National Curriculum is very different. The new National Curriculum Handbook begins with a four-page statement of aims and underpinning values. In the original draft of this (QCA, 1999), the first of these values mentioned is 'a belief in education as a route to the well-being and development of the individual'. (This became somewhat more complex in its final version (DfEE/QCA, 1999: 10), but the basic notion is still the same.)

* * *

What, then, is personal well-being? What is it for an individual to lead a flourishing life? This is an ancient philosophical question. The fact that it is shows how essential philosophy is for educational policy. If foremost among the values which underlie a national education system is the well-being of the individual, policymakers need to be able to say what that well-being consists in – and this plunges them immediately into issues of great depth and complexity that go back to Plato.

A condition of personal flourishing is that, by and large, one's basic needs are met. No one can lead a fulfilled life without food or shelter or money. What a fuller list of such needs would be – to what extent, for instance, it should include health or liberty – is an issue I shall bypass here in favour of another question: what counts as a life of well-being given that one's basic needs are broadly met?

Here a core issue – and one of great significance for everyday educational decisions – is this. Can one draw up a reliable objective list of the components of personal well-being, components which apply to any human being whether they are attracted to them or not? Or is well-being a subjective matter, consisting in the satisfaction of those desires of the individual which matter most to him or her?

The significance of this distinction for education should be clear. Suppose we take some common elements among those contemporary philosophers who favour the objective view. A quick survey of leading writers reveals that most of the following items appear on list after list:

1   accomplishing things in one's life which make that life meaningful;
2   being self-directed or autonomous in the conduct of one's life;
3   knowledge and understanding;
4   the enjoyment of beauty;
5   deep personal relationships;
6   moral goodness;
7   sensual pleasures.

Suppose it could be conclusively shown that these are the main components of anyone's well-being. Educators would then have a good reason to steer pupils towards these things as ends in themselves. Not that all of them typically depend on institutionalised learning. Where schools *can* contribute to them, teachers have reason to be confident that, in equipping their charges with different kinds of understanding, with aesthetic sensitivity, with dispositions towards self-directedness and accomplishment, they are enriching their lives. They need not fear that they are paternalistically imposing ends which may be important to themselves, the teachers, but simply reflect their own subjective preferences. For on the account we are considering the values are universal components of human well-being.

This does not imply that teachers must lead pupils to believe that, come what may, they cannot turn their backs on any of the items, that is, that they must all continue to be involved in aesthetic and intellectual matters or deep relationships throughout their lives. For the existence of an objective list of personal goods is compatible with differences in the way individuals weigh these goods. For some, for instance, aesthetic matters may be of maximum significance in their lives while intimate relationships count for much less. But at least these learners would have to adopt a certain attitude towards rejected or downplayed values: they would still have to come to see them as objective constituents of human well-being, valuing them as such when they see them highlighted in other people's lives, even though they do not highlight them themselves.

It is one thing to draw up allegedly objective lists of personal goods, another to *show* their objectivity. How far do lists merely reflect the subjective preferences of their proponents? Moore's (1903, ch. 6) ideal values – the pursuit of beauty and of personal intimacy – were those of the Bloomsbury group with which he was connected. In philosophy of education, the 'intrinsically valuable activities' favoured by Peters (1966, ch. 5) are those to do with the pursuit of truth, Peters' own master passion, rather than, say, the arts.

One reason for adopting a cautious scepticism towards objective lists is their potential significance, already mentioned, in shaping social, including educational, policy. If they are well-founded, state partiality towards, say, the worlds of academe or the arts, or towards an intellectually biased school curriculum may well be in order. But until such well-foundedness can be shown to exist, why should public policy favour the listed goods?

* * *

A challenge to the objective list view is the characterisation of personal well-being in terms of the satisfaction of an individual's major informed preferences. Personal good is now a function of an individual's desires – and not determinable independently of these as on the objective theory. *Major* preferences come into the picture, since any individual's desires are hierarchically structured and if a particular person attaches a lot of weight to the place of watching football in his life but much less weight to eating oysters, then his well-being is more a function of success in the former project than in the latter. *Informed* preferences are important, because even major desires can be based on illusion or insufficient understanding – for instance, wanting to be a poet while imagining that one is blessed with a poetic gift and knowing nothing about the craft and its traditions – and it would be odd for success in deluded activities of this sort to count towards one's flourishing.

What might be the educational applications of this subjective theory of the good? One application is this. In a liberal society we may assume that individuals will themselves choose which major informed preferences they wish to satisfy. A key aim of education here is to equip them for such choices. This entails providing them with whatever acquaintance is necessary with a wide range of possible intrinsic goods from which to make informed choices. Items favoured on most objective views – such as engagement in aesthetic activities – will be included, but they will not be privileged over other items. As on the objective view, individual pupils may reject or downplay such items as aesthetic activity. But they do not have to reject them for other objective list goods. If their major preferences are for the acquisition of material goods or others' recognition and they have no place for intellectual or other objective list pursuits, they can still lead a flourishing life if successful in attaining their preferred goals.

* * *

I would like to connect this discussion of the two perspectives on personal well-being with recent arguments by John O'Neill about well-being and the market. Here, as in the argument so far, my main interest will be in applications to education.

O'Neill's 1998 book *The Market: Ethics, Knowledge and Politics* examines notions of individual well-being embodied in various arguments in favour of the market. I will not run through them all here. The most defensible account in O'Neill's eyes turns out to be the subjectivist view I sketched earlier.

> Well-being can be identified with the satisfaction of fully informed preferences. The position allows for error but still holds that whether something is good for a person depends ultimately on what they would want or value. What is good for us is still determined ultimately by our preferences.
> (O'Neill, 1998: 47)

O'Neill's argument is interesting because, if one assumes a subjectivist framework on the flourishing life, it enables one to see education as much more intimately connected with the market than it is often taken to be. The two institutions are sometimes treated as mutually antagonistic, or at least in uneasy tension with each other. O'Neill's discussion suggests a wider perspective – of the education system as one branch of social activity working with other agencies, both public and private, in the pursuit of common ends.

A partial version of this ideal is familiar enough. Like other public services, the health service is intended to provide one necessary condition of a flourishing life – good health, just as the education service is intended to supply another – which includes acquaintance with possible options. The private sector, if sufficiently controlled, can also work towards the same end, providing the wealth necessary for personal flourishing as well as employment opportunities which enlarge a person's range of life-choices.

O'Neill shows – by implication – how a more radical version of this ideal is possible. The private sector is not now merely an agency, like the health service, for the satisfaction of *basic needs* – in its case, adequate wealth and material goods. The market can bring with it, too, an ethical conception of the *final ends* of human life. It locates these, in the most sophisticated version, in the satisfaction of fully informed individual preferences. As such, it is itself an educational vehicle, reinforcing in each of its everyday transactions this message about the *summum bonum*. Schools, universities and families are not the only, or even the most important, educational institutions. Neither are they champions of 'eternal human values' which stand opposed to the acquisitive values of the market. For schools and families and the market are, or should be, all working together in the same direction. They are all promoters of individual well-being, as conceived on the subjectivist theory. Schools, colleges and families open up new options, steering as clear as they can from paternalist privileging of some over others. The market, in opening up its own ranges of options to meet the consumer's autonomous preferences, reinforces the implicit messages about personal well-being that the educational bodies have been transmitting.

* * *

How adequate is the picture just presented?

A large part of the answer has to do with the adequacy of the subjectivist theory of personal well-being. This is O'Neill's chief target. He supports an objectivist view, founded on the commonalities of human nature. If he is right, what he calls the strongest justification for the market collapses and there is a strong case for basing educational aims on objective goods. If they were so based, the education system and the market would tug, after all, in different directions.

I will look at O'Neill's objectivism later. First, though, I would like to stay within the subjectivist framework and ask whether, *within this framework*, educational aims and the market could not still be at loggerheads.

Behind the *version* of subjectivism adopted by leading market theorists – that individual well-being (utility) resides in the satisfaction of one's major informed preferences – is the assumption that one's preferences are revealed in the choices one makes in the market place (Sumner, 1996: 115–16). This effectively rules out preferences which cannot be costed in monetary terms (p. 118). While it caters for my preference for a Mercedes over a Volkswagen Golf, it cannot encompass the value I attach to my relationship with my wife over that with a colleague at work. The economists' narrow definition of well-being in monetary terms fits some of the ways we commonly think about the topic: if you are 'better off' than someone else, for instance, that means you have more money than them. But it fails to fit what we normally understand by 'flourishing'. This is partly because there is a whole range of goods that are left out – friendship, for instance, or self-understanding, aesthetic enjoyment of nature, personal autonomy or bodily pleasures. These are all goods that may be prized as making for a more fulfilled life, whether on a subjectivist or an objectivist account of well-being. It is also because the satisfaction of informed market-place preferences, in itself, may not count towards one's own well-being as normally understood: one may buy goods not for one's own benefit but out of some motive of altruism or obligation (Sumner, 1996: 120).

All this supports the thesis that within a *broad* subjectivist framework, that is, one not necessarily tied to choices in the market place, educational aims and the market could still be in tension. If the relevant aim of education in this context is to open up options from which students may select their preferences, on many of these options – aesthetic and intellectual enjoyments, say – no price can be put.

Even so, the education system and the market could *still* work together towards the same overall aim of helping people to satisfy their major informed preferences. The two agencies would be providing *different sorts* of intrinsically desired options: those that cannot be bought or sold, like aesthetic awareness or scientific understanding, and those which can, like owning a yacht. (If we include extrinsically desired goods, the education system can come even closer to the market: a student may seek scientific understanding as a commodity whose use can be sold in the vocational market place.)

* * *

If we are working within a broad subjectivist framework, the idea that education and the market are cooperating promoters of individual well-being may then be hard to resist. But will the subjective account do?

One much-discussed problem is that the satisfaction of *some* informed major preferences seems to have no bearing on one's well-being. Suppose I want people living two centuries hence to lead lives of great personal fulfilment. Let us take it that this is indeed what happens. How can something which occurs in the twenty-third century affect my well-being in the twenty-first (Griffin, 1986: 23; Sumner, 1996: 126)?

Could one cope with this problem by ruling out desires for happenings after one's death? Perhaps. But another difficulty may be more recalcitrant. It is not inconceivable that someone may want most of all in life to engage in some activity which many of us would call bizarre or trivial. John Rawls (1972: 432) famously invented a person whose greatest joy was in counting the blades of grass in city parks. Or take people always glued to patchinko machines, television game shows or computer games. In practice there may well often be pathological reasons why people do some of these things. But let us imagine we are talking about rational, informed choices. Would we be willing to say that these people are leading nourishing or fulfilled lives?

Insofar as we have doubts, is this because we are working with some richer notion of the contours of a flourishing life? If so, does this cast doubt on the idea, implicit in subjectivism, that the only authority on the prudentially good life can be the individual himself or herself?

Doubts like these can urge one in the direction of objectivism. O'Neill is, as already stated, an objectivist. He holds that an individual's well-being is objectively rooted in human nature, 'in the development other characteristically human capacities'

(O'Neill, 1993: 73). The inspiration for this is Aristotelian. He describes his view as:

> an Aristotelian conception of well-being according to which well-being should be characterised not in terms of having the right subjective states, as the hedonist claims, nor in terms of the satisfaction of preferences as modern welfare economics assumes, but rather in terms of a set of objective goods a person might possess, for example friends, the contemplation of what is beautiful and wonderful, the development of one's capacities, the ability to shape one's life, and so on.
>
> (O'Neill, 1993: 3)

O'Neill's adherence to an objective list of personal goods enables him to support the existence of a network of non-market institutions and practices alongside the market. These have to do, among other things with the promotion of science and other forms of knowledge, the arts, respect for the natural world, friendship (see, e.g. O'Neill, 1993: 88–9, 143). Education plays a vital role in developing the specific human capacities involved in such pursuits. It 'increases the well-being of the agent since it widens her powers to realise significant goods and achievements' (ibid.: 80).

* * *

O'Neill's position faces several difficulties. First, what are these 'characteristically human capacities'? In the long quotation above O'Neill's examples include capacities for friendship, the contemplation of what is beautiful and wonderful, and the ability to shape one's life. All these are certainly phenomena absent in other animals. But, notoriously, there are also capacities absent in other animals and found only in humans like the capacity self-consciously to enjoy another's suffering. Is the development of this capacity an aspect of a human being's flourishing?

No doubt any item which makes a contribution to human flourishing – enjoyment of art, say, or physical pleasure, or having a deep personal relationship – must be the kind of thing that human beings can desire and for which we have a capacity. But this is not to say that an objective list of values can be *read off* from a list of our characteristically human capacities.

Does this latter term exclude capacities we share with other animals, like capacities for physical pleasure? O'Neill's 'characteristically human capacities' only include more high-flown items like the contemplation of beauty and the ability to shape one's life – items of which other animals are incapable. But why should the pleasures of food, drink, sex and exercise not count towards a flourishing human life?

O'Neill's example of 'the ability to shape one's life' also brings up another problem. He is talking about the value which he refers to elsewhere as 'autonomy' (O'Neill, 1998, chs 5, 6). There are grounds for thinking that autonomy is a peculiarly modern ideal of personal fulfilment, which, although it had its seeds in ancient Greece, has come to prominence especially with the rise of liberalism and modern industrial societies over the past four centuries (see Raz, 1986, ch. 14). How valid is it, then, to read this value into *human nature itself*?

If these difficulties strike home, O'Neill may be not so much deriving values from human nature as giving an account of human nature which fits values independently posited. If this is so, the objectivity of his list of goods is in doubt.

* * *

In his 1998 book O'Neill modifies his position on human well-being. He still holds on to an objectivist account dependent on Aristotle, but denies that 'the objective standards of the good are ahistorical and fixed' (p. 51). He is attracted now by

> the kind of historicised Aristotelianism one finds in Kant, Hegel and Marx, which with Aristotle claims that it is the exercise of human powers and capacities that is constitutive of human well-being, but argues that these develop historically and are not determined by some fixed biological fact... On this account there is an objective standard of well-being given by our human powers, but this is not a given standard.
>
> (ibid.)

O'Neill says that he would endorse this view, but only given major qualifications – that passive as well as active powers are taken into account, that human nature is not infinitely plastic, and that it is not to be assumed that later is better, that is, that historical progress is inevitable (p. 52).

This modification certainly takes the edge off the two criticisms of O'Neill's 1993 position, but it faces a further difficulty of its own. What criteria are there for identifying when the historical changes which produce alterations in the objective standard of well-being occur? O'Neill clearly rejects any developmentalist account, such as that found in Kant (ibid.: 52), which implies that later is better. He still wants to hold on to a notion of historical development, but in the absence of the criteria just mentioned, we have no reason for embracing this.

* * *

All this has consequences for the issue raised earlier about the relationship between educational institutions and the market. If O'Neill's argument for an objective account is unconvincing, which way shall we move? In the interests of keeping education and the market as separate spheres, we could look for another, less porous, objective account. Or we could see if subjectivism could meet the objections levied against it above (thereby reviving the possibility of education and the market as co-promoters of personal well-being).

Is there a third way? The subjectivism with which we have been dealing has been individualistic, in that a person's well-being is taken as a function of the satisfaction of *his or her* wants. Could there be a subjectivism of a more inclusive sort, dependent on *many people's* rather than an individual's major informed desires?

Let us go back to Rawls' grass counter and the thought that satisfying his passion *just couldn't* make him better off. The problem with him seems to be that we cannot make any sense of him: his preference is so bizarre that it does not fit into any picture we have of what makes a human life go well. Our touchstone here is not some objective account of the good based on human nature. It is, rather, what *we* desire, where the 'we' refers to a more delimited collection of people than humanity as a whole. Let me explain.

The bizarreness of the grass counter is that he has no time for any of the ordinary pleasures which many people in, say, contemporary Britain would see as part of what makes our life worth living – things like physical exercise, socialising, eating and drinking, sex, being entertained, deep personal relationships, living autonomously, a degree of self-understanding, love of the arts, including their popular versions, love of the natural world. The grass counter is unmoved by any of these pleasures and commitments.

It should be clear that the people mentioned do not constitute a tightly knit group. The group they constitute, if indeed it can be called a 'group', has ragged edges. Internally, it is not all of a piece, some values being shared across the whole spectrum, others not. Some people will be more *au fait* with poetry, mountaineering, classical music or the subtleties of intimate relationships than others. But there is no clearly bounded elite which has a monopoly of the more recondite fulfilments. The people in question shade gradually into those who – perhaps being cut off by poor education from more reflective and contemplative activities – would see the good life more Marbella-style in terms of a villa in the sun, sex, sangria and a handy golf course.

This loose group of people exists not only in Britain, but also across much of the contemporary world. It also, most importantly, has a history. It includes not only contemporary inhabitants of modern, liberal societies, but their ancestors, too, stretching back to the origins of such societies over the past four or five hundred years. It has been over these centuries that such values as autonomy, depth in personal relationships, the pursuit of self-understanding and an understanding of the world, love of the arts and of natural beauty have become articulated as important goals of human life – in addition to its more ordinary pleasures.

There is an indebtedness here to more ancient thinking, such as that of the Greeks. The group has honorary members in Socrates and Plato. It cannot be understood except in terms of the breakdown of the medieval world order and the recovery of Greek ideals from the Renascence onwards. New values have had to be forged to fit an increasingly secular world and changing views about man's place in nature and the meaningfulness, if any, of an individual human life. Our being in the world has over these centuries become an object of increasing fascination to us – a disposition which has found expression not only in the arts, in contemplation of nature, in science and in scholarly forms of self-reflection like philosophy, history and psychology, but at a more everyday level in self-examination and in the mutual explorations of intimate relationships, these finding literary embodiment in the new poetry of the late eighteenth century and beyond, the novel, biography and autobiography.

At first the new values were the province only of the leisured classes, and no doubt of only few of them, but as more of us have risen above the level of subsistence, not least in the twentieth century, they have filtered down into the population at large, often in more popular forms, the poorest-off being the least touched by them.

The items I have mentioned are roughly those found in O'Neill's objective account. But they do not derive from human nature, either in itself, or modified through historical development, but from what the roughly delineated group of people just mentioned thinks and desires.

The individual on his or her own is not the final authority on what counts as his or her flourishing. There is a centuries-long continuous tradition of thought about this topic to guide us. In this tradition all the various goods mentioned are elements which could be included in a flourishing life.

This position has affinities with that of John Stuart Mill (1861, ch. 2) in *Utilitarianism*. Notoriously, he argued that mental pleasures constitute goods higher in value than physical pleasures, because this is what those who have had experience of both would claim. I think it is true that there are people relatively untouched by the post-Renascence values, whose experience is broadly confined to what were grouped together earlier as 'ordinary pleasures'. It is also true that there are those who are also at home among the profounder satisfactions. I suspect (from experience) that very few who are well acquainted with the latter would willingly jettison all interest in them for the sake of ordinary pleasures alone. So far all this is compatible with Mill's position. Mill also goes on to claim that those who have experienced both mental and physical pleasures tend to prefer the former and that these are therefore more desirable than the latter. Here, it seems to me, Mill goes too far. As has often been said, he cannot legitimately derive the conclusion that mental pleasures are qualitatively superior from empirical facts about preferences. Further, to say that those who know both pleasures markedly prefer mental ones makes things too black-and-white. There may be scholars and poets who live for scholarship and poetry alone and have little room for physical pleasures. But there are plenty of other intellectuals and artists for whom sports or sex or carousing are activities pursued with passion.

We need not follow Mill into arranging personal goods into a hierarchy to agree with him that those who have wider experience of the range of goods within the tradition are in a better position to make judgements about what constitutes human flourishing than those who lack this.

Mill was a liberal. He also held that some people are better placed than others to make judgements about the components of personal well-being. (This is not to say that they are well-placed to judge in detail about specific individuals.) Some may see a paradox in such 'liberal elitism' (see Skorupski, 1992), but if they do, are they right to do so?

* * *

Is this third solution – the non-individualist subjectivist account – really viable? It faces two challenges. First, could not the superior judges simply be better at discerning objective values – that is, values which pre-exist their preferences for them? Second, could not their judgements simply reflect their own idiosyncrasies and thus provide no basis for a more general notion of well-being?

In this increasingly speculative and schematic part of this paper, I would like to suggest a model for prudential judgements which might avoid these two difficulties. I have in mind judgements of artistic value (see Budd, 1995: 38–43). Here we also have grounds for saying that some people are better placed than others to make such judgements. They must have had extensive experience of works of art, across the board or in a particular mode. They must have reflected on the features, general or specific, which add to or subtract from artistic value. They must be prepared to substantiate their judgements by reference to these features, as found in particular works. No doubt there will be disagreements among them, but there exists at the same time an intersubjective discourse of artistic judgement which seeks to resolve these differences where possible, or to reveal different weightings among values which may help to account for them. The enterprise of revising, refining, extending, deepening judgements of artistic value is ongoing.

Such judgements are neither idiosyncratic nor about features of works which can perceive in the straightforward way that colours can be perceived. They require evaluation in the light of reflection and are subject to others' critical assessment. In this way they are intersubjective judgements rather than straightforward perceptions of objective features of the world.

The social practice of making and challenging judgements of artistic value is not culturally confined. As we know it in Europe, it is certainly a cultural *product*, having developed with the rise of aesthetics as an autonomous domain in the eighteenth century. But its discourse is universal in intention and also in practice. This is shown by, among other things, its capacity to engage and sometimes fuse with other traditions elsewhere in the world.

If there is a model here for prudential judgements, it must also be sensitive to differences between the two spheres. Prudential judgements are about valuable features of human lives, not works of art. Their object is therefore less delimited, more amorphous. It is also, partly for that reason, something on which a less tightly defined group than a community of artistic judges can be expected to have views and contribute to a fuller delineation of human flourishing. As suggested earlier, nearly all of us in our kind of society will have *some* thoughts on what makes for a flourishing life; while amongst us there will be those of wider experience and greater reflectiveness whose views often carry more weight.

It should be clear by now that this account of personal well-being does not confine prudential values to a particular community. New personal goods have been coming into being over the past four or five hundred years, originating in many cases in Western Europe. But this is a point only about origins, not about any limitation on scope. As with the sub-class of aesthetic values mentioned earlier, once in existence the new values have been able to transcend their original social confines. That is why I have been cautious about labelling the widening number of people with this broader approach to well-being a tightly-definable 'group'. The values in question are theirs, certainly, in that they hold them; but this does not mean they are not potentially values which anyone in our world can hold.

* * *

This is only the briefest of sketches of an alternative. But if it can be adequately defended, what might be the implications for the aims of education and the relationship between education and the market? This is a big subject and I can only put up one or two signposts.

First, it means an end to an individualistic framework on personal well-being. Individuals are not the final authority on their flourishing, but can only defer to the accumulated wisdom described earlier. This is not to say that any authority will force them to lead such and such a life. We are still working within a liberal framework, if not an individualist-subjectivist one. People will be free, indeed encouraged, to make their personal weightings among the handed-down values (which come down to them with views attached about the relative importances – in general – of different values). They will also be encouraged to join in the ongoing social process of assessment and reassessment parallel to that in the arts, mentioned earlier.

Over time all this should give parents, teachers and educational policy-makers greater *confidence* in judgements about well-being. There is a source on which they can draw – and indeed on which they have already drawn throughout their lives. They should be able, gradually, to leave behind the uncertainties which have tended to beset us all in an age when the philosophical study of personal flourishing has been in its infancy, having had little attention in the Judaeo-Christian culture from which we in Britain, as elsewhere, are rapidly disentangling ourselves (Griffin, 1996: 66–7).

In that part of their endeavour concerned with personal well-being, schools and families should direct pupils, *inter alia*, towards the intrinsic goods within the tradition mentioned. These would no doubt include among other things such items as close personal relationships, a love of beauty in art and nature, understanding of oneself, human beings and the world they inhabit, self-directedness and simple bodily pleasures, including the pleasures of physical exercise.

The aims of the English/Welsh National Curriculum to do with the child's well-being should become less the well-meaning but unargued list of items which they are now and more a philosophically and historically informed set whose rationale is fully stated, public and revisable. How good a shot could be made at this at first, given the remark just made about the infancy of the philosophy of well-being, is another question. But a first shot is perhaps better than no shot at all. The education system cannot be as aimless throughout the next century as it has been throughout the last.

More generally, teachers and parents should wholeheartedly encourage children to engage in activities subserving these ends. They would not be favouring their own idiosyncratic preferences, but inducting children into time-tested values. They should also leave children free to reject elements in this tradition in favour of values which lie outside it, such as obedience to God. Does this mean that the (on the whole secular) values of the tradition are privileged? There would be nothing wrong about teachers' encouraging a commitment to art or friendship. What could it be? But encouraging wholehearted devotion to a personal god is problematic, as the religious clauses of the 1944 Education Act and subsequent guidelines for religious education in English schools testify. Love of works of art is directed to objects about whose existence there is no doubt; but whether the same can be said about love of God is moot. This said, there is everything to be said for *revealing* this value to the pupil, in case he or she wishes to adopt it.

On this view the education system would not be all of a piece with the market. Schools, colleges and the market would not all be reinforcing the same meta-ethic, leading people to think that their flourishing consists in the satisfaction of their major desires, whatever these may be. Education would be driven by an independent set of values. The values of the market would have to be reassessed – and altered or abandoned accordingly – in the light of wisdom already accumulated within the culture about what makes for a flourishing human life.

Acknowledgements

This paper is a substantially revised version of a keynote presentation to a symposium on *Economy, Public Education and Democracy* held at Ascona, Switzerland, in September 2000 and organised by the Pedagogical Institute of the University of Zürich.

References

Budd, M. (1995) *Values of Art*, London: The Penguin Press.
DfEE/QCA (1999) *The National Curriculum* (handbook for teachers), London: Department for Education and Employment, and Qualifications and Curriculum Authority.
Griffin, J. (1986) *Well-being*, Oxford: Clarendon Press.
Griffin, J. (1996) *Value Judgement*, Oxford: Clarendon Press.
Mill. J. S. (1861) 'Utilitarianism', in *Utilitarianism, Liberty and Representative Government*, London: Everyman.
Moore, G. E. (1903) *Principia Ethica*, Cambridge: Cambridge University Press.
O'Neill, J. (1993) *Ecology, Policy and Politics: Human Well-being and the Natural World*, London: Routledge.
O'Neill, J. (1998) *The Market: Ethics, Knowledge and Politics*, London: Routledge.

QCA (1999) *The Review of the National Curriculum in England: The Consultation Materials*, London: Qualifications and Curriculum Authority.

Peters, R. S. (1966) *Ethics and Education*, London: Allen and Unwin.

Rawls, J. (1972) *A Theory of Justice*, Oxford: Clarendon Press.

Raz, J. (1986) *The Morality of Freedom*, Oxford: Clarendon Press.

Skorupski, J. (1992) 'Liberal elitism', in D. Milligan and W. W. Miller (eds), *Liberalism, Citizenship and Autonomy*, Aldershot: Avebury.

Sumner, L. W. (1996) *Welfare, Happiness and Ethics*, Oxford: Oxford University Press.

CHAPTER 13

EDUCATION AND NATIONALITY

Journal of Philosophy of Education (1996), 30(3): 327–43

Introduction

When I first began to think about the topic of this paper, in July 1993, the new state of Belarus was in the midst of devising a national system of education based on the Belarusian language, history and culture. Since 1988 England and Wales has had a National Curriculum. It is based on the English and Welsh languages; its history is to a large extent British history, and texts by British writers – along with those of some American and other overseas writers in English – make up the literature syllabus. Yet, despite its name, we do not tend to think of our National Curriculum, as the Belarusians do their new system, in terms of nationality. Indeed, it has not been presented to us in that way. Its aims have to do with the promotion of pupils' spiritual, moral, cultural, mental and physical development and with preparing them for adult life: they do not mention cultivating national sentiment.

If they did, we would be in greater difficulties than the Belarusians in knowing which nation was intended. The National Curriculum is for England and Wales, but we do not think of ourselves as part of an English + Welsh nation. Do we belong to England if we are English, Wales if Welsh? And what if we call ourselves neither English nor Welsh, but Greek Cypriot or Bengali? Whoever we are, is our nation Britain? Or is it the UK?

Like many of my countrymen and -women (whoever precisely they are), I am not sure what to reply. Unlike the Danes or the Hungarians, I do not belong to a well-defined nation. More fundamentally, I am radically uncertain how far nationality should matter to me or other people. Would I want a National Curriculum that encouraged national attachments?

Three sets of issues need sorting out. There are general ones about the place of national sentiment in ethical and political thinking, specific ones about nationalities in the British Isles and ones about educational applications in this more local context. I shall discuss them in this order, except that, having educational matters centrally in mind, I shall sometimes refer to these in the next two sections before dealing with them specifically.

National sentiment in general

This century national feeling has been an emotion often associated with the political right, especially the extreme political right: we think first of the Nazis, Mussolini, the National Front in Britain. Left-wingers and liberals have been wary of privileging the interests of particular national groups over others, being attached to universalistic principles like equality of respect for all human beings, or, in the case of some Marxists, the interests of the working class the world over. Recently, however, from a socialist perspective, David Miller (1989) has called for a reassessment of the left's traditional attitude towards the nation.

How might one defend national sentiment? First, via a distinction between it and nationalistic sentiment, or chauvinism. Love of one's nation does not necessarily bring with it a belief in the superiority of one's nation over other nations. The latter should be condemned on the principle of universal equality of respect mentioned earlier. But love of one's nation does not contravene this principle, any more than any other particularistic attachment does. If I can love my own family without thinking it superior to other families, the same can be true of my nation.

Someone may object that although this distinction can be made in logic, the more national feeling is encouraged the more it is liable to turn into nationalistic feeling. We know from every international sporting event we see on television how ardently people can want their national side to beat the rest. More seriously, we have seen this century, and not least in the last few years in the former Yugoslavia, how quickly and powerfully nationalism (using this term to connote feelings of superiority) can take hold.

How solid is this argument? There are dangers in encouraging any feeling beyond a certain point. You are delighted by your daughter's attachment to her friends; but you will not want her to be so exclusively devoted to them that she neglects her school-work or follows them into crime. If fostering love of one's nation were urging people to become exclusively devoted to it, one could understand that it might tip over into chauvinism. But national feeling could be encouraged as one value among many without according it any privileged place. In this way it is like friendship, commitment to personal projects, attending to the needs of strangers, global justice: each of these values may properly weigh with us, but all must take their due place in company with others.

Again, we may need to know more about the content of the national feeling in question. The Finnish National Curriculum, unlike the English/Welsh, aims at pupils becoming among other things 'cooperative and peace-loving human beings and citizens'. One may love one's nation because one sees it as on the side of world peace, of equal respect for all peoples. Promoting this type of national feeling in schools seems unlikely to turn students into chauvinists.

National sentiment, then, must not be confused with nationalism. But there is no point in going further into outlining the case for the former without clarifying what is meant by 'nation'. The first thing to stress is that a nation is a group of people: the French constitute a nation and so do the Poles. It is not some kind of supra-personal entity, something that should be written with a capital 'N'. Just as a family is a group consisting of its members and nothing above these, so too is a nation. Being attached to one's nation, like being attached to one's family, is all to do with one's bonds with other individuals – and nothing to do with adulation of some abstract entity.

What binds a national group together? A common language is one link, but, as with the Swiss or Belgian nations, not a necessary one. The same is true of ethnic origin. Some nations, notoriously today the Serbs and the Croats, define national membership in their cases in terms of descent from ancestors of the same blood. But others are more inclusive, granting nationality to people of diverse ethnic origins provided that they meet certain other conditions. The American nation is a supreme example of this, although the same is true, to a lesser and less constitutionally celebrated extent, of many other nations. Neither can 'nation' be defined in terms of possessing a measure of political autonomy. Many nations – the Danish, Australian, the Chilean – also have independent states, but the Palestinians do not. True, the latter want political autonomy, and this has indeed long been a key aspiration of all national movements. If, as seems to be the case, the desire for political independence, if not its actuality, is part of our understanding of nationality, this underlines the subjective nature of this concept.

What holds a nation together, as Miller (1988) argues, is the shared beliefs of its members:

> a belief that each belongs together with the rest; that this association is neither transitory nor merely instrumental but stems from a long history of living together which (it is hoped and expected) will continue into the future; that the community is marked off from other communities by its members' distinctive characteristics; and that each member recognises a loyalty to the community, expressed in a willingness to sacrifice personal gain to advance its interests. We should add, as a final element, that the nation should enjoy some degree of political autonomy.
>
> (p. 648)

On this last point, in line with remarks in the last paragraph, I would weaken 'enjoy' to 'enjoy or aspire after'.

It is because nationality is subjective in this way that new nations can come into being, as people living in the same territory and used to seeing themselves as part of more local communities are persuaded to reconceptualise themselves, perhaps through the education system and the mass media, as co-nationals. This process is at work in much of Africa today, but, as Hobsbawm (1990) has shown, it lay behind the formation of many European nations in the nineteenth century.

What bearing has the subjectivity of nationality on its acceptability? Some would baulk at the myths that it tends to bring with it – shared beliefs about historical origins or about past triumphs that are either untrue or wilful exaggerations; stereotypes about alleged national characteristics of one's own group or one's neighbours. But how far is myth a necessary feature of the concept? How far is it possible to subject the shared beliefs to objective control? Our own experience in Britain is cause for optimism here. Older images of Britishness to do with effortless superiority over other peoples, Protestant virtuousness and victoriousness over Catholic enemies, and so on, while still powerfully at work among us, are increasingly under challenge from a reasonably objective education system and mass media.

The subjectivity also gives political power-seekers a weapon. Control of education and the media has enabled many of them this century to foment national movements to serve their own ends. We know too well the intolerance and xenophobia that this creates and the horrors in which these can end. But should this cause us to turn our back on national sentiment altogether?

Its subjective nature is also a clue to its ethical importance. The political structuring of the world, a century or two ago based largely on dynastic states, colonial dependencies and indigenous tribal structures, is now a mosaic of largely autonomous nations. Although there are growing pressures to amalgamate into transnational units, the European Union for instance, this is not favoured if it threatens the continued existence of national identities. It is unrealistic to think that this near-universal preference for living in national groupings has been wholly engineered by political power-seekers, that it does not reflect some deep-seated desire on the part of people themselves.

Nationality has become, for many of us, closely connected with a sense of our own identity. It is a commonplace of political philosophy that individuals are not atomic entities but social creatures, in the sense that the concepts employed across their mental life are acquired, and perhaps necessarily so, from the society in which they have grown up. In addition, their goals, activities and relationships are inescapably shaped by social institutions and traditions, including traditions of radical thought that question other traditions. This social framework is multiplex. We live not in one society but in several: we are shaped by our families, our schools, local communities, the wider national community, international institutions and other influences. Without some such framework we could not exist.

But how far is the national community a necessary feature of the framework? Communitarian thinkers often look in other directions – to smaller-scale communities, or to ones like the Roman Catholic church, which cut across national boundaries, but that possess, like the smaller communities mentioned, clear and deeply rooted traditions of how human beings should live and the virtues they need to flourish (MacIntyre, 1981). Critics of such communitarianism have drawn attention to the threat it can pose to the central liberal value of individual self-determination (Mulhall and Swift, 1992). If we assume that this is important, then we need to look towards more open forms of community.

Yet this does not necessarily get us to the nation. Academics need other academics, but they can be in other countries; supporters of world peace or ecological improvement can attach themselves to international organisations.

Belonging to a nation is not essential to personal well-being, perhaps, but it can contribute to that end. A large part of the social, cultural, economic and political framework of our lives is the national community. Across the world we find national governments managing national economies, running national education, health and welfare systems. Mass media, whether public or private, operate largely within national frontiers, keeping each part of the nation in touch with all the others. Writers, dramatists, actors, painters, especially in the English-speaking world, are less confined within national boundaries than they used to be, but even so, much that artists produce is intended in the first place for a national audience and is reviewed by national critics.

For many of us the work that we do, our attachments to other people, our personal interests and our values would lose much of their point if this national framework were removed. We need it to make sense of our lives, to help us towards a sense of who we are. It is in this way that nationality is important for personal identity, and not because it is metaphysically necessary to it in a Hegelian or some other fashion.

As David Miller (1989) has argued, there is a good reason why socialists should re-evaluate their traditional attitudes towards the nation. Socialists favour a redistribution of resources and other benefits from the more to the less affluent. This means action by the state in the shape of things like progressive income taxes and ensuring better housing, income, education, health, etc. for the poor. However, in a liberal democracy, some way has to be found to motivate a sufficient number of citizens to favour redistribution, especially where it is against their financial interest to do this. If they feel themselves to be part of the same community as those in need, their emotional bonds with them may outweigh narrower considerations of advantage and disadvantage. National sentiment can help to provide this bonding.

On this argument, it is not enough for socialists – or, indeed, any non-socialists moved by the plight of fellow-citizens – to pin all their hopes on the institutions of the democratic state that can promote redistribution: for these institutions to be able to do this, behind the state there has to be communal sentiment, the feeling that everybody's fate matters to each. There is no reason in logic why this community must be a nation. But the fact that nations exist and, through the attachment to political autonomy that is part of their nature, do now often coincide in their boundaries with the boundaries of states, provides a strong pragmatic reason for relying on them.

Following Miller, I have been arguing that there is nothing intrinsically amiss with national sentiment, but that, on the contrary, it can be politically beneficial, as well as helping to meet needs in the area of personal identity, mentioned earlier. But there will still be those suspicious of it, perhaps for fear of how it might get out of hand and slip into chauvinism. They will include those in favour of redistribution. Some of these may say that the argument so far has conflated national sentiment with civic friendship. Certainly, the liberal democratic state needs widespread feelings of fraternity to animate it. But these can be fostered by building up attachments to the democratic polity itself, for instance by citizenship education in schools: the more aware people become of the importance of democratic life and government for their own lives and for the lives of fellow-citizens, the more committed to their own particular democracy they will become.

I do not want to deny the possibility or desirability of a community founded on civic friendship. But this does not rule out a community based on national sentiment. Indeed, the latter can be the undergirding of the former.

The civic community needs some kind of emotional tie to bind it together. This could be a shared commitment to democratic ideals, including more specific political emotions like a hatred of injustice, pride in the proper workings of the polity, concern to better the living and working conditions of the less fortunate. Let us suppose that the binding emotions are only ones of this sort, tied to universal moral/political principles.

The question arises why these feelings are directed specifically towards members of *this* community as well as towards injustice and misfortune elsewhere in the world. The answer may be that one has a greater chance of doing more good at the local level than globally: the levers of action are easier to operate. This would be to look at the matter as perhaps a utilitarian would. It would seem to imply that if the levers were different, if through some technology which we cannot now imagine politicians in this community were better able to help people in some distant country than those around them, this is what they should do.

Is a community bound together only by attachment to principles conceivable? Perhaps but for many people, including myself, it would not be an attractive one. I would not like to be a younger member of a family bonded in a similar principle-orientated way, aware that my parents were attentive to my needs not out of affection but only because they saw this as a parental duty. Neither, I suggest, would virtually anyone else. Similarly, like most people I would feel more comfortable in a wider community where people felt a more immediate sympathy for each other. A national community can provide this more spontaneous, less intellectualised kind of attachment, thus strengthening bonds at the civic level.

The defender of civic friendship may well reply that its ethical commitments need not be restricted to universal principles but may also include particularistic concerns – indeed, the 'immediate sympathy' mentioned earlier. This sympathy would be directed, however, not to fellow-nationals, but to fellow-citizens. The deprivations of the long-term unemployed in North East England would affect one not as a Britisher or an Englander, but as a citizen, because it is part of the civic ideal in a liberal democracy that everyone's basic needs for a flourishing life should be met.

It may be possible to divorce civic sympathy from national sentiment in this way; and it may be that this civic sympathy needs no further underpinning. I do not deny this. It seems more likely, however, that the two emotions are conceptually hard to disentangle, assuming that we are dealing with a political community that has existed for some time. The longer the shared history, the more its particular features help to provide the social cement that binds it together. Unemployment and poverty in the North East affect one not only civically, as obstacles to people's well-being in those parts, but also against the background of the rise and fall of British shipbuilding since the industrial revolution, the 1930s slump and the Jarrow marches. I see no reason why civic feeling should not be strengthened by thoughts of how, as a people, we have lived and suffered together.

Has enough been done to make the case for national feeling? Opponents may still be anxious about exclusiveness towards minorities. If nations undergird civic polities, will this not mean that those who are not co-nationals but who live in the same country are likely to be treated as less than full citizens? Not necessarily. That there is a danger of this is undeniable. It is already happening in the Balkans and threatens to happen elsewhere in Eastern Europe. But it is not inevitable; and steps can be taken to try to prevent it. The outsiders, perhaps recent immigrants, can be welcomed on equal terms into the national community. This will involve them and their children coming to share some of the beliefs and attitudes of community members and therewith gaining some acquaintance with the history and culture of the community and some ability to communicate in its national language(s). Over time the traditions, values and historical perspectives of the host community may be expected to be modified and enriched by the contributions of outside cultures. The education system will play a crucial role in all these developments. This policy does not demand total assimilation, as joining the national community is wholly compatible with remaining a member of one's original community: nationality requires shared beliefs, but not an exclusive attachment. Neither does the policy necessarily demand that everyone living permanently in the territory join the national community: part of the self-concept of the nation could be that it allows within its midst groups of people largely untouched by its own way of life. These people would indeed be treated as less than full members of the national community for the obvious reason that they themselves preferred to keep out of it; but there is every reason why they should be treated as full citizens in the civic sense: they would be subject to the laws of the land and qualify for rights and benefits to which they were entitled, to the extent that they wished to receive them. Given the kinds of arrangement outlined in this paragraph, I hope enough has now been done to allay fears that encouraging national sentiment will lead to the demeaning and disadvantaging of those outside the national group. It should be a central objective of any nationally based state to see that this does not happen.[1]

In this section I have tried to show that liberal-democratic values are not incompatible with national sentiment and, more strongly, that promoting the latter may help to promote the former. I have *not* argued that national sentiment is always desirable, having assumed throughout that the only kind worth considering is that constrained by liberal values.[2]

For the most part I have argued for national sentiment on the ground of its contribution to democratic, or left-liberal, politics. But there may be other, equally unsinister, reasons. I heard recently that in Denmark and Malta there are moves to make Danish and Maltese culture respectively more salient in school curricula. National sentiment is encouraged in these cases not only for civic reasons but also, and more centrally, to prevent the further erosion of a threatened culture. This does not seem to me to be an objectionable goal.

The meaning of Britishness

Now that the general case has been made for encouraging a certain sort of national sentiment, what applications might this have to our own national community and to its educational arrangements?

The first problem, as noted at the beginning of this paper, is to know what 'our own national community' is. And here we should not assume that we are each members of only one. Many Scots think of themselves as both Scottish and British: there are shared beliefs binding them to both groups, including beliefs about a measure of political autonomy. Whether dual nationality is so prominent a feature of the English psyche, I doubt. Far fewer English people think that England should be (to some extent) politically autonomous than Scots think Scotland should be. I suspect – on impressionistic evidence only – that the English do not tend to distinguish themselves so sharply from the Scots, Welsh and to some extent the Irish as many Scots do from the three other groups. As for other communities – Greek Cypriots, West Indians, Sikhs, Bangladeshis, etc. – we need to make a distinction between 'cultural' or 'ethnic' community and 'national' community. Some people in these groups may feel themselves to belong to two nations – if, for instance, they see themselves as part of the home community of Bangladesh as much as they do Britain; others may identify themselves exclusively as British, while living in a community of other West Indians or Jews.

Despite these complications, and further ones arising from the mixed ancestry of so many of us, there may seem to be a short and definitive answer to the question about what our national community is. It is Britain. There are Scottish, Irish and Welsh nationalists who would reject this suggestion; and many Northern Irish people who are not Irish nationalists would also be unhappy with it on the grounds that being part of the UK is not the same as being part of Britain. But all these apart, everyone else is a part of the British nation, to whatever other nation they may also belong.

This short answer is really too short. If the shared beliefs we have mentioned are central to nationality, what shared beliefs unite the British? As the historian Linda Colley (1992) has recently argued, it is easier to spell this out for the eighteenth and early nineteenth centuries than it is for our own time. Great Britain came into existence with the Act of Union of 1707, uniting the previously independent kingdoms of Scotland and England/Wales. Over the next century the British nation was forged. A large part of its formation was played by the shared Protestantism of the three countries, coupled with the century and more of wars with Catholic France. Britishness was thus defined partly in contradistinction to a hostile other, which all Britons could unite in withstanding. Colley draws our attention to the place that fighting has had in Britain's self-understanding, both actual warfare and the spiritual struggle to uphold true Christianity – embodied, for instance, in the eighteenth-century image of Britain as a new Israel. A related belief at this time was that Britain was richer and politically freer than the rest of Europe. The growth of the British Empire throughout the two centuries strengthened the shared assumption of Britain's invincible commercial supremacy in the world and of its imperial hegemony.

Britain is no longer the powerful nation it was. The twentieth century has seen its pretensions and power dwindle dramatically. The story is by now painfully familiar to us all. Our imperial decline, coupled with the now overwhelmingly secular nature of our society and the long-past ending of hostilities towards the French has meant that central features of our earlier self-definition have no foundation in reality.

Some of us cling to tattered remnants, the Falklands War revivifying in miniature submerged imperialist proclivities and feelings of righteous antagonism towards the Other, in this case, indeed, one Catholic in origin. For many people 'immigrants', especially 'coloured immigrants' from ex-imperial countries like Jamaica or Trinidad, have now taken, the place of French, and more recently German or Russian Others: the pretensions of such people to Britishness are anathema to those attached to the notion that Britain's role is to keep the likes of them in imperial subjection. For others (overlapping with the anti-immigrants) Europe is now the Other. Old feelings of national and racial superiority, of suspicion and antipathy towards the Continent, lie deep in our psyche, affecting, no doubt, many of us who would reject the traditional British identity.

This brings us to the sceptics, among whom I count myself. There are two unassailable reasons why the old view of Britishness will not do. One: the world is now different. Two: the view is ethically ugly anyway – we would not want to live in a nation of such arrogance and self-righteousness.

The sceptics have turned their back on Britishness as traditionally conceived. For many of them this has been equivalent to turning one's back on Britishness *tout court*. With Britishness has gone the ideal of nationality itself. They have felt we can well do without the notion, redefining ourselves, if micro-inclined, as commune-dwellers, family-men and women, decent schoolteachers and bank employees, or, if macro-, as socialists, citizens of the world, environmentalists, crusaders for peace or animal rights. 'The idea of the nation, though a potent one, belongs to the realm of the imaginary rather than the real' (Samuel, 1989b: 16).

But some sceptics, and here again I include myself, are less negative. Given the benefits of national sentiment discussed in the last section, how far can one reconstitute the idea of Britishness so as to exclude many – perhaps not all – of the old associations? As Linda Colley (1992) writes, our neighbours in Europe, the French and the Germans, have a greater confidence than we do about their national identity. How can we go about 'consolidating a deeper sense of citizenship on the home front'? (p. 375).

We need, above all, clarity about the issues, raising a reasoned discussion of the place of national sentiment in general to greater prominence in public debate. We also need to redefine Britishness in more acceptable terms. Part of our heritage we can retain: the association with freedom. The liberal tradition of tolerance, of promoting individuality and personal autonomy that has come down to us via Locke and Mill, is one part of our intellectual history of which we can reasonably be proud. Although much is still imperfect here, since some people – some women, members of minority ethnic communities, gays and lesbians, poor people – benefit less from this tradition than others, progress is being made and foreigners who come to Britain for the first time often compare us favourably in this respect with more repressive parts of the world. Foreigners also tend to comment on the marked decency of British people, the politeness and friendliness with which strangers interact with each other. Again, we know of innumerable counterexamples; but these notwithstanding, there is probably enough truth in the generalisation to justify our including it in our collective self-image. (On positive aspects of our past, see also Hill, 1989: 4.)

These are two examples of how we may begin to construct a new identity. They both involve ethical ideals, and ideals that are realised, at least to some extent, in actual states of affairs. This is one way we can move forward. We might think of other values that can be realistically incorporated: benevolence and social justice, for instance. These have been salient in our Christian heritage, at least in certain strands of it: we think back to the ending of the slave trade, to Dickens, to the social reform movements of the later nineteenth century and the origins of the welfare state. We might transmute our erstwhile national bellicosity into a national virtue – as in the Finns' or Swedes' self-concept, for instance – of peacelovingness (which does not mean peace at all costs). Again, there is sufficient, if patchy, evidence of this in our history since Waterloo on which to found such a shared belief.

As is evident from these examples, our attitude towards our own history will be important in this self-redefinition. This need not, and should not, bring with it the fanciful notion that Britain has always been ethically unspotted. On the contrary, it will be important explicitly to detach the image of the new Britain from that of the old. It will become part of our shared consciousness that Britishness *did* connote the unattractive features we have described and that these have now been deliberately replaced. History lessons in schools will show our warts and wens as well as beauty spots: there is no cause for deviations from historians' normal standards of objectivity.

Another example: Ralf Dahrendorf's (1982) picture of Britain from his vantage point of a German who has come to live here stresses the confrontational character of so much of our national life: the lines between workers and management in industry, between the social classes, between left and right in politics are etched so much more sharply than in comparable European countries. How far this might be an introjected form of the self-definition via the Other located in Linda Colley's account of Britishness, I do not know. At all events, a history of Britain should bring out this oppositional aspect of our nature, so that, if as I am assuming this proves desirable, we can identify it in order to transcend it in the direction of greater fraternity.

This is only a brief first indication, not of course a complete account, of how Britishness might be reconstituted. Some will object to the artificiality of the whole enterprise. How can a national character be painted in by numbers, adding this virtue, removing that fault in the way I seem to have espoused? My answer would be, first, that the artificiality should not be exaggerated: to a large extent the shared beliefs are already in place and the main task is to encourage commitment to the more acceptable of them. Secondly, nation building has more often than not been to some extent artificial and there is nothing necessarily wrong with that. Where things have gone wrong is where fantasised national definitions have been imposed on people by an autocrat or oligarchy for self-seeking purposes: one thinks of Hitler's vision of the German as a willing martyr to the honour of his people. Not only should any artificial constructions have some root in historical reality, it is also preferable on liberal-democratic grounds if they arise as far as possible from a broad social consensus. More centrally, I do not see what is wrong in deliberate self-definition if the ideals and beliefs on which this is founded are worthy ones. The United States is an artificial foundation, but the aspirations touching universal liberty and pursuit of happiness written into its constitution are nonetheless admirable for that. As for Britain today, we are notoriously short on positive directions in which we can go forward: strong in negative criticism, too ready to dismiss with a cynical smile any suggestion that we need a new vision to lead us into the future, we waste our energies in public bickerings or look for our salvation to purely private commitments. A conscious resolution to refashion our national identity may be exactly what we now need.

Out of this first objection may spring another. I have mentioned the Finns' attachment to peace and suggested that the British might emulate them. More generally, the values recommended for our new self-definition – social justice, tolerance, personal autonomy, benevolence, fraternity – are likely to be among the ideals of other enlightened liberal-democratic nations across the world. But what sense does this make when part of the notion of nationality is that nations claim to have their own peculiar characteristics, that its members see themselves as different from members of other nations?

My answer is that they do not have to see themselves as in every way different. This would in any case be an impossible – a logically impossible – demand. Even though Britons held some values in common with other peoples, there would still be many unique bonds between us. Our history is not that of Italy or Sweden; neither is our landscape or climate; our jokes are different; we are attached differently to Constable and Jane Austen than to Monet and Tolstoy; our language has ways of putting things with which we all feel at home.

Although these objections can be met, other problems remain. Some of these are practical: for instance, how do we soften the class-divisiveness that makes some look down on others almost as if they belonged to a different tribe? Others are partly practical, partly conceptual. I have suggested that we seek a new version of Britishness applicable to all sub-groups dwelling on this island. The biggest of these sub-groups is the English. How are they to see themselves? Scots will continue to belong to two nations. Can we say the same of the English? This is problematic because the English have never clearly distinguished Englishness from Britishness. Like many other English people, I personally would find it hard to say to which nationality I belonged: in a formal sense, like any Scot I hold a British passport and am obviously British in a formal sense. Yet many Scots, if asked their nationality more informally, would immediately answer 'Scottish'; while I, like many of the English, would dither. Is there an English nation? Should any English national sentiment that there is be benignly remoulded? After the 1707 Act of Union fears that England and Englishness would dominate over Scotland and Scottishness were met by playing down Englishness and playing up Britishness (Crick, 1988). The process has continued. But has it gone too far? Should English people ignore the English in them and think of themselves as unmediatedly British, in a way that the Scots do not? Or should they do more to celebrate what binds them uniquely together? (For an argument in favour of British nationality rather than 'cultural Englishness', see Miller, 1995.)

We are left with Northern Ireland. Its continued problems underline our reluctance to dispel the fog surrounding our nationality: the distinction between GB and UK makes it hard to throw ourselves wholeheartedly into the cause of Britishness, but the suggestion that we should see ourselves as Ukanians has little appeal. Not surprisingly, I offer no magic solution. But if, as urged, we now redefine our self-conceptions, this is a major issue that we should face.

Nationality and education

The education system could play a large part in helping us become clearer about our nationality. So far there is little sign of this happening. I have already mentioned the absence of any reference to national sentiment among the aims of the 1988 National Curriculum. More surprising is its equal absence from the National Curriculum Council's (NCC) (1990) document *Education for Citizenship*. For the most part the booklet is about specifically civic matters – about the rights and responsibilities of individuals and societies, about principles like freedom and equality of opportunity, about democracy, law, wealth creation and public services. There is one mention of the 'national community' among the 'variety of communities to which people simultaneously belong' (p. 3), but this is not taken up elsewhere and no guidance is given to teachers about how they could develop an understanding of it. This is in stark contrast to the family, also included in the list of communities: work on this is recommended as one of eight essential components of education for citizenship. So it is not as though the publication is wholly wedded to universalistic subject-matter and eschews particularistic perspectives relevant to self-identity. The family is in, even though the nation is out.

Perhaps this is not so surprising, after all, in the light of what was said in the last two sections on ambivalence about national sentiment in general and Britishness in particular. For the NCC to recommend practice in this area they would have had to take a stand on a topic where there is no consensus – not so much because there are sharply divided views, although these do exist at the margins, but because most people are confused or have given little thought to the matter.

Debates on and changes to the National Curriculum and Religious Education (RE) since 1988 have put nationality somewhat more under the spotlight. Some have argued that British material should be given more prominence in the History syllabus. The legal requirement that the RE syllabus put the main weight on Christianity probably reflects the older view that Britain is essentially a Christian, indeed Protestant country. Both moves have come from the right, from those holding traditional beliefs about Britishness. They have been opposed by those on the left suspicious about national sentiment. We will come back to history and RE later.

More broadly than the National Curriculum, what role should education in general play? Children's earliest education is in the home. It is here that they begin to acquire a sense of who they are in relation to the various communities of which they will form a part. Among other things nearly all parents will consciously or unconsciously be inducting them into the way of life of our national group. This is true of those parents from ethnic communities who encourage some integration into British life while holding firm to their own cultural identity, and excludes only those who want their children brought up wholly outside British patterns. Virtually every family will bring up children in the English language and not French or German; they will learn to play games and hear jokes and stories that children across the Channel will not experience (which is not to deny all sorts of things they will have in common). They will also become aware of the existence of foreigners, perhaps through seeing sports on TV, perhaps through travelling abroad. All this will begin to help them to define themselves in national terms.

Schools should pick up from this. Part of their role is to help pupils discover who they are, and they risk leaving them unnecessarily confused if they do not equip them to understand their national identity, or, if there are doubts about this, to understand the causes of doubt more fully. There are several ways in which more specific activities and school subjects may help.

Personal and social education is a part of the curriculum tailor-made for this sort of work, because here the focus is on the children themselves rather than on some more external subject-matter. Self-understanding is so closely connected with discerning the cultural horizons that frame one's existence that national horizons must come into the picture. The presence of children from other national and cultural backgrounds, more marked in some of our big cities than elsewhere, can be put to good use in exploring issues of nationality.

In a well-structured school, personal and social aims pervade every part of the curriculum (see White, 1990). History is a subject especially relevant to nationality. The aims of school history are currently under dispute in this connection (Lee *et al.*, 1992), one side arguing that history has its own internal aims and any attempt to subordinate it to the requirements of citizenship or patriotism tends to pervert it, the other seeing nothing reprehensible in such a policy. Without going into the details of this debate, I think it will be clear from earlier remarks that I support the latter position. If pupils are to come to understand their Britishness, they need to see how this has come into being, historically speaking. They need to understand the importance of the Act of Union, something of the separate national and pre-national histories which lay behind it, the original connotations of Britishness, and the historical roots of more acceptable versions of it which may replace it. As they grow older, applying their historical knowledge to political issues, they need to be engaged themselves in the debate about our nationality and the future of our national community. They will, of course, also be studying the history of other countries.

I take that as read. (For a defence of teaching English/British national history in schools and the sketch of an A level/GCSE syllabus in the subject, see Howkins, 1989. For him a course in national history 'should set up the nation as the object of study, problematise the very idea, and then examine aspects of that problematic in more detail', p. 24.)

A word on patriotism: the idea that history should be taught partly for patriotic ends is hateful to many history teachers, not least those on the left. They will point to the corruption of school history under the Nazis, to the indoctrination of pre-war British children into the imperial myth and the rites of Empire Day. But there is nothing intrinsically wrong with patriotism.

Love of other people: caring for their welfare, being concerned about their future – is generally taken to be a highly desirable emotion. We laud it in the shape of parental and other love within the family, in sexual relationships, in more global concerns for humanity at large. Why should we not laud it also at the intermediate level of the national community – in the anxious concern we have, for instance, for our homeless and unemployed and for abused children? True, love of one's own people can be accompanied by hatred of outsiders. Yet this is not a necessary feature of it, but an atavism that we should by now have learned to outgrow. Not only in *Romeo and Juliet*, but also in some societies today, attachment to one's own family goes with antagonism towards others; but in the way that we do not reject the institution of the family and family love just because some families are and have been morally repellent, so we should not turn our back on the nation and on national sentiment simply because some nations have been filled with hostility for others. History teachers exercised about patriotism and the dangers of indoctrination are keen on objectivity. Yet more objective than a blanket refusal to have nothing to do with patriotism would be a decision to help students to see, via conceptual distinction and historical illustration, that patriotism is not one thing and that more benign and more odious forms of it can be separated from each other.

Now to English: the very name of this subject seems to carry national connotations, as do its subdivisions English Language and English Literature. The former's value partly resides in its indispensability for other academic subjects and for work and other activities in later life; but it is also the basis of our national community and could be taught more explicitly as such. In this area, too, issues are cloudier for the British than for other nations. It is easy for outsiders like ourselves to grasp how teaching children the Hungarian language is vitally connected with making them members of the Hungarian nation. Yet we are less inclined to apply similar thinking to British children. This is largely for reasons already given about our coyness towards nationality and uncertainties about Britishness. However, it may also have something to do with the fact that we do not own the English language as the Hungarians own theirs. Many other nations – the Americans, Irish, Jamaicans, Australians, New Zealanders and others – rely on it as much as we do. This together with its invincible position as the chief international language must make it hard for all of us to see it as our language in particular, rather than a more globally useful instrument – even though it *is* our language and vital to our self-identity.

Perversely, at the one place where the traditional school curriculum has been constructed largely on national lines more outward-looking attitudes would be desirable. Literature in schools is always labelled 'English Literature'. In practice this means the literature of Great Britain (rather than England) plus a few works by American, Australian, South African, Caribbean and other writers, which suggests that the term 'English Literature' can be taken to mean 'literature written in English' as well as 'literature from England (or Great Britain)'. Clarifying where we stand on nationality would help us to know what the aims of teaching literature should be. I am far from out of sympathy with the idea that its literature is an important facet of a nation's make-up, reinforcing the shared beliefs which we have discussed and enabling us to appreciate this sharing across time. Yet I can also see good reason for extending the range of literature beyond the national. However great the intrinsic aesthetic and spiritual merits of Estonian literature – and I know nothing about these – I am sure that Estonian students would be badly deprived if their schools and universities introduced them only to their own literature. The case for adding to this repertoire the translatable part – largely fiction and drama – of the world's finest writers is too obvious to need delineating. Obvious or not, it is rarely made in Britain. Whether people feel that English literature is so superabundantly rich that there is no point in going beyond it, I do not know. Meanwhile students leave school, even after A-level English Literature, knowing nothing of Chekhov or Ibsen, Tolstoy or Stendhal. Not only would this wider acquaintance be valuable in itself in revealing aspects of human nature of universal significance, but penetrating other national cultures could also support education for nationality in particular, in two ways. It could impede identifications of Otherness with evil, and it could make us more aware by contrast of what makes us us.

These same two objectives are attainable by factual studies of other national groups. In Britain we are well-placed for this, with a score of nations within an hour or two's flying distance from London, our membership of the European community and the new links it brings compounding this advantage. (Contrast a child living in New York or Sydney.) History, geography, social and political studies and literature can join forces in this work. Enlightened teaching under the rubric of foreign languages also includes work – conducted in English – on the life and culture of our European neighbours.

Whether teaching compulsory foreign languages in the way we traditionally do it is as helpful is more doubtful. Most children spend several hours a week for several years learning French or, less frequently, German or Spanish, but few achieve more in the end than being able to string together a few simple phrases and many get vastly bored on the way. For all we know, from the point of view of cultural education, their experience could be counterproductive. It might associate things French with pain and tediousness, perhaps even reinforcing traditional antipathies towards that nation rather than breaking them down. There are independent reasons against compulsory foreign languages (White, 1990; Williams, 1991). They do little to extend understanding as distinct from teaching certain skills: unlike many other subjects, the concepts that pupils employ in them are mostly already familiar to them, because what they are learning is new words to express concepts for which they have the words in English. As for skills, since English is the chief world language, there is far less motivation for British than for, say, German children to learn a foreign language. Even leading figures in the foreign language teaching world have thought it would be better if the work was voluntary rather than compulsory (Hornsey, 1969). On the compulsory side they favour 'language awareness' classes, where the objective is to introduce students to aspects of – perhaps several – foreign languages, not so as to equip them with skills but in order to give them insight into language in general and make them more reflective about the nature of their own language. The cultural significance of one's native language in shaping one's membership of a national community could be one aspect of this work.

I have concentrated on some subject-areas of closest relevance to education for nationality. But the role that every curriculum activity could play in this deserves review. Film is an underestimated art form in education. Classic French, Italian, Russian, Polish, Mexican (etc.) films are excellent means – in some ways better than foreign literature in translation – of introducing pupils to other nations and making them more conscious of their own. Media teachers can direct students to aspects of British films which shed light on what and who we are. Art lessons can, *inter alia*, open children's eyes to British landscapes and townscapes and changes in these over the years. Science, maths and technology and economics can deepen understanding of the industrial base of British society, so crucial to the ambivalent way we see, and have always seen, ourselves – now as a 'manufacturing nation', now as industry-haters yearning for the green and pleasant land of Blake's poem (Wiener, 1981). Religious Education has now, owing to recent legislation, to make Christianity its main focus. As suggested earlier, the impetus behind this probably reflects the traditional association between Britishness and Christianity, especially Protestantism. But the new law can be put to the service of a very different, more reflective and humane, picture of ourselves than this eighteenth-century throwback: RE classes can study the role that Christianity has played in forming this older conception of Britishness and in this way fit us better to transcend it.

These are only some of the ways in which the school curriculum could be remodelled to meet the demands of a defensible education for nationality. The task is an unfamiliar one for British educators and there is a lot to do, beginning with changes to deep-set attitudes towards national sentiment in general and in its British form held by those with power to make policy.

I suspect the Belarusians may get there before us.[3]

Notes

1   Bhikhu Parekh (1994) has provided a provocative critique of liberal as well as conservative defences of national sentiment, seeing as a particularly weak point in both their antipathy to outsiders. But his claim that 'whether it is conservative or liberal, nationalism cannot avoid being exclusive and hostile to immigration' seems more telling against conservative than against liberal views. He argues, indeed, that national identity can be thickened and enriched by incorporating some elements of immigrant culture.

2   This thesis has many affinities with that presented in Tamir (1993). She, too, argues for the compatibility of liberalism with national sentiment. But her notion of 'nation' is different from mine, being detached from the notion of possessing or aspiring to political autonomy and closer to the notion of a cultural group. For a critique of her position see White (1994).

3   I am most grateful for ideas helpful in writing this paper provided by Tanyo Buiko, Matthew Clayton, Alan Cribb, Ruth Jonathan, Ian McPherson, Sven-Erik Nordenbo, Yael Tamir, Ken Wain and Patricia White.

References

Colley, L. (1992) *Britons: Forging the Nation 1707–1837*, New Haven and London: Yale University Press.

Crick, B. (1988) 'An Englishman considers his passport', *The Irish Review*, Vol. 5.

Dahrendorf, R. (1982) *On Britain*, London: BBC.

Hill, C. (1989) 'History and patriotism', in R. Samuel (ed.), *Patriotism: The Making and Unmaking of British National Identity*, Vols I–III, London: Routledge.

Hobsbawm, E. (1990) *Nations and Nationalism Since 1780: Programme, Myth, Reality*, Cambridge: Cambridge University Press.

Hornsey, A. (1969) 'Why teach a foreign language?', *University of London Institute of Education Bulletin*, No. 18.

Howkins, A. (1989) 'A defence of national history', in R. Samuel (ed.), *Patriotism: The Making and Unmaking of British National Identity*, Vols I–III, London: Routledge.

Lee, P., Slater, J., Walsh, P. and White, J. (1992) *The Aims of School History*, London File Series, London: Tufnell Press.

MacIntyre, A. (1981) *After Virtue*, London: Duckworth.

Miller, D. (1988) 'The ethical significance of nationality', *Ethics*, Vol. 98.

Miller, D. (1989) 'In what sense must socialism be communitarian?', in E. F. Paul, F. D. Miller, J. Paul and D. Greenberg (eds), *Socialism*, Oxford: Blackwell.

Miller, D. (1993) 'In defence of nationality', *Journal of Applied Philosophy*, 10(1).

Miller, D. (1995) 'Reflections on British national identity', *New Community*, January, 21(2).

Mulhall, S. and Swift, A. (1992) *Liberals and Communitarians*, Oxford: Blackwell.

National Curriculum Council (1990) *Education for Citizenship: Curriculum Guidance*, [8], London: HMSO.

Parekh, B. (1994) 'Politics of nationhood', in K. von Benda-Beckman and M. Verkuyten (eds), *Cultural Identity and Development in Europe*, London: University College Press.

Samuel, R. (ed.) (1989a) *Patriotism: The Making and Unmaking of British National Identity*, Vols I–III, London: Routledge.

Samuel, R. (1989b) 'Continuous national history', in R. Samuel (ed.), *Patriotism: The Making and Unmaking of British National Identity*, Vols I–III, London: Routledge.

Tamir, Y. (1993) *Liberal Nationalism*, Princeton, NJ: Princeton University Press.

White, J. (1990) *Education and the Good Life: Beyond the National Curriculum*, London: Kogan Page.

White, J. (1994) 'Liberalism, nationality and education', in *Proceedings of 4th Biennial INPE Conference*, Leuven, Belgium, August 17–20.

Wiener, M. (1981) *English Culture and the Decline of the Industrial Spirit 1830–1980*, Cambridge: Cambridge University Press.

Williams, K. (1991) 'Modern languages in the school curriculum: a philosophical view', *Journal of Philosophy of Education*, 25(2), pp. 247–58.

PART 4

SUBJECTS

CHAPTER 14

THE ROOTS OF PHILOSOPHY

The Impulse to Philosophise (1992), A. P. Griffiths (ed.). Cambridge: Cambridge University Press

I

Some people think that the impulse to philosophise begins in early childhood: Gareth Matthews, for instance, in his *Philosophy and the Young Child* (1980). His book begins 'TIM (about six years), while busily engaged in licking a pot, asked, "Papa, how can we be sure that everything is not a dream?"' 'Tim's puzzle,' he tells us, 'is quintessentially philosophical. Tim has framed a question that calls into doubt a very ordinary notion (being awake) in such a way as to make us wonder whether we really know something that most of us unquestioningly assume we know.'

Matthew Lipman, Director of the Institute for the Advancement of Philosophy for Children at Montclair State College, New Jersey, also sees the starting point for children's philosophical development in their questionings and wonderings. 'Children begin to think philosophically when they begin to ask why' (Lipman *et al.*, 1977: 35). Children wonder constantly about all sorts of things. They try to cope in various ways – by scientific explanation, by fairy tales, and stories, and 'by formulating the matter philosophically' (p. 14). They do so in the latter case when they ask questions like 'What's space? What's number? What's matter? What's mind? What are possibilities? What's reality? What are things? What's my identity? What are relationships? Did everything have a beginning? What's death? What's life? What's meaning? What's value?' (p. 70).

Part of the impulse behind Matthews' promotion of philosophy for children has been the thought that philosophising is an activity which is natural to all of us. He writes:

> I first became interested in the philosophical thought of young children by worrying about how to teach introductory courses in philosophy to college students. Many students seemed to resist the idea that doing philosophy could be natural. In response to their resistance I hit on the strategy of showing them that as children many of them had already done philosophy. It occurred to me that my task as a college philosophy teacher was to reintroduce my students to an activity that they had once enjoyed and found natural, but that they had later been socialized to abandon.
>
> (Matthews, 1980: vii)

Lipman, too, first turned to philosophy for children (PFC) through dissatisfaction with teaching philosophy at university. In his case he was concerned about poor reasoning abilities of students (Lipman, 1989). In 1969 he wrote a novel for

11–12-year olds called *Harry Stottlemeier's Discovery* in which children discover logic for themselves (Lipman, 1974). Since then he has used this and other such novels in training programmes for preparing teachers of philosophy in schools.

The literature of PFC stresses the opposition between the idea that young children can be interested in such an abstract subject as philosophy and Piaget's theory. Will Robinson, a British follower of Lipman, says that 'at four years of age my kids would ask me questions that I thought were deeply philosophical; but I knew they couldn't ask those questions because Piaget had said they couldn't!' (Robinson, 1988: 86). He goes on to say that youngsters 'can and do ask important questions which are philosophically substantial' and that 'any day now, even the youngest child may come up with a contribution that is going to be philosophically revolutionary'.

So much for some of the claims of enthusiasts for children's philosophising. How sound are they?

We need, first, to test whether the accounts that theorists give of what children do match the facts. A first issue here is whether children in fact say what they are alleged to say. *Do* young children typically – or indeed ever – ask 'What are possibilities?' 'What is my identity?' 'What's value?'? Since we are given no further evidence we cannot judge, but it is rather hard to swallow.

A second issue is whether the descriptions theorists give of what children say are always well-grounded. Take Tim's question about dreaming with which we began and Matthews' comment on it. It is true that in a certain context this could be a philosophical question – if asked by a philosophy teacher in an undergraduate seminar, for instance. It is true that, in that context, the speaker 'has framed a question that calls into doubt a very ordinary notion…(etc.)'. But does it follow that because this is a philosophical question in that context it is a philosophical question in every other context? How in general do we identify a philosophical question? We cannot go by the mere production of a sentence like 'How can we be sure that everything is not a dream?', since a person could be parroting something picked up elsewhere. We have to presuppose that the speaker understands what he is saying and is saying it with a certain intention in mind, in this case an intention to become clearer about a topic about which he is puzzled or confused. We have to say more than this, of course, for not every confusing or puzzling topic is philosophical. This is not the place to embark on the wild goose chase of producing a non-circular definition of the philosophical. I perhaps need only remark that the person who asks the question about dreaming must at least be affected by doubts of a categorical sort about the distinction between appearance and reality. I am not arguing that any of this must be very sophisticated, such that, say, only those acquainted with the literature of philosophy can be said to ask philosophical questions. But something like this intention, perhaps only in a very inchoate form, must be present.

It *may* be that six-year-old Tim has this intention. I do not want to deny that he does. The issue is only Matthews' warrant for inferring from the data that he has it. Should one go so far, for instance, as to talk of Tim's 'puzzle'? Or of his having 'framed a question that calls into doubt…(etc.)'. What *I* find puzzling about all this is that professional philosophers like Matthews, who must be acquainted with philosophical discussions about the wealth of intentions that can be hypothetically attributed to the same piece of overt verbal behaviour, can insist without further ado that a philosophical intention rather than some other lies behind a question like Tim's.

When Matthews describes three-year-old Denis, talking about not being able to have bread without butter if it's buttered already, as 'exploring the modal notions of possibility and necessity' (p. 14), the gap between behaviour and interpretation seems very great indeed. If all that Matthews is implying is that such a young child can reason in a logical way, that is not news; but it is misleading to describe this in such a way as to suggest that the child is adopting something of the *higher-order* stance to reasoning taken by philosophers of logic. Lipman, it seems to me, similarly conflates reasoning and philosophising in saying that children begin to philosophise when they ask the question 'why?'.

Philosophers are interested in the criteria for the application of concepts. Another of Matthews' examples records 'an instructive moment of puzzlement over the concept of life':

> DAVID [aged five] worries about whether an apple is alive. He decides that it is when it's on the ground but not when it has been brought into the house.
>
> (p. 6)

We all know that when children are learning new concepts they are often at first uncertain how they are to be applied. But the remarks they make and the questions they ask to reduce this uncertainty must be distinguished from philosophers' comments. Once again, different intentions are at work. Children want to know how to use the concept; philosophers, who have no trouble using it, are interested in mapping it from a higher-order perspective, and usually in the pursuit of larger theoretical enquiries. Needless to say, too, philosophers are only interested in those concepts which present philosophical problems, whereas the point just made about children can apply to their acquisition of *all* kinds of concepts – of cats, rivers, computers. Matthews' example, the concept of life, happens to be one which is of interest to philosophers also. But this is coincidental. David is not puzzled about the concept of life as a philosopher might be who is reflecting on the possibility of survival after death or the ethics of abortion. He is simply on the way to acquiring the concept. Or so it would seem. I do not want categorically to deny that he is really philosophising in something of the way we would describe an adult as doing this. It is just that I see no evidence that this is what he is doing.

To come back to Matthews' comment, in the quotation about his students, that philosophy is something which as children they found enjoyable and natural, but which they had later been socialised to abandon. There is a hint here of the view, often associated with Rousseau, that educators need to strip away the corrupting influences of social conventions and get back to children's 'natural' propensities, when thus unspoilt, to explore their world and make their own discoveries. The same child-centred orientation may lie behind Will Robinson's heady comment that any day we may expect some really young child to make a philosophically revolutionary contribution. (I have begun eavesdropping on our neighbour's toddler in the garden next door, and am almost sure I heard her say 'Slab!' when playing with her bricks.)

Difficulties with this kind of child-centred theorising are well known, having been dissected with exemplary clarity by Robert Dearden (1968), and I will not dwell on them here. Whether it is true or not that there is this ideological thrust behind some of the manifestations of the movement for children's philosophising, the latter does seem to suggest that philosophy is something that virtually *all* children would want to engage in, given the opportunity. There are epistemological difficulties here about how one knows that this is so. But there are also ethical considerations. If, as in some PFC courses in schools, it is not only children with a clear philosophical talent – if they exist – who are obliged to participate, but all the members of a school class, then, if the remarks I have made about confusions of purpose in the movement are correct, it is not clear to me how beneficial it will be to the ordinary child to be engaged in philosophical discussion. That is, if we are indeed talking about teaching them philosophy rather than improving their reasoning powers or building up desirable interpersonal dispositions. PFC programmes often have these latter two aims, bringing them under the umbrella of teaching philosophy. But they are surely separable from it. Good teachers in most areas of the curriculum want to develop their students' reasoning abilities and to encourage them to listen with respect to others' points of view. But to come back to the main point, how justified is one as a teacher in obliging young children to engage in philosophising when there are such slim grounds for thinking it suitable for them?

Before we bid farewell to Gareth Matthews, reading his nine-year-old son to sleep with Augustine's *De magistro* (p. 97), one last thought. Advocates of philosophy for children, like Matthews in the quotation from him above, treat children's philosophising as an *enjoyable* activity. If so, that would immediately make it very different from the experience which adults typically have of it. Or, at least, if we talk of enjoyment in their case, it is often only in the broad sense that one may apply to a boxer or a marathon runner. Philosophy often brings bewilderment, despair, painful struggles for understanding. Just as one may wonder whether sitting a class down in an English lesson to write a poem after listening to Honegger's *Pacific 231* may not give them a totally false idea of poetic creation – as something that can be done to order and en masse, so I cannot escape the thought that presenting philosophy to children as a fun activity may impede rather than promote any understanding they may come to have of what philosophy is all about.

II

After writing the last section I came across an excellent article by Richard Kitchener, called 'Do Children Think Philosophically?' (Kitchener, 1990). I commend it as a thorough and scholarly discussion of claims by Lipman and Matthews among others that children can philosophise. Like me, Kitchener is sceptical, on the grounds that young children are by and large incapable of the reflective, higher-order kind of thinking crucial to doing philosophy and that what is labelled 'philosophising' in children is often confused with thinking critically. I will not go over the many points where I find myself in agreement with him, but will focus instead on what seems to be an issue that divides us.

As an expert on Piaget's genetic epistemology (see Kitchener, 1986), he is especially interested in the claim often made by supporters of philosophy for children and instanced above that the existence of young children's philosophising casts doubt on Piaget's cognitive-developmental theory. According to the latter, younger children, say below the age of ten, are capable of concrete operational thought but not formal operational thought. Since philosophising requires critical – reflective abilities impossible before the formal stage, Piaget's stage theory of development must be wrong (see Matthews, 1980, ch. 4).

Kitchener's arguments that there is no evidence of young children's higher-order thinking, if sound, are enough to rebut the claim that data on children's philosophising have undermined Piaget's theory. But he goes further than this critical move, giving an embryonic sketch of a Piagetian account of the development of philosophical abilities. For this purpose he makes a distinction between 'concrete philosophising' and 'abstract philosophising'. The former is exemplified in the dialogues found in Gareth Matthews and others about such things as death, dreaming, whether plants have feelings, whether computers think, and so on. This thinking remains at the concrete level since young children cannot grasp the principle *qua* principle underlying the concrete case. 'Abstract philosophising' requires the skills underlying concrete philosophy, i.e. the mental operations Piaget characterised as 'concrete operations', but also additional ones as well – those involving 'formal operations' (p. 430). Kitchener goes on to suggest that formal operational thinking is not sufficient for doing philosophy since one also needs still higher-order, meta-philosophical abilities, those called in Piagetian circles 'post formal operational skills'. He concludes

> If there is a stage of reasoning higher than formal-operational thinking, then the development of philosophical skills may indeed [proceed] by a stage-like sequence involving lower-order logical skills, higher-order logical skills (formal operational skills) and post-formal operational skills.
>
> (p. 430)

This goes further than showing that Piaget has not been refuted and suggests that there may be Piagetian stages in philosophical development just as in other spheres, for example in moral judgement or in understanding the physical world. But this raises a difficulty. Is the notion of philosophical development coherent? In some ways of taking the term there are no problems. It may be said of a student that her philosophical skills have developed markedly over the year when all that is meant by this is that she has made great strides in learning the subject. But the Piagetian sense of 'development' is tied to a biological conception of organisms and their powers unfolding from within in the presence of appropriate environmental factors. While we familiarly use this notion in the context of plants growing and the physical growth of young children, it is not at all clear how it can be applied to mental phenomena. The notion of biological development brings with it the concept of some initial state out of which unfolding occurs and also the concept of some mature end-state towards which the unfolding is directed and beyond which it cannot go. But if we apply this to, say, moral judgement, this teleological conception gains no purchase. There is no evidence of a moral seed out of which children's moral learning springs; and ideas of what counts as maturity of moral understanding are very diverse, dependent not least on cultural factors: there is no biologically based mature state comparable to the fully-grown oak tree which has developed from an acorn. But this is not basically an empirical issue: given what we know of the necessary dependence of moral learning on social involvement, the atomism implicit in the Piagetian conception of individual unfolding is inconsistent with this. Difficulties along these lines in Piaget's cognitive developmentalism in general have been pointed out by other philosophers, notably David Hamlyn (1967, 1978, ch. 4). If this critique is sound, then the notion of philosophical development is a myth; and so *a fortiori*, is the notion of stages of philosophical development.

Although he is a powerful critic of the views of Lipman and Matthews, Kitchener is still at one with them in holding that young children can philosophise, if only concretely and not, as Lipman and Matthews think, abstractly. He writes, indeed, of the 'very insightful and interesting philosophical discussion' that young children can engage in at the concrete level (1990: 427). As an example of concrete philosophising he quotes a dialogue from Gareth Matthews about whether cheese is made of grass:

> 'In a way it is true,' said Donald. 'We do not really notice what stuff is actually made of,' suggested Esther…'You know,'…. [cows] have four different stomachs.' [Donald said] 'It sounds unusual, but grass *is* cheese in a way; it is

just the first stage of what becomes cheese – the second stage is milk.' 'Cream!' put in someone as a correction. 'The third stage is cheese,' Donald continued. 'It's all the same really, it's just different stages as it matures.'

(p. 428)

Why does Kitchener call this kind of discussion 'philosophical'? His reason is 'the underlying similarities – their family resemblances' – between it and abstract philosophising (p. 430). He does not expand on what these similarities are. He is, of course, entitled to use the word in this way if he pleases: but to me there seems so *little* resemblance between the two, for reasons that I have already referred to, and especially over the crucial feature of higher-order reflection, that it is less misleading to restrict rather than extend the use of the term.

I suspect, in any case, that Kitchener's reason for extending it has to do not only with perceived family resemblances but also with a pre-commitment to a Piagetian paradigm. If one takes as a starting point that philosophising is a category of thinking, like moral or scientific thinking, to which cognitive – developmental theory can apply, then one will be understandably drawn to seek out its early manifestations among young children.

One last point on Kitchener. Piaget's own accounts of different kinds of children's thinking are universal in their scope. They are intended to apply to every child: *all* children develop through the stages of moral development or an understanding of space or number. Does Kitchener want to follow this through into the philosophical area? If so, just as we would, within a Piagetian framework, expect everyone – unless there are special internal reasons why their growth is stunted, and always provided external circumstances are favourable – to develop towards higher levels of moral or scientific understanding, so we should expect everyone to move towards more sophisticated levels of philosophising. Usually, however, doing philosophy is seen as very much a minority activity: only a relatively few people seem to come to have the peculiar cast of mind which it demands. Kitchener's view appears to be out of line with this common conception. That is not enough, of course, to show that it is wrong.

III

Is the argument of Sections I and II quite fair to the view that the impulse to philosophise begins in childhood? We know that some children do seem genuinely affected by matters to do with the infinite, about numbers going on for ever, or about whether space or time can come to a stop. It is interesting to speculate about why it is issues like these that tend to crop up in this context, rather than questions about, say, logical validity, the objectivity of ethical judgements, or the nature of substance. A plausible answer is that an interest in infinity is continuous with, or grows naturally out of, children's widening understanding of their world, whereas an interest in the other things requires a shift to a higher-order stance. If children's concern with the infinite were to do with the *nature* of mathematical, spatial or temporal infinity, this, too, would require higher-order thinking. But this is not what grips them. In arithmetic they begin with numbers from one to ten, go on to larger and larger numbers and by the time they hit the billions and trillions and quadrillions, not surprisingly begin to wonder where it is all going to stop. The same with space: once they move outwards from the planetary system and past the Milky Way, it would be very odd if they *did not* ask themselves what lay beyond. Similarly for time.

I have been suggesting that simply having thoughts about infinite magnitudes is not to engage in philosophising. This may begin when something more is added – some kind of conceptual conflict – between the thought, for instance, that space must go on for ever and the thought that when it was created or came into being it must have been limited in extent. We should not assume that all those children who reach beyond the supernovas – and such children may not be so numerous, we do not know – experience any such conflict: they may just register that space does not stop and turn back to collecting cards of footballers. Some children may well experience some kind of conflict in these situations, but it is likely to be pretty inchoate, since to formulate the issues with any precision depends on resources that we cannot expect many eight- or eleven-year olds to possess. Whether these children begin to think philosophically when faced with such conflicts cannot be taken for granted. To judge from my own personal experience of children, they are quite likely, even the most intellectually lively of them, to want to put a rapid end to the discomfort of thinking about such head-breaking matters.

This is not to deny that a vague sense of unresolved, deep and important issues may linger with some of them in the obscurer parts of their minds and impel them towards philosophy at a later time. It may be that some children get further than this – that their thoughts about infinity (or something else) start them off down a philosophical road along which, no doubt with tuition, they then make unbroken progress, just as they might make in mathematics, say. What interests me is that, as far as I know, we never hear about any children like this. Do they exist?

One way of throwing light on this, on the topic of children's philosophising in general, and indeed on wider questions about the impulse to philosophise, is to turn to biographical material about how adult philosophers first came into contact with philosophical issues and at what age. I have been suggesting that the number of children who get anywhere near to philosophical thinking is likely to be small. Among them, one might hypothesise, one would expect to find future fully-fledged philosophers and certainly the philosophical stars. Is this borne out in fact?

The earliest age I have been able to discover is five. Colin Radford (1989) describes, in his *The Examined Life*, how an older friend tried to quell his fear of cows by telling him 'Cows have got magnifying eyes, so you look very big to a cow and that is why they are frightened of *you*' (p. 3). Radford tells us that

> I suddenly felt – dizzy. There was something wrong, something *terribly, profoundly, wrong*, with what Cecil had said, but although I had stopped, and was grimacing and gritting my teeth in my effort to work out what was wrong, I could not do so.

In fact it was only years later that he was able to sort out the conceptual confusion in Cecil's remark. We cannot, it seems, claim this as an early example of children's engaging in the activity of philosophising, since as he says he was quite unable to cope with the problem. It seems at most an instance of the inchoate awareness of some kind of conceptual conflict that I mentioned above. All this is assuming that his recollection of how he felt and behaved at five is accurate. One can readily imagine that a young child might be fascinated and perhaps frightened by an animal with strange eyes, but it is harder to credit that he could already be operating with a concept of the profound logical wrongness of some-one's statement. Of course, there can be different degrees of conceptual under-standing and it may be – I would not want to deny this – that Radford possessed this concept in some minimal sense. If you told a child that a certain tree was called a yew tree and the next moment you told her that it was not a yew but a hawthorn, one might expect her to look puzzled and upset. Would one say that she possessed, in some minimal sense, the concept of logical wrongness? Perhaps. The difference between this example and Radford's is that the former is structurally simpler. The child is confronted with an instance of p immediately followed by *not-p*, and it would be surprising if she did not see a discrepancy. But Cecil's statement, as reported above, is a complex little argument. To see its incoherence one would have not only to grasp how p *is* presented as a ground for q and q as a ground for r, but also to follow through the implications of having magnifying eyes and see that these would make everything larger, not just oneself, so that one did not look large in comparison to other things. The incoherence here does not leap to the eye as in the former example.

This may raise a difficulty for Radford's description of the case. To see, even at a minimal level, the logical oddness of Cecil's remark seems to involve having traced through – at least at some minimal level – the connections just mentioned. Yet Radford writes that it was many years before he succeeded in working out what was wrong with the account. But perhaps he means by this working through to an explicit, higher-order, understanding of it. And perhaps this is compatible with working through the connections in some more intuitive way at an early age and seeing some kind of logical oddness here. If Radford did do so, this would indeed show that he possessed unusual thinking abilities for his age, perhaps even some proto-philosophical abilities.

How could we ever know? Our only access to the event is Radford's memory and this, as I am sure he would be the first to agree, may be inaccurate. Whether this is indeed the earliest recorded example of a future philosopher's first philosophisings must be left an open question.

Radford is also a contestant for the *second* prize in this competition, for I have found no other contender younger than six, the age at which for the second occasion in his life he encountered what strikes him now as a philosophical problem (p. 15). He was a new pupil at an infants school and found himself behind the other children in arithmetic. Asked to take 48 from 13, he could not do so because he had not come across negative numbers. Recording his bewilderment and despair at not being able to make any headway, he writes

> My difficulties will seem childish misunderstandings, but what I hope to have demonstrated is that the solution requires extensions of techniques and concepts. So my difficulty was not just a consequence of stupidity, or a blind spot for maths, it was philosophical. I did not find it natural to go on, to take the right approach here, on the basis of what I already knew and could do.
>
> (p. 18)

Was his difficulty indeed philosophical? If so, it would seem to follow that any learning difficulties that young children have where they need to extend their conceptual schemes can be labelled in the same way. Many children would be facing philosophical problems in learning to read, to count, to talk about things happening in the past or in the future; and those struggling the hardest – the slowest and most handicapped – would be those with most exposure to philosophical difficulties. But this seems to make little sense.

There is *a parallel* between the sort of learning difficulty that Radford describes and the experience of some kinds of philosophising. In each case one feels at a loss, not knowing which way to turn; and in each case this feeling is relieved by coming to see things in a new way. But there is also a difference. Young children – or, for that matter, adults with these kinds of learning difficulties – are aware that even if they are stumped, their teachers are not. When Colin Radford 'burst into a further paroxysm of sobs, which allowed me to nestle into the exquisite, warm, firm softness of Miss Davies' right breast' (p. 17), he knew that she knew some way of taking 48 from 13. But when Wittgenstein was wrestling with how the elements of atomic propositions are related to the world, he knew that he was on his own. There are no authorities in philosophy to tell one how to go on.

Perhaps, though, we should compare the subtraction example not with the experience of fully-fledged philosophising but with that of *learning* philosophy. If an undergraduate is thoroughly confused over whether the mental is distinct from the physical or identical with it, she knows – or thinks she knows – that her teacher knows what moves to make to illuminate things. This may well be true, but the philosophy student is still a world away from a young Radford. She knows that her tutor is not privy to the right answer, to the right way of doing things: philosophy is not that kind of subject. She also knows that her tutor has deliberately set up the radical confusion she is suffering, that this is all part of what it is to become a philosopher. Related with this, the headaches she experiences in finding a way out are not wholly painful to her: she enjoys the activity, bewilderment and all. None of these things could be said of the child learning arithmetic.

Radford writes that 'it will be clear to any professional philosopher reading the above that my thinking about mathematics and philosophical problems about mathematics has been influenced by Wittgenstein' (p. 20). Perhaps what he has in mind is that, reflecting on his childhood difficulties in learning arithmetic, he sees in them illustrations of Wittgensteinian themes. They may well provide them, but they can do this without any implication that any philosophising has been going on on the part of the child. The experience of trying fruitlessly to solve problems by following well-worn tracks when a radical shift of perspective is what is required is an object of philosophical interest for a philosopher: the notion of a change of perspective can help to dispel a whole range of philosophical difficulties. These are philosophical difficulties for the philosopher. There is no implication in this that any difficulties which the *learner* faces are philosophical in nature, or at least, are philosophical difficulties *for him or her*.

If these points about the five- and six-year old Colin Radford are correct, we still have not discovered a clear case of philosophical activity or experience among very young, future philosophers.

The next earliest age I have discovered – and this applies to both Collingwood and Popper – is eight. Collingwood found a translation of Kant's *Groundwork of the Metaphysics of Ethics* among his father's books. As he began reading it

> I was attacked by a strange succession of emotions. First came an intense excitement. I felt that things of the highest importance were being said about matters of the utmost urgency...Then, with a wave of indignation, came the discovery that I could not understand them...Then...came the strangest emotion of all. I felt that the contents of this book, although I could not understand it, were somehow my business: a matter personal to myself, or rather to some future self of my own.
>
> (Collingwood, 1944: 8–9)

Karl Popper (1976: 15–16) records that he first stumbled on; a philosophical problem about the age of eight:

> Somehow I heard about the solar system and the infinity of space (no doubt of Newtonian space) and I was worried: I could neither imagine that space was finite (for what, then, was outside it?) nor that it was infinite. My father suggested that I ask one of his brothers, who, he told me, was very good at explaining such things. This uncle asked me first whether I had any trouble about a sequence of numbers going on and on. I had not. Then he asked me to imagine a stack of bricks, and add to it one brick, and again one brick, and so on without end; it would never fill the space of the universe. I agreed, somewhat reluctantly, that this was a very helpful answer, though I was not completely happy about it. Of course, I was unable to formulate the misgivings I still felt: it was the difference between potential and actual infinity, and the impossibility of reducing actual infinity to the potential... It did not, of course, occur to me that what was worrying me might be an open problem. Rather, I thought that this was a question which an intelligent adult like my uncle must understand, while I was too ignorant, or perhaps too young, or too stupid, to grasp it completely.

It seems this was an isolated experience: Popper remembers similar problems when he was a few years older, about twelve or thirteen.

In accounts of philosophers' early childhoods I have discovered only occasional experiences like these. It is not until we come to the twelve-year old J. S. Mill that we find hard evidence of philosophising proper. Having been given an extraordinary comprehensive and rigorous education by his father until that age, he tells us

> I entered into another and more advanced stage in my course of instruction; in which the main object was no longer the aids and appliances of thought, but the thoughts themselves. This commenced with Logic, in which I began at once with the Organon, and read it to the Analytics inclusive...
>
> (Mill, 1873: 15)

Mill is exceptional in the earliness of his acquaintance with philosophy, even among well-known philosophers. There is little evidence of an early interest in philosophy on the part of T. H. Green (Cacoullos, 1974: 26). G. E. Moore became interested in it in his second year at university (Levy, 1979: 51). Russell writes

> I began thinking about philosophical questions at the age of fifteen. From then until I went to Cambridge, three years later, my thinking was solitary and completely amateurish, until I read Mill's *Logic*...
>
> (Russell, 1959: 28)

Augustine (1909: 51) discovered the subject through reading an exhortation to philosophy in Cicero's *Hortensius* about the age of eighteen. Kant first became interested at university, having shown no signs of philosophical precocity:

> Even those of Kant's boyhood friends who thought they perceived in him the earmarks of future greatness saw then only the eminent philologist-to-be.
>
> (Cassirer, 1981: 14–15)

Wittgenstein was considered to be a dull child and did not even start speaking until he was four years old (Monk, 1990: 12) (incidentally, only one year before Colin Radford's philosophical experience to do with bovine vision). At eight or nine he remembered having paused in a doorway to consider the question 'Why should one tell the truth if it is to one's advantage to tell a lie?' and concluded that there was nothing wrong with lying under such circumstances. Apart from this one incident, which – again if his memory is correct – shows him gripped by a philosophical question if not arriving at a characteristically Wittgensteinian answer, there is no further evidence of philosophical interests on his part until after the age of fourteen.

A more comprehensive survey might tell otherwise, but with the exception of Mill, all these philosophers first began to philosophise in their teens, and not always in an organized way. Conflicts of one sort or another often seem to be the first triggers. Russell was affected by theological doubts; Augustine by the unsettled nature of his wayward life. For several of these men, Green, Moore, Russell and Wittgenstein among them, adolescence was a lonely time. Mill's every minute was so taken up with studying that he may not have felt lonely, but in his early years he was certainly much on his own, having been educated by his father – as was Collingwood. I mention all this because solitariness, perceived sometimes, as with Green and Collingwood, as 'indolence' or 'idleness', may be linked with the troubled detachment characteristic of the philosophic turn of mind. Collingwood is explicit:

> I know now that the problems of my life's work were taking, deep down inside me, their first embryonic shape. But any one who observed me must have thought, as my elders did think, that I had fallen into a habit of loafing, and lost the alertness and quickness of wit that had been so noticeable in my early childhood.
>
> (1944: 9)

All the people I have just reviewed became well-known philosophers. But not all those who begin to think philosophically in their youth make their mark as philosophers, or primarily as philosophers, in later life. Some of them are drawn towards other things. Pasternak is an example. Another great Russian writer, Tolstoy, has left us a vivid description of the philosophical thoughts which began to assail him about the age of fifteen or sixteen (Tolstoy, 1854, ch. 19). His account strikes many a chord in me and, I suspect, in others of similar inclination. He writes of his solitary interior life, shut in on himself; of his 'weak childish intellect with all the ardour of inexperience' striving to solve abstract questions about man's destiny, the future life, the immortality of the soul; of deciding to live for the present and lying on his bed for two or three days reading novels and eating gingerbread; of fancying that nothing existed in the universe except himself and 'glancing sharply round in some opposite direction, hoping to catch unawares the void where I was not'. For Tolstoy the experience was painful and destructive:

> My feeble intellect could not penetrate the impenetrable, and in that backbreaking effort lost one after the other the convictions which, for my life's happiness, I ought never to have dared disturb.
>
> All this weary mental struggle yielded me nothing save an artful elasticity of mind which weakened my will-power, and a habit of perpetually dissecting and analysing, which destroyed spontaneity of feeling and clarity of reason.

Advocates of encouraging young people to philosophise, please note. He goes on:

> My fondness for abstract reasoning developed my conscious being to such an unnatural degree that frequently, thinking about the simplest things, I would fall back into the vicious circle of analysis of my thoughts, entirely losing sight of the question that had occupied my mind at the outset, and thinking, instead, about what I was thinking about. Asking myself: 'Of what am I thinking?' I would answer: 'I think of what I am thinking. And now what am I thinking of? I think that I am thinking of what I am thinking of.' And so on. I was at my wits end.
>
> However, the philosophical discoveries I made vastly flattered my vanity: I often imagined myself a great man discovering truths for the benefit of humanity, and gazed upon other mortals with a proud consciousness of my own worth; but strangely enough when I encountered those other mortals I felt shy of each and every one, and the higher I rated myself in my own estimation the less capable I was not only of displaying any consciousness of merit but even of schooling myself not to blush for every word and movement, however simple and unimportant.

In these examples of future philosophers and non-philosophers, the impulse to philosophise is first manifested in adolescence, not in early childhood. No doubt there is more to be said about the conditions in which it flourishes and its origins in individuals' earlier lives, always bearing in mind that it may not be one thing, but may take different forms: some may be drawn into philosophy through religious doubts, others through the quest for a worthwhile life, others – like Wittgenstein, perhaps – through reflections on the nature of mathematics. It may be that some germ of what comes later can be found in early childhood, although I know of no evidence for this. It may also be argued that empirical findings such as I have put forward show very little. The fact that Kant did not start philosophising until late adolescence does not show that engaging him in the activity at eight or nine would have been fruitless. (It might have helped him reach even greater heights.)

This may well be true as a logical point, and I am not ruling out the possibility or desirability of young children's philosophising. All I have been claiming is that the grounds on which these things have been proposed are shaky.

It is interesting to me that it is general philosophers, not philosophers of education, who have been most prominent in advocating children's philosophy. A recurring trigger, found in Matthews, Lipman and others, has been the difficulty of getting undergraduate students of philosophy to think philosophically. But starting them young is not the only way of trying to cope with it, and, in the light of the higher-order nature of philosophy, not the most obvious. Improving secondary education so that more emphasis is put on thinking than on fact-learning across the whole curriculum may have more to be said for it. So, for all I know, may the discouragement of those undergraduate students who show no aptitude for the subject.

The idea that young children can philosophise or naturally are philosophers is arresting. Even more than the earlier idea, associated with Herbert Read (1943) and others, that young children are natural artists, it shocks by its counterintuitiveness. This may help to explain the attention which children's philosophy has attracted – from the media as well as philosophers and educators – in recent years. But does it exist?

Acknowledgements

I am grateful to Professor Matthew Lipman for his kindness and generosity of spirit in sending me a copy of Kitchener's critical discussion of his and Gareth Matthews' work.

References

Augustine (1909) *The Confessions*, London: Chatto and Windus.
Cacoullos, A. R. (1974) *Thomas Hill Green: Philosopher of Rights*, New York: Twayne.
Cassirer, E. (1981) *Kant's Life and Thought*, New Haven, CT: Yale University Press.
Collingwood, R. G. (1944) *An Autobiography*, Harmondsworth: Penguin.
Dearden, R. F. (1968) *The Philosophy of Primary Education*, London: Routledge and Kegan Paul.
Hamlyn, D. W. (1967) 'Logical and Psychological Aspects of Learning', in R. S. Peters (ed.), *The Concept of Education*, London: Routledge and Kegan Paul.
Kitchener, R. F. (1990) 'Do Children Think Philosophically?', *Metaphilosophy*, Vol. 21, No. 4.
Levy, P. (1979) *Moore: G. E. Moore and the Cambridge Apostles*, Oxford: Oxford University Press.
Lipman, M. (1974) *Harry Stottlemeier's Discovery*, New Jersey: IAPC.
Lipman, M. (1989) 'The Institute for the Advancement of Philosophy for Children – Looking Backwards and Looking Forward', *Cogito*, Vol. 3, No. 12.
Lipman, M., Shary, A. M. and Oscayan, F. S. (1977) *Philosophy in the Classroom*, New Jersey: IAPC.
Matthews, G. (1980) *Philosophy and the Young Child* Cambridge, MA: Harvard University Press.
Mill, J. S. (1873) *Autobiography*, The World's Classics 1924 Edition. Oxford: Oxford University Press.
Monk, R. (1990) *Ludwig Wittgenstein: The Duty of Genius*, London: Jonathan Cape.
Popper, K. (1976) *Unended Quest*, London: Fontana.
Radford, C. (1989) *The Examined Life*, Aldershot: Gower.
Read, H. (1943) *Education through Art*, Aldershot: Gower.
Robinson, W. (1988) 'Philosophy for Children', in A. Fisher (ed.), *Critical Thinking: Proceedings of the First British Conference on Informal Logic and Critical Thinking*, Norwich: University of East Anglia.
Russell, B. (1959) *My Philosophical Development*, London: Allen and Unwin.
Tolstoy, L. (1854) *Boyhood in Childhood, Boyhood, Youth*, Harmondsworth: Penguin.

CHAPTER 15

THE ARTS, WELL-BEING AND EDUCATION

Beyond Liberal Education (1992), P. H. Hirst and P. A. White (eds).
London: Routledge

What should be the purposes of education in the arts? This is a big question. Fully to deal with it – and bearing in mind, the kinds of art activities most commonly found in educational institutions – would require asking why, if at all, students should make art (write poems, paint pictures, compose music), perform on musical instruments, engage in literary and other forms of art criticism. In this chapter, I shall not be exploring these questions, but limiting the investigation to what we might call sensuous engagement with works of art and why it should be held to be educationally desirable.

The starting point for this enquiry, as for so many contemporary philosophical enquiries about the content of education, must be Paul Hirst's article on 'Liberal Education and the Nature of Knowledge' (1965). At the time of writing, Hirst's interest, too, lay exclusively in engagement with the arts, 'literature and the fine arts' constituting one of the forms of knowledge into which every liberally educated person was to be inducted. The justification of the artistic form of knowledge, like that of the others, lay in its indispensability for personal well-being. For Hirst, as for the Greek philosophers, this resided in the flourishing of the mind, which in turn consisted in being in a state of knowledge rather than mere belief; and since knowledge was not all of a piece but was found in logically discrete forms, individual flourishing depended on induction into *all* these forms.

While I see difficulties both in the view that art is a form of knowledge and in tying personal well-being so closely to the possession of knowledge, I find Hirst's claim that engagement with the arts is an essential ingredient of personal flourishing intuitively appealing. If true, it may give us a powerful argument for the place of the arts in education, including their place in the school curriculum. In this chapter, I shall begin to put this wider claim of Hirst's to the test, drawing also on recent philosophical writings about the arts which likewise emphasise the latter's role in human well-being.

Osborne's argument

Harold Osborne (1986: 298–9) has sought to justify the 'expansion and enhancement of aesthetic sensibility' as an educational aim. This goes further than, but includes, a justification of engagement with the arts, since it also covers aesthetic experience of nature and of the human environment. Osborne sees the current transition towards a society in which work loses its old salience as enabling the cultivation of 'cultural values' not only in a leisured elite but also in the population as a whole. 'Culture' consists in the cultivation for their own sake of faculties originally developed for purposes of evolutionary survival, such as intelligence, intellectual curiosity and altruistic fellow-feeling. Another of these originally practical faculties is perception of the environment. In its intrinsic form it has become aesthetic experience: this is virtually definable as perception for its own sake.

Aesthetic experience is thus in the same category as the cultivated pursuit of intelligence in mathematics and logic, of intellectual curiosity in science and history, of religious awe and reverence in organised religion. The increasingly leisured individuals of the future will be able to devote themselves to one or more of such cultural activities. Will aesthetic concerns have any privileged place among them? On this Osborne states that 'aesthetic appreciation is the most important (cultural value) and has an even more general appeal than the acquisition of knowledge for its own sake' (p. 299). He does not say why it is the most important value. If he had done so, we might – it is not clear – have had a reason for making aesthetic experience an indispensable ingredient in human flourishing as distinct from an option which some might adopt and others ignore.

As it stands, Osborne's position would seem to point to an educational justification of aesthetic engagement which consists in acquainting pupils with cultural pursuits among which they will later choose which they prefer. The arts would presumably be an important element within the wider field of the aesthetic because of their 'high cultural value' (p. 298), in that it is in aesthetic experience of works of art that perception for its own sake is most fully developed.

The 'opening-up options' justification of educational, including curriculum, activities is in its general form a familiar, and to my mind sound, argument, given some kind of background commitment to the value of personal autonomy as an element in personal well-being. It may, *inter alia*, be relied on to justify engagement with the arts. But it falls short of what is needed to support Hirst's stronger claim, to which this essay is directed, that such engagement is a *necessary* part of our flourishing. Can this stronger position be defended?

On the way to tackling that question, we need to look more closely at Osborne's account of aesthetic experience. For him it comes close to the exercise of our perceptual powers for their own sake. This would seem to imply that the aesthetic qualities of a work of art – or natural object – are confined to those which can be perceptually discriminated. But this is a contestable claim about the scope of the aesthetic. Others have held that this also covers other features of a work, its expressive powers, for instance, or its capacity to reveal truths about the world or about human nature.

If we accept the narrower account of the aesthetic, it is indeed hard to see engagement with the arts as anything more than an option for those drawn to that direction. It will be a matter of developing ever more skilful powers of discriminating such things as patterns of musical sound and their interrelationships, or connections and contrasts among lines, tones, spatial forms and colours in visual art. Those who do not choose to cultivate such connoisseurship need not feel that they are excluding themselves from something vital to their well-being – any more than they need feel this if they decide not to go in for chess or bacteriology.

The conclusion *seems* to be that if the arts are to have any deeper significance in our lives as objects of aesthetic concern a broader account of the aesthetic must be adopted. Whether this conclusion is true, will occupy us through the next section.

Beyond options: further claims for the arts

It is often claimed that engagement with the arts can contribute to personal and social well-being in ways beyond its value as an option for those attracted by it.

It has been variously said to help resolve psychological tensions and foster inner harmony; to help us to understand our own existence; to promote mutual sympathy and understanding; to break down feelings of isolation from the rest of mankind; to reinforce socially accepted values; to promote morality. Some writers see it as performing the redemptive role in society today which religion played in earlier times.

If valid, these claims provide educational justifications of some moment. We will be examining them in more detail in the rest of this chapter. Many of those philosophers who make them, hold the wider view of the aesthetic just mentioned. But not all do. In addition, some people would argue that the benefits referred to depend on a specifically *aesthetic* engagement with works of art; while others would agree that reading literature, looking at paintings and so on might have a moral or psychological spin-off, but urge that this need have nothing to do with relating to the works as aesthetic objects. We need to separate these different strands.

Beardsley's argument

First, let us look at the position of Monroe Beardsley (1958). He writes about the 'inherent values' of works of art, that is, their 'capacity to...produce desirable effects by means of the aesthetic experience they evoke' (p. 573). He has in mind such effects as the relief of tension, the refinement of perception, the development of the imagination, the fostering of mutual sympathy. Unlike other writers with whom we will be dealing, Beardsley holds the narrower view of the scope of the aesthetic. Like Osborne, he restricts aesthetic qualities of a work to certain perceptual features, in his case broadly classifiable under the headings of unity, complexity and intensity of human regional qualities in the work (p. 462). Although the third of these, which he exemplifies by such things as vitality, forcefulness, tenderness and irony, seems to point beyond perceptual qualities to emotions expressed in the work, he emphatically denies this, attracted by the thought that what we call the sadness or joyfulness of a piece of music is an objective feature of the work, dependent on perceptual qualities like tempo, rhythm, interval and pitch.

Beardsley's view is, then, that aesthetic experience as so defined can produce the desirable effects he describes. How sound are his arguments?

1 He admits that the claims that aesthetic experience relieves tensions, quiets destructive impulses and helps to create an inner harmony are speculative rather than soundly supported 'by empirical evidence, although he does mention a remarkable feeling of clarification that we feel when aesthetically absorbed – 'as though the jumble in our minds were being sorted out' (p. 574). We will come back to views about tension and harmony when we turn to writers with a wider view of the aesthetic.

2 His next claim is that aesthetic experience refines perception and discrimination. This seems to follow logically from his perception-based conception of the aesthetic. He further contends that 'if we can be made more sensitive and perceptive by aesthetic experience, then this would have a wide bearing upon all other aspects of our lives – our emotional relations with other people, for example' (ibid.). For this he produces no evidence and *prima facie* the claim seems implausible; just as a developed skill in throwing darts can remain a self-contained achievement with no spill-over on to the improvement of one's personal life or social relationships, should we not say the same of the skills

of aesthetic discernment? We must not be misled by language in all this. When Beardsley says that aesthetic experience can make us 'more sensitive and perceptive', this is obviously true if we take these terms in a perceptual sense; but whether it makes us more sensitive to others' needs and more perceptive in our judgements of character is quite another matter.

3   A similar verdict should be passed on the statement that 'aesthetic experience develops the imagination and with it the ability to put oneself in the place of others' (ibid.). It is true that in aesthetic experience (in Beardsley's sense) 'we must be open to new qualities and new forms'; but the kind of imaginative capacity which this requires has to do solely with aesthetic perception and is not the same as the sympathetic imagination which enables us to put ourselves in others' shoes. One cannot assume a transfer of learning between one kind of exercise of the imagination and another: to show this, too, empirical evidence would be needed and Beardsley does not provide it.

4   He then argues that aesthetic experience 'fosters mutual sympathy and understanding'. We have to be careful here. We will come across similar claims when we turn to authors with a wider conception of the aesthetic. The latter are talking about sympathy and understanding among people generally, or at least among people generally within the same community or culture. But Beardsley's claim is more limited. He has in mind people listening to the same music or seeing the same paintings and so on. 'Insofar as they have learnt to make similar responses, they share an experience' and this tends to bring them together in friendship and mutual respect, to create a bond between them. In adjudicating Beardsley's argument, we should not think of aesthetic experience in individualistic terms, as a transaction between a solitary person and an aesthetic object. If we did, then it would become an empirical matter, and one where evidence is probably not forthcoming, whether lovers of art tend to develop friendship and respect among themselves. We should rely, rather, on MacIntyre's concept of a 'practice', as a co-operative activity with its own internal goods, included among them the recognition of various personal qualities among participants. If we conceive engagement with works of art as a practice, then it follows logically that those who pursue it are bonded together by ties of co-operative endeavour, respect for each other's abilities and that broad sense of friendship, transcending intimacy, to which Aristotle has drawn our attention in the *Nicomachean Ethics*. In sum, we can accept this claim of Beardsley's as conceptually true – as long as we remember that it has only to do with attitudes and behaviour among the aesthetically initiated and has no bearing on whether aesthetic experience fosters mutual sympathy and understanding outside this circle.

5   Beardsley's last claim is that aesthetic experience offers an ideal for human life – of an activity 'in which means and ends are so closely interrelated that we feel no separation between them' (p. 575). He counterposes this to the gap which often exists between means and ends in other parts of our social life, especially in more boring kinds of work. Aesthetic experience gives a clue as to how this undesirable state of affairs can be transformed.

I find this argument attractive, but wonder whether it gives aesthetic experience any privileged place in presenting this ideal over other activities where participants see what they are doing as intrinsically rewarding, such as theoretical enquiry, sports, community service. If it is not so privileged, we come close to Osborne's position, described above. We may have a good reason for including engagement with art in the content of education in that it helps to extend the range of life-options; but we are not helped in our search for its *further* contribution to personal and social well-being which is the topic of this section.

Taking all five of Beardsley's arguments together and assessing the light they shed on this further contribution, we can rule out (5), as we have just seen. Claims numbers (2), (3) and (4) fail to deliver what they seemed to promise: where they are at their most convincing, the sensitivity, perceptiveness, imagination, sympathy and understanding which they mention are not qualities found in ordinary human intercourse, but are confined within the circle of aesthetic experience itself. This leaves (1), the speculative, empirically unsupported argument about the relief of tension and the promotion of inner harmony. All in all, Beardsley has given us next to no reason to think that engagement with the arts has any value for human life outside its own autonomous domain.

Other arguments

Osborne and Beardsley both adhere to the narrower conception of aesthetic experience which confines it to acquaintance with perceptual features of aesthetic objects, detaching this from everything lying outside the work itself. Not everyone sees the aesthetic as belonging to a world of its own – Anthony Savile (1982: 86), for instance, quotes with approval Stuart Hampshire's remark that empiricist philosophies 'have detached aesthetics as an autonomous domain, only contingently connected with other interests.... The enjoyment of art, and art itself, is trivialised, as a detached and peculiar pleasure, which leads to nothing else. Its part in the whole experience of man is then left unexplained' (Hampshire, 1959: 246).

On a broader conception, the objects of aesthetic experience are not limited to perceptible features, still less to such formal features as Beardsley describes, like the complexity and unity in which sensuous phenomena – tones, colours, sounds, etc. – are bound together. The work of art is not, or is not always, an objective, completed entity, requiring only our trained aesthetic perception to yield its aesthetic fruit. On the contrary, for the latter to be possible we must often make a contribution of our own in the shape of an imaginative involvement with the work which brings it to completion. On one such conception, that of R. K. Elliott, one role of imagination is to enable us to experience works 'from within', as if we were participants in their worlds, or were entering into intimate communion with the characters portrayed in them or with their creators. In these ways we experience works as delivering situations (as in painting) or as expressing emotion (as in music) or both (as in poetry) (Elliott, 1972: 157).

If one conceives aesthetic experience as not only of perceptual, including formal, features of works themselves, but also, at least in many cases, of imagined human feelings and situations, this helps to provide that non-contingent link between aesthetics and other human interests of which Hampshire wrote. Educationally, it enables us to see cultivating in young people a love of art not only as opening up new options, but also as helping them to live a fuller human life.

In what way? In recent writings, both Anthony Savile (1982) and Anthony O'Hear (1988) have discussed the wider value to us of engagement with the arts. I will now examine and assess some of their claims. As we shall see, several of them are superficially reminiscent of those of Beardsley; unlike Beardsley's, however, they do not shepherd us back inside a narrow perceptual fold.

O'Hear writes:

> Art, on the other hand (i.e. unlike science), is intimately involved in our sense
> of the value of things. First, by means of its sympathetic re-enactments of
> anthropomorphic perspectives on the world, it can play; a central role both in
> value enquiry and in coming to an understanding of the nature of one's own
> existence and the meanings available in it. And, then, through its ability to
> resolve, at least for a time, certain fundamental tensions in our existence, it is
> well fitted to play a role in fostering harmony in one's own existence.
>
> (1988: 162–3)

The first of these claims is that art promotes value-enquiry and self-understanding;
the second that it resolves certain tensions and fosters harmony. Are they both
sound?

The first claim might seem to suggest that art is valuable to us for theoretical
reasons, that is, that it helps us to uncover truths with which we were not previously acquainted. It certainly can do this. In the field of value-enquiry, we can
come to learn about the ethical values of other cultures or sub-cultures or other
historical periods through their art, especially through their literature. But putting
things like this underrates the importance that the arts can play in our ethical life.
It appears to make engaging with them instrumental to something else, the pursuit
of knowledge; and to suggest that if non-aesthetic evidence about values were
superior to that furnished by art, the latter might prove dispensable. In addition, it
is not even clear that in order to attain these theoretical benefits, one needs to
engage *aesthetically* with a work, as distinct from mining it, as a scholar, for the
light it might shed on other things.

But perhaps O'Hear has other things in mind than theoretical enquiry. He also
writes of the contribution art can make to self-knowledge, and self-knowledge is
perhaps more a form of practical wisdom than a theoretical achievement. As
David Hamlyn (1977) has implied, it can scarcely be modelled on forms of understanding, like science or mathematics, where a distinction can be drawn between
the knowing subject and an independent known object. Knowing oneself better is
to have got one's priorities more into order, to have come more clearly to see what
concerns weigh with one more than others. It involves having dwelt not on one's
scheme of values, or hierarchy of desires, as a whole – for this would take us back
to the misconception of self-knowledge as confrontation with some kind of
inspectable object; but on particular values and on conflicts between them. One
role of art is to enable us to dwell on, or better, perhaps, to dwell in our values or
desires and their associated emotions in this more particular and less global way.
Since works of art are produced to be enjoyed by a public, the desires, emotions
and conflicts between them which they express are typically those which many
have experienced; and one mark of the greatness of a work is its ability to strike
such chords in all of us. In aesthetic engagement with art, we come to a more profound self-awareness, of ourselves as unique individuals and at the same time of
ourselves as members of a particular community or culture, and as human beings
in general. We come to dwell not only in what we *do* feel but also in what we
would feel if our circumstances were different, or became different. Art both reinforces feelings and priorities we already have and also shakes them up, unsettles
established patterns and allows us imaginatively to entertain alternatives – a state,
for instance, where grief dominates over everything, or where murder no longer
belongs to the unthinkable.

This kind of argument for the ethical import of art may be charged with turning it into a vehicle for moral improvement, and therein treating it just as instrumentally as it is treated in the claim, examined earlier, that art can help in theoretical value-enquiry. We have to tread carefully here. There is no suggestion in this context that through the arts we may come to possess values that we did not possess before, for example, altruistic values where previously we were egoistical. It may or may not be true that art, or some art, can have this power: to determine this would require empirical investigation. The point to be made is not that engagement with the arts gives us *new* values – although it might do this but that we have to bring to it desires, feelings and the values they enshrine, which we *already* possess.

Even so, the claim may still look instrumental – it may seem to be saying that we sometimes have recourse to art so as to dwell on our desires and feelings and the conflicts and priorities among them. Does this not overlook the intrinsic interest in it which we must always have if we are to engage with it aesthetically? It is important to defuse this charge of instrumentalism. Aesthetic engagement with a work *is* something pursued for its own sake. But on a broader conception of the aesthetic, since part of what we *understand* by aesthetic engagement is imaginatively dwelling in feelings and desires, the experience of art cannot be divorced from ethical contemplation. We do not choose to read poems as aesthetic objects *in order to* reflect on the ethical life, where the latter is a further goal to which the former is a means; but in choosing so to read them we may well have such ethical ends in mind, accruing as part of our intrinsic experience of the work.

This kind of relationship between the aesthetic and the ethical can be obscured by too narrow a conception of either or both of these terms. Just as objects of aesthetic experience can be confined to perceptual qualities, so the ethical can become restricted to that sense of the moral, recently identified by Bernard Williams (1985), in which duty or obligation becomes the central concept: on a wider view of the ethical, this would cover all aspects of how we are to live our lives, including not, only obligations into which we have entered, but also our commitments and enthusiasms for our own projects as well as, what is often inseparable from these, our attachments to persons and communities. If we work with a narrow conception of both terms, the aesthetic and the ethical do indeed constitute seemingly impermeable different worlds: of, on the one hand, a rarefied kind of perception, and on the other of attention to certain kinds of obligation. It is hard to see how aesthetic perception, pursued for its own sake, could be expected to have anything to do with our adhering to moral principles of, say, fairness or non-maleficence. On a broader view of both, however, they come much closer, so close that the aesthetic comes to presuppose the ethical in the way we have seen above (which is not to say that the ethical presupposes the aesthetic, although it may do). What is significant about the conceptions of both the aesthetic and the ethical in their narrow senses is the negligible place both have for the emotions. Just as aesthetic experience on this view has nothing to do with expression, so in moral experience the emotions are seen not as motivators of moral conduct – for only the sense of duty could fill that role, but as forms of passivity which have the potential to interfere with our acting morally and so must be kept firmly under control. (A modern version of this Kantian theme is found in R. S. Peters' account of the education of the emotions in Peters (1972).) On a wider view of both areas, the emotions become of central importance: in respect of expression, in the case of the aesthetic, and in the shaping of our fears, hopes, joys and sorrows into settled dispositions of behaviour and response in the case of ethics.

It is because we bring to our experience of art concerns that we already possess in life that art can play an often-remarked role in binding us together. Beardsley's claim in this area is confined to mutual understanding among the aesthetically initiated; but we now see how this circle can be both deepened and widened: deepened, because those who engage with a particular work of art can become conscious not only of a shared exercise of skills of discrimination but also of the shared life-emotions and values they bring to the work; and widened, because the sharing now goes beyond the initiated and includes others society unacquainted with this work, or perhaps, indeed, with any works of art. The public character of works of art, their role as a focal point for shared experience, is from an ethical perspective an important feature. Since the ethical values which individuals possess come to them, often in complex ways (see Taylor, 1990), from the cultures and communities in which they live, art can help to bind us not only as fellow human beings, but also as members of more localised groups. As O'Hear puts it: 'through art, indeed, the individual can come to a powerful realisation of the truth of Bradley's claim that a community enters into his essence' (1988: 148). This adds a further dimension to O'Hear's point about the role of art in fostering self-understanding. This mutual binding is not exclusively a matter of shared awareness; for experience of art/ in encouraging us to dwell on the springs of our ethical life, recommits us to what we value, thereby strengthening their role in our life, both individually and communally. Savile (1982: 107), drawing on Hume, gives an interesting example: the tapering of pillars upwards from a broader base insensibly reinforces a shared desire for security.

In these ways, through their common roots in our desires and emotions, art reflects and fosters our ethical life. It has not been proposed, so far at least, that all art does this. Music, and among it the greatest, can be aesthetically interesting for its patterns and complexities of sound, even when we do not hear it as expression. This said, it may still be the case that the patterns and complexities themselves are ethically relevant, but in a different way. We shall be taking up this point in the next section.

O'Hear's second claim is that art can play a part in resolving certain fundamental tensions in our existence and thereby foster harmony. He has in mind such tensions as those between the self and the objective world, between feeling and reason, between the natural and the conventional, between the individual and the community. He writes of the redemptive powers of art, its ability to save us from 'gazing into the horrors of the night' (p. 140).

Elsewhere he makes a significantly different claim to do with tensions, that 'art can help us creatively to express and explore the tensions caused in us by the fundamental dualisms of our nature' (p. 148). Expressing and exploring tensions is different from resolving them. Can art do either?

A claim about resolution we also noted in Beardsley. Quite what resolution means in O'Hear's context would need further exploration, but, as with Beardsley, the claim in question, whether applicable to a narrower or a broader conception of the aesthetic, would seem to depend on evidence, which O'Hear does not provide. For him art seems to have powers once ascribed to religion – redemptive powers, as he puts it, of transforming our life from a meaningless jumble of conflicting elements into a harmonious unity. This may well bring art *too* close to religion. It suggests perfectibilism. The ideal of human perfectibility, as Passmore (1970) has reminded us, has deep roots in our history, not least in the history of our religious and political ideas, from ancient times, but is in his view to be shunned, not welcomed. 'To achieve perfection in any of its classical senses, as so many perfectibilists have admitted, it would first be necessary to cease to be human, to become godlike, to rise above the human condition' (p. 326).

Quite another outlook on human life sees conflict and tension as ineradicable from it. In contemporary ethics, one sees this in writers like Williams (1985) who stress the irreducible diversity of values. From this perspective, O'Hear's second suggestion, that art helps us to express and explore basic tensions, may be more fruitful: it seems a surer vehicle of self-understanding than when viewed from the perfectibilist standpoint, since there it may lead us into a false conception of what we are.

At the same time, in any individual's life conflicts have to be managed somehow. Balances have to be struck, values weighted, all within some kind of personal system of psychological regulation. On this view of human flourishing, conflicts co-exist within a unitary framework, one which is constantly changing with experience as balances are struck in different places. This has its obvious parallel in the contrasting elements held together within the framework of a work of art. Like a self, a work of art is nothing fixed. Both are endlessly open to being seen from new perspectives, to new features coming to the fore while others recede. Art may speak to us not only in its sensuous delights and its links with our emotional life, but also in its mirroring of our psychic constitution as a whole. If this is on the right lines, then even the least expressive music may still be ethically important to us. Music, indeed, may be a more faithful mirror of ourselves than painting. In the latter, the whole work is laid before us simultaneously for our contemplation. But we never see ourselves at any one time as a complete entity; to think in this way is to resort to that misconceived notion of self-understanding with which we dealt above. Music, flowing through time, never graspable *in toto*, but only in more local stretches and contrasts, is closer to our self as we know it.

Perhaps, after all, O'Hear has something more like this, and not perfectibilism, in mind in writing about art's contribution to our inner harmony. If so, it would be better not to link this with talk of redemption and salvation. Art may indeed have replaced religion in our age as a central element in our flourishing and in our self-understanding; but what it can do for us should not be exaggerated: our lives are not in danger without art, only vastly poorer.

Conclusion

The purpose of education in the arts cannot be restricted to enlarging options. They can have a more intimate connection with our flourishing – with fostering self-knowledge reinforcing our ethical values, binding us together as members of communities. For these reasons alone, acquaintance with works of art should have a central place in the school curriculum, although not necessarily to an equal extent for pupils of different ages. This essay agrees with Paul Hirst, but for different reasons, that engagement with the arts is, at least, an *important* element in personal well-being. Whether it is an *indispensable* element, as his theory may suggest, is, after all, another question. Given that flourishing is not an all-or-nothing matter and that there can be different degrees of it, it would be hard to show that people could not flourish at all without art. With respect to poetry at least. Kit Wright (1989) is sceptical:

> When they say
> That every day
>
> Men die miserably without it
> I doubt it.

References

Beardsley, M. (1958). *Aesthetics*, New York: Harcourt Brace and World.
Elliott, R. K. (1972). 'Aesthetic Theory and the Experience of Art', in H. Osborne (ed.), *Aesthetics*, Oxford: Oxford University Press.
Hamlyn, D. W. (1977). 'Self Knowledge', in T. Mischel (ed.), *The Self*. Oxford: Blackwell.
Hampshire, S. (1959). *Thought and Action*, London: Chatto and Windus.
Hirst, P. H. (1965). 'Liberal Education and the Nature of Knowledge', in R. D. Archambault (ed.), *Philosophical Analysis and Education*, London: Routledge and Kegan Paul.
O'Hear, A. (1988). *The Element of Fire*, London: Routledge.
Osborne, H. (1986). Review of H. B. Redfern *Questions in Aesthetic Education, Journal of Philosophy of Education*, 20(2), pp. 296–9.
Passmore, J. (1970). *The Perfectibility of Man*, London: Duckworth.
Peters, R. S. (1972). 'The Education of the Emotions', in R. F. Dearden, P. H. Hirst and R. S. Peters (eds), *Education and the Development of Reason*, London: Routledge & Kegan Paul.
Savile, A. (1982). *The Test of Time*, Oxford: Clarendon Press.
Taylor, C. (1990). *The Sources of the Self*, Cambridge: Cambridge University Press.
Williams, B. (1985). *Ethics and the Limits of Philosophy*, London: Fontana.
Wright, K. (1989). 'Poetry' in *Short Afternoons*, London: Hutchinson.

CHAPTER 16

SHOULD MATHEMATICS BE COMPULSORY FOR ALL UNTIL THE AGE OF 16?

Why Learn Maths? (2000), S. Bramall and J. White (eds). London: Institute of Education, University of London

I

Mathematics is a subject held in high esteem. It has traditionally occupied an unchallenged role within our culture. No other subject can match it in intellectual prestige. It is the hardest and most abstract of disciplines. Who could top a Cambridge wrangler?

According to research surveyed in a recent Qualifications and Curriculum Authority (QCA) review of curricular aims, 'parents, governors and employers all saw mathematics and English as the most important subjects' (QCA, 1998: 35). Is mathematics' high position in the academic pecking order justified? Are there good reasons to support it? In particular – and this is the main topic of this chapter – are there good reasons for its being compulsory from the age of 5 to 16?

Other chapters in this book examine different kinds of reasons for teaching and studying the subject, past and present. They can be divided into two broad groups, namely instrumental and non-instrumental. 'Instrumental' reasons – as I am using the term here (I realize it can have other uses) – are about the harnessing of mathematics to the demands of everyday life and of the economy. Non-instrumental ones are about other aims than these, for example about mathematics as a vehicle of mental training or as intrinsically interesting.

We need to assess these reasons insofar as they are still alive in current thinking. This is partly a matter of seeing whether the reasons will do at all – or whether there are intellectual or moral flaws in them which rule them out for anybody. But it is also partly a matter of examining the scope of the reasons which pass this first test – of seeing how far they are merely good reasons for some people in some circumstances, or whether they are powerful enough to justify compulsory mathematics for everybody up to the age of 16.

To start with non-instrumental reasons. The first task here is to separate the sound reasons from the dubious. Mathematical thinking has for millennia been closely associated with our unique nature as human beings. Both Plato and Descartes believed that the essence of the human is our ability to reason. Whereas emotions and desires belong to our bodies, we ourselves are only contingently associated with the latter and can continue to exist in their absence when the body dies. What we are essentially are souls or minds and the distinguishing feature of a soul or a mind is that it engages in ratiocination. For both thinkers the highest type of reasoning is that furthest removed from anything to do with our bodily existence, that is, maximally abstracted from our ordinary social life as embodied creatures. For both of them, mathematical thinking occupies the highest rungs of the ladder, only to he superseded by philosophical reasoning in Plato's case and the certainty of the 'Cogito' in Descartes'.

It is from within this tradition that Fred Clarke, the eminent British educationalist who was Director of the Institute of Education between 1936 and 1945, wrote that 'the ultimate reason for teaching long division to little Johnny is that he is an immortal soul' (Clarke, 1923: 2). Few of us living in a more secular age could go along with the religious assumptions in this. Yet many more of us are insensibly influenced by other aspects of the Platonic–Cartesian theory. Especially the notion that mathematical thinking is in some way *superior* to other forms of thinking – both academic forms like those of the historian or literary critic, and the practical reasoning on which we rely day-to-day in the planning of our personal and institutional lives. In the Platonic–Cartesian tradition there was a reason why mathematical reasoning had this high status: its abstraction from the realities of embodied existence. Today, we rightly take more seriously the fact of our embodiment: nearly all of us see ourselves not as minds which happen to be attached to bodies in this earthly life, but as sharing some bodily and some mental attributes with other animals and capable, owing to our linguistic capacities, of forms of social life not found in other species. Against this background, there is no reason to elevate mathematical thinking above the many other sorts on which we depend, not least the practical reasoning mentioned above.

It is a myth, then, that if we want to develop young people's minds, one of the best ways of doing this is to give them a rigorous training in mathematics (see Peter Huckstep's (2000: 94–5) comments on Sir Joshua Fitch). If we want them to act in the social world, there are better ways of equipping them mentally to do this than by making them adept in abstract operations which have least attachment to that world. In his *Republic*, Plato made his philosopher kings study mathematics for ten years in early adulthood to help equip them for statesmanship. Yet despite the attractions of Plato's educational ideas for those responsible for elite education in Britain over the past 150 years, we have no reason to follow him in this. Getting into mathematics helps you, unsurprisingly, with mathematical reasoning, but there's no evidence that it makes you better at thinking about, say, history, current affairs or personal relationships.

Suppose we discard the mental training reason for learning mathematics? Are any other kinds of non-instrumental reason more convincing?

As Peter Huckstep (2000: 89) shows, Plato also held that studying mathematics gives us a direct insight into the structure of reality. In our own age, Bertrand Russell spent his early years exploring the foundations of mathematics in the belief that these would lead him towards the contemplation of eternal logical forms and a quasi-mystical sense of union with the universe (Monk, 1997: 159).

However, the idea that pure mathematics – on its own, not as handmaiden to science – is the key to understanding fundamental reality is now dead. Russell himself came to see his work as an exploration of language rather than the cosmos.

So far we have been looking at non-instrumental reasons that have proved to be failures. Are there others which are more successful?

II

I can think of three. The first is the intrinsic delight in mathematical thinking which many people have experienced and which Richard Smith (2000) has evoked so well. Part of this delight, especially in the upper reaches of the subject to do with matters such as pattern, simplicity and elegance of proof, has an aesthetic quality.

The second reason, not separable from the first, has to do with the necessary role of mathematics within science taken as intrinsically interesting in its own right apart from its technological applications.

The third reason, again inseparable from the first two, concerns the place of mathematics in our culture and, more generally, as a human achievement.

All three are good reasons in general why mathematics should be studied by some people. Yet, this is where considerations of *scope* come into the picture. We are looking for good reasons why *everyone* should have to study mathematics until the age of 16. Do these three provide them?

At the very least, they do not show why mathematics should be privileged in the last Key Stage of the present National Curriculum in the way that it is. If we take the ten foundation subjects as our baseline, all of them are compulsory between the ages of 11 and 14, while between the ages of 14 and 16 mathematics, English, science, technology, physical education and a modern foreign language are compulsory and history, geography, music and art are not. In this scheme, mathematics is privileged over these four non-compulsory subjects.

The first of the three good reasons for mathematics, about intrinsic delight, does not elevate mathematics above art and music, for these too provide this for some people. This point also undermines the second reason, as there is nothing to show that an interest in science for its own sake is privileged over an intrinsic interest in one of the arts or in history. The third reason, about the place of mathematics in our culture and as a human achievement, fails to show why mathematics should be privileged over history at Key Stage 4. Quite the reverse. This is because the reason only makes sense if the student has some kind of historical framework in which he or she can place cultural phenomena or great human achievements. I am assuming that history up to and including Key Stage 3 (age 14) does not provide enough of such a framework.

Perhaps we should abstract from current curricular arrangements in one country. Indeed, in the first version of the National Curriculum after 1988, *all* the foundation subjects were compulsory until the age of 16, so there was no issue then of privileging mathematics over the arts and history. Less parochially then, should all students be compelled to study mathematics from, say, the age of 11 to 16 for one or other of the three non-instrumental reasons?

The first reason for studying mathematics has to do with its intrinsic delights. No one would want to argue that a persisting love of mathematical thinking for its own sake is a *sine qua non* of any fulfilled life. A stronger argument would be that education should open every pupil's eyes to a number of *possible* intrinsic delights which they may or may not decide to take further as a major life commitment; and that mathematics, along with a range of other intrinsic goods, should be something to which everyone is exposed.

The argument is a powerful one in general; but not powerful enough, I think, to support compulsory mathematics for all until the age of 16. Three considerations speak against this: the need to prioritize within the school curriculum; children's inclinations; and the likely pattern of adult commitments.

On prioritizing: the general case for mathematics applies to a host of other activities, for example, the arts, physical activities, chess, philosophy, physical science and anthropology. There is no space for all of these to be compulsory for all until the age of 16, so reasoned choices will have to be made.

On inclinations: by the age of 11, some children really take to mathematics as an intriguing subject in its own right, others do not. If those who lack inclination are compelled to persevere with the subject until the age of 16 in the hope that a taste for its non-instrumental aspects will develop, this may well be counterproductive for some, perhaps many, children, especially as they become attached to intrinsic delights in other areas.

On the likely pattern of adult commitments: common sense suggests that, however well-run and extensive any school courses in mathematics were, the proportion of adults who delighted in mathematical thinking for its own sake would be likely to be very small. Few would be willing to devote the time and effort required for such abstract and difficult activity. Human beings being what they are, most would prefer to spend any free time in their short lives on pleasures closer to the sensuous surface of life, for instance on those to do with relationships, sports and the arts. Common sense may be wrong about this, of course, and it would be interesting to see what evidence could be adduced to test it. One test would be to find out the proportion of mathematics graduates who continue to pursue the subject for intrinsic reasons as against those who abandon it in favour of other ends-in-themselves.

These considerations point towards a compulsory taster course in mathematics after the age of 11 rather than a compulsory five-year course. This would enable those who don't already have an inclination for it to see if one develops. If they find no hint of joy in it despite the taster course, it would be sensible to let them drop it. After all, there are plenty of alternatives among which they might find something more appealing. Beyond the taster courses, there would be voluntary courses, perhaps within some constrained option system, for those who like the subject. If teaching on the taster course has been sufficiently inspiring, one may expect many, perhaps most children to want to take the subject further, but it would be unrealistic to expect every child to do so.

A word on the voluntary courses. There is every reason, given what we know of how people's intrinsic interests shift, why entry to these should be at any point, up to and indeed beyond the end of compulsory schooling. School voluntary courses in mathematics and other subjects could be meshed into a wider system of further and adult education, with a right to opt in being available, and courses free of charge for younger people and some other groups.

The second non-instrumental reason is that a knowledge of mathematics is necessary for the pursuit of science for its own sake.

The three considerations of prioritizing, inclinations and likely pattern of adult commitment also apply to some extent to science, speaking against its being a compulsory subject for intrinsic reasons from the age of 11 to 16 (although there may be other reasons why it should be compulsory for this period). The combination of taster and voluntary courses in mathematics already referred to seems appropriate for both the first and second non-instrumental reasons described above.

I turn to the third of our non-instrumental reasons, to do with the place of mathematics in our culture and as a human achievement. I am excluding from this utilitarian reasons for mathematics to do with citizenship and the world of work, but will be looking at these in the third section of this chapter.

A leader from the *Daily Telegraph* (19 August 1998) about the award of the Fields Medal in mathematics to two British academics sets the scene. It begins:

> Mathematics is the master key to the Universe. Its mysteries may seem arcane to the layman, but without it we would still be living in a pre- scientific, pre-industrial world. Most educated people have little grasp of the arithmetic and geometry of the Ancient Greeks, yet none of their legacies has a more direct impact on our lives than those of Euclid, Archimedes or Diaphantos. As for the modern immortals, the great discoveries in physics of a Newton or an Einstein would have been impossible had they not also been superb mathematicians. Our society is shamefully ill-equipped to comprehend the mathematical mind.

I am sure all this is true. The only question is: does it provide a good reason for compulsory school courses in mathematics from the age of 11 to 16?

If it does, parallel arguments could be mounted for such pillars of our culture as philosophy, law and architecture. Should there then be five-year courses in all these subjects? (To say nothing of music, the visual arts, history and politics.)

Another issue is how much of the cultural importance of mathematics can one grasp from outside the subject? The *Daily Telegraph* leader communicates *something* of this to its readers, many, perhaps most, of whom probably know little mathematics. How much further could its account be filled out without requiring an insider's understanding of advanced mathematics?

Part of mathematics' cultural significance lies, as indicated in the excerpt, in its contribution to science. Many of those lacking a scientific education acquire some insight, often considerable insight, into the way the scientific advances of the last four centuries have radically transformed human life. They realize that many of these advances have depended on advanced mathematics, even though they lack an insider's knowledge of the latter.

In saying this, I am not, of course, claiming that mathematical knowledge adds nothing to one's appreciation of its cultural role. It surely deepens one's understanding considerably. The only issue, once again, is whether a five-year secondary course in mathematics is justified for cultural reasons. If one takes into account the considerations already mentioned about curriculum priorities and about children's inclinations, taster-plus-voluntary courses in mathematics with a cultural dimension to them seem the best answer.

III

I turn to the teaching and learning of mathematics for instrumental reasons, meaning by this its contribution to everyday life and to the world of work. First, to sort out the good from the bad arguments. Elizabeth Anderson tells us that in nineteenth-century British universities:

> Students did learn some mathematics, although rarely at an advanced level. And math classes were valued more for the discipline and obedience they instilled through boring drill and rote exercises, than for their potential to sharpen students' analytical reasoning skills or to enable them to understand the basis of physical laws.
>
> (Anderson, 1998: 336)

There is no doubt, either, that discipline and obedience help to explain why arithmetic occupied so prominent a place in English elementary school codes from 1862 onwards. Richard Aldrich and David Crook (2000) have drawn our attention to the large amount of time spent on the subject and to endless practice sums that did not teach children anything new but kept their heads well down.

Obedience to orders and getting used to boring, mechanical tasks are personal characteristics tailor-made for the Work Culture of the nineteenth and early twentieth centuries. Schooling based on them treats pupils not as ends in themselves, but only as means to economic ends. I hope I can safely take it that this reason for teaching mathematics, usually arithmetic, can be ruled out on ethical grounds.

This leaves us with the sound instrumental reasons for studying mathematics.

(a) It is a commonplace that we all need some understanding of simple arithmetic to manage our personal finances, measure areas around the house, etc. How much we need, especially in the age of the calculator, is a further question. Even before calculators came on the scene, most adults had little cause to tap into their knowledge of long division or long multiplication or square roots.

(b) We also all need some mathematics from a civic point of view. We have to be able to think in terms of millions and billions in order to grasp anything of national housekeeping; we need to understand graphical and other representations of quantitative data on policy matters such as are found in the media; we need some insight into how such statistics can be misleadingly presented.

(c) Mathematics is also a *sine qua non* of very many jobs. (i) Sometimes the arithmetical knowledge already mentioned covers this, as in work on check-outs and simpler craft activities. (ii) More advanced mathematics is necessary for mathematics- and science-based jobs. (iii) Richard Noss, in his inaugural lecture (Noss, 1997), has also drawn attention to the 'hidden', unobvious, presence of mathematical thinking in various jobs. I will go into this further below.

There are three good reasons, therefore, (a), (b) and (c) for learning some mathematics. As before, the issue of scope now becomes salient. Do all these reasons apply to everybody? Insofar as they do, do they furnish a good reason for compulsory mathematics up to the age of 16?

(a) Most children can be expected to have mastered most of the basic arithmetic needed for everyday purposes by the end of primary schooling (age 11). There may have to be some remedial work for a few pupils, but beyond that a compulsory course for all would only have to cover a few areas not taught at primary level.

(b) Civic mathematics is important for everybody. There is a plain case for a short, focused compulsory course, preferably tied in with courses in education for citizenship.

(c) In discussing work-related mathematics, I shall use the same three categories, (i), (ii) and (iii) as above. (i) The basic arithmetic required for many jobs will be largely acquired by the end of primary school. (ii) Only a minority of students will be learning the advanced mathematics needed for mathematics- and science-based jobs. They will include those who show an early aptitude for the subject and want to do more of it, either for its own sake, or for what it leads on to, or both. They will opt for voluntary courses in non-basic mathematics in secondary schools. Other students may decide to take up mathematics later in the secondary school, or indeed after secondary school, having first become interested in some area of employment and then seen the necessity of advanced mathematics for that work. Voluntary courses would also be suitable for them.

There is a good case, based on the value of personal autonomy, for making sure that all secondary students have access to knowledge about the academic requirements for different jobs. These include mathematical requirements. It would be going too far to compulsorily equip all students early on with the academic requirements for a whole range of jobs, just in case they decided to choose one of these later. The first reason for this is that so many compulsory subjects would have to be included – not only advanced mathematics, but also criminal and civil law, geology, psychology, linguistics, Asian studies, etc. The second reason is that virtually all the compulsory studies would be vocationally useless for most students. Rather than thinking of pre-equipping students for vocational possibilities, we should ensure that they can take up voluntary courses in requisite subjects once their vocational preferences are clear. (iii) We come back to Richard Noss's idea of the hidden presence of mathematics in many jobs: 'mathematics is not always visible, it lies beneath the surface of practices and cultures' (Noss, 1997: 5). He gives examples of nurses' use of a simple mathematical model of drug level; and of the growing use of computers in many jobs, where workers need to operate beyond a routine level: 'the massive computerization of systems... will mean that more and more people will need to modify and rebuild systems with their own variables and parameters, not just plug in values to someone else's' (Noss, 1997: 17).

Given Noss's case, what implications does it have for the extent to which mathematics should be compulsory in secondary education? He does not explicitly draw any himself, but his call for a new conception of 'numeracy' which goes beyond basic arithmetical skills and equips people to understand the 'invisible' mathematics just described suggests that he *may* (?) think that all pupils should become numerate in this new sense.

Noss's own views on this aside, the case for a compulsory course for all does not seem to have been made. What proportion of the population will require the modelling and other job-related abilities that Noss mentions? We have no reason to think it is anywhere near 100 per cent. The further it falls short of this, the more pupils who are compulsorily inducted into this area of mathematics are learning something which will turn out to be useless to them. There is much more of a case for building this learning into voluntary courses which learners can choose to follow at any time from early secondary education onwards, including the time after they · become attracted by career options which require this sort of mathematical attainment.

It is time to draw together the threads of the argument about acceptable instrumental reasons for studying mathematics. There is an unchallengeable argument that all children should learn the basic mathematics, that is arithmetic, necessary for everyday life. This is a job almost exclusively for primary schools. If the current government's policies on numeracy succeed, by the year 2002, 75 per cent of British children will have reached Level 4 in the area by the age of 11. That will provide them with the basic arithmetic they need to get by.

What role does that leave for the secondary school? None of the vocationally orientated arguments we looked at, justify compulsory as distinct from voluntary classes. The only powerful case for compulsion concerns a short, focused course in civic mathematics.

IV

A little more thread-gathering. We have so far examined separately the non-instrumental and the instrumental reasons for studying mathematics and their curricular consequences. The instrumental arguments, as we have just seen, point to a compulsory basic course for all at primary level and a short course in civic mathematics somewhere in secondary education. The non-instrumental arguments suggest a taster course in mathematics for its own sake and for cultural reasons. At secondary level, the two proposals – instrumental and non-instrumental – taken together add up to a drastically reduced role for compulsory mathematics. At the same time, there would be a massively *increased* place at secondary level for voluntary courses, perhaps for various voluntary courses with different orientations, on the lines suggested by Richard Smith above.

I am far from advocating that compulsory curriculum time vacated by one subject should automatically be filled by other compulsory subjects. There is a general case for keeping compulsion down to the level at which it can be adequately justified-1 say more on this later. However, if Steve Bramall (2000) is right – as he surely is – that mathematics cannot give us insight into the ends of human life in the way that humanities subjects can (except, presumably, for the insight it can give us into the intrinsic features of mathematics), there is a strong case for letting more classes in compulsory literature, history, sociology and perhaps philosophy take up some of the slack.

One of the most intellectually courageous colleagues I have known in my time is Alan Hornsey, who before his retirement was Head of the Modern Languages

Department at the Institute of Education. Alan has never wavered in his belief that the case for a compulsory modern language in the school curriculum had not been made. I know there are mathematics educators similarly sceptical of the conventional wisdom that mathematics should be compulsory for all 11 years of compulsory schooling. It would be good if their voices were heard more often.

Whatever stance mathematics educators take on this issue, I do not wish to imply that only those who are in mathematics education are authorities on how much and what mathematics should be compulsory. The issue is one for the citizen, not only the specialist. With the coming of the National Curriculum in 1988 this was recognized – in a way – via the *political* decision that mathematics should be compulsory from ages of 5 to 16. The trouble was that the political decision was not made on good enough grounds. After all, it was not only mathematics that was made compulsory for 11 years: the same was true for all but one of the other foundation subjects. This fact alone should be enough to cast doubts on the well-foundedness of the government's decision, for if that decision *had been* well-founded, what a coincidence it would have been that pros and cons about the length of compulsory courses in art, science, English, technology, history, music, geography and physical education were resolved in each case in exactly the same way to produce the 11-year recommendation. Surely, one is inclined to think, a careful review of the arguments would have led to very different proposals for the different subject areas.

The extent to which children are compelled to attend school classes is no trivial matter. In the adult world, we rightly refrain as far as possible from compelling other people to do things. True, people are obliged to pay income tax, go to prison for certain offences and drive on the left. However, good reasons have to be provided for such compulsion: we do not see it as an arbitrary matter. We should take the same stance towards children at school. The system should not arbitrarily oblige them to do this course or that. There have to be good reasons why constraint has to be used. There is no doubt in my own mind that such good reasons are available in many, many cases. I am not suggesting at all that children should be at liberty to do – or not do – whichever courses they want. There is nothing to be said in favour of such an ideological stance. I am calling, instead, for the piecemeal, careful examination of arguments, most of which are likely to differ from subject to subject.

It may be that, in the case of mathematics education, such judicious investigation will come up with a copper-bottomed argument for compulsory mathematics for all from the ages 5 to 16. I promise you, I will believe it when I see it.

References

Aldrich, R. and Crook, D. (2000) 'Mathematics, arithmetic and numeracy: an historical perspective', in S. Bramall and J. White (eds), *Why Learn Maths?*, London: Institute of Education, University of London.

Anderson, E. (1998) 'John Stuart Mill: democracy as sentimental education', in A. O. Rorty (ed.), *Philosophers on Education: New Historical Perspectives*, London: Routledge.

Bramall, S. (2000) 'Rethinking the place of mathematical knowledge in the curriculum', in S. Bramall and J. White (eds), *Why Learn Maths?*, London: Institute of Education, University of London.

Clarke, F. (1923) *Essays in the Politics of Education*, Oxford: Oxford University Press.

Huckstep, P. (2000) 'Mathematics as a vehicle for "mental training"', in S. Bramall and J. White (eds), *Why Learn Maths?*, London: Institute of Education, University of London.

Monk, R. (1997) *Bertrand Russell*, London: Vintage Books.

Noss, R. (1997) *New Cultures, New Numeracies*, London: Institute of Education, University of London.

Smith, R. (2000) 'Insight and assurance', in S. Bramall and J. White (eds), *Why Learn Maths?*, London: Institute of Education, University of London.

INDEX